16

—

The Development of
African Drama

Hutchinson University Library for Africa

General Editors: Michael Crowder and Paul Richards

The Development Process: A Spatial Perspective
Akin Mabogunje

Forced Migration: The Impact of the Export Slave Trade on African Societies
Edited by J. E. Inikori

A Handbook of Adult Education for West Africa
Edited by Lalage Bown and S. H. Olu Tomori

A History of Africa
J. D. Fage

Indigenization of African Economies
Edited by Adebayo Adedeji

Peasants and Proletarians: The Struggles of Third World Workers
Edited by Robin Cohen, Peter C. W. Gutkind and Phyllis Brazier

Rural Development: Theories of Peasant Economy and Agrarian Change
Edited by John Harriss

Rural Settlement and Land Use
Michael Chisholm

Studies in Nigerian Administration
Edited by D. J. Murray

Technology, Tradition and the State in Africa
Jack Goody

Twelve African Writers
Gerald Moore

West Africa Under Colonial Rule
Michael Crowder

West African Resistance: The Military Response to Colonial Occupation
Edited by Michael Crowder

in association with the International African Institute

Islam in Tropical Africa
Edited by I. M. Lewis

The Drums of Affliction: A Study of Religious Processes among the Ndembu of Zambia
V. W. Turner

The Development of African Drama

Michael Etherton

Hutchinson University Library for Africa
London Melbourne Sydney Auckland Johannesburg

HUTCHINSON UNIVERSITY LIBRARY FOR AFRICA

Hutchinson & Co. (Publishers) Ltd

An imprint of the Hutchinson Publishing Group

17–21 Conway Street, London W1P 6JD

Hutchinson Group (Australia) Pty Ltd
30–32 Cremorne Street, Richmond South, Victoria 3121
Po Box 151, Broadway, New South Wales 2007

Hutchinson Group (NZ) Ltd
32–34 View Road, PO Box 40-086, Glenfield, Auckland 10

Hutchinson Group (SA) (Pty) Ltd
PO Box 337, Bergvlei 2012, South Africa

First published 1982

© Michael Etherton 1982

Set in Times Roman by
A-Line Services, Saffron Walden, Essex

Printed in Great Britain by The Anchor Press Ltd
and bound by Wm Brendon & Sons Ltd
both of Tiptree, Essex

British Library Cataloguing in Publication Data
Etherton, Michael
    The development of African drama.
    1. African drama – History and criticism
    I. Title
    809.2′0096   PL8010

ISBN 0 09 146420 X cased
        0 09 146421 8 paper

For Mary

Contents

Acknowledgements

This book is the result of a continual sharpening of perceptions shared by friends and colleagues through discussion, team teaching and criticism of each other's work. I am most deeply indebted to John Reed who, as professor of English in the University of Zambia where I first taught, and subsequently, has shaped my thinking over the past fourteen years. I am especially grateful to him for his painstaking criticism of the manuscript while he encouraged me to complete it. I am also grateful to James Currey who has encouraged my creative writing, and helped me to understand, practically and theoretically, the problems of publishing African plays while providing me with the opportunity to put my own ideas about this into practice. I am greatly indebted to my colleagues in drama at Ahmadu Bello University: Brian Crow and Salihu Bappa, Tony Humphries, Oga Abah and Saddiq Balewa, Tunde Lakoju and Sandy Arkhurst. We have worked together collectively and creatively; in addition, they not only read and criticized chapters but also gave me time to write by taking on an extra burden of work. I must also acknowledge stimulating interaction with other colleagues in ABU and with our drama students. Many colleagues elsewhere have offered and given help, especially Atta Annan Mensah in Ghana who has helped me to understand the function of African music in performance, and Ross Kidd in Canada who has opened to me a broader Third World context through contacts and travel opportunities.

The editors of HULA, Michael Crowder and Paul Richards, encouraged me to write the book I wanted to write; though of course I am responsible for any inadequacies and errors.

Finally, I wish to thank Joe Eke Udo for readily making available to me the secretarial facilities of the English department, ABU. I sincerely thank Joan and Franklyn Bellamy and Margery Abrahams who made their houses available to me to write; and my long-suffering family who made many sacrifices, often unacknowledged by me.   *Zaria, July 1981*

Glossary

This glossary contains short definitions of some of the theatre terms which occur in the text. Words which appear in bold print within definitions in the glossary have a separate entry.

Act (*n./pl.* *-s*)   a division of a **play** into sections. European theatre has tended to divide plays into either one, two, three, four or five acts, labelling the divisions thus: Act 1, Act 2 etc., depending on the number of divisions. In time, playwrights have come to structure the action of their plays in accordance with the division into acts. (See also **scene**.) To act (*v.*) is to assume a role.

Action (*n. sing.*)   refers to events within a play. E.g. the action of the play takes place inside a prison.

Alienation effect (*n. sing.*)   the English phrase for the German 'Verfremdungseffekt', 'V-effekt', which was the term coined by the playwright Bertolt Brecht, for a type of acting and theatre presentation which avoids creating the illusion of reality on stage in order to make the audience more critical of the action in the play. For instance, (1) the actor does not 'become' the character he or she is playing, (2) all the technical devices by which illusion is created are in full view of the audience, and (3) the action can be stopped in order to sing songs about relevant issues.

Allegory (*n. sing.*) and **allegorical** (*adj.*)   in drama and theatre, allegory is the process by which abstractions, like 'wealth', 'salvation', are made concrete on stage, using characterization (including the use of **costumes**, **masks**, **props**) and story.

Anti-climax (*n. sing.*)   see **climax**.

Apron (*n. sing.*)   that area of the **stage** between the **proscenium arch** and the audience in a conventional theatre building. (See illustration on page 16.)

Art Theatre also **art theatre** (*n. sing.; as pl.*, Art theatres, refers to theatre buildings)   a term somewhat loosely used to refer to either (1) experimental dramatic production by intellectual playwrights and theatre artists (in this sense a 'new' theatre), or (2) established elitist theatres which produce the 'great works' of the culture, including opera and ballet, in contra-distinction to the 'new' theatre; or (3) both 1 and 2, especially in societies where all receive state subsidies and are, therefore, differentiated from the purely commercial theatre.

Aside (*n./pl. -s*)   a comment made by an actor in **role** which is clearly audible to the audience but is not meant to be heard by the other **characters** on the stage.

Backcloth (*n./pl. -s;* also N.Am., **backdrop**)   a large piece of fabric, generally with scenes painted upon it, which is behind the actors, dividing the scene from the **back-stage** area (except in a **theatre-in-the-round** production). Useful also in outdoor performances. (See illustration on page 19.) **Flats** can serve the same purpose as backcloths.

Black-out (*n. sing.*)   the total elimination of light on stage and in the auditorium, usually to indicate the ending of a scene. Some playwrights conclude scenes in their play-scripts with the term 'black-out'. (See also **curtain**.)

Box-office (*n. sing.*)   the place in the **foyer** of a conventional European theatre where tickets for performances are purchased. A more idiomatic use is in the sense of the amount of money taken for a performance, e.g. 'the box-office was good tonight'. In anglophone West Africa the more common word for 'box-office' is 'gate'.

Cast (*n. sing.*)   generally refers to the group of actors who each have a part or parts in a play. Sometimes refers to the list of characters in a play, an abbreviation of 'cast-list'. To cast (*v.*) is to give actors their roles, or characters they are to play, in a particular production.

Character (*n./pl. -s*)   a person within a play; people whom the play is about: e.g. the character of a corrupt party secretary; a group of prisoners whose lives the play explores. Characterization (*n.*) refers to the process by which the playwright creates the play's characters.

Choreography (*n. sing.*)   the composition of the movements for a new **dance** or **dance-mime**, to be performed either by one person or by an ensemble of dancers. The choreographer choreographs the movements, working closely with the composer of the music for that dance.

Chorus (*n. sing.*)   in western theatre the chorus derives specifically from the ancient Greek dramatists and refers to a group of characters in a play, such as elders, who collectively comment on the action of the play, either in formal spoken verse, or in song and dance, or as individuals.

Climax (*n./pl. -es*) the moment of supreme tension in a play, after which matters are in some way resolved. A playwright usually shapes his play to the moment of climax so as to engage the audience's attention fully. Some new forms of drama question the use of climax. **Anti-climax** (*n.*): a failed climax in a badly-directed play; but sometimes deliberately contrived by the playwright for a purpose.

Comedy (*n./pl. -ies*) a form of drama in which matters work out well at the end of the play, proceeding to this conclusion by way of humour and wit. (See **farce, satire**, as specific forms of comedy.)

Company (*n./pl. -ies*) refers to (1) an *ad hoc* group of actors or players who have presented a play; (2) a commercial or subsidized group of actors, directors, designers, managers, musicians, technicians, and anyone else on the pay-roll, which regularly presents performances to the public.

Concert party (*n./pl. -ies*) a small group of travelling actors who travel from village to village in coastal West Africa (mainly in Ghana) presenting short comedies, staged simply but with vigorous acting and accompanied by jazzy music.

Costume (*n./pl. -s*) an actor's costume enables the audience to identify the character through appearance, which conforms to the image of that type of person. In plays incorporating history or fable or myth, costume has the added function of providing spectacle on the stage. (See also **props, make-up**.)

Dance (*n./pl. -s*) broadly defined as rhythmic movement to music, ranging from the traditional and ethnic dances to contemporary ballet. In the performance of plays dance is used less than songs. **dance-mimes** (*n.*) are closer to drama than 'pure' dance, partly because there is a strengthening of the **story** (**plot**) and **characterization** at the expense of a specific dance aesthetic or of ritualistic dances and traditional **masquerades**.

Dénouement (*n. sing.*) the resolution of the action in a play so that the 'truth' is at last revealed. The dénouement usually follows the **climax**.

Deus ex machina (*n. sing.*; from the Latin = 'god, out of a machine') a contrived ending by the playwright: matters are sorted out in the play usually through the introduction of a new character, who enters the action near the end with privileged information. In ancient Greek (and, later, Roman), theatre a 'god' came down from 'heaven' (on a 'cloud' or a 'bird' – the **stage machine**) and told the other mortal characters what was what.

Dialogue (*n. sing.*) the discussion which takes place between characters on stage. It may be scripted already, or **improvised**.

Dimmers (*n. pl.*) see **stage lighting**.

Director (*n./pl. -s*) a person who is concerned with the aesthetics of a performance and who shapes the production of a play through a series of rehearsals. 'Producer' is sometimes used in this sense (but see **producer**, and also **stage manager**).

Drama (*n. sing.*) defies precise definition; it can refer to (1) a type of performance, e.g. African drama, as opposed to African dance; (2) an intellectual discipline, e.g. a drama course; (3) a particular play, e.g. Aidoo's *Anowa* is a drama about freedom and slavery; and (4) the more intense parts of a particular play, e.g. the drama at the end of *Anowa*. (See also **theatre**, which is sometimes confused with drama in usage.)

Dramatic irony (*n. sing.*) information about certain characters and events in a play which the audience have, but which the characters themselves don't have. (Not to be confused with **irony** which is more generally defined.)

Dramaturge (*n./pl. -s*) a resident playwright of a theatre company who will shape and adapt scenes, in writing, for the director and the actors while they are rehearsing his (or someone else's) play.

Dress rehearsal (*n./pl. -s*) usually the last rehearsal before the first performance of a new production. All other aspects of the production are combined at this point with the acting: **sets**, **costumes**, **props**, **music**.

Effects (*n. pl.*) certain stage devices which create apparently fabulous and magical happenings on stage, e.g. explosions, the appearance of ghosts, fire-spitting gods, monsters and levitation. Sometimes referred to as special effects; see also **sound effects**, **stage machinery**.

Entrance (*n./pl. -s*) and **enter** (*v.*) an actor 'makes an entrance' on coming into the acting area in role. In some productions, actors can sit on the stage, in view of the audience, and 'enter' simply by getting up and assuming their roles.

Exit (*n. and v.;* from Latin = 'he/she goes out'; **exeunt** = 'they go out') when an actor leaves the acting area 'he exits', and when more than one go out 'they exit' – the word is now completely anglicized. We also refer to actors' 'entrances and exits'.

Farce (*n./pl. -es*) a type of frenzied comedy in which the humour lies in the complicated situations and exaggerated characterization.

Festival theatre (*n. sing.*) a term suggested by Oyin Ogunba (Nigerian critic) to describe a traditional African performance mode which occurs at traditional festivals.

Flats (*n. pl.*; rarely *sing.*) screens of varying sizes from 2m × 1m to 4m × 2m, lightweight and with a taut surface which can be painted. Flats are linked or hinged together as walls, doors, arches, etc., painted accordingly, in order to form the setting for the action. (See **backcloth**, **scenery**)

Folk media (*n. pl.*) a term, used mainly in UNESCO publications, to refer to a variety of live traditional performances as communication media; and to differentiate these from film, radio and television which are referred to as mass media.

Freeze (*v.*) in multiple staging or a **split scene**. A group of actors can end a scene or part of a scene, and still remain on the stage, by 'freezing', i.e. by becoming absolutely immobile while another group of actors take over the scene. This gives the impression of actions in different locations happening simultaneously.

Gate (*n. sing.*) a term, especially in West Africa, for **box-office**, which refers to (1) the entrance to the auditorium; and (2) the charges for admission.

Hero (*n./pl. -es*) also **tragic hero**, **anti-hero** the principal character in a drama, who has qualities of leadership. The tragic hero struggles against adversity, fate or evil; and often becomes a sacrifice, or victim. The anti-hero is someone who is unlikely to become a hero, but despite himself does. (All tend to be male; the female 'heroine' plays a more limited and limiting role.)

Improvise (*v.*), and **improvisation** (*n. sing.*) to act out situations in role, making up dialogue and developing characters as the improvisations proceed. Some improvisations can be entirely open-ended, others can be within a tightly-controlled **scenario**. Often, a play which has been developed by a group of actors through improvisation can become 'stabilized', and eventually transcribed as a play-script.

Irony (*n. sing.* mainly) but also **ironies** (*pl.*) a word with a wider, complex meaning. Briefly, in drama, it is the means by which audiences achieve a wider consciousness through unlikely and strange (though subsequently most appropriate) developments in the action and characterization within a play.

Joker system (*n. sing.*)   a term deriving from the work of Augusto Boal (Argentinian theatre activist) which refers to a mode of rehearsing and performing a play, through characters who are both within and outside the dramatic action, and through actors who exchange roles.

Lead (*adj.*, as in lead roles, or leading roles)   the principal characters in a play. Other characters are referred to as 'supporting roles' in this context.

Make-up (*n. sing.*)   the means by which an actor emphasizes or changes his or her facial features in order to look more like the audience's conception of the character which he or she is playing, e.g. whitening hair to look older; painting lips to look voluptuous.

Mask (*n./pl. -s*)   the covering for part or all of an actor's face (and sometimes for even the whole head and shoulders) to present to the audience strange features and a frozen expression which the movements of the body alone can animate.

Mask (*v.*)   accidentally to obscure the character on stage who is speaking from the view of the audience; the actor doing so is said to be 'masking the speaker'.

Masque (*n./pl. -s*)   a word deriving from sixteenth and seventeenth century courtly performances and entertainments, somewhat removed from more standard drama and theatre performances in the sense that the masque involved the courtly members of the audience, masked, as the performers. It was sophisticated and formal play by them, rather than a play for them.

Masquerade (*n./pl. -s*)   an English word, closely related in origin to masque, which now describes a widespread and important African mode of performance and entertainment; the formal presentation of the (sacred) masks to the community, accompanied, variously, by music, dance, chants, acrobatics and rituals.

Melodrama (*n./pl. -s*)   a type of drama in which the playwright underlines the emotional impact of the play by the use of music, and in which 'good' finally triumphs over 'evil'. Some critics find melodrama to be sentimental and escapist.

Mime (*v.*)   to act without using any words or sounds; mime (*n. sing.*) is the performance by an **actor** (or **mime**, or mime-artist) using gestures, facial expression and body movement only.

Musical (*n./pl. -s*)   a more popular form of music theatre than opera or ballet. Musicals have spoken dialogue between the songs; but the actors keep in character throughout the performance.

Narrator (*n./pl. -s*)   in traditional performances, a story-teller; in a play, the narrator provides a link between scenes, and also between the audience and the drama itself. In plays which seek interaction with their audiences the narrator plays a crucial role in restating arguments which might have been missed, stopping the action, and bringing members of the audience into the performance.

Naturalism (*n. sing.*)   in drama and theatre, naturalism is a form of stylization in performance which makes a pretence of not being stylized at all but showing things 'exactly as they are'. This refers not only to the settings of a play (e.g. seemingly real fires under the real pots in the peasant's hut) but also to the content of the play (e.g. the 'real' motivations of the characters).

Pacing (*n. sing.*)   in play direction, refers to the way the performance is shaped, in terms of the pace of the action and the dialogue, speeding it up, slowing it down, the use of silences, the creation of tension. In the performance of individual actors the related term is a sense of 'timing' which is, in fact, one of the main acting skills.

Performance (*n./pl. -s*)   refers (1) generally to any presentation before an audience, be it a traditional dance or a contemporary play; and (2) specifically to one showing of a particular production of a play. **To perform** (*v.*) has a wider term of reference than to act because it applies not only to actors but also to musicians, dancers, masqueraders, traditional story-tellers – the demonstration of each person's art.

Perspective (*n. sing.*)   first developed in the architecture of the theatres of the Italian Renaissance (fifteenth and sixteenth centuries), it is today, in theatre, specifically related to the painting of **scenery**, usually in **proscenium arch** theatres. Through perspective a comparatively shallow stage is given the impression of immense scenic depth. (See illustration on page 16.)

Plot (*n./pl. -s*)   a story restructured so as to fit into the scenes of a play for performance.

Producer (*n./pl. -s*)   strictly speaking one who arranges the finances for a particular production (and who *ipso facto* has some say in its final form); but also loosely used instead of **director**.

Production (*n./pl. -s*)   a series of performances of a play by a theatre company or *ad hoc* group of actors.

Projection (*n. sing.*)   technical acting term for the audibility of the whole range of an actor's voice to all members of the audience, and, by inference, the accessibility of the actor's character to the whole audience. The actor is said to project (*v.*) his or her voice, or his or her character.

Props (*n. pl.*)   short form of 'properties' (seldom used now): the accoutrements, implements and various objects which actors require both in their characterization and in the action of the play.

Proscenium arch (*n. sing.*)   and proscenium arch stage (*n./pl.* – – stages) a development in theatre building during the Italian Renaissance: the arch at the front of the stage provides a structural support for the curtain (which closes off the scene from the audience) and an aesthetic 'framing' of the perspective scenery. It also enables all the mechanical means by which theatre illusion is created to be hidden from the gaze of the audience, so that the illusion of reality is complete.

Ramp (*n./pl -s*)   ramps provide access to different acting levels on stage other than by steps. (See illustration on page 19.)

Ritual theatre (*n. sing.*)   in Africa, the term refers to what are seen as the traditional origins of African theatre in ritual performances which co-exist today with contemporary drama. (But there is debate over this.)

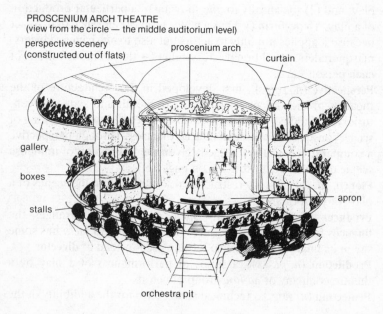

PROSCENIUM ARCH THEATRE
(view from the circle — the middle auditorium level)

perspective scenery
(constructed out of flats)

proscenium arch

curtain

gallery

boxes

stalls

apron

orchestra pit

Role (*n./pl. -s*) and **role-play** (*n.* and *v.*)   role means any character or part which an actor plays; role-play is specific to group improvisation and drama-in-education (N.Am.: **creative dramatics**): open-ended and non-scripted exploration of situations and roles, using the collective imagination of the group (not necessarily actors).

Rostra (*n. pl.*)   the removable structures which create different acting levels on stage. (See also **ramp**; and illustration on page 20.)

Saga (*n./pl. -s*)   an account of heroic deeds, in verse, in song or in dramatic performance, which belongs to a particular community and relates to their collective past.

Satire (*n./pl. -s*)   also **to satirize**, (*v.*)   satire in drama is the humorous presentation on stage of individual vice and human weakness for the purposes of social and political criticism. The tone of satire is often bitter or 'fierce', usually sophisticated, and seldom moralistic.

Scenario (*n./pl. -s*)   in drama, an arrangement of what will take place within each scene; in film, a summary of the action.

Scene (*n./pl. -s*)   in drama and theatre, refers to (1) a further division of a play within each Act, thus: Act 1 scene ii; (2) a particular setting on the stage relating to the action within a play, e.g. the surgery in the basement of Dr Bero's house; (3) a particular incident or series of incidents between specific characters, e.g. the scene between Bero and the Earth Mothers; and, more idiomatically, e.g. Aafaa's big scene near the end of *Madmen and Specialists*.

Scenery (*n. sing.*)   the means by which a specific place, a general area, or a special atmosphere is created within which the action of a particular play takes place. Sometimes 'sets' is used in a similar sense (from 'settings', 'setting the scene').

Scrim (*n. sing.*); also N.Am. **scenic gauze**)   loose-woven material hung as a backdrop on stage, which can appear solid if stage lighting is thrown on to it, but which seems to disappear if bright stage lighting illuminates the area directly behind it. By switching between lighting systems, people or objects can seem to disappear and reappear as if by magic.

Sight-lines (*n. pl.*)   the view of the stage from all parts of the auditorium. Sight-lines are important for directors and actors since they must collectively ensure that every member of the audience is able to see all the action in a production.

Soliloquy (*n./pl. -ies*)   a speech made by a single actor, alone on the stage, in role, as though speaking aloud that character's thoughts.

Sound effects (*n. pl.*)   sounds which it would be inappropriate for actors to make in role on stage (e.g. announcements on the radio, thunder and rain, the voice of a character's conscience) are either made live off-stage by other actors or recorded on tape and played back during a performance over the theatre's sound system.

Spectacle (*n. sing.*)   the use of a number of illusionistic devices which together with costumes, settings, dance and music creates a dazzling show, sometimes referred to as 'total theatre'.

Split-scene (*n./pl. -s*)   parts of the acting area created as separate locations in a composite scene, for the action to move back and forth, from one to the other, as appropriate. (See also **freeze**.)

Stage (*n./pl. -s*)   technically a raised platform for performance, but in fact any acting area, be it raised, sunken, or a piece of canvas laid on the earth.

Stage directions (*n. pl.*)   in a play text, the instructions to actors (and information for readers), usually in brackets or italics, indicating (1) actions appropriate to their lines; (2) the tone of voice required; and (3) a meaning contrary to the literal meaning of the words (sometimes referred to as the 'sub-plot').

Stage lighting (*n. sing.* and *pl.*)   a means of illuminating the action of a play to heighten dramatic impact. The most elaborate lighting systems are in conventional theatre buildings; but there can be effective portable stage lighting as well. The following are the main types of lanterns: (1) spots, which 'throw' very bright, concentrated light on to a small area; (2) floods, which give a bright, general light; (3) battens – rows of ordinary light bulbs, backed by simple reflectors, arranged above the actors' heads or below their feet ('footlights').   The lanterns are wired into dimmers and a control panel, which enables the lighting technician to vary the intensity of individual lights, and to 'fade up' and 'fade down' sets of lights which have previously been 'set' to light different scenes. Some lighting systems in big theatres are so complicated that computers are used to light elaborate productions.

Stage machinery (*n. sing.*)   mechanical devices, such as winches and pulleys, or, more recently, hydraulically operated platforms which can be raised, lowered, or revolved, so as to lift people and scenery on to and off the acting area. The mechanical devices are in various ways obscured from the audience.

Stage manager (*n./pl. -s*)   the person in complete charge, back-stage, of a performance, to whom the producer and director cede their authority. (Not to be confused with theatre manager who handles the administration of the theatre company and theatre building.)

Street theatre (*n./pl. -s*)   performances given in *ad hoc* situations, by the roadside, in the market-place – wherever people congregate in the normal course of events.

Stylization (*n. sing.*)   forms of drama established between actors and audiences, including stage conventions, symbols and acting techniques – all as a way of depicting 'reality' on the stage.

Theatre (*n./pl. -s*)   difficult to define in ways appropriate to different cultures. Basically two meanings in western European theatre, (1) the circumstances of a live dramatic performance; and (2) a building for live dramatic performances.

Theatre-in-the-round (*n.*), **traverse stage** (*n.*), **thrust stage** (*n.*) different actor-audience relationships for a dramatic performance, which are all alternatives to the *proscenium arch stage*. In theatre-in-the-round the audience sit all a-round the actors; the traverse stage has audience on two opposite sides; the thrust stage has audience on three sides, or in a 250° semi-circle, with a **backdrop**,

THEATRE-IN-THE-ROUND
(a possible purpose-built structure)

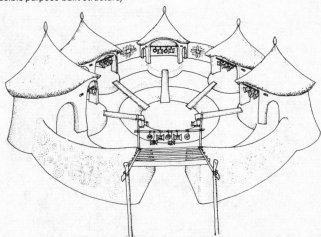

Note the **sunken stage** in the centre and the levels for audience seating rising up to the walled periphery. The thatched-roofed **backstage** areas for actors, and entrances and exits (with *ramps* drawn in), as well as additional seating for the audience.

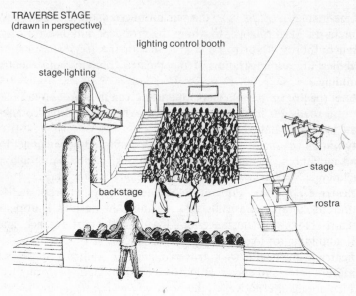

TRAVERSE STAGE
(drawn in perspective)

stage-lighting

lighting control booth

backstage

stage

rostra

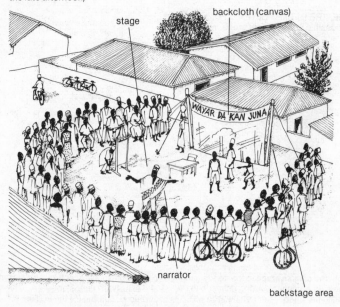

THRUST STAGE
(created for an ad hoc street performance in
the late afternoon)

stage

backcloth (canvas)

WAYAR DA 'KAN JUNA

narrator

backstage area

or back-stage wall, which gives actors access to the stage and screens off the backstage area.

Tragedy (*n./pl. -ies*) deriving from the Greeks (like so much of European theatre) tragedy reduces the great to death or disgrace through the working out of fate, and holds them, ironically, responsible in some way for their misfortune. (See also **hero**.)

Transposition (*n./pl. -s*), **to transpose** (*v.*), **translation** (*n./pl. -s*), **to translate** (*v.*) transposition of plays from one culture or era to another differs from translation of the texts from one language to another in that the former attempts specifically to relate the plays to a new social milieu.

Travelling theatre (*n./pl. -s*) a theatre which goes out to the people rather than expecting the people to come to the theatre.

Introduction

This book attempts to analyse the way African drama is developing within the context of African societies. A starting point might be the tensions which now exist in African countries between a number of playwrights and their governments: Wole Soyinka and the government in Nigeria; Ngugi wa Thiong'o and the government in Kenya; Amadu Maddy and the government in Sierra Leone. These, and other examples which are less well known, do not refer to crises past and now resolved but to an ever-widening rift.

The increasing economic and political contradictions in most of the nation–states in Africa are reflected in crises in their post-independence theatre. Established playwrights are discredited by students, their work no longer conceived relevant even in the context in which it was written. Academic theatre departments are despised by both employed professionals as well as the graduates of those departments who cannot find jobs in theatre. African governments have become much more nervous about theatre than any of the other arts; and playwrights who work in Pidgin or a vernacular find themselves harassed or sometimes even imprisoned.

These playwrights begin to perceive, objectively, the nature of the elite, the class-in-formation of which they have inevitably become a part. Their commentary upon their societies now takes on a new dimension and assumes a new focus: the sufferings of the poor can be related to them through a theory of exploitation by the elite. This process by which the creative artist or intellectual in the society discovers links with the oppressed in that society is taking place in many parts of the third world; with it there is a growing consciousness of the *cultural* dependence (as well as an economic dependence) which the elite have upon the developed world. And whereas, at the time of independence, it was art which tended to establish the goals for the revolution (especially in negritude), now it is seen to be the social revolution which will dictate the goals of art.

This study of African drama tries to relate the growing politicization of the playwrights and theatre activists to the development of the most social of the arts.

In relation to this I do not think that it is particularly helpful to think of African drama as 'things' like plays, productions, actors, texts. Even '*a* history of drama' reifies what is essentially a process through which many minds and imaginations interact with each other, in the process changing the 'thing' being studied. For this reason few definitions of culture ever achieve any measure of agreement; and the words 'drama', 'theatre', 'tradition' are no exception.

I have not offered any definitions, therefore, and have tried to present the development of drama on this continent as a process. I see it as a process in terms of individual plays: how an idea becomes a performance in front of an audience committed to watching it; how a problem becomes dramatized. I also see it as a wider process of the development of new dramatic traditions within specific communities, leading to a wider consciousness. This process is specific to the history of colonialism and neo-colonialism in Africa during this century.

The study seeks to present this process through an analysis of a number of contradictions. First, there is the contradictory relationship between the traditional performing arts and the new elites. On the one hand the cultural bureaucrats and theatre artists transform the art of the people into a product for bourgeois and international consumption – whilst at the same time professing to revive the traditional cultural values of the people. On the other hand, traditional performances with a highly conservative or reactionary function are often made to appear radical in the politics of the new nation–state, and the new urban culture of the proletariat is derided even by those who manoeuvre themselves into marketing it. This is the subject-matter of the first chapter.

Second, the tendency towards the creation of play-texts as dramatic literature appears to tie the development of drama to the western tradition of 'great works', with the emphasis on individual achievement. This contradicts the nature of the live performance with its own emphasis on communication with a particular audience speaking a particular language and at a particular time. The second chapter approaches this problem in the context of existing performance traditions.

The 'great tradition', including the somewhat self-conscious reaction to it, has helped create what is sometimes known as the Art Theatre (or art theatre). On the one hand this is a professional and technically proficient theatre (which can make money), and on the other hand it is a serious and artistically experimental theatre (which loses money). The Art Theatre actually holds these two opposing tendencies in tension.

Within the 'great tradition' an apparently new play may be more derivative than an actual adaptation into a contemporary African context of a 'great work' from another culture. These adaptations are also referred to as transpositions. Chapter 3 compares some notable transpositions of ancient Greek and European plays by contemporary African playwrights.

Related to this are a number of contradictions in the development of the Art Theatre. Plays about African history which claim their function is to return to the people their history, end up alienating them even more by embedding their history in an artistic process (as well as an economic process) which effectively excludes them from understanding it. Four history plays, from East and West Africa, are analysed in Chapter 4.

It seems that all too often what the academic critics judge to be an 'exceptional' play is not at all 'popular'. However, this concept of 'popularity' is actually restricted to an appreciation by those who are formally educated, the elite. The playwright's sensibility reaches beyond this group, this class-in-formation, which has ironically, through its economic function, enabled the playwright to achieve intellectual distinction.

As plays become increasingly bitter and critical about the levers of power within the state, and those who control them, their authors retreat into those institutions – in fact, the university, specifically – where their salaries are protected through the currency of such concepts as academic freedom, which they increasingly support. Their criticism of the state, in the metropolitan language, is contradicted by their increasing identity with the most elitist institute of higher learning. Those whom they criticize, in English or in French, usually leave them alone. However, when the playwright goes out into the communities and works directly with and among peasants or workers, using their language and dramatizing matters from their point of view, state governments act with brutal swiftness and incarcerate the offending play-wright.

Theatre in the third world, like the third world economies in which this theatre is based, is, in some aspects, over-developed rather than under-developed. Nigeria, for example has constructed elaborate theatre buildings with hugely expensive equipment inside them without having appropriate commercial companies or viable patronage to provide the product for which they were built. Smaller and poorer nations than Nigeria each fund their own national dance troupe which all too often becomes a corps de ballet trained overseas or by foreign professionals to make tours abroad. The rationale behind this is said to be the marketing of the particular country's image abroad, for which the traditional dances have to be 'brought up' to 'international standards'. Finally, countries as different economically and ideologically as Tanzania and Nigeria produce graduates in the performing arts from their universities for whom there are no professional jobs. These graduates then go into the broadcast media (for which they are inappropriately trained) or the bureaucracy or the private commercial sector.

It is appropriate to mention this here for the following reason. This book is intended primarily for African students interested in the study of drama in Africa, who may indeed be embarked upon a career in some aspect of drama or theatre; the book's function, therefore, contradicts its message. It helps compound the problem which it seeks to analyse. There is, for the moment, no way out of this, except to try to understand more clearly the processes by which society shapes its art.

Greater understanding, greater consciousness on the part of all members of the society, is the intention of an alternative type of theatre which is now emerging in different parts of the third world. This has come to be known amongst those involved in it as 'popular theatre'. A description of this sort of popular theatre in Africa forms the substance of the last chapter of the book.

The analysis presented in this book has a number of limitations. It would have been difficult to overcome some of these without creating other limitations in their place.

First, the analysis is largely restricted to theatre in anglophone African countries. This is partly to do with the length of the book, partly to do with the geographical limitations of my own experience, and partly to do with the fact that the study is quite deliberately not *regional* (for example, East Africa, West Africa, North Africa, Southern Africa) and it only considers the drama and theatre *nationally* when this is seminal to the analysis (for example, the protest drama in Nigeria). Regional studies produce their own anomalies, for example, should the region surrounding the Sahara desert be seen as culturally homogeneous (partly because of Islam, the spread of which was itself the result of trade routes across the Sahara), instead of including the Sahelian nations under West Africa in a francophone/anglophone categorization?

Another limitation, perhaps, is my own subjective involvement in the development of African drama. This may be seen in opposite ways: by those who feel that any committed involvement destroys the 'objective' basis of the study; and by those who feel that an expatriate can never be effectively involved in the culture. I do not believe that there can be 'scientific' objectivity in any cultural analysis without our losing an understanding of it as a process. Furthermore, the dispassionate observer can also distort the process in a way which may be more serious because it is unacknowledged and even unperceived.

The academic observer of a people's traditional performances, or of serious theatrical experimentation, who goes away and presents the analysis of these 'objective' observations in a foreign place, is in fact something of a thief. This applies not only to the foreign scholar but even more so to the indigenous researcher from the local university, who has greater access to his or her people's own art, whose research benefits those people not at all whilst providing the researcher with academic honours, high salary and international travel. Some African activists now maintain that recording a traditional performance, even preserving it 'live' in some form or other, is less relevant to the peasant owners of that art than a growing ability *by them* to make it contribute to a better society *for them*. The research which has this latter concern is now referred to as participatory research. This participatory research approach (which, for example, is the basis for a cultural research project in the western Bagamoyo District in Tanzania called *Jipemoyo*) is a pointer to the sort of research in drama and theatre in the future. It is likely to come into sharp opposition with the more conventional research objectives of the bourgeois African universities.

This is not a contrived radical position, or in any sense rhetorical, on the part of such intellectuals. For someone like Ngugi wa Thiong'o, or in the urban context Amadu Maddy, it is a stage in an inevitable process which begins the moment one seeks to make the art of drama available to the people, either based on their traditional performances or not, but always with a contemporary social relevance as its justification to them. In our own much more limited experience in Kaduna State, Nigeria, we have been told time and time again by the peasant farmers that they would prefer the fertilizer to plays about how they are not getting the fertilizer. They would prefer us to come and organize them into effective co-operatives, instead of presenting plays about how co-operatives are undermined. They would want us to help them regain land taken from them for speculative purposes instead of making plays about how they lost their lands. And after the plays have been enthusiastically developed, presented and received, the question always is: 'What is the next step forward?'. For those at the bottom of the social heap, and ultimately for the intellectuals and creative artists who seek to engage with them, the art of drama cannot be separated from the greater political task, and, in its function, from social reality.

At every stage of the process there are great difficulties. It is difficult to make lasting contacts. It is very difficult to formulate the plays so as to lay bare the contradictions. This type of drama work is just beginning in Africa. It is much more developed in parts of Latin America and South East Asia. The limitation of the final chapter of this book is that I have chosen not to discuss work of a greater scope in other communities in Africa. This is because we have not been able to analyse the processes in the way in which we continue to analyse our own, along with the people with whom we work.

The notes carry a wider reference where necessary to a particular aspect of the analysis; the glossary of theatre terms is not comprehensive but covers references in the text.

1 Traditional performance in contemporary society

The various definitions of 'performance', 'drama', 'theatre', and of 'tradition' and 'traditional', come to exercise a tyranny over students. Very often they proceed to use the definitions and categories not so much as a means of conceptualization but as a yardstick to measure how 'dramatic' and how 'theatrical' each performance item is. It is with this in mind that we need to take note of the approaches to the study of African drama; and in the process try to set out a framework for the discussion of African theatre and drama as a complex phenomenon of social and cultural change. The African student of drama is, by the very process of *reading* about drama, part of this phenomenon. Those of us who are engaged in practical theatre projects, and those who study and criticize the play texts, are all engaged, wittingly or unwittingly, in transforming that which we have previously defined. Ironically, many who are keen to see their society changed radically – even through revolution – are also concerned to keep the culture, and especially the performing arts, intact. And there is another irony too, for the deeper we are within the culture, the more committed we are to it but the less we 'see' it. That which has been 'seen' as worth preserving has already been prised apart from its original social setting.

Rural traditions for drama and theatre

The following somewhat lengthy example will perhaps set forth this phenomenon of 'tradition', 'performance', 'African drama' as a process, together with the problems of critical and social perception. A group of university drama students presented three plays, which they had written and directed collectively, in a small village near their university's rural campus. These complete plays, presented largely in the Hausa language, were well received.

Some time later another group of drama students from the same university joined with young farmers (all men) from the same village in developing plays together about the farmers' problems. The whole exercise had been established on the basis of a political perspective on the part of the organizers.

Some months after this, the drama staff at the university were invited as guests to witness the annual *Kalankuwa* festival which is held every year in the village, and which every year is dominated by the role-play performances of the young adults of the village who are the organizers. I and my colleagues accepted the invitation and attended the 'traditional' performance which opened the festival in the village of Bomo.

Each year the road through the village is sealed off at both ends and the visitors, and those residents who are not 'actors' or 'organizers', are charged an admission fee. In the village, on either side of the road, booths of guinea-corn stalks have been erected, but in outline only so that the decoration and activities within each booth are readily apparent to the spectators strolling down the road. The booths are variously labelled 'Hospital'; 'Min. of Agriculture'; 'Office of the President'; 'Alkali Court'; and so on: a depiction in each case, directly made, of the agencies of government at local, state and national levels. They are all muddled up, however, and the Alkali's Court is right next door to the Office of the President of Nigeria.

At 5.00 p.m. there was a procession into the village by the young peasant farmers, many of whom also work in the nearby university as messengers or cooks or labourers. They were dressed up in the costumes of the roles they were intending to play: military of all ranks in excellently made uniforms; nurses, newsmen, politicians. The procession moved through the crowds of villagers to the centre of the village where two pavilions were set up. The 'military' and 'civilian politicians' sat in front of the one facing the other in which the chief organizers of *Kalankuwa* were stationed to control the proceedings.

The role-play was entered into very seriously. At this particular *Kalankuwa*, which was on 19 and 20 December 1980, the 'military' gave a report and handed over to the 'civilian politicians' – an obvious reflection of what had taken place in Nigeria in October 1979. This 'ceremony' – in role – was followed by the award of prizes to those who had performed best in the role play (which was still to take place, since this was only the beginning of the festival), or excelled in the organization which had preceded it. There were a very large number of prizes, awarded both to the children who were dressed up (mainly as nurses) and to the young adult farmers themselves. The prizes ranged from cash which was in excess of £50 each, to tea-sets, lamps, transistor radios and televisions. The farmers had raised the money for these prizes among themselves, and also from the proceeds of a farm which they had worked collectively during the previous farming season.

Following this, the group processed out of the village. After the prayers at sunset (Bomo is almost entirely a Muslim village), the people, still in their costumes, returned to the booth-lined street and took up positions in their respective booths and remained in role. Spectators could visit them and enter into role-play with them: they could 'petition' the 'President of Nigeria'; they could be 'tried' in the 'Alkali Court'; see a slide-show in the 'Ministry of Agriculture'; be 'charged' in the 'Police Station'; be attended to in the 'Hospital'; and so on. Many of the villagers thronged through the booths; but their entry into corresponding roles appeared to be limited.

Kalankuwa is also a variation of a 'Lord-of-Misrule' festival,[1]* and there is licence within the village enclosure to gamble, smoke and take other liberties in public normally proscribed by Islam. Many of the villagers do not go to sleep at all that night, and indeed throughout the processions and the performances the serious gamblers, within the gambling booths also made from guinea-corn stalks or simply on the ground, pursue their sport.

I have attempted a sketchy outline of what was described by the farmers themselves, in their publicity in English, as 'village drama'. It seemingly bore no relation to the drama which we had done for and with the villagers; nor was it in any way affected by that, despite the fact that a few of the village personnel were involved in both our work and their own festival. What then was our own perception of their festival 'drama'?

First of all, the role-play was so serious and so meticulously observed that we had some difficulty knowing who was in role and who was actually a member of the village hierarchy. It was also difficult to know when people were in role and when they were not. Initially, all of us thought that the prizes were part of a central dramatized satire on the hand-over by the 'military' to the

---

* Notes and references to the text occur at the end of each chapter.

'civilians'. We thought that *empty* cartons and envelopes were being used in the 'presentation of awards'. We were therefore rather disconcerted to discover that the radios, televisions, money etc, were all new and were actually prizes for organizational effort and good acting.

One of our colleagues commented that the peasant participants should be told that this was not 'drama' after all. However, perhaps it is possible to see it differently, from the farmers' point of view: after seeing university students performing plays for them ('drama') and also after participating in making 'plays' themselves with the students (also 'drama'), they have appropriated the word 'drama' to describe their own cultural presentation. This has been and is still undergoing a process of transformation, which we will comment on in a moment.

We also had some politicized social science students with us from the university, who commented afterwards that the young farmers 'needed to be organized'. Again I think it is possible to see this rather differently, from the peasants' own point of view; for, in fact, effective organization was the one thing which their 'drama' – and indeed the whole festival – demonstrated. This organization was at the grass roots, at the very lowest social and cultural level. The ability of these young adults to form such a grass-roots organization that mobilized *cadres* to raise money, collect costumes, improvise imaginatively on decoration, borrow expensive equipment, and then ensure that the two-day festival ran smoothly, probably exceeded the organizational capability, at a comparable level, of the professional theatre and drama units in the university who have more resources at their disposal. It certainly exceeded these units' ability to present performances in rural villages.

The farmers acknowledged their ability to organize themselves by presenting prizes for organization within the context of the performance itself; and it is interesting to see why this is so.

The name *Kalankuwa* suggests that it was originally a harvest festival. However, the symbolic connection with the harvest now seems tenuous – except, ironically, that funds from the harvest are now used to organize a 'drama'. A festival will continue to exist only if its organization is guaranteed from year to year. This is much more likely to be the case if the traditional hierarchy orders the festival and maintains it. A grass-roots organization for a specifically cultural (as opposed to a purely economic) objective is an achievement and it is appropriate that it should be celebrated within the context of the final performance.

We have become accustomed to the separation of 'art' from its means of production, which is a significant feature of the culture of advanced technological societies. In particular, in most bourgeois forms of dramatic art (the classical theatre, opera, ballet, musicals) the means of production are deliberately masked. As we sit, for example, watching a performance of an elaborate production we are kept unaware of the hard-nosed bargaining between the writer/composer/choreographer and the backers (state or commercial, it makes little difference) which has preceded its staging and which, in the case of non-established playwrights, has certainly determined and transformed what they wanted to say. It is one view of contemporary African theatre that a great deal of it is the result of, and a further contribution towards, the establishment of an artistic mode of production for theatre which requires university-trained specialists and elaborate facilities, and an elaborate system of state subsidies where such a theatre is inevitably not commercially viable.

The standard definitions of 'drama' and 'theatre' even within different social systems define it specifically as an *art* and ignore the way in which its organizational capacity has developed. This is not just because the *organization* of the established forms of theatre, and the study and production of drama both for live theatre and other media like radio and film, has been situated within the economic framework of the society. It is actually enshrined in the western theatre aesthetic. The definitions for western dramatic art derive from the model and precepts of Aristotle, the ancient Greek philosopher and teacher who formulated his analysis 2300 years ago. Aristotle's critique concentrates entirely on the final dramatic product, the art manifest in a performance; and any socially coercive function for drama is based on this analysis of an aesthetic. It is the surviving portion of this critique, specifically on tragedy, which has been mediated by later European theorists of the art of theatre, through enormous commentaries on this text, most notably by the scholars of the sixteenth century. All this has coalesced today into hard and fast 'rules' for the successful and effective 'play'. For example, a play has a beginning, a middle and an end (described as the 'unity of action'); the central 'tragic' character always has a 'tragic flaw'; the theory of katharsis sees tragedy as a 'purging of the emotions'; the 'representation' of an action follows certain patterns of probability; and so on. These rules help to consolidate the specialized and professional status of the dramatic arts without ever articulating *how* such a theatre and drama might develop in terms of its economic organization.

Even the twentieth century reaction to the Aristotelian notions of theatre tends to concentrate on the final artistic form. It seems that in defining theatre we are predisposed to look for an *art form* (which may follow certain rules or deliberately reject them), and in the process we ignore completely the way in which the production of that art form has been accomplished.

This has considerable significance for the definitions which are produced for African drama and theatre. The definitions generally come from the Aristotelian model for Western dramatic art, either absolutely, or as a modification of the Aristotelian 'rules'. In the end, that which is absorbed by the students – becoming a critical orthodoxy over a period of time – is a system of categorization based on a set of rules. Students then want to be told by their teachers all the 'right' answers; and the dramatic works, the play-texts, which are said to constitute African drama, are reduced to such questions as: Is Soyinka's play *The Road* a tragedy, or a comedy, or a tragi-comedy, or. . . .? Is Kurunmi in Ola Romtimi's play of that title a tragic hero? What are the formal elements of drama in the traditional *Nyau* dance, and how are they used in Zambian plays?

A modification of the Aristotelian 'rules', which may even include opposition to Aristotle's theories generally, is often the starting point for an attempt to relate the traditional arts of performance to contemporary African culture in terms of a redefinition of drama. This has been manifest, for example, in the continuing academic argument over whether *ritual* or *festival* (or both) is historically and in essence 'African drama'. In the argument it is the final product, the ritual or the festival observed in performance, which provides a new definition of drama or an alternative method of categorization. This leads to such statements as:

This ceremony can serve as a paradigm for kings' festivals not only in Yorubaland but much wider afield in Africa, especially in West Africa, for it contains several of the typical elements of the African 'royal drama'. First there is a string of loosely connected events lasting for a few days, all in an atmosphere of general merriment. Then, there is a central event of a historical and military nature which is usually mimed. The king may conclude the ceremony by dancing in full pomp and pageantry for the whole community.[2]

and:

The Chorus, called *Akunyungba*, was an essential part of the perform-ance. During the early part of the development of the theatre when the masque-dramaturge was yet an officer at court the chorus was composed mainly of the women of the palace. Later, when the theatre moved out of court circles and the troupe had to travel about entertaining the general public, the masque-dramaturge had to rely on his younger players to play the chorus. . . .

. . . The importance of the chorus to any performance was never in doubt since without it the drama was fragmented, episodic, and incomplete.[3]

Both these quotations come from influential studies of the tradi-tional performing arts as drama and theatre. They are primarily concerned with the aesthetics of the particular performances being studied. However, the description in each case does not indicate how a festival or ritual performance has achieved its present organizational level; nor does it suggest how its personnel may be able to change its basic mode of performance in order to depict the changes taking place in the society itself. Indeed, these social changes may have already rendered the festival or ritual meaning-less in terms of present-day realities.

The present-day *Kalankuwa* performance in Bomo village might seem to be trivial, inconsequential, and even a corruption of tradition for it is changing from a harvest festival into a more satirical festival with licence to 'break the rules' for the duration. What we are observing is the usurpation of the function of a cultural activity – a festival – by the grass-roots elements in the society. The village is hard against the boundary of the university which is a major agent for change in the society, both locally and nationally. There is obviously a 'hot-house' effect with regard to social change within the village; and there may be other factors which make the cultural development in this village unique. The Bomo *Kalankuwa* is not, therefore, necessarily representative of the way 'drama' is developing from the traditional culture. Rather, it is intended to show how complex is contemporary performance even in its most modest form.

There is a final observation which perhaps needs to be made

before we move away from definitions of 'traditional drama' and 'traditional theatre'. Those academic critics, as well as ourselves who are readers, who talk of African 'ritual theatre' and African 'festival drama' as fixed entities or as the embodiment of cultural history, are nevertheless contributing to the transformation of an oral culture into a literary culture. And we are doing this organizationally. We do it through our careers in the universities, through our academic research, through publications, and through policy-making in arts councils and ministries of culture. The trouble is that this high-level reorganization of traditional art is rendered more or less invisible by its very rapid inclusion within the overall educational framework of the new nation-states. The paradox is that while we advocate social change for ourselves, who have benefited most from the educational system, and the establishment of a new society in which we will figure prominently, we also strive to keep the traditional culture intact and unchanging, and justify doing so by the ideology of cultural independence.

If much tradition-based critical analysis of African drama is limited by focusing exclusively on the artistic product and omitting its social and economic organization from the discussion, so too are a number of sociological and anthropological studies of African societies severely limited by their exclusion of the plastic and performing arts from their analyses. The sociologist's definition of 'culture' has been narrowed down to include that which can be assessed scientifically: descent groups, lineages, kinship patterns, the functioning of magic and religion, the systems of kingship and other formalized social and political institutions. For example, a generally illuminating study of the Yoruba in western Nigeria[4] indicates the contrary tendencies of extensive urbanization of the Yoruba heartlands since the middle of the last century, and their diaspora throughout West Africa this century; but there is no discussion at all on the amazing popularity of the Yoruba travelling theatres amongst local and expatriate Yoruba communities during the last three decades. Research by the Yoruba theatre scholar, Joel Adedeji, whom I quoted above, has shown that these companies had a traditional and historical precursor in the *Alarinjo* theatre: travelling groups of entertainers which grew out of the Yoruba court and cult performances of the sixteenth, seventeenth and eighteenth centuries. Any sociological discussion of Yoruba urban consciousness should surely include the travelling theatres. These articulate this consciousness whilst being made economically viable by the very existence of towns. But the author of this sociological study is silent on the Yorubas' ability to organize and present theatre, as well as on the aesthetics of the performances.

There is also an opposite tendency, which is to write at length on African cults, rituals and masquerades either anthropologically (and as reflecting social structures) or as adjuncts of the traditional plastic arts (and artefact remains). However, once again there is a growing silence when the use of cult objects, costumes and masks in *secular* public performance come into prominence. One such study, by Dennis Duerden,[5] specifically seeks to relate African traditional art (represented by masks, cult objects, regalia) to contemporary African literature (represented by a handful of West African novels and play-texts). But the study is silent on the actual dynamics of traditional and contemporary performances. The author, through a philosophical analysis, postulates a theory of aesthetics which binds the creative principle that lies behind traditional African art to the creative principle that formulates the content of modern African literature. The absence of any extended discussion on the art of performance in the specific context of a theoretical discussion of the relationship between art and literature in Africa reflects two crucial problems which are central to any process of trying to define theatre and drama:

1   Live performances – whether they be performances of dramas, songs, dances, music, stories – are the most ephemeral of all art. They vanish within moments of being brought into existence, and only remain as a memory.
2   It is very difficult for someone outside the specific culture to know what he or she is looking at and listening to during a particular performance: the very *style* of a performance is a shorthand of actual meaning which has been established jointly by artists (composers and performers) and their audiences over a period of time.

There is a common solution to each of these problems, but in each case I think it is a *false* solution:

1   The live performance is recorded. It is generally recorded as a written text; though occasionally it is recorded on sound tape and on film. I would describe it as a false solution because what is being preserved is not the total experience of the actual performance but only one of its ingredients: that is, the final artistic product in

itself, isolated from the social act of its performance which gives it its full meaning.

2 Traditional styles of performance are rendered *exotic*, which means that the incomprehensible elements – to an outsider to the tradition – no longer need to be understood, because they have been taken out of context, 'cut loose' as it were, and can now be accepted merely as 'local colour', framed by the more easily comprehensible international or inter-cultural style of the rest of the show.

There is another sense in which these apparent solutions to the ephemeral qualities of performance and the inaccessibility of traditional material and style can be described as false. In each instance the problem relates to the *meaning* of a performance. For many anthropologists and ethnographers secular performance seems to lack substance and appears not to have any great significance for their respective communities. It appears to have no meaning in the way, say, a ritual has a meaning. If a performance is transient, is its ultimate meaning transient as well? Obviously the text of a play, which has been written down, has a meaning, or meanings in its textual form; and this meaning may be enhanced by abstract reference to the text's cultural background. But is it the same meaning that the play has for the audience collectively assembled at a performance of it? And is this meaning always the same for each performance, irrespective of the circumstances and of who constitutes the audience?

The answer must be no, for the meaning of each performance is tied up with the particular and unique experience of that perform-ance. We are now beginning to set the objective meaning of a play-text in opposition to the subjective experience of it in performance.

The other problem, of the inaccessibility of traditional material, suggests that meaning is deeply embedded in forms that custom and repeated use have loaded with a detailed significance, which is now intuitively rather than consciously perceived. The crucial question is whether the meaning is now so culture-bound that it cannot be decoded to yield a more generalized meaning. To render these elements merely exotic avoids the real meaning.

We have not quite finished with the written analysis of the traditional performing arts. There are some studies of the tradi-tional arts which do in fact address themselves to this central issue of meaning where   (1) there is no text;   (2) the performance is secular;   (3) the performance is a transformation of ritual and ceremony into entertainment;   (4) the performance is a depiction of social realities, and, perhaps,   (5) a satirical comment as well. Some of these studies also address themselves to the way the performance and its artistic quality have been organized.

J. Clyde Mitchell's study of the *Kalela* dance on the Zambian Copperbelt in the 1950s[6] showed that the organization of the societies that presented the dance in organized competitions at weekends was a response to the process of urbanization, and a further extension of the 'joking relationships' which had previously existed between rival ethnic groups. The competitiveness of these grass-roots dance groups amongst the mines' labour force was a kind of *metaphor* for traditional animosities – in much the same way as some team sports are. There is another dimension to the metaphor which exists in the actual dance itself; its use of specific role-play, costumes and dance-steps, all suggested the colonial authority, so that the dance itself became a metaphor for the colonial presence.

These concepts were carried much further in T. O. Ranger's study of the *Beni* dance in East Africa,[7] based upon the research and observations of a number of people in Kenya, Tanzania, Malawi and northern Zambia of rural dance societies, which, in their evolving organization over the eighty years of colonialism first reflected, metaphorically, the colonial authority, and then later mounted a satirical critique of it. The dance itself was a dazzling stylization of the colonial brass band. The musical instruments were approximated out of scrap metal; the white tunic and short pants of the colonial DOs were parodied; and the dance's choreography transformed the parade into an extravaganza of inventiveness, borrowings from traditional dances, and acrobatic embellishments. It was in no way like the high-stepping female bands of the American ball-games. Rather, the whole body of the dancer was used creatively and the performance was much closer to pure dance than to military marches. Since independence it seems that the dance societies have dissolved; and the dance itself has ossified into a less skilful and less interesting performance by 'amateurs' or old men.

The two key performance elements which were omitted from both *Beni* and *Kalankuwa* were (1) songs and (2) stories, and we need to note briefly some studies of these.

Of the studies made of traditional songs in African societies two may be mentioned which are, in fact, quite different from each other. One is by Charles Kiel, who analyses the songs of the Tiv peoples in central Nigeria,[8] and the occasions and ways in which the songs are performed. From this composite analysis, Kiel is able to show a deeper, metaphorical meaning that comes not just from the words, or the 'texts', of individual songs, but also from the nature of the occasion of an evening of song performances. The study is interesting, not least because it attempts to place song-composition and song performance in the context of social change; and it is relevant to Iyoruese Hagher's recent research into the Tiv *Kwagh hir* puppet theatre which we will come to in a moment.

The other study is by Andreya Masiye, a Zambian broadcaster, playwright and diplomat,[9] who shows how songs were used by the Party in the struggle for independence, especially through the medium of radio broadcast. Songs were broadcast, through record request programmes, to the rural areas; and it took the colonial authorities who controlled the networks some time to realize the subversion which was going on under their noses. Like the Tiv songs, as Kiel's study shows, these songs were heavily metaphorical in content (they had to be), as well as being metaphorical in the circumstances of their performance, such as radio DJ record requests programmes which mixed real requests with fake ones that contained covert seditious messages.

What about the use of narrative in performance? Most societies in Africa have story-telling traditions. For example, the Akan in Ghana have the stories of Ananse the tricky spider. The Ijǫ in southern Nigeria have an epic narrative tradition, which requires many evenings for the saga to be told in its entirety.[10] Very often, the story-teller is a lone performer (with, perhaps, some accompaniment by musicians) and his art lies in his ability to get his audience to participate in the telling of the story without the story-teller himself losing the 'ownership' of it. Some traditions have pairs of professional narrators who move about the countryside with musicians accompanying them. Some of these narrators, as in the case of the Hausa, are praise-singers as well.

Iyoruese Hagher describes the *Kwagh hir* puppet theatre amongst the Tiv people as a story-telling theatre.[11] He suggests that the *Kwagh hir* is a purely rural traditional art even though it appeared in its present highly active form only in 1961, in response to the Tiv riots of 1960 (which, together with the 1964 riots, he shows to be linked to the earlier cult riots of the colonial period). Hagher sees the *Kwagh hir* as a modern – but rural and wholly indigenous – theatrical art of performance. It combines *spectacle* and *performance*. The spectacle derives from the plastic arts: the masks and figurines, of monsters and of humans, and relating to the *Adzov* and *Mbatzav*, spirits whose world images the human world. The performance milieu is that of the songs, dances and stories, all now transformed from their traditional mode of performance. Hagher indicates that the programme of 'events' or 'turns' or 'stories' during a night of performance is metaphorical, in terms both of individual 'stories' and of the entertainment as a whole. The stories and their presentation as spectacle are a metaphor for the Tiv world view. This involves the traditional beliefs in magic, and in the acquisition, by individuals, of 'powers' and influence, being secularized and commented upon in public: the dolls and masks, which were part of the cult world are brought out into the public gaze in a stylized but essentially non-affective way.

The owners of the *Kwagh hir* companies, which tend to have a lineage or kinship base, involve their companies from season to season in fierce competitions with other companies; and referees determine the best. Best in performance, that is. The referees who are drawn from within the competing communities judge the performances in their own terms: are the animated puppets (i.e. the dolls and the articulated limbs of the gigantic mask-figures) life-like? Do they embody in their actions and movements the quality which they visually present? Does the mask do, in the dance, what its introductory song announces as its potential? Are the proverbs and stories accurately interpreted in the spectacle of their performance? Hagher's study indicates an extensive vocabulary in Tiv in which the aesthetic qualities of performances can be critically assessed. It opens up a new area for research which discovers within the changing rural society a performance dynamic which combines the various traditional artistic elements to depict that change metaphorically. The *Kwagh hir* lies in the interstices between the traditional and essentially rural arts inherited from the past, and the fully-fledged urban theatre performances of travelling theatre companies like the Ogunde Theatre company, which are grass-roots artistic products by urban folk for their own communities.

Before moving on to a discussion of these theatre companies I will try to summarize my argument so far:

1   The phenomenon of African drama developing out of traditional art is complex, as the example of a modest village festival performance tried to show.

2   The various critical approaches to the sources of African drama generally involve research into the oral traditions and traditional performances, but often there are limitations manifest in the various methodologies:

   a   a great deal of research by theatre specialists concentrates almost exclusively on the final artistic product; and ignores the means of production. This research modifies or reinforces Aristotelian 'rules' for drama;

   b   some sociologists and social anthropologists use a measurable definition of culture, in their description of a particular society, which often excludes totally that society's artistic production;

   c   other anthropologists and ethnographers tend to discuss traditional art purely in terms of its function, or its structure, or both, solely within the context of affective ceremonies and rituals.

3   This may be the result of two problems concerning the meaning of secular performance:

   a   performances are ephemeral; and their meaning is experiential;

   b   it is difficult for outsiders to 'see' and 'hear' a traditional performance, because meaning is established between actors and audience through agreed stylistic conventions in performance which have been established over a period of time.

4   A few studies are, however, concerned with the dynamics of performance, that is to say, with the way in which performances for entertainment are organized at the grass roots, and how this organization affects the development of the final product, which itself is subject to change.

5   The development of the use of metaphor, both in terms of the grass-roots reorganization of traditional art, and in terms of the transformation of content, is crucial in the analysis.

We have now reached the point at which we would need to consider a performance art in which the elements of traditional performance have been so transformed, and recombined in so many new ways, that it can scarcely still be called traditional –

even though it may so advertise itself. The most significant development here is the way in which story-telling and role-play have been combined into dialogue drama. We will look at this in terms of two urban travelling theatres: the Yoruba travelling theatres and the theatres of the black South African townships.

Urban influences on drama and theatre

Yoruba travelling theatres have been eclectic: the influence of Western dramatic modes has been combined with the *Alarinjo* theatre historically, described by Adedeji.[12] The masquerades (particularly *Egungun* and *Gelede*) and the music traditions of the different kingdoms in Yorubaland exercised a great deal of influence especially at the formative stage of Hubert Ogunde's company. Dialogue drama also developed through Ogunde: after 1945 his improvised plays caught the Yoruba imagination (though there had been a tradition since the middle of the nineteenth century in Lagos of dramatized Bible stories and religious plays). There have been a very large number of companies over the past twenty-five years; but the main ones have been those of Hubert Ogunde, E. K. Ogunmola, Duro Ladipọ and Moses Olaiya Adejumo (alias 'Baba Sala'). We shall concentrate on Ogunde's company; and I shall attempt to summarize the achievements of the other three in order to indicate the similarities and the differences. However, for the travelling theatres generally we need to establish three factors which contribute to the concept of them as part of the system of free market enterprise which goes some way to explaining the limitations of these theatres.

1 First of all, we are not dealing with a play-text, or a body of play-texts belonging to a particular author. We are concerned in the case of each theatre company with a 'personality'. It is the personality of Ogunde, or the personality of 'Baba Sala', which actually constitutes the substance of their dramatic work. This notion of 'personality' involves two aspects: the character on stage – which is basically a fiction – and the public image of the man in real life. These two aspects are inextricably bound up with each other.

2 The second factor concerns the nature of each man's company's organization. The more successful the 'personality', the more detailed and complex are the business and commercial

structures of his enterprises. These facilitate not only the production of more performances on tours, and on the radio and
television, but also the production of records, magazines and even
films – which, in turn, boost this 'personality'. The performances
of the plays become the occasion to market these other products.
3   The third factor is quite different and concerns the relationship
between these theatre companies and the universities, especially
the University of Ibadan. There were two units in the University of
Ibadan which involved themselves with one or more of the popular
theatre personalities, and attempted to shape their art. One was
the extra-mural department which, through Ulli Beier, set up the
Mbari Clubs; and the other was the school of drama, which
eventually became the department of theatre arts, awarding
undergraduate and post-graduate degrees in practical and theoretical theatre. The Mbari Club in Oshogbo first accommodated
Duro Ladipo and his company, and then eventually became the
embodiment of his personality. The school of drama brought in the
late Kola Ogunmola to develop his art, according to Geoffrey
Axworthy, then the head of the school, free from the commercial
pressures of the day-to-day existence of his company. However
opinions are divided over the measure of success of this experiment;
and it could be argued that these theatre personalities are in fact
sustained by the commercial milieu in which they flourish and
through which their art is defined organizationally. It is quite
possible that the social isolation of the university campus in Nigeria
is inimical to their art. Thus, in one way or another, the University
of Ibadan attempted to engage with some of these commercially
successful enterprises whose theatre art was so popular in the towns
throughout Nigeria wherever there were concentrations of Yoruba
people. However, Hubert Ogunde, who was really the pioneer of
this development, seemed largely to have kept himself apart, until
quite recently, from the academics. Latterly Ebun Clark, of the
University of Lagos, won Ogunde's confidence and accomplished
some painstaking and detailed historical research on Ogunde's
work over thirty-five years.[13]

Hubert Ogunde

From Ebun Clark's study it would appear that Ogunde's theatre
very closely reflected the prevailing mood of the people, especially
in the West of Nigeria (the Yoruba heartlands) from 1946 to the

beginning of the Nigerian civil war in 1966. The style, the form, the content of his work changed as the mood changed in the territory, which was itself responding to the changing political climate. This ability to key in to the main preoccupations of the emerging political leadership in Nigeria in the years before independence, and to give it expression in front of large Yoruba audiences, specifically defined Ogunde's 'personality'. He put his local audiences 'in touch' with the aspirations of those who were operating at a national level. What he did was to *fictionalize* himself in his own dramas, while appearing before the public in the flesh. In this way he was able to personalize and concretize issues – through characterization, story and metaphor – so that the audiences could engage directly with these issues.

Furthermore, the ability of Ogunde's theatre company to travel all round Nigeria, and even beyond its boundaries, meant a wider circulation of these issues – which certainly made him a thorn in the flesh of the colonial authorities. This led to his theatre being banned in certain parts of the country, and his arrest and interrogation by the colonial authorities. Through this persecution his 'personality' was greatly enhanced.

For the sake of discussion we can probably identify four phases in the development of Ogunde's theatre to the present time: (1) The phase of cultural nationalism from 1944–50: (2) consolidation of the company through independence 1954–64; (3) post-independence party politics 1964–66; (4) the company since the civil war 1972 to the present day.

1   The period of cultural nationalism from 1944–50

Ogunde's first plays were folk operas with titles like *The Garden of Eden* and *Throne of God*. They were presented for the Cherubim and Seraphim Church while he was still a member of the Nigeria Police Force. In 1945 his performances took on a political dimension. His play *Strike and Hunger*, for example, was an allegory that expressed the hopeless conditions of labour in colonial Nigeria which led to the general strike of 1945. In 1946 he gave up his job and established The African Music Research Party as a fully professional company with a play called *Tiger's Empire* which was another attack on colonialism.

The titles of both his theatre company and of the play indicate the direction Ogunde's creative energy was taking at this time. He wanted to revive the Yoruba music which had been downgraded by the colonialists and to reawaken interest in the indigenous culture. At the same time he specifically saw his company as the means by which he could help establish the cultural independence of the Africans in Nigeria as a back-up to the growing movement for political and economic independence, or, as it was called, self-government. Both the content of his plays and the organization of his company would show that Nigerians could be 'self-sufficient' in the arts.

Even at this stage his art was eclectic. He took the old stories, enlivened them with songs which he himself composed, transformed Yoruba musical forms by mixing indigenous instruments with others from elsewhere in the country, and dramatized the story in such a way that it set forth an obvious political theme (*Tiger's Empire*) or social message (*Mr Devil's Money* – an African version of the Faust theme of a man who signs a pact with the devil for money) which was highly appropriate for the times. His shows were both traditional and modern at the same time. They appealed to Yoruba audiences because they clearly reflected the desire for the creation of a modern state, independent of the colonial authority, on the basis of the Nigerians' present achievements and collective abilities. There was no need to become more 'civilized': Ogunde's plays framed the insult of colonialism for all to see it as such.

In 1947 Ogunde changed the title of his company to the Ogunde Theatre Company; and although the content of the shows continued to shift between overly political themes and more general social themes, the main form of his work had been established. The show comprised an opening glee – a lively musical number including perhaps the song which Ogunde had composed as the theme song for that particular play – and the play itself: an allegorical story with songs, dances and dialogue. There was also a closing glee.

The plays were moralistic. Even the political dramas were presented in the form of obvious moral issues: colonialism which Ogunde attacked in play after play, was shown to be immoral. Thus a non-political play like *Half and Half* (1949), which tells the story of a changeling, half deer, half beautiful woman, is not a different sort of play from *Bread and Bullet* (1950), which was a play based on the Enugu coal-miners' strike of 1949 in which eighteen miners were shot dead by the police. It seems from accounts of the play that Ogunde overlaid the issue of the strike with a love story. And even the politics of the piece are construed in terms of an obvious good confronting an obvious evil. At the time this was appropriate enough. It inflamed passions and caused the performances to be banned in the North.

During this period Ogunde also established the Ogunde Record Company (1947) which recorded and marketed his songs; and he also extended his theatre company into a regularly travelling troupe. Both of these developments led to the consolidation of his 'personality' as an entertainer (singer, actor and musician), who spoke with the voice of the new nationalism. His various brushes with the colonial authority – the denial of a passport to travel to England, the banning of *Strike and Hunger*, the trouble over the tour of *Bread and Bullet* in northern Nigeria – all contributed to the projection of this 'personality'. In the shows, the fictionalizing of his personality in the different roles situated it within a moral framework. Both his personal success and the roles he played embodied the aspirations of the people. It gave their rising expectations a specific form and a moral justification.

2   Consolidation of the company through independence: 1954–64

During the 1950s cultural nationalism gave way to a more specific process of political organization in the regions of Nigeria in anticipation of independence. Ogunde does not seem to have responded to this development directly; and the presentation of new plays tailed off towards the end of the 1950s. Perhaps it was less easy to see the political lobbying and jockeying for power in the simplified moralistic terms in which he framed his earlier plays about colonialism and social evils. He had worked out a formula for stabilizing the membership of his theatre company, for refining and modifying a repertoire of established plays and for executing extensive tours around Nigeria. This formula had proved success-ful, both financially and in terms of his growing popularity.

Clark, however, feels there was a change. She contends that Ogunde eventually gave up operatic work (a series of songs, dances and mime, without spoken dialogue) in favour of the style of the concert party from Ghana. She suggests that Ogunde was responding to a challenge from Bobby Benson in the early 1950s and that this led him to introduce such innovations as new types of songs, new rhythms and fashionable dance-steps into the existing

repertoire of plays. The influence of American pop music produced a jazzy urban style. However, Bobby Benson didn't really
develop a touring theatre company; he didn't share Ogunde's
enthusiasm of the earlier years for cultural nationalism; and
eventually he turned completely to night club entertainment and
to developing Nigerian pop music. His heirs are the contemporary
Nigerian pop stars.

3 Post-independence politics: 1964–66

Ogunde's most famous play belongs to this period: *Yoruba Ronu*
('Yoruba – think!'). Ironically it has been performed much less
than most of his other plays in repertory. It was first of all a song,
composed by Ogunde, which deplored the increasingly bitter party
strife in the western region of Nigeria. The play itself was written
as a result of a commission from the break-away party of one of
the political rivals in the territory, Chief Akintola. In fact the play
was highly critical of Akintola, and Ebun Clark comments that he
and his entourage walked out during its première performance on
28 February, 1964. The play had further performances in March
and April and then Ogunde and his entire company were banned
from performing in the western region. The Ogunde Concert Party
was declared an unlawful society. The ban did a great deal for
Ogunde's public image but nothing for his pocket. It was lifted
after the military coup of 1966, and Ogunde gave the military
governor a command performance of his by now celebrated but
little known play.

In 1966 Ogunde formed the Ogunde Dance Company, for the
purpose of taking his shows on tours overseas; and those tours
confirmed his position as an integral part of the Nigerian theatre
establishment.

4 The Ogunde Theatre Company since the civil war: 1972 onwards

Hubert Ogunde is wealthy and successful. In 1980 a BBC film was
made of him, his family, and his Theatre Company, and broadcast
in Britain.[14] The film showed Ogunde with his fans, his wives and
his children; and the rehearsal of a play based on a folk tale.

Shows I have seen in Zaria have been of older folk operas

recently revamped. *Half and Half*, which dates from 1949, was the most dynamic in performance. The large audience almost entirely of university students and mainly Yoruba, greatly appreciated the comic techniques of Ogunde and his actors. They neither found, nor looked for, any significant content or deeper meaning in the play. There were one or two topical political jokes worked into the performance. It would seem that most of the political plays of the period of cultural nationalism have been dropped from the repertoire of the company. Following the assassination of the Nigerian head of state, General Murtala Mohammed, in 1976, a wave of deep regret swept over the country for the untimely death of the man who had given a much needed focus to Nigerian national life; and Ogunde produced a bland play, *Murtala*, which toured the country, but which encountered some opposition to its performance in the North.

Ogunde's theatre company is Hubert Ogunde. His theatre is a Yoruba theatre, performed in Yoruba which embraces wit and poetry. The fans come to see and hear him; and to an outsider it appears that no member of his cast can steal the focus of the audience from him. This is the essence, it seems, of the most successful of the travelling theatres: the creation of a 'personality', a unique person, through whom Yoruba of all walks of life can find a central image of their contemporary world. Ogunde is the entertainer, the successful businessman, the cherished head of the family. He is now frequently described as 'the father of Nigerian theatre'. It is probably more accurate to describe him more generally as a father-figure, an embodiment of success, and his art as a popular expression of Yoruba sensibility.

Other Yoruba companies: E. K. Ogunmola and Duro Ladipọ

Both Ogunmola and Ladipọ are dead – both died unexpectedly in mid career – but they had a memorial to their respective talents in the records of their work that resulted from their association with the University of Ibadan. There are written texts in Yoruba and in English translation; sound tapes of various productions and a film record of some of their work. However, this record of their work is seen as archival rather than as the means to accomplish more performances.

It was the opinion of many who saw Kola Ogunmola perform his plays that he was the most brilliant actor of the 1950s and 1960s.

He greatly admired Ogunde; and Ebun Clark reports that Ogunde gave him financial help when he needed it most, after a long illness. There is a published text of his dramatization of *The Palm-Wine Drinkard*, Amos Tutuola's novel. Apart from this his two best-known plays were *Love of Money* and *Conscience*, both in the style of Ogunde's moralistic theatre.

His arts fellowship at the University of Ibadan was apparently an attempt to enrich his theatrical art; and *The Palm-Wine Drinkard* was the result of that collaboration. The adaptation was suggested by Geoffrey Axworthy, the head of the school of drama, and the eventual staging of it realized the best design and production talents in the school. But whereas Tutuola's fiction was a quest for self, with a view of the world from a somewhat tilted point of view, Ogunmola's play makes this serious work superficial, for it is set as the dream, or the nightmare, of the central character, Lanke, the 'drinkard'. Lanke falls asleep in his armchair at the beginning of the play, after the supposed death of his favourite palm-wine tapper; and is awakened at the end of the play by his friends who tell him that his tapper is alive after all. This prosaic attempt at providing some sort of naturalistic credibility reflects a deep-rooted misunderstanding of the bizarre but significant world of the original.

By contrast, Duro Ladipọ plays have a detailed structure of meaning through their imaginative dramatization of key Yoruba myths. For example, in his most famous play, *Oba Kò So*, different elements all contribute quite specifically to the play's overall meaning, such as symbolism, both in the dialogue and the spectacle on stage, and the play's formal rhythm through which characterization is established and the story unfolds. The play recounts how Shango, as King, is increasingly unable to curb the destructive influence of his two powerful generals. In the end he commits suicide; but in being transformed into the God of Thunder he negates his act of self-destruction: 'the King does not hang!' – the title of the play.

Although Ladipọ toured with his company, performing his plays, he was never as popular with audiences as the other theatre personalities, and his plays were much more consciously artistic. The publication of his major productions as written texts will ironically establish him as a playwright, and the one most likely to be remembered from this time. His Yoruba version of *Everyman*, *Èdá* is discussed at some length in Chapter 3.

Baba Sala

Moses Olaiya Adejumo, alias 'Baba Sala', his abiding stage name, is the most recent of the Yoruba travelling theatre personalities. According to his biographer and researcher, the playwright Tunde Lakoju[15] he claims to have been 'made' by his early appearances on Nigerian television. He won a Yoruba theatre contest on Ibadan television to find the best company; and the first prize was to be a sponsored tour abroad to Europe. However, although the referees agreed that in the Yoruba milieu in Nigeria, he was undoubtedly the best, his theatre would not be good for Nigeria's theatre image abroad. So an agreement was cobbled together whereby he got the first prize and a television contract for weekly shows by his company; and someone else went to Germany. Moses Olaiya went on to become a very wealthy man. He too, like Ogunde, has established a number of successful enterprises and ancillary companies besides the main theatre company.

When he began his act he portrayed himself comically: his 'personality' was that of an enterprising fellow, often ingenuous, and way down the social ladder. As Baba Sala, his fictionalized self, he exposed, sometimes by accident, sometimes by design, the venality, devices and schemes of Nigerians on the make. 'Baba Sala' himself, caricatured in gigantic revolving bow-tie and funny hats, was included in the satire.

It is interesting to note that as the man himself has become well-off so has his fictional 'personality' Baba Sala. This development should be seen alongside the introduction of motion-picture inserts into the live performances of his plays. 'Baba Sala' has quite literally become a film star. (On tour the company carries the entire equipment necessary for a performance outdoors with them, including stage, cinema screen, a curtained-off back-stage area, and a generator.)

Thus, Yoruba audiences will be given the following 'package' at a performance, like, for example, the one I attended in the Railway Club Yard in distant Zaria.[16]

As they arrive the audience can listen to records of performances of other plays – which are stopped at the critical moment so that people will want to buy them. Young members of the company move amongst the swelling audience selling them. To begin the play there is an opening glee[17] – a lively dance by the dancers in the company attired in skimpy costumes which represent traditional dance costume. Then the cinema screen is draped over the back-cloths and we see the first film insert – in this example Baba Sala picking up a girl by the roadside in his Mercedes (his own car) after serenading her in a deliberate send-up of the Indian love-movie. The back-cloth is revealed again and Baba Sala arrives 'home', which is on stage, and the scene is acted live. It really does seem as though he has stepped out of the screen for he is in the identical costume.

And so the story unfolds, alternating between film and live performance, without the flow of the narrative being interrupted. This particular play showed Baba Sala as a well-off older man planning to take as another wife the young woman whom his son was intending to marry.

Baba Sala's theatre is more eclectic than Ogunde's. Anything which is likely to be popular with the audience is brought into the performances. The autocratic nature of Moses Olaiya's rule over members of his company allows him to determine everything from touring schedules to the content and style of the plays to the detailed conduct of each performance.

Two things stand out in the work of Ogunde and Baba Sala: both have been dependent on the mass media (radio, television and newspapers) for the promotion of their 'personalities'. Baba Sala established his particular 'style' and comic persona through both radio and television, while the newspapers projected Ogunde in the 1950s as an entertainer who was part of the political struggle. But although both have become wealthy neither halt their strenuous tours around the country in which they remain the 'star' of the show and the reason for it being on the road.

The large public performance provides them with an opportunity to market their other products. The fact that they continue to interact with their audiences directly shows that they recognize their 'personality' as the base of their commercial enterprises. The 'fictionalizing' of themselves through dramas based on the contemporary experiences of their audience creates the product, their travelling theatres, which they market so successfully.

The tradition of urbanization among the Yoruba, and also their willingness to travel in search of jobs and success, has undoubtedly provided a fertile ground for the growth of this sort of urban grass-roots theatre. The existence of a similar theatre in the black South African townships reinforces the idea that the scattering of populations in the context of urbanization for entrepreneurial activity provides a collective experience at the bottom of the social heap to which theatre is uniquely able to give expression, while it paradoxically places severe constraints upon that theatre, through its economic organization, making it seemingly incapable of offering its audiences a valid critique of their increasingly disadvantaged position. The concept of the 'personality' enables the owner of the theatre company, who is also that personality, to exploit his fellow actors, his 'workers'. The dramas produced can therefore be critical of obvious social injustices like colonialism or racialism which fit into a simple moral framework, but they are unable to attack the root causes of social coercion. Instead they provide an illusion of individual success once the obvious injustice has been removed.

Black theatre in Soweto

In an introduction to a collection of South African people's plays, Robert Kavanagh[18] describes the development of black grass-roots urban theatre. He categorizes the popular theatre tradition into three groups which he describes as (1) 'town theatre', involving both blacks and whites in experimental and often highly political theatre; (2) 'the theatre of Black Consciousness' which involved the South African Students Organization and the Black People's Convention who were concerned to develop the cultural dimension to the politcal struggle in which they were engaged; and (3) 'township theatre' (not to be confused with 'town theatre') which Kavanagh describes as being commercial, involving music and dance, and reflecting 'the life and culture of the urban townships . . . created and performed in the townships, rarely emerging from them. . . .'

The main theatre personality in the township theatre is Gibson Kente. In another article Kavanagh specifically compares him to Hubert Ogunde.[19] However, there seem to be differences which reflect the different political situations in Nigeria and in South Africa. Kente's early theatre work was non-political but was transformed into a politicized theatre in 1974, according to Kavanagh, by unemployment and inflation and by the influence of the Black Consciousness Movement and of the more radical mixed-race theatre.

In his play *Too Late* (1975) Kente sets up a group of characters: a woman, her friend, her daughter, a young fellow who is a relative of the woman but now orphaned and homeless; some cynical young people who have chosen a life of petty crime rather than go to a Boer-controlled blacks-only university; a preacher, a doctor; and a policeman called Pelepele, and his associates. These people reflect the township milieu. The oppressive nature of the white South African regime is indicated by the constant harassment of blacks by the police. This is presented in a casual sort of way that makes the violence seem inevitable; and it is continually set forth in jazzy songs, dances and music. This tone is not contrived for a deliberate artistic or political effect; it is a direct depiction of the violence that is the norm for blacks in that society. It appears bizarre only to those of us who are outside it. For instance, the orphaned young man is on one occasion caught by Pelepele the policeman and is physically defended by his young female cousin – whom the policeman kills, deliberately, with a blow on the head! Furthermore, the most dramatic moments in the play are not to do with this wanton violence, totally unprepared for within the play, but with the non-arrival of a letter which causes a misunderstanding.

In fact the play's story is tentative; the narrative is much more to do with the way in which this group of people cope, moment by moment, with the undertow of arbitrary violence which epitomizes apartheid for blacks. There is no beginning and no end to the play in the conventional sense. Between the start and the finish there are a series of crises affecting the characters, which are merely part of a continuing crisis throughout their lives. The woman is put in jail for running a shebeen; the cynical and bitter young men shop-lift and are remorselessly pursued; the woman's daughter gets killed; the orphaned young man, who witnesses this, is put in jail for not having a pass and eventually he comes out. The play concludes with one of the characters asking the question which gives the play its title:

'Can't something be done to curb the bitterness in both
young and old before it's
TOO LATE?'[20]

Another township play in the anthology is *uNosilimela* by Credo Mutwa, a play which has profound significance for the revival of African culture in South Africa. It has considerable scope, involving in the experiences of the central character, uNosilimela, the daughter of a mythical princess, the destiny of all black South

Africans. The story-teller begins the play in the traditional manner of story-telling, with songs and dances, creating an atmosphere in which all manner of things are possible. The beginning truly does have magical and mythical dimensions: he gives an account of star wars that result in the Earth-destiny of one of the victims, the princess Kimamereva. uNosilimela is the daughter of this princess of the stars, born in the present time:

Story-teller: Thus it was that Magadlemzini's son, Solemamba, left the land of his forefathers for Johannesburg. And in due course, after much pain and difficult labour, Kimamereva, voyager of the sea of time and queen of a thousand galaxies, gave birth to a baby girl and because she had had the habit of sitting outside each night during her pregnancy, staring fixedly at the Silimela constellation, the stars of Spring, which were her distant home, the child Kimamereva bore was known as. . . . [*uNosilimela stands dressed in the clothes and adornments of a young Zulu girl*]

Song: uNosilimela!
Uyeza uNosilimela. . . . (uNosilimela is coming. . . .)[21]

uNosilimela is a child of destiny. Her being is hedged by taboos which she breaks by having an illicit love affair. Then she strikes her earthly 'mother'; and for this outrage she must be exiled. She moves deeper and deeper into urban South Africa, is corrupted and abused. She gains education only by being Christianized by some nuns; but in the townships she is utterly debased. Finally she is warned, in a vision, by the Earth Mother (not to be confused with her father's wife whom she struck) that death is imminent:

> Listen, death stalks you as a lion stalks an impala in the darkness. Leave Johannesburg at once. Go out to the pure open spaces where the truth about you and your people will be revealed to you. Now go![22]

She returns home; questions the ancestors about her destiny (and the destiny of her people); and witnesses a great conflagration in which white oppression is swept away and there is the promise of peace.

Like Ogunde's plays, *uNosilimela* is concerned with the traditional performing arts – especially story-telling and music as a traditionally composite art – and their use allegorically in depicting the contemporary urban world. But Credo Mutwa differs from the Nigerian Hubert Ogunde in two respects. First, Mutwa is primarily a *writer*; and he does not run a professional theatre company to stage his plays. Certainly he is a public figure; but it is more as an intellectual than as a theatre 'personality'.

Secondly, Mutwa is profoundly resentful of the urban milieu. *uNosilimela* is an attack on the city and all its values, and it advocates a return to the precolonial rural world which he has now romanticized. This romanticism of rurality is tied up with a political consciousness with which it sharply conflicts. In fact, as we will see in the final chapter, it is a critical problem not only for black South Africans in their revolutionary overthrow of the present racist regime, but also, in another dimension, for all Africans across the continent.

We have moved from the rural, traditional milieu to the contemporary, urban milieu, both of which are experiencing social change. We have seen the growth of traditional performing arts into drama and theatre as a phenomenon which is not easy to define. Drama is a process – a process of realizing a performance, a process of responding to cultural change to make some sense of it – rather than a categorization of parts and a series of limiting definitions. In many ways it actually helps to keep words like 'theatre' and 'drama' fluid, as indeed they are in reality, as the many conflicting attempts to define them show.

But we do need to understand the process of how *actuality* (that which happens) becomes *drama*, in a performance.

This process is not simply one which occurs every time a new play is devised. It is not merely the conscious techniques of the individual dramatist, although it may seem to have become this in the present time. Rather, it is much more significantly a historical process which stretches through time. Drama is unlike a poem, or a song, or a melody on a Fulani's flute. It is not the response of an individual to an experience involving individual sensibility. Each drama is instead a corporate and social act reflecting a collective experience.

As such, the circumstances of a performance must needs be organized, whether it be the Lozi ceremony of *Kuomboka* on the flooding Zambesi, or a 'first night' at the Lagos National Theatre; and each performance will have a frame set about it, even though it may be unperceived through custom and familiarity, within which the spontaneous elements may emerge. Furthermore, the group's collective experience of actuality becomes in time an expression of its social sensibility, and ultimately of its history. Thus drama, as a recurring process from actuality to performance, stretches backwards and forwards in time beyond the lives of individual dramatists and actors who mediate it.

We must resist a reduction of this view into 'content' and 'form', as alternative categories within each dramatic work. We have to keep in mind (1) the process by which each 'play' is realized as such; (2) the process by which some plays become 'great works' (and others are irretrievably lost); and (3) the *historical* process, by which the collective recreation of life as art in the oral tradition, which was previously passed from one generation to the next, has become, ironically, the individual's depiction of his or her individuality in the bourgeois theatre.

The following schema might be useful in approaching what is presently recognized as the main body of African drama, namely, the play-texts of contemporary playwrights. The schema has no other validity than as a formal attempt to situate the process of dramatic composition within the social processes.

$$\text{ACTUALITY}$$
$$\downarrow$$
$$\text{STORY}$$
$$\downarrow$$
$$\text{SCENARIO}$$
$$\downarrow$$
$$\text{FORM}$$
$$\downarrow$$
$$\text{PERFORMANCE}$$
$$\downarrow$$
$$\text{[PLAY-TEXT]}$$

Actuality is what is to be depicted. It is life, viewed by those who would seek to interpret it to their audiences through their art. The first step in the process of transforming life into art, into a drama or play, is to cast it in the form of a story.

A *story* involves particularization (a time, a place, characters) and causality (one event leading to another). However the story in itself is not the drama or the play. The story which particularizes life now needs to be transformed into a scenario.

The *scenario* gives the story its dramatic impact by its dramatically effective reorganization of the story's events into scenes which cope with problems of time and space. Two other elements in scenario-making need to be mentioned here: (1) Some scenes develop in quite unexpected ways, and sometimes even the exact opposite to what one would imagine. Afterwards, however, the unexpected can be seen as curiously appropriate, and reveals a deeper truth which was previously hidden. This is *irony*. (2) Some scenes present us with characters who know less about what is happening to them than we the audience do, or other characters on stage do. This is called *dramatic irony*. Scenario is sometimes referred to as *plot*; but both scenario and plot refer to a part of the process which is specific to the story. The next part of the process is specific to the social milieu in which the performance of the drama or play will take place: this is the finding of an appropriate form.

Form requires that the writer or group making the drama take account of specific performance traditions and particular actor-audience relationships. It involves them in deciding what theatre style they are going to use and what performance conventions. It also, obviously, involves them in deciding what language and language registers they are going to use.

Performance is the presentation of the dramatic work to an audience. Although an audience is made up of individuals, the performance of a play usually invokes a collective response, even if that response sometimes divides into those who approve of what the play is saying and those who disapprove. Even a run of performances, which is generally before a different group of individuals on each successive night, achieves over the run a collective response (which may again divide into those who support the play and those who oppose it).

The *play-text*. Individual playwrights can, on the basis of a successful performance, realize a play-text. The play-text is, historically, performance in a finalized literary form. In the present economic organization of bourgeois theatre successful playwrights can submit a more or less finalized play-text to a theatre management for performance, and by virtue of their previous (commercial) success, insist on it being performed unchanged. New playwrights, however, are deceived if they imagine that they can present wholly autonomous texts for first performances. Powerful theatre managements of both the commercial and state-subsidized theatre, actually intervene at the *form* stage (in terms of this schema) and insist on changes being made in accordance with what they think their audiences will pay money to see. The situation is in fact little different from what we have already observed with regard to the Yoruba travelling theatres.

This, then, is the process of depicting actuality (life) in plays for the theatre (art). However, we have not quite finished with the process, for we have to see it not only as a process which concerns each playwright every time he or she creates a new play but also as a process in time. Once the play-text is published in the form of a book, it can intervene between *scenario* and *form* in the continuation of this process. A new performance of a play-text which has come from an earlier age must take cognizance of the *form* of performance which is both possible in, and approved by, the new society; and this new form may actually change the original play's *meaning* (i.e. the actual situation to which it once referred). But even as a new performance changes the original meaning, the play-text itself gathers an aura of 'greatness'. As it passes from era to era, culture to culture, language to language, it gradually comes to embody 'absolute truths' which are not specific to any society; and although the form is continually changing (and changing the play) the play itself is paradoxically thought of as 'complete'. One result of this is that a genuinely new theatre in a new society, which is trying to depict an unprecedented social reality, finds itself contradicting the established theatre which has already predisposed audiences to what 'theatre' ought to be.

In this chapter we have seen how the owners of contemporary grass-roots performances struggle to depict a new reality through the transformation of existing performance traditions. Inevitably they will be in the shadow of the literary African playwrights who have inherited the established theatre's 'great tradition'. The next chapter specifically considers this tension between the literary play-text and the indigenous performance traditions.

Chapters 3 to 7 analyse some of the published play-texts. For the framework for these chapters we must look again, briefly, at the *story* stage of my schema.

The story may be derived from 3 sources:

1   *Myth*, which is actuality from those closest to its source; and which is a model of actuality for playwrights in later times and other cultures, who treat it as a representation of actuality. Occasionally a playwright may attempt to approach a foreign myth

directly, or through cultural comparison; but generally it is through an established play-text, a 'great work', which in its original culture approached the myth directly or through a non-dramatic source – such as existing rites of passage, rituals and affective masquerades.

2 *History*, which records actuality specific to a particular society; and which is verifiable, either from written records or from the oral tradition. This can also include existing festivals and cere-monies, and non-affective masquerades.

3 *Fiction*, which seeks to reach actuality through a fiction. Observation of contemporary society often provides the substance for fiction.

I have found it convenient to look at the body of literary African drama in terms of the source of the story. Chapter 3 analyses some examples of plays which return to myths already handled in plays from other cultures. Chapter 4 analyses examples of plays which turn to recent history – specifically the history of colonialism and of the struggle for independence. Chapters 5, 6 and 7 analyse examples of plays in which fiction attempts to discover a deeper reality.

As the chapters progress, the term 'literary' theatre gives way to the concept of the 'art' theatre. Broadly speaking the terms are interchangeable. More specifically, however, in the theatre which works directly from reality, fictionalizing it, meaning is seen as 'artistic truth'.

The literary theatre of Africa is not accessible to the mass of the people but neither, on the whole, is the 'art' theatre with its own vision of the truth. The final chapter returns us to the people, both as the makers and consumers of drama and theatre, and to the need to indicate how drama, through a new creative and organiza-tional dynamic, might itself be transformed so as to effect the transformation of social consciousness amongst the mass of the people.

Notes and references

1 *Aboakyer*, the annual deer-hunt festival in Winneba, Ghana, is also linked to a Lord-of-Misrule festival. After the victorious team has returned with the captured deer, the whole commun-ity, many of whom are in elaborate or bizarre costumes, makes

a procession around the town with guilds, clubs, age-sets and so on, performing satirical shows within the main body of the procession. This procession is more than a mile long and takes several hours, and the victorious group can ridicule the losers in any way they wish.

2 Oyin Ogunba, 'Traditional African festival drama', in Oyin Ogunba and Abiola Irele (eds.), *Theatre in Africa* (Ibadan: Ibadan University Press 1978), p. 15.

3 Joel Adedeji, 'Traditional Yoruba travelling theatre', in Ogunba and Irele, 1978, p. 43.

4 J. S. Eades, *The Yoruba Today* (Cambridge: Cambridge University Press 1980).

5 Dennis Duerden, *African Art and Literature: the invisible present* (New York: Harper and Row 1975, also London: Heinemann Educational Books 1977).

6 J. Clyde Mitchell, 'The Kalela Dance: aspects of social relationships among urban Africans in Northern Rhodesia', *The Rhodes-Livingstone Papers*, no. 27 (Manchester: Manchester University Press 1956).

7 T. O. Ranger, *Dance and Society in Eastern Africa 1890–1970: the Beni Ngoma* (London: Heinemann Educational Books 1975). See also, in connection with this, Margaret Strobel, *Moslem Women in Mombasa 1890–1975* (New Haven: Yale University Press 1980).

8 Charles Kiel, *Tiv Song* (Chicago: Chicago University Press 1979).

9 Andreya Masiye, *Singing for Freedom* (Lusaka: NECZAM 1977).

10 *Ozidi* is the Ijo saga. It is discussed in Chapter 2 of this book.

11 I. O. Hagher, 'The Kwagh hir: an analysis of a contemporary indigenous puppet theatre and its social and cultural significance in Tivland in the 1960s and 1970s' (PhD thesis, Zaria: Ahamdu Bello University 1981).

12 Adedeji, in Ogunba and Irele, 1978.

13 Ebun Clark, *Hubert Ogunde: the making of Nigerian theatre* (London, Oxford University Press 1979). Some of the material was published previously in *Nigeria Magazine*, no. 114 (1974), and nos. 115–16 (1975).

14 The BBC, London, produced a film on Hubert Ogunde, made by Tony Isaacs: *Ogunde: Man of the Theatre*, which was broadcast on 7 September 1980.

15 Tunde Lakoju, 'Travelling Theatre in Nigeria: a study of Moses Olaiya and his Alawada Theatre International of Nigeria' (MA thesis in preparation, Zaria: Ahmadu Bello University).

16 The play was *Kase Kuro* ('Remove your legs'); it was staged at the Railway Club, Zaria, on 29 November 1980.

17 For a discussion of this see Joel Adedeji, 'Trends in the content and form of the opening glee in Yoruba drama', *Research in African Literatures*, vol. 4 no. 1 (1973), pp. 32–47.

18 Robert Kavanagh (ed), *South African People's Plays* (London: Heinemann Educational Books 1981).

19 'Mshengu', 'After Soweto: people's theatre and the political struggle in South Africa', *Theatre Quarterly*, vol. 9 no. 33 (1979), pp. 31–8.

20 Gibson Kente, *Too Late*, in Robert Kavanagh (ed.), *South African People's Plays*, p. 122.

21 Credo Mutwa, *uNosilimela*, in Robert Kavanagh (ed.), *South African People's Plays*, p. 18.

22 ibid., p. 48.

2   Drama as literature and performance

What is the relationship between literature and peformance? The relationship is complicated by seeing drama as a process of social development in the way we represent ourselves and our society to ourselves.

Our initial question then breaks down into three specific questions:

1   What is the relationship between the traditional performances and modern African play-texts?
2   What is the relationship between the traditional performances and modern African drama in performance (which may or may not be performances of those play-texts)?
3   What is the relationship between modern African play-texts and modern African drama in performance?

In attempting to answer these questions and discover these relationships, this chapter considers also the various ways by which the growing body of what is called African drama is evaluated: as play-texts, as performance, as cultural dynamics and as a social phenomenon.

We will approach these questions, initially, in the context of the following observations, namely: (1) the development of the study of drama in African universities; (2) the extensive influence of classical (Greek and Roman) and European forms of drama on African playwrights; and (3) the establishment of the play-text as the dominant mode of drama.

The establishment of university departments studying drama

From the establishment of the School of Music and Drama, at the University of Ghana, Legon, and the department of theatre arts at the University of Dar es Salaam in the early 1960s, and the subsequent establishment of the department of theatre arts, separate from literature studies, at the University of Ibadan,

Nigeria, a number of universities, at least in the anglophone African countries, experienced increased pressure to create distinct courses in 'drama' and 'theatre' studies. These pressures tended to come from recently created ministries of culture who were themselves giving expression to the rediscovery of the African personality, after the long years of colonial domination, through a revival of African culture; and also from the students themselves. Research into the culture was centred in the institutes of African studies, which a large number of universities set up under a variety of names, many of whom were able to support traditional performers and even whole performing companies.

The undergraduate curriculum was rigidly controlled in the early years of a new university by its founding university overseas. This was all right for those subjects whose content and methodology existed quite separately from whoever was studying them – such as medicine or engineering – but was less appropriate in the case of subjects whose content was related to the student – such as history – and quite disastrous in the case of those subjects which were creative and wholly dependent on the student: fine art, music, and drama or theatre. In the case of fine art and music there was no argument over their creative and practical character, only over the extent to which European techniques should be allowed to influence them. But drama and theatre encountered opposition straight away as to whether in fact, within the university curriculum, they were creative or practical at all. Wasn't drama simply a part of the discipline of literary criticism? Wasn't theatre to be studied historically? It was the usual argument over whether or not a university ought to, or even could, teach creativity but it was complicated by political pressures from governments on the universities to generate African creativity. The response of the universities has been muddled and often a compromise: a combination of theory and practice, often taught quite separately, a mixture of literary criticism, history of the theatre and some practical performance skills.

The influence of classical and European drama

The connection between the development of drama and theatre and educational syllabuses is extensive. On the one hand it stretches beyond the university through the whole system of secondary and primary schooling to basic literacy. On the other hand it can predetermine the form and content of new creative work. Formal education is almost always seen as the key to personal advancement, and, where resources are limited, for economic or political reasons, it is competed for vigorously. A school syllabus can quite arbitrarily limit the extent of the study of drama because at a higher level of study it has not yet been defined. The course is geared towards a qualifying examination which has the effect of making the pupils studying it uncritical of its content. One result may be to divorce drama and theatre from the real cultural situation of the people and, in those societies where schools reinforce an elitist tendency, to make drama itself elitist. Another result is the perpetuation of uncomprehended, and therefore incomprehensible, information.

An example of the latter is the perpetuation in Africa of the analysis of a certain form of drama, tragedy, given by Aristotle, which I pointed out in Chapter 1. In writing about tragedy Aristotle was commenting on the texts of performances of Greek playwrights writing over a hundred years before Aristotle formulated his theory. He was not merely concerned to find a way to evaluate the 'dramatic' quality of these play-texts but to justify them as being socially corrective in performance. Those which could support his theory were analysed in detail; those which could not were either criticized or ignored. His theory of tragedy was 'literary' and schematic;[1] it was part, a small and incomplete part, of his vast body of philosophical writings which in turn were part of a highly literate tradition of Greek thought which lay hidden in libraries while the Greek and Roman civilizations collapsed and Christianity and feudalism reorganized Europe. When the writing of the Greeks and the Romans came back into circulation in Europe, about 600 years ago, Europeans were interested in it *as writings*, as literature, and interest was awakened in play-texts as literature. In this context, Aristotle's literary criticism, especially *The Poetics*, had considerable appeal.

There was, too, a feeling of cultural inferiority on the part of the Europeans in the face of the sophisticated and literary classical culture. Their response was to devise education systems based upon the surviving classical literature. Thus the influence of Aristotle, with his theory of tragedy, was perpetuated intellectually and at the expense of another sort of drama in England, namely the Elizabethan and Jacobean theatre which all strata of English society had helped to formulate.

Obviously cultural reactions to educational and social developments were more complex than a brief statement like this would
suggest. However, it serves to suggest two things. First, how
Aristotle and the Greeks came to be part of syllabuses in African
education systems, and, second, what their effect has been on the
development of African drama. In the same way as the Europeans
felt a sense of cultural inferiority when confronted with both a
classical literature and a classical criticism with which to evaluate
it, so also did African intellectuals accept initially the cultural
implications of a foreign system of intellectual analysis through its
educational structures. There is, however, a crucial difference
between the two processes. The Europeans were not being
colonized by the Greeks or the Romans when they came upon
their culture. By that time the social formations of the Greek and
Roman world had passed. But in Africa today, western colonialism and neo-colonialism has created a serious disjunction within
the process of cultural development. Ruling elites criticize western
acculturation whilst proceeding apace with it. This paradoxical
situation serves to create a profound cultural uncertainty.

The influence of the Greeks on the development of African
drama has been in two directions: (1) Greek plays have served as
models for African plays; and (2) the theory of Aristotle has
become a basis for dramatic criticism. An example of the former is
the transposition by the Nigerian playwright, Ola Rotimi, of
King Oedipus by the Greek playwright, Sophocles, into a play
in a Yoruba setting (but in English) called *The Gods are not to
Blame*. An example of the influence of Aristotle's theory is the
analysis by John Pepper Clark (a Nigerian critic and playwright) of
the Ijo̲ saga of *Ozidi* (which is extensively discussed later in this
chapter).

In general, though, the main problem is that many African
writers approach the Greek plays through Aristotle's analysis of
them, rather than responding to the text directly. The result is that
the subsequent transposition into an African setting can frequently
become socially prescriptive and mechanical, and not really a
response to the actual social preoccupations of the audience.
Almost without knowing it, the playwright finds himself using
Aristotle's theories to think about his own audience's reactions;
and this may be completely inappropriate.

Some African critics are aware of this, and desire a more
intellectual response to Greek culture. Michael Echeruo, the

Nigerian critic and academic, makes the following suggestion in his essay on *The Dramatic Limits of Igbo Ritual*:

The Igbo should do what the Greeks did: expand ritual into life and give that life a secular base. That way we may be able to interpret and reinterpret that serious view of life which is now only dimly manifested in our festivals.[2]

In his support for the Greeks (and Aristotle) Echeruo seems to be suggesting that there should take place within the context of Igbo performance culture a process of turning *festival* into *literature*, in the same way as the Greeks turned their oral and performance traditions into literature when they started to analyse in a written form the *play-texts* which had been written down. These play-texts had come to exist in the place of actual performances. We need to look at the process a bit more closely.

When Greek thinkers began to ponder the moral and social meaning of their legends and myths, they were actually seeking to expand the significance of their ancient traditional culture so as to reach a truth about their own contemporary social realities. In a similar way they began to question the moral and social purpose of recurrent and seasonal festivals. The dramatization of the myths and legends brings performance and the oral tradition together; and this dramatization becomes *questioning* and *interpretative*. This in turn leads to subtle changes in the myth or legend, and the emphases within it. The desire to give these performances at the festivals a semantic quality which is intellectualized and precise, requires that the new bits be written down, so that the 'actors' can learn it off exactly, word for word. That way there would be no confusion. There was no need to write down or record what was being used unchanged in the performance.

The written-out version of the play became the text for perform-ance, and subsequently the text for literary analysis. The text was linguistically complete, though it lacked a record of all other elements of performance, such as a notation for the music, another type of notation for the choreography, and a description of the spectacle. It seems to me that this is the process to which Echeruo is referring: Igbo festivals should be used by Igbo thinkers as a basis for the generation of a *literature*.

The disappearance of traditional modes of performance

The Greek play-texts survived but the traditional performances were forgotten. The texts survived the destruction of the societies in which they were generated, and they survived the passing of subsequent civilizations.

Why is this so? Why should a dance or a masquerade which is popular in conception and repeatedly performed be so easily lost, while a play-text which is the product of one mind and given only an occasional performance survive? If this is a general pattern of cultural development in civilizations, then we must expect masquerades like *Egungun*, dances like *Nyau*, story-telling like that of the Akan to disappear soon. On the other hand, the plays of, say, Wole Soyinka could outlast African society as we know it today and as we imagine it will become in distant centuries. Is it simply to do with the fact that one is written down and the other isn't? If this were so then all that would be needed to preserve a masquerade or a dance would be some form of notation, a 'score'. Indeed, today we can record such a performance on sound tape and film; but do we preserve the performance itself? Surely all we preserve is a *record* of the performance. The existence of a dance on film does not in any way guarantee that the dance will continue to be performed, while the existence of a play-text, in many instances, actually encourages subsequent performances, enabling that play-text to gather an aura of 'greatness' as it moves from one era to the next, contributing in the process to the establishment of a 'great tradition' in drama.

Performance is a social act. In an increasingly literate society live performances will continue to take place which attract enthusiastic and socially mixed audiences. This fact, however, does not guarantee that such performances will be approved of in the new social order. If performance is a social act, drama as literature becomes increasingly individualistic, as the society becomes more and more literate. This dramatic literature certainly does not have to be performed in order to find approval in the new social order. And by linking the development of drama with the education system through its various syllabuses, drama – even in live theatre performances – is likely to become less and less accessible to the 'uneducated' masses. Your reading this book on 'African drama' is an indication of how far this process has gone in contemporary Africa. In fact, the production of the book is a contradiction of what it is attempting to say.

It is ultimately impossible for you, the reader, to consider the relationship between performance and literature in the development of African drama today, without taking into account your own contribution to the process.

Traditional performance into modern drama: a comparison between *Ozidi* and *The Contest*

The way forward at this point is, probably, to make a comparison between two play-texts (which have been published), both of which seek their inspiration in, and derive from, the traditional performing arts. In the process of making the comparison we will seek to evaluate the methodology by which we make the analysis of each play. The first play is *Ozidi* by John Pepper Clark. It was first published in 1966; and there has, subsequently, been quite a lot written about it. It exists primarily as a play-text, for there have been few performances of it so that little useful comment about it in performance can be made. However, and this is important, it is not to say that the play cannot be performed. I believe it can; but its analysis here will be literary criticism, that is, a close analysis of the text.

The second play is *The Contest* by Mukotani Rugyendo, a playwright who was born in Uganda but who now lives permanently in Tanzania. *The Contest* was first published in 1977 in a collection with two other plays by him in a volume called *The Barbed Wire and other plays*. It is not clear whether *The Contest* has ever been performed. However, it is impossible to analyse the text of this play as literature; it can only be evaluated in performance. This is one of the reasons for including it in the comparison; for I hope that at the end of the comparison the relationship between literature and performance will have been established not only in terms of the development of African drama but more specifically in terms of methodology for evaluating this drama.

Ozidi

Clark's play derives from the traditional Ijọ saga, or epic, centred on Orua in the Delta region of Nigeria where it is still told and enacted today. The saga has engaged Clark for most of his life. He first heard the story when he was 9 years old, a school-boy and far from home, narrated by a story-teller called Afoluwa, and it made a deep impression on him. Years later, after he had graduated from university and achieved various academic honours, he set about rediscovering the story. Afoluwa had become a seaman on ships plying between Lagos and Liverpool, but when Clark finally tracked him down and got him to tell again the saga, to him and his friends in Lagos, it was a terrible disappointment. The man had forgotten it. He has subsequently disappeared without trace.[3]

A much more successful attempt at getting the saga told in its entirety, with the intention of tape-recording it, took place in Ibadan. This time the story-teller was a man called Qkabou, who, prompted by one Madame Yakubu, was able to tell the whole dramatized story – which traditionally took seven nights to re-late – in the course of one long day and night. Qkabou is now dead, but the whole saga as he told it was painstakingly tran-scribed, and the Ijǫ then translated more or less word for word into English. Clark published this in 1977 with the title *The Ozidi Saga* with his English translation alongside Okabou's Ijǫ version of the epic. It is not to be confused with Clark's own English language play, *Ozidi*, which we are presently going to consider, which was of course based on the saga.

Whilst making the Qkabou transcriptions, Clark travelled with the film-maker Frank Speed, in 1964, to Orua, to make a film of a performance there of the Ozidi saga. It is important to note that the Ozidi saga exists, traditionally, in two forms: as a story narrated by a story-teller who assumes all the roles and who may or may not be accompanied by musicians; as a community performance, in Orua, in which certain members of the commun-ity take certain roles in the saga, according to tradition. What was filmed, therefore, in Orua was not the *narration* of the story but its *enactment*. The leading actor and organizer of the performance was Erivini. Clark comments that the linguistic quality of Erivini's version was very thin – 'although a fine performer, he had not the gift for words'. The film was edited down to forty-five minutes and was issued under the title *Tides of the Delta*, in 1964. Erivini, too, is now dead.

There are also three long-playing records called *Songs from the Ozidi Saga*, released by EMI for the Institute of African Studies, the University of Ibadan.

And, finally, there is Clark's own play in English, *Ozidi*, published in 1966, which uses all the versions of the traditional saga. His involvement has been sustained for over thirty years, and reveals a two-fold commitment: first, to record the saga, and to preserve it, as accurately as possible, in its traditional narrative and performance forms; second, to transform it into a modern work of art.

How well has he succeeded in his first intention? He has made a record of the saga on cine film, on sound tape and on long-playing records, in written transcriptions of it in Ijọ and translated into English. However, the means by which the various recordings were made were frequently inadequate – as Clark himself admits – both in a purely technical sense (the microphones were not sufficiently sensitive; there were not enough cameras) and in terms of the inevitable limitations of the actual media themselves, such as the need for the film to be as long as it is appropriate for a documentary film, rather than the actual length of the whole saga. Inevitably, some of the images photographed during the live performance in Orua were condensed or even discarded in the film. However, even if the recording were perfect, the experience of the saga for one outside the Ijọ saga would be much less than for one who was a part of the tradition and familiar with its forms. It is perhaps in recognition of this ultimate limitation that Clark turned to a recreation of the saga in a contemporary English idiom.

To appreciate what he has done with the saga we would need to start with the basic story which I would summarize as follows:

A council of the warriors and elders of Orua gather together to select a new king – their previous kings having died almost as soon as appointed – and they choose an idiot, Temugedege, who is the elder brother of the all-powerful warrior Ozidi. It is the turn of Ozidi's family to provide the king, and it ought to be Temugedege, because he is the elder. But he is an idiot, and Ozidi advises against this selection; his idiot brother accepts, and he is overruled. The warriors think that by this move they will retain their own power and autonomy, and they ignore King Temugedege whom they have created. When Ozidi insists on due recognition for his brother, the warriors band together and destroy Ozidi, and serve up his head to his idiot brother. Ozidi's wife, Orea, is with child, and gives birth nine months later in the town of her mother, Oreame, who is a notable witch and an agent of Tamara, the ultimate godhead in that region, a female deity. Oreame rears the boy as an agent of vengeance, and turns him into a warrior full of strength and cunning, protected by very strong magic. He comes of age and learns his name: Ozidi. He returns to Orua with his mother and grandmother and slays his father's murderers, one by one. However, this is not the end of it. He provokes further challenges, either deliberately or by virtue of his reputation; and seems unable to stop killing people. He even strikes down his grandmother, by whose power he thrives, by accident; but they have been forewarned of this eventuality and she is miraculously brought back to life. It is through her powers, and his mother's love, that Ozidi is able, finally, to defeat the Smallpox King and drive him from the town, thereby purging Orua.

Stating the story as baldly as this hardly makes it seem a riveting experience. To be compelling, as a story told by an itinerant story-teller, it needs a strong narrative line, rich in incident and unexpected developments as the central sequence of events is unfolded, and, in addition, it needs a great deal of visual detail – descriptions which add to the significance of the tale for the whole community. Inevitably, there is some tension between the demands of the narrative and the discursiveness of the detail. The gifted story-teller will even play up this tension and so compel his audience to listen more intently. In the Ozidi saga the strong narrative line is supplied by the revenge theme; and the technique is to tell the story in such a way that the listeners, the audience, themselves will vicariously desire revenge.

This is done by creating an unsettling and amoral world in which the person who gets murdered, Ozidi the father, is the only person with whom the audience can identify. A society is evoked in which the ultimate sanction is not justice but might. Temugedege, the idiot brother of Ozidi the elder, is not so stupid that he cannot recognize the advantages of being king – but he is too stupid to see why the other warriors have chosen him. They are pursuing their own self-interest. Ozidi pleads for sanity, but his objections are over-ridden both by his brother and the other warriors. Then when Temugedege is grossly insulted, Ozidi puts aside his original opposition and rails against the other warriors and elders, arguing for his brother's rights. The response of the other warriors, and indeed of the whole community, is to plan his murder. Ozidi does not even suspect their malevolence, and he innocently responds to the ruse to get him out of doors. He falls into the trap laid for him and is quite brutally killed. The community which he served so well has destroyed him. Again, Temugedege is not so crazy that he cannot recognize the ultimate outrage committed against him when they serve him up his brother's head, but he is too feeble-minded to do anything about it and seek revenge. Ozidi's wife flees when she discovers that she is pregnant. This alone gives the audience some hope, whereas, the rejoicing by the whole community at Ozidi's death compounds the sense of injustice. Evil seems to work circumstantially, and there is no force within the community to check it.

It would be impossible to leave the story there. The audience need to be reassured that blatant injustice cannot ultimately go unchecked. Ozidi's death must be revenged. However, the audience are aware how difficult it is to fight the strong and the powerful, particularly if they are protected by strong magic and motivated only by self-interest. The preparation for revenge must, therefore, be as thorough as possible. Nothing must be left to chance. So the next part of the story tells how the young Ozidi is prepared for his great task of avenging his murdered father.

He starts as a normal child, and it is only as he grows to manhood that he acquires the strength, cunning and magical protection which he needs. He is recognizably good, and essentially innocent. He is taught to have no fear, and is introduced to the powerful charms and potions of the world of magic which will give him the might and courage which he will need. He goes through all his trials and accepts everything which is done to him because he believes implicitly in his grandmother's superior knowledge. The only thing which he complains about is his apparent lack of identity. Finally, when he receives his name, which is his father's name, he accepts without question the burden of avenging his father's death. The young Ozidi's reactions and responses are exactly those of the audience. And so the family of son, mother and grandmother, together with their retinue, return to Ozidi's home town, Orua, to the ruined homestead and the doddering Temugedege.

Revenge is now possible, but it is still not yet finally accomplished. At this point, the teller of the tale draws his audience further into the world of the story by the device known as dramatic irony. This is where the playwright places the audience in a situation in which they are in possession of certain facts which certain characters within the play are ignorant of, and whose behaviour would be remarkably different if they knew what the audience knows. Here, the story-teller reintroduces the warrior-elders and shows them to be complacent, arrogant and secure. His audience knows, however, that the agent of vengeance is already in their midst. Eventually they are told of the arrival of young Ozidi in town, together with his grandmother, the witch. Complacency gives way to a certain amount of anxiety. However, Ozidi still has to find out who exactly murdered his father, and dramatic irony is further used to reveal it to him. He falls asleep on the way to the market and is awakened by the three wives of the three warriors who murdered his father. The wives do not know who this young man is – though, of course, the audience does. In their ignorance the wives reveal who they are and brag to him about the brutal manner in which their husbands killed the senior Ozidi. His son now knows everything he needs to know, and can reveal his identity to them. All the while the audience have been anticipating the discomfort of these foolish wives when they find out who the young man is. Ozidi's slaughter of their wives provokes the warriors into facing the young man in combat.

The battles themselves, the successive fights which Ozidi has with his father's murderers, are the opportunities for virtuoso performances by the story-teller and his musicians, or the community actors; and they provide the audience, as do all organized fights, with the vicarious enjoyment of violence. Here, the violence is extreme, but it is simulated, and the outcome is known and desired. Vengeance has been carried out and justice has been done. Were the saga merely a tale of magic and revenge it would end here, order having been restored. But the Ijọ saga is not simply a tale of revenge. The diversions and elaborations on the main thread of the story over the seven nights and days of its telling, have served to evoke, for the audience, a whole community, a whole world together with its cosmos and special ambience 'where the land meets the sea and the sky'; and it is this community which is the focus of the story.

At the height of young Ozidi's triumph a subtle transformation takes place in the saga. The community, with a supreme champion in its midst, now begins to melt away. The champion seeks out monsters and does battle with them but it is in an increasingly sterile milieu, within his own compound and the barrenness of his eventual marriage, and within the town itself which is soon emptied of people. The story-teller is now presenting his audience with two opposing directions in the story, which interact with each other in such a way as to distance the audience from the hero, Ozidi. Even the slaying of the Smallpox King is in a city long since deserted by its populations. Ozidi's actions, and indeed his character, which in the beginning seemed to embody good, now seem to have progressed into a dual existence of both good and evil. It is a complex view, but it is matched, in fact, by the demands of telling the story; the audience are initially drawn into the saga by the adroit handling of the revenge theme in a strong narrative line, and by the excellent characterization through the extensive detail.

Once their attention has been engaged they are identified with the community that has been created for the narrative, and the narrative line weakens. There is alternating comedy and violence which drifts to an open-ended conclusion in which the members of the audience will find the meaning they want to find.

This is the oral version of the Ozidi saga, and it is thanks to Clark that we have such full and complementary records of it. However, not even the film of the Orua performance can really match the experience of a live performance of the story. Clark's English-language play, *Ozidi*, does something different from his various recordings of the oral tradition: it makes the oral version into a literary work of art. How has Clark changed the perform-ance into literature? And why?

We can take as the starting point Clark's story-teller, who plays Ozidi, father and son, as well as Temugedege. The story-teller starts the play by referring to a hitch. The company need seven young virgins to placate the hosts of the sea before the play can begin. 'Perhaps you think this is a quaint custom . . . that . . . we ought to sweep clean out of the house. . . .' he says, and adds that we can think that if we like, 'for aren't we living in a free democratic country?' He performs the oblations while maintaining this wry tone – 'Don't you people kneel to any gods?' – and extends it into a plea to the gods to help them to share in the materialist offerings of the modern Nigerian state:

> . . . So grant
> Us good money, good children, good women. . . .[4]

This speech, and the accompanying 'ritual' which is performed, is not intended as a parody. It is a secularization of the ritual, a turning of 'ritual into life' as Echeruo suggests. As if to underline the point, it is followed by an old woman symbolically sweeping out the 'evil' from the theatre or outdoor acting space. She is interrupted and sent off by the story-teller: 'We men have important affairs of state to consider right now.' By this single line he transforms the stage into the locale of the first scene which is the meeting of the Council of State in Orua. The chorus and the whole group of people who have been participating in the per-formance of the 'ritual', now assume the first roles which they are going to play, though, of course, as people performing a 'ritual' they have been playing a role as well.

Indeed, there is a double paradox in all this. In the first place, although Clark has brought the ritual into modern-day reality by using a matter-of-fact tone and contemporary references, it is in fact expressed in English, which would neither be used in a ritual enactment itself, nor in a performance of that ritual enactment within the relevant community. Thus, to achieve something that looks natural on the stage, and just like real life, Clark uses a greater degree of artificiality. Second, we, as readers, are not actually at a performance of the play. We are sitting somewhere relatively private, and reading a book. Perhaps, if our imaginations are powerful enough, we can imagine that we are at some performance of the play – though we shall come back later to the problems of the play in performance. Is the story-teller really Clark himself, addressing us, the readers – 'Perhaps you think this is a quaint custom. . . .' – or another group of people altogether? If so, who? Certainly, he has written lines for the story-teller in a most sophisticated tone, a tone that would appeal to the sort of people likely to *read* this play. It is deferential yet slightly cynical.

In fact, Clark has maintained this tone throughout the play. The utterances of all the main characters are marked by a quality of understatement that comes only from the urbane and worldly-wise. At the same time the language is richly metaphorical. The wit itself is an interaction of understatement and metaphor, as the following examples show. In the Council of Elders, for instance, Azezabife is speaking about appointing a king, and arguing with another elder:

Azezabife: . . . This state needs a head to put
  It on its feet.
Elder: I was not aware we were lying down.
Ofe: You were never one to care in what position
  You stood in the eye of the public.[5]

Later, in a scene saturated with the atmosphere of desolation, the young Ozidi discovers his father's decayed compound for the first time, inhabited by the human wreck his uncle, Temugedege, who tells him:

Temugedege: . . . It was not my fault,
  Oh my brother, my brother, it was not
  My fault, I tell you, or don't
  You hear me, don't you? Don't you?
  [*He falls down, a bundle of rags, at the feet of* **Ozidi**]

Oreame: There, you see, Ozidi, it is not
The family house alone requiring
Prompt repair.

Ozidi: [*Picking up the old idiot and addressing his men*]
Start clearing the bush; on this spot
Let us raise again the compound of my fathers.[6]

The ruined compound is mirrored in the pathetic Temugedege and
Ozidi's tarnished name. All require, as Oreame succinctly puts it,
'prompt repair. The pithiness of these exchanges, which is almost
a shorthand, is present even in violent and passionate scenes – for
example, in the scene in which the messengers are sent to Orea,
the wife of Ozidi the father, to find out how to cut off the head of
her husband, which is protected by charms, without telling her that
he has been cruelly murdered by his fellow-citizens:

Orea: . . . Did you say he has
Suffered a small wound?

First Messenger: Of course, that's only
To be expected; in war it's give and take,
You know. . . .

Second Messenger: Your man is all right. All he asks
Is that you send some medicine down to staunch
A small sore on his foot.

But Orea knows that they are lying, that her husband Ozidi is
dead, and when they intimidate her she tells them about the
special medicine:

Orea: . . . Stop on your way and pluck seven leaves
Of the coco-yam. When you have covered up
Ozidi's face completely with them, then
You may again try cutting his neck.

First Messenger: Nobody's going to cut your husband's neck,
Don't you understand a word we say? But thanks
All the same.

They run out, making a cruel pun as they leave:

. . . You'll be convinced when . . . Ozidi returns
At the head of Orua in triumph.[7]

This scene is paralleled by scene 3 in Act 4, near the end of the
play, when Ozidi (the son) and his grandmother, Oreame, visit the
sister of the monster Tebesonoma whom they have just killed.
They intend to kill the sister and her baby son as well. The woman

welcomes them as strangers and friends of her brother. The vulnerability of Orea, in the earlier scene, is now echoed in this woman's sudden awareness of her own vulnerability. She lies down with her son on her breast and prepares to die. The callous comments of those earlier messengers is carried to the extreme in Oreame's utterances in this scene. Only Ozidi is struck by doubt and some feeling of compassion. 'Let me be,' he tells his grand-mother, 'I don't want to kill anybody again.' Nevertheless, he does.

Even in the sombre final scene of the whole play this tone of understatement is consistently maintained. One neighbour tells Orea:

> Orea, it's a thorough purification ceremony
> You of this house require.

When they've taken a look at Ozidi they say not a word and tip-toe out, 'each with hand to mouth'. Orea addresses the supreme God, Tamara:

> My mother no longer lives in this house,
> So it cannot contain you.

And the Smallpox King announces to his retinue:

> She called me Yaws!
> The woman mistook us for common Yaws!*

One of the members of his grisly crew replies:

> You've been too gentle with her; let's go
> Ashore and take the whole town captive.

But everybody has fled. 'Phew,' says Okrikpakpa, 'a wretched race!'[8]

The metaphors link the characters with the world of nature, suggesting typical traits and universal characteristics. On the other hand, the use of understatement and of the swift verbal exchanges conveys the self-awareness of the characters and their almost cynical expectation of the worst; it makes the characters human and contemporary. And so, while the metaphors take us back to legend and rurality, the understatement is modern and sophisti-cated. In fact, the matter-of-factness of the dialogue is so effective

---

* A tropical skin disease which is contagious. It is ironical that something as deadly and feared as smallpox should be 'mistaken' for the relatively harmless and common yaws.

that it could almost be taken for granted. If the reader did so he would miss a significant development of the saga which Clark has achieved through it, namely a register in the common language of Nigeria, English, which is appropriate both for the content of the original oral model and for an exploration of contemporary themes. Through this tone, or register, of English the past itself becomes an elaborate metaphor for the present.

Clark, it seems, has attempted to give his fellow Nigerian intellectuals an experience of his own powerful imaginative response to the saga which comes from the heart of his own regional culture. He has endeavoured to write into the English version of the saga the meaning, or layers of meaning, which he has foraged out of its deeply traditional cultural appeal for him. In identifying the following three layers of meaning we are specifically not discussing themes, but resonances, rather, or intellectual motivations.

The first is an emotional one, an ultimate point of reference for his continuing involvement in the saga. It is a nostalgia for his youth, for a time when his young imagination first encountered the performance of the story of Ozidi, and for the circumstances of its telling in the pre-independence world of the Delta region of Nigeria. Both his childhood and that Ijo̱ world are now lost to him; the former is a metaphor for the latter.

The second layer of meaning is, by contrast, an objective one. The saga can be transformed into an account of an incipient morality. It is not the simple revenge theme of the legend, though this is the means by which he explores a more complex moral order; but it springs from the deep respect which he has for 'the serious view of life' deeply imbedded in the saga. The moral development which Clark articulates he sees as being already implicit in the original oral tradition.

The third layer of meaning, the deepest resonance, seems to return to the personal significance of the saga for Clark. It seems to have become a fabulous parable of the talented individual in Africa today, a growing awareness of the ambiguous nature of his destiny, and a search for his identity. The young Ozidi is, at the deepest level in Clark's version, a very modern African, and, as a characterization by Clark, it involves his own ambiguous relationship with (English) literature and the (Ijo̱) oral tradition. By developing in himself the highest level of literary proficiency – in order to *preserve* the traditional performing arts – he nevertheless contributes to the development of an elite literary culture which spells the decline of that which he would preserve.

These layers of meaning, these resonances, emerge as a result of a close consideration of the *text*, rather than from an experience of the play in performance. The point is, that with the text in front of you it is possible to probe the constituent elements such as language, the characterization, the structure of the scenes and acts, and the use of dramatic devices at your leisure, rather than experience the work as a whole at a single continuous perform-ance. The probing of the text, which we are doing now, is part of the literary process. It is an intellectual activity, and it forms part of the methodology of this book – though paradoxically I am critical of the literary process and fearful of its implications for the performing arts in Africa. It is the same dilemma faced by those playwrights who would seek to intellectualize their art while retaining a cultural rapport with both the oral tradition and its mass audiences – with, in fact, the people.

Bearing in mind these paradoxes, let us look again at the text of Clark's *Ozidi*, starting this time with the character of the young Ozidi. Although the stage directions indicate that he is to be played by the story-teller (who also plays Ozidi the father), the writing indicates that the young Ozidi is very different in tempera-ment from his father. First of all, the young Ozidi, unlike his father, is very dependent upon women: upon his mother and grandmother, but particularly on his grandmother, Oreame. Orea provides her son with a mother's love and devotion, but it is Oreame who educates him and initiates him into the world of the warrior with its dual emphasis on bravery and magical powers. She creates in him a dependence on her own superior magical powers and divine support. Continually, he has to call her to his aid, but at the same time there is a growing rejection of her role in his life. For instance, his final act of revenge against his father's murderers is the slaying of Ofe. When it seems that Ofe is likely to win, Tamara herself intervenes, then Oreame adds her spell, and it is only then that Ozidi is roused to a state of possession and hacks the old warrior up. The crowd fall back horrified, and leave Ozidi and his grandmother alone on the stage. There is an interesting stage direction:

[*The old woman falls on her knees, overwhelmed by events and bewildered by her grandson who is possessed. . . .*][9]

It is Ozidi's horn-blower and other personal attendants who bring him back to normal.

The next contest, which is with the seven-headed monster, Tebesonoma, begins with Ozidi being trapped by the monster whilst he is asleep. He calls for his mother (that is, his grandmother) who flies in (with a sound like an aeroplane coming in to land!) and saves her grandson. Tebesonoma and Ozidi fight and after losing six of his seven heads, the monster begs Ozidi not to cut off his last head. Ozidi is about to comply, but Oreame cuts him short:

> Not so my son! This cannot happen! I
> Was tending at home a client bleeding to death when
> Tebesonoma dragged me forth. And do
> You want to let him go who brought you here,
> Your feet trailing in dirt?[10]

They fight on; but it requires Oreame's cunning to distract the monster so that Ozidi can enter a state of possession again and hack him to death.

They move on to the home of Tebesonoma's sister, and Ozidi is now sullenly arguing with his grandmother – 'Let me be! I don't want to kill anybody again . . .' He requires to be put into a manic state of possession physically, by a slap of Oreame's magic fan, before he will carry out the murder of the woman and her baby. The next contest is with Odogu, whose wife Ozidi has tried to seduce, and it is Ozidi's last fight. Clark makes it a formal and almost emblematic affair: the mortal combatants are evenly matched in magic, and each are backed up by their half-mortal female progenitors. Behind them all is the voice of the wizard Bouakarakarabiri, the source of their magical potions and strategies. The contest inevitably reaches stalemate. Boua taunts the witches and finally sends them on a race for a magical herb which will decide the victor. Oreame wins the race. The magic herb enables Ozidi to triumph over Odogu, but it so blinds him with manic rage that he kills his grandmother as well. There is a very interesting stage direction:

> [**Ozidi** *staggers out shouting his name* . . .][11]

Out of the random and discursive acts of violence and comic exaggeration which form the latter half of the saga, Clark has discovered a thread of logic which expresses his concept of the central character: Ozidi's realization that he lacks a personal identity. Clark has drawn this thread right through the play. Let us see how.

In the very first scene in which we meet the young Ozidi he is a boy-without-a-name. He remains nameless for the next six scenes, right throughout the time of his preparation as a young warrior. In fact, a name is specifically denied him, despite his boyish protests. It also worries him that he doesn't seem to have a father and he couples the two deprivations in his mind. As far as Oreame is concerned, and in terms of the magic which saturates the world in which he is growing up, he cannot carry his murdered father's name until he proves himself to be an adequate agent of vengeance. However, Oreame permits him no alternative course and he, in his innocence which Clark is at pains to emphasize, totally accepts his grandmother's superior wisdom. He finally acquires his father's name by a magical process. He is now committed to his immediate destiny as an avenger. He has an identity which he positively assumes.

However, once he has accomplished his revenge he pursues the logic of this identity in a crucial conversation with his mother Orea (*not* his grandmother):

> I cannot farm or fish; nor as others
> Exchange fruits from both for profit. I was born
> With a sword to hand, fists clenched firm for fight.
>   This course
> I have followed without deviation
> Doing my duty by my dead father. But now
> Like a river at a whirlpool I am come to
> A spinning stop. . . .

Orea replies that she is not going to let him fight again, now that his father is avenged. Ozidi then succinctly points out the problem to her:

> Yes, my father sleeps well but what
> About me? I have only to step out and children
> Are running to hide their faces in between the feet
> Of their mothers . . .
> Oh yes, my father, all set up now and free from the grove of night
> Sleeps well indeed, while I walk here awake, for
> I have only to close my eyes and heads of those
> I have slaughtered tumble forth, rolling and

Hopping about my feet like huge jiggers
Screaming to suck my blood.[12]

After this, and for the rest of the play, Ozidi remains outwardly a
hero, but inwardly a nonentity.

Clark does not shirk the issue. He shows us Ozidi sexually
thwarted and curiously exposed in two separate scenes. The first is
Ozidi's own telling of his sexual dream concerning the Scrotum
King. He admits that it is his grandmother who in the end has to
come and rescue him from the giant testicles and the flood the
Scrotum King has released. The second scene shows Ozidi's
impotence more poignantly and more extensively. It is the scene
where he tries to seduce the wife of Odogu. When he fails to take
the woman he has abducted, he admits to her his dependence on
his grandmother:

And of course my grandmother, she is
The sea that fills my stream. . . .

As soon as he admits this the woman begins to treat him
coquettishly, almost as though he were a child – 'Oh, come now,
play with me. . . .' – and Ozidi, who would seduce her and not
rape her, finds that her change of attitude signifies nothing more
than that she is prepared to trade sex with him for the secrets of his
might. Again, an attempt at achieving a normal life fails and he is
forced back into his vengeful self. As his mother Orea says at the
end of the scene:

Leave the woman alone, Ozidi!
Now is there nothing else you can do but kill?
Oh, no more sleep for us again in this house.[13]

Finally, after his last frenzied act of destruction which destroys
his grandmother, he staggers out, *shouting his name*. It is a
grotesque parody of that earlier scene in which he discovered his
name and his identity for the first time in his grandmother's house,
and performed a triumphal dance, chanting his name to the
applause of his grandmother, mother and retinue. The two scenes
have deliberate parallels which are evoked by their respective
stage directions. The destruction of Oreame by Ozidi is one of the
most significant changes which Clark has made to the saga. In the
traditional story, Ozidi is magically warned of the possibility of
accidentally killing his grandmother. He takes the advised precau-

tions, so that when he falls into the trap, she is able to escape from actual death and continue to advise him. Clark perceives that with her influence over him, Ozidi has no individual identity, and he makes his own Ozidi increasingly aware of this constraint upon his life. Clark's Ozidi knows, if only at a subconscious level, that he must kill her if he is to find his true self. But in killing her he cuts off the source of his power and the magical protection which he has enjoyed. Clark sees the arrival of the Smallpox King and Ozidi's affliction with the disease as being a result of this act of virtual self-destruction. His mother Orea says that this is the first illness he has ever had in his life, and it is an indication of Ozidi's losing, at last, his divine protection, and acquiring common humanity. In the saga it is Oreame who cures Ozidi – admittedly on Orea's own suggestion that he has common yaws – and then helps him slay the Smallpox King. But in Clark's play it is Orea alone, with her own enduring humanity, who cures him, and the Smallpox King and his retinue depart without the fight.

In Clark's development of the character, the vengeful Ozidi, the manic scourge, is a personality which has been overlaid on the character of the man himself. For a time, when it seemed that everybody wanted revenge, it was possible for there to be a total identity between Ozidi the scourge and Ozidi the man, and to find no conflict between the man's destiny and himself. We have already seen how, in the saga, Ozidi's presence within the community becomes deeply ambiguous for that community. In the play, Clark is less concerned with the community than he is with the man. After Ozidi has achieved his revenge Clark turns the public man upon his private self, in order that the play might reflect the theme of man's divided self, which Clark sees as a condition of the modern world. The ending of the play, nevertheless, leaves this problem unresolved.

These existential problems are the ones that seem to lie at the core of the play, and they are the ones which have taken Clark farthest away from the spirit and intent of the saga. On a less problematic level, he has been able to pursue the development of moral issues which he finds in the saga. He accepts the metaphysical world of Orua, with its parallel experience of magic and mortality through the divinity – Tamara, the half-mortal, half-magical beings like Oreame, and the mortals whose powers are enhanced by magic, as well as the ordinary mortals of the community who are not. The affairs of the mortal world are ordered by custom . . . and also by self-interest, mainly on the part of the leaders.

At the beginning of the play, the basis on which the community leaders decide to appoint the idiot Temugedege as king appears to be irrational. It's your family's turn, they tell Ozidi, but custom forbids the appointment of a younger brother. Ozidi declines on behalf of his idiot elder brother, who, at that moment, staggers in and contradicts him. He agrees to be king, and the elders so appoint him. This apparently unthinking pursuance of custom actually appears to be motivated by self-interest on the part of the most powerful warriors. Another elder has in fact suggested that before they select a new king they should find out why all the others have died so soon after election, but his objections are brushed aside. The deliberate selection of someone wholly unsuitable suggests that the community's traditions are being used against the community's best interests. Ozidi himself is pushed into a contradictory position by having to support his feeble-minded brother against the community, when they refuse to pay tribute to the man whom they elected. The community seems collectively unable to sort out its problems, and in the impasse allows itself to be led further astray by the immoral warriors. The whole community plays a part in the slaughter of Ozidi, who, bound by honour and custom, walks into the trap and then stoically accepts his fate.

The slaughter of Ozidi and the hacking off of his head is followed by a grotesque scene. Temugedege waits with Ozidi's wife Orea to receive the customary tribute. He is a parody of a king – 'He wears a dirty brown tunic over his cloth, and about his brow is a garland which has withered in the course of the day. . . .' He holds a stick as a staff of office. The procession comes in bearing his awful tribute:

All (*With one voice*):   Here is our tribute to you,
  King Temugedege, take it and rejoice!!! [**Temugedege**, *with a fixed stupid smile on his face, steps down and opens the parcel dumped at his feet. He shrieks at the sight, tottering back in a fit*][14]

Orea is left to cradle the head of her husband in her lap, while Temugedege 'with finger in his mouth cries his way into the house'. He comes out again, his erstwhile staff of office now over his shoulder with a bundle tied to it, wandering off, aware at last of his own pathetic uselessness.

At this point in the play, the good and evil in the world of the drama are clearly distinguished one from the other, and the whole community at Orua is seen to be corrupted by the evil in its midst. In defeating the murderers of his father, the younger Ozidi overturns the evil in the community. Or does he? It would seem that Clark sees the magic which is at the heart of the play as amoral. It is not a thing in itself but merely a medium, through which superior might and cunning are channelled to whoever seeks these powers and is capable of absorbing them, be they good or evil. The use of magic in all of Ozidi's subsequent battles is shown to be morally sterile. It is one of the community elders, an ordinary mortal who tricks Ozidi into fighting his battle with Tebesonoma, but it is Oreame who advocates a fight to the death:

> But better finish off the fight today
> Than clash on another: this forest cannot contain
> Two champion lions.

But the slaughter of Tebesonoma leads to further and even more gratuituous killing: Tebesonoma's sister and her baby. As Tebesonoma himself says:

> . . . Take it from me, Ozidi, except you murder them too,
> Twenty years from now, as you did
> With your father's assassins, you shall be called to account. . . .[15]

Clark establishes the woman's innocence and essential good nature unequivocally; and when she is threatened he brings in the neighbours to support her. The audience have now been turned through 180°: Ozidi now embodies evil, and the community is seen as good. Oreame manifests her morally blind pragmatism and strikes the woman and her family down by magic. In the same way as Ozidi's father accepted his immiment death, so too does this poor woman.

The final contest, with Odogu, is utterly sterile because it is the logical outcome of an amoral source of strength: the magic of the witch progenitors. The fight, and the magic, has ceased to have any relevance to the affairs of men. Ozidi's killing of his grandmother, at the end of this fight, seemingly by accident, restores the human dimension. Orea, too, manifests a recognizable moral goodness in her caring, selfless nature. In the final scene, Ozidi is deserted by his retinue and racked by disease and it is Orua's simple human care which helps him survive the illness. The mortals, Orua and Ozidi, are now totally unaware of the presence of the fabulous barge of Engarando, the Smallpox King, filled with his retinue of shadowy allegorical figures. That world now exists in another dimension altogether. Morality, Clark seems to be saying, rests with human beings, within the world of their common humanity, and not with magic.

Clark has tried to create for the modern stage a dazzling spectacle to delight the imagination of audiences, as much as his own imagination was stirred by the telling of the legend in his childhood. It is ironical, therefore, that for many readers of the play it is this element of extravagant staging, suggested in the stage directions, which is their greatest obstacle to understanding the play. There are two sorts of difficulties. One is the difficulty of actually visualizing the totality of music, dancing, costumes and transformations while reading the play. The other is a disbelief in the possibility of achieving the stage directions in a performance in even the best-equipped theatre. The effect of this second difficulty is to lead the reader into trying to discover the correlative action for which the stage direction must be some sort of metaphor, and then, when this fails, to doubt the validity of the theatrical form which Clark has chosen for his reworking of the saga.

There is no doubt that the highly technical theatres of the wealthy industrialized societies, with the vast range of professional performance and artistic skills which they can employ, can cope with every scenic effect called for in *Ozidi*, but such theatrical resources are yet in their infancy in Africa. Although *Ozidi* has been performed in Nigeria, it has not been given the costly and elaborate staging which it calls for. For example, scene 5 in Act 2, when Ozidi acquires his personal charm, needs an actor who has trained professionally in acrobatics to play the role of Bouakar-akarabiri, so that he can act upside-down as he is initially required to do. The huge lizard, eagle-hornbill, and monkey, are played by actors wearing masks; the eagle-hornbill would be played by a trapeze artist (who would be able to fly around the stage on trapezes on a pulley system) while the monkey would be played by another acrobat. The gigantic pestle would be over a trap-door on the stage, and when these weird creatures were put into it they would pass through the false bottom of the pestle, then through the stage trap-door, unseen by the audience. The colossal pestle would be made out of lightweight synthetic material like poly-styrene, painted to look like solid wood. The unearthly sounds which signify the onset of Ozidi's state of possession can be recorded on a synthesizer and then amplified around the auditorium. Many theatres have complicated stereophonic sound systems which enable the recorded sounds to swirl around the theatre, and come from different directions.

The other complicated scene, as far as staging is concerned, is the fight with Ofe in Act 3, scene 8. Ofe's repeated disappearing act can be effected by having a second actor dressed identically to Ofe, and by using special lighting effects. There is, for example, a type of gauze curtain called scrim which seems to disappear when light is thrown on to a person or object behind it, and yet looks very solid when light is thrown on to it and on to whatever is painted on it. So strong lights on Ofe 1 in front of it will make him the target for Ozidi to strike at; and then strong lights on Ofe 2 behind the scrim, with the sudden fade of the first lights, will give the audience the impression of one person suddenly disappearing in one place and reappearing in another.

It is a complicated imaginative process trying to visualize not only these detailed scenic effects taking place but also the mechanics by which they are achieved, while reading the text. However, grasping the visual spectacle of the play on stage is not actually essential to an understanding of it as literature – in my analysis of the layers of meaning I did not have special recourse to the spectacle. On the other hand, it is important to realize that the play can be staged, and that it does not provide any insuperable problems for a competent theatre director, provided he has access to very extensive theatre resources.

The Contest

It is necessary now to place Clark's *Ozidi* in the context of the various attempts elsewhere in Africa to develop a modern African theatre from the rural traditional performance modes. We can see a very different approach to the oral tradition to Clark's in Mukotani Rugyendo's play in English, *The Contest*. Rugyendo's initial concern is not with a particular example of the oral tradition, or its preservation for its own sake. 'This play,' he writes in the production note to it,[16] 'sets out to explore what can possibly be done to maintain the *popular* nature of theatre.' It is Rugyendo himself who has emphasized the word 'popular'. His basic premise is that traditional performances are by their very nature popular, because of their function in society:

Theatre in societies that have not suffered heavy fragmentation and class divisions is a popular activity. It is the expression of the spirit of the collective; the embodiment of their struggle for survival in a hostile environment. In societies with low scientific and technical knowledge, this is confined to the expression of the people's experiences in the production of the very basics of their existence. And art is necessary to bridge the gap that prevails as man grapples with these hostilities.

Rugyendo's other premise is that theatre in technologically advanced societies, especially capitalist societies, becomes less and less popular:

But the problem is that as capitalist society becomes more and more complex, and thus more alienating, art forms instead of being richer and more dynamic, become stale and removed from concrete reality.

Thus, in turning back to the African performance traditions, Rugyendo has shifted the emphasis from the peasants' oral traditions to the peasants themselves, today, as the audiences for modern theatre. What is to be preserved is not a particular saga or dance or masquerade, but the peasant audience itself; and they are to carry over to the contemporary theatre their growing social and political awareness. Rugyendo is not an isolated example of a playwright anxious to retain the popular dimension of traditional performances in the modern forms of theatre. The Zambians, Kasoma and Chifunyise, the Kenyan, Ngugi wa Thiong'o, the Tanzanian, Hussein, as well as the Botswana movement, *Laedza Batanani*, whose work is dealt with in subsequent chapters, are concerned to address the peasantry and the urban proletariat about their present disadvantaged position.

The Contest is, however, an appropriate play to consider alongside *Ozidi*, particularly in the terms which this chapter is attempting to set forth, namely, the relationship between literature and performance in the development of an African drama.

Clark's play can be subjected to literary analysis, to a close and rewarding consideration of the play-text. Rugyendo's play cannot. To read Rugyendo's play in the context of a study of African dramatic literature can be a disillusionment, and lead to a dismissal of it as glib and inconsequential. The critic cannot find anything like 'themes' and 'plot', 'characterization' and 'relationships', in the text on which to hang his analysis. Even the traditional element seems weak. In fact, *The Contest* is not intended for reading, except as an indication of the nature of the experiment in performance which Rugyendo is suggesting. Although both *Ozidi* and *The Contest* use a traditional performance respective to their author's particular indigenous culture, with the aim of preserving some aspects of it, the results are diametrically opposed to each other. *Ozidi* is basically literary (though it can be performed); *The Contest* is basically a performance (though an account of it can be read).

This crucial difference between the two plays is evident on at least three levels of analysis, namely; (1) in the role of the audience in terms of the references to audience participation given in the stage directions; (2) in the structure of each play; (3) in the use of English, that is, in the linguistic texture of each play. I propose to give an analysis of *The Contest*, and a comparison of it with *Ozidi*, under these three headings.

1   The role of the audience

Rugyendo tells us in the production note that his play derives from something which he calls the 'heroic recitation', 'a poetic theatrical form which is found among the Bahima, Banyankole, Bakiga and Bayarwanda in Western Uganda, the Bahaya in north-western Tanzania and in Rwanda and Burundi'. He is not concerned with one specific 'recitation', or one special saga, but with the genre, which 'deals with heroic feats of adventure in war, cattle-raiding, hunting. . . .' The way an adventure is told is more important than the actual content of the recitation, and the performers are supposed to 'win the spectators' admiration and honour depending on how they excel in their recitations'. This is Rugyendo's own response to the recitations, and it reflects his delight in an audience's response to a performance. Clark's response to Okabou's telling of the Ozidi saga, whose version he favours above all others, is significantly different:

Herein lies precisely the strength of the Okabou text – its observance of Aristotle's old canon for a thundering good story to stir the heart anywhere – and it is outstanding not just in comparison with the Erivini and Afolua versions. As a story, Okabou's version has a beginning, a middle, and an end in a total structure where no segment is super-fluous. . . . Okabou . . . preserves the Ozidi epic as a unified work of art . . .

For Clark, the quality of the saga lies in the textual arrangement of a plot. In fact, Clark complains that in the enacted version in Orua there was very little 'text' – 'The narrator/protagonist, the late Erivini of Bolou Orua, although a fine performer, had not the gift for words'.

Rugyendo's concern is with the form of theatre appropriate to a peasant audience today, and so all other traditional elements relate to this overriding concern and can be changed to suit peasant societies elsewhere in Africa. He specifically states this:

The producers and actors should feel free to exploit to the full what they can possibly imagine of the limitless possibilities of this form. It is supposed to establish very easy communication between performers and spectators so that the latter can actively respond to the rhythm of the performance. It aspires to minimise to the lowest degree the hollow distance between actors and the silent audience in the modern theatre.

Clark, however, speaks of his own English version *Ozidi* in a different mode, which reveals a remarkably different intent:

In my play, *Ozidi*, I treated the combined accounts of the Ozidi myth given by Okabou, Afolua, and Erivini, just as Shakespeare in his Roman and English plays handled history that Plutarch and Livy on the one hand, and Hall and Holinshed on the other, had written up. The parallel may be stretched to the Greek playwrights in their exploitation of a body of myths that was the public property of their people.

If Clark uses the myth to 'mirror the continuing state of man', and to explore the contemporary restraints on man's individuality, Rugyendo uses the 'heroic recitations' to show the choice which is idealistically presented to the contemporary masses in Africa between socialist and capitalist forms of development.

The contest of the title is between two heroes, known as Hero 1 (the son of the Mungwes) and Hero 2 (son of the Nkozis) for the hand in marriage of the beautiful daughter of the village, Maendeleo. The leading drummer is the master of ceremonies; the villagers themselves, who have assembled to enjoy each hero's defence of his claim to the bride, are the final arbiters, though Maendeleo herself has a choice in the matter. Each Hero is assigned a girl who will sing his praises, stir up the crowd on his behalf, and generally encourage him. Maendeleo is the society of the African masses; Hero 1 is, if you like, African capitalism; Hero 2 is African socialism. The Heroes are each expected to develop their arguments in concrete terms, providing an analysis of what they did before and since independence, and suggesting how future development will go in terms of their guiding philosophies.

Obviously, because of the nature and composition of the peasant 'audience' within the play, Hero 2, the socialist, will win the bride, since what he has to say has greater relevance and applicability to the peasant than what the urban capitalist has to say. In fact, Rugyendo allows Hero 1 to present a positive and somewhat idealized view of capitalist development, in order to strengthen the significance of the 'audience's' response. Hero 2 wins; Hero 1 shakes his hand, and everyone proceeds to a feast. This is clearly an idealized vision of peasant society, and an idealized version of the nature of the choice for future development for the masses. It is quite deliberately so. Rugyendo himself has shown in another play, *And the Storm Gathers*, that the peasantry really have very little say in their affairs; that when there is a choice for them to make it is always between two equally unsatisfactory alternatives; and that socialism is never as strong as capitalism on the African continent, backed up and manipulated as the latter is by international capitalism and Western economic imperialism. However, in *The Contest*, he is concerned to present the ideal rather than the actual.

For this to be valid, the nature and composition of the real audience, of whom the 'audience' within the play will become a part, is crucial. The play is intended for performance before and with villagers: farmers, herdsmen, traders. It is not intended for performance in a conventional proscenium arch theatre – 'It is supposed to establish very easy communication between actors and spectators. . . .' – and it is not intended for an elitist audience. If the 'audience' within the play, who are taking the roles of peasants, and the actual audience at a performance of it have the same social identity, the response of the former will be very close to what is already written into the text for 'the people' to say and do. This is clearly what Rugyendo intends when he says that the play 'aspires to minimise to the lowest degree the hollow distance between actors and the silent audience in the modern theatre'. Comments, therefore, in the stage directions which refer to the responses of 'the people' are to be taken to refer to the whole audience present at a performance of the play. The 'audience' within the play will be able to encourage and focus the response of the real audience who are seeing the play performed for the first time. Thus, their role bridges the gap between actor and spectator, and the dramatic form which Rugyendo is reaching towards begins to materialize. The play would be meaningless to a middle class

African audience in a conventional theatre. By choosing to make the contest a contemporary political one, of critical importance for the least articulate section of African society, and by presenting it from their point of view and in their terms, the author has bound together traditional form and contemporary content in an uncompromising radical way. If there is to be no sense of distance between actors and spectators, then there should be no distance, likewise, between actors and performers on the one hand, and the subject-matter of the performance on the other. In this sense, therefore, the 'heroic recitations' can be modified. Producers and actors, Rugyendo says, 'should feel free to exploit to the full the limitless possibilities of this form'.

Thus, the many forms of praise-singing, which occur in many different African cultures, could be appropriated to the form of the play.[17]

The extent of audience participation in *Ozidi* is much less than it is in the two versions of the saga, the film of Erivini's performance and transcription of Okabou's narration (which Clark himself has given us). Throughout Okabou's version there are constant interruptions by the spectators, both on the formal level of what Clark calls 'story reminder' and on the informal level of individual interjections and comments. In describing the function of the 'story reminder', Clark is, perhaps unconsciously, revealing that the audiences of the saga are interested in the manner of telling the story as much as in the unfolding of the narrative:

The 'story reminder' is self-explanatory. Antiphonal in form, it carries the story forward all the way to its end. It keeps in constant view the immediate aim of the gathering – to see a good presentation, and to revel in the high spirits of the adventure transmitted. Occasionally the form is extended to include a citation of probable difficulties and the prompt regulation of these. 'Are you strong? If you see, will you act? Are there men in Ijo?' often comes the challenge. In each case, the response, of course, is an emphatic 'Yes'.

But when we turn to Clark's play, the 'story reminder' has disappeared, as have all other interjections by the audience. All that remains is the story-teller's introduction in the first scene and the accompanying ritual which we have already analysed. He makes two other brief appearances as story-teller, but these have nothing to do with audience participation. They are instead devices to shape the drama as a text. And who is the story-teller addressing at the beginning of the play? From both the comments and the tone it appears to be addressed to readers and Clark's fellow intellectuals.

But the same people will read the text of *The Contest* (the same people, by and large, who are reading this book). Furthermore, *The Contest* has a detailed explanatory production note while *Ozidi* has none. This is odd because the traditional performance from which *Ozidi* derives is much more specific and esoteric than the generalized 'heroic recitations' that *The Contest* develops. This would seem to argue for more explanations for *Ozidi*. Again, the theme of *The Contest* is contemporary and explicit, while the theme of *Ozidi* is complex and its relevance to the present is not immediately apparent. This too would argue for more explanations for *Ozidi*. Yet it is the other way around. Why?

The reason is that *Ozidi* is ultimately contained in its textual form; *The Contest* is primarily a performance – and, moreover, a performance for an audience other than the readers of the text of it. *Ozidi*, therefore, needs no introduction. Students and readers, who are familiar with the methodology of literary criticism will discover its meaning, or layers of meaning, and derive their insights from the study of the text. Subjected to the same scrutiny, the text of *The Contest* will fall apart and yield no further meaning than the obvious one. So an explanation is required: this play in performance – the author is saying – is not actually meant for you, the reader of the text of it, unless you wish to share in its intent and experiment with how the theatre can be made accessible again to the mass of the population, for whom the play is intended.

2 Structure

It is when we come to compare the structures of these two plays that we begin to see the ambiguities inherent in the development of drama in Africa from its traditional modes of performance to the ways in which it now exists.

We have already noted that Clark finds a unity – which he defines as a beginning, a middle and an end – in the original epic, and that this is reinforced in his own play through Ozidi's search for an identity. In fact, the one major change which Clark makes is to have Ozidi kill Oreame irrevocably. This becomes inevitable, in the way Clark has structured his play, because he shows Ozidi's purpose in life, and his identity, change from the identity which his grandmother gave him and subsequently sustained. It is clear that the focus, for Clark, is the character of Ozidi, who is given an existence both inside the epic and also beyond it: we can, after reading the play, consider Ozidi's problem of identity entirely on its own, and quite separately from the fact that it happens in a particular society at a particular time. Ozidi is predominant over the social forces which might control him. Those forces outside him which control him are bound to his ego and are manifest in ever more extreme forms of anti-social behaviour. The play offers no comment on the impact of Ozidi on his community (whereas, as we saw, there is a community perspective in the saga). Are the problems of an individual as compelling as the problems of a community, and especially an oppressed social class? They are for those who are aware of their own individuality and find it checked within their society, but they are not for those at the bottom of the social heap. Therefore, and more specifically, if *Ozidi* is about an individual's identity and in disregard of any social forces acting upon him, can it be of any compelling interest to Africa's peasants (even if it were performed in their own language)? The answer, logically, is no. We can go further and ask if it will be as interesting as the original saga, in Orua? And the answer again is probably no. Nor has it been Clark's aim to return the saga to Orua in a new form. After all, they have their version of it already. He is more concerned to make the saga 'accessible' to a wider African audience – he states as much – and, as far as his own play is concerned, to indicate to whoever is interested his own intellectual and aesthetic response to the tradition. However, it is possible that the way he responds to the saga and what he wishes to see happen to African drama might prove something of a paradox: the attempt to preserve the traditional forms may well hasten their demise.

The structure in *Ozidi* is concerned, then, with the structuring of the *story itself*: an internal textual organization. The structure in *The Contest* is concerned with the structuring of *performance*. There is an extended 'introduction' between the drummer and the audience, which is in fact more than a quarter of the length of the whole play. It is much longer than the story-teller's introduction in *Ozidi*; and, unlike the need for seven 'virgins' from the audience if the performance is to be a 'success', the introduction by the drummer is, *in reality*, and not in pseudo-reality, crucial to the success of the performance. The audience need to be put in the right mood. As the drummer says:

Before our visitors come forward to show themselves to us, we will first have the flute-player to play a bit and enliven the atmosphere. [**Flute-player** *gets up*] It is still dull. It must be warm. Let us shake our bones first. Draw our visitors and ourselves into the throng. Eee!   People there to dance to the flute! Where are they?[18]

People start dancing. There is an extended and specific stage direction; and all the while the Flute-player and the Drummer encourage the people:

'This is it. The thing we want. Or isn't it, wananchi?'

'It is! We can feel it coming up! The heat!'. . . .

'Now wananchi . . . let us continue with the heat. Here we have our visitors – Hero 1 and Hero 2 – I can see them getting into the heat, too. . . .'

The whole passage may well strike the reader as boringly long-winded and rather odd, especially when compared with the opening speech of the story-teller in *Ozidi*. The point is that it doesn't matter, in a performance of *Ozidi*, who acts the part of the virgins. It is not a 'real' sacrifice, but an acted one. The whole story-teller scene is a reference to the traditional culture – a stage convention, if you like – and the performance will continue because the producer will make sure beforehand that there are seven women in the audience, be they virgins or not, who will 'volunteer'. The audience, too, will know that the sacrifice has been organized, 'produced', and they will accept the 'spontaneity' of the scene on the level of an imitation of reality, like the rest of the play.

But in *The Contest* the opening scene requires the audience to get themselves in the mood, to dance if they want to, and to become part of the actual celebration. This is something which cannot be recreated on the page through the written word. It does not matter how detailed or precise the stage directions are, the reader is not going to get out of his or her chair and start dancing. On the other hand, in an actual performance, the drummer and the flute-player will establish a mood and pace which will be different in each performance. Rugyendo acknowledges this in the production note when he admits that the best results 'will be got if both the actors and the producers go beyond the few directions given in the text and introduce whatever movements may fit their particular context'.

There is a long stage direction which describes the ways in which the Heroes are to comport themselves while delivering their 'recitations'. These stage directions possess no literary qualities but they must be followed in essence if the performance is to be successful wherever in rural Africa it is staged. It is in the actual arguments of the Heroes that the substance of the play is to be found, and the structuring of these has nothing at all to do with narrative or plot or beginnings, middles and ends. Instead, the structure is that of a debate, and each of the two parties structures his own argument in the most convincing way possible. It is only the circumstances of any given performance of the play which can allow the outcome of the debate to go in favour of the socialist candidate (which Rugyendo himself, of course, supports). This is a most important point: the debate is only 'rigged' in so far as the performance of the play takes place in front of disadvantaged rural audiences. For the argument is open-ended: it is the audience who decides in favour of one contestant over another. On one level, the choice between socialism and capitalism is not actual but metaphorical, and given in the context of a recognized perform-ance mode. On another level, however, it is an indication of choices which *do* exist in reality, though hitherto obscured, not only by existing economic and political institutions, but by the very development of the type of performing arts which those economic and political institutions encourage.

3　Language

Finally, the way English is used in *The Contest*, and in comparison with the English of *Ozidi*, reveals that the language used in African drama is a problem for which there is no easy solution. The choice of language is a problem which faces each African playwright every time he sits down to write a play, just as it is a problem for each director every time he has to choose a play for production. First of all, playwrights and directors are themselves seldom monolingual: their day-by-day experience is multi-lingual. Because they are linguistically versatile, playwrights and directors do indeed have a real choice of language for their drama. Second, the choice of language is not one which can be made on its own, but must be related to other factors over which the playwright or producer may have no control.

For instance, if the playwright is hoping to get his play published it will have to be in a language which the publishers will regard as marketable, that is, with enough potential readers of the text to make the publication of the play economically viable. In practice in Africa today, this means the likelihood of the play being a 'set-work' on a university or school syllabus; so his choice of language in which to write the play is tied up with the language policies of a particular country's educational system. Related to this initial sense of restriction is the more generalized linguistic consideration of which language will be read by other intellectuals, not necessarily in the same country: a desire to communicate ideas and experiences through a creative literature, and to manipulate and develop the form of the creative medium in the process. These considerations will tend to push the playwright into writing in English (or French or Portuguese).

Directors and producers respond to quite different considerations. The first problem concerns the cadence of speech. Obviously, this varies in different parts of Africa and it is probably more marked in anglophone than francophone countries. There is a general conception, in anglophone countries, of different sorts of English: Nigerian English, Kenyan English and so on. There are also different sorts of Nigerian English, which depend on a wide variety of factors. This variation in English usage is distinct from the existence of varieties of Pidgin even in Coastal West Africa, and Creole in Sierra Leone. A Pidgin is a contact language. A Creole is a Pidgin which has become a first language for its speakers. Although African linguists are taking Pidgin and Creole seriously now – as languages in their own right and therefore worthy of their close professional scrutiny – students (and indeed many of their academic masters, too) still regard Pidgin and Creole in a derogatory way, as an unexpressive bastardized form of language or as baby-talk. Pidgin and Creole are almost exclusively languages of oral communication. This has positive implications for their use in dramatic performance and negative implications for writing plays.

For a director, the production of a play in English involves a consideration of such elements as alternative stress patterns, variations in the morphology and phonology of Standard English, and structural and lexical differences: all to make it easier for the actors to speak the play's dialogue.

African playwrights have experimented with a number of solutions to the problem of writing in English, and yet in an English that will be appealing to their African audiences in performance. One solution is to try to forge a poetic diction which will be high-sounding but have the right cadences. Another solution is to use a variety of English registers within one play, making, say, the main characters speak normal and 'correct' English, those who are pompous and elitist, a pedantic form of 'proper' English, and the servants Pidgin. A third solution is to lard the dialogue with proverbs and axioms, making it heavily metaphorical with an emphasis on nature and the rural routine. In this last option the authentic tone is achieved lexically rather than structurally, but it is rather inappropriate for plays with a contemporary urban setting. There has been a great deal written on how English can be developed as an appropriate language for African drama. The Nigerian critic, Akanji Nasiru, for instance, has analysed the problem in the context of Nigerian drama and focused on the achievement of the playwright Ola Rotimi,[19] Kaabwe Kasoma, the Zambian playwright has commented that the mixing of English with other languages has less to do with the social categorization of characters than with the comprehension of the play by a linguistically mixed audience.[20]

This brings us back to the problems facing directors and producers of plays. Often their options are not between appealing to an English-speaking audience on the one hand, and a non-English-speaking audience on the other, but between a linguistically homogeneous audience (usually a very rural one) and a linguistically heterogeneous audience (usually urban). A director's problem will be acute if he is touring a production in both rural and urban communities, except among communities, like in coastal Ghana where Akan is a *lingua franca*, which have a prevailing, widely-spoken language.

It is extremely difficult, therefore, to find a language which matches the linguistic complexity of the African milieu. Ironically, it has only become a central issue recently, when playwrights began belatedly to address themselves to the problem of developing a wider audience for contemporary drama. The first efforts have tended to be with the linguistically homogeneous rural audiences such as in Botswana with the *Laedza Batanani* popular theatre movement. The established popular theatre traditions of coastal West Africa, like the various Yoruba travelling theatres, do have, it is true, an urban orientation, but the companies tend to perform in Yoruba and to draw their audiences exclusively from the particular regional group. Occasionally, people like the Yoruba playwright and performer, Hubert Ogunde, will perform in Pidgin, in the hope of bringing in a wider urban audience.

Pidgin and Creole are in fact becoming a significant linguistic medium for popular urban performance. Young Nigerian playwrights are writing and performing serious plays and political satire in Pidgin. A significant experiment was by the Sierra Leonean novelist and playwright, Yulisa Maddy, whose Krio play, *Big Berrin*, got him into political trouble in Freetown.

Those playwrights who have decided to write plays now in the language of their people, like the Kenyan Ngugi wa Thiong'o, have done so because they have tended to have a political commitment which over-rides a specifically literary objective. Rugyendo appears to have such a political commitment. Yet he writes *The Contest* in English; and he feels compelled to apologize for it:

Rendition [of the heroic recitations] into English certainly curtails much of the poetic quality, especially the even relationship between the dance and the gestures with the tonal structure of the recited word.

Clark makes no apology for his use of English in *Ozidi*, for his intention is to render the Ijo saga into a modern Nigerian play in English. We have earlier observed how controlled the language is in the play, and how Clark has found a tone and a register of English which matches his intent. However, some Nigerian critics have found the language of the play 'Shakespearean'. They are critical of passages like the following:

> You
> Could say of the storm that a giant wind
> Had taken the sea as an orange by the mouth
> And sucking it, had spat in the face of the sun
> Who winced lightning, and then hurled it all back
> At earth as rain and bolts of thunder. . . .[21]

and

> **Oreame**: . . . Take
> The boy into your shrine so, like his late father,
> No sword wielded by man may cut through
> His skin nor any spear or bullet wound pass
> Beyond a bump. . . .
>
> **Old Man**: Shall we go in
> Then, Oreame? And you come on, boy.
> One thing though: it was no pretence
> Or malice on my side, you must understand. . . .[22]

The criticism springs from literary criteria, but it is bound up with the problem of cultural identity: African drama, these critics are saying, ought not to be 'Shakespearean' drama.

Rugyendo makes a curious comment about the English of his own play:

But even with what we are left with, there is something more popular, magical and more precipitately involving than the formalism and staleness of modern African theatre.

There is a confusion here, for it seems that Rugyendo accepts that the play in English is a work of literature. This would be a contradiction of all that he has previously said about it, and, more important, a contradiction of the text itself. The fact of the matter is that the play cannot be performed for the audiences, for which it is intended, *in English*. A peasant or rural audience, anywhere in Africa, will require the play to be performed in their own language.

Thus not only does the director have to transpose the heroic recitations into equivalent performance traditions in his audience's own culture, but he also must translate the play entirely into their language. We are left, finally, without a single word of the original text. Instead of being a work of literature, a work of art, the text has become a collection of performance ideas – but in support of a very definite purpose, namely to help create a drama for the people in terms of what it has to say and the way in which it is presented.

Notes and references

1 Aristotle, 'On the art of poetry', T. S. Dorsch (trans.), *Aristotle, Horace, Longinus: Classical Literary Criticism* (Harmondsworth: Penguin Books 1965). See also Augusto Boal's criticism of Aristotle's *Poetics* in Boal, *Theatre of the Oppressed* (New York: Urizen Books 1979); and, especially, Brecht's criticism of Aristotle in Brecht, John Willett (ed. and trans.), 'Short Organum', in *Brecht on Theatre: the development of an aesthetic* (London: Eyre Methuen 1964).
2 Michael Echeruo, 'The dramatic limits of Igbo ritual', paper presented at the First Ibadan Annual African Literature Conference: Drama in Africa, 6–10 July, 1976.
3 J. P. Clark, *The Ozidi Saga: collected and translated from the Ijọ*

of Okabou Ojobolo (Ibadan: Oxford University Press and Ibadan University Press 1977). See especially the introductory essay by Clark, pp. xv–xxxvii, from which the information and later quotations in the chapter are taken.

4 J. P. Clark, *Ozidi* (London and Ibadan: Oxford University Press 1966), p. 4.

5 ibid., p. 6.

6 ibid., p. 62.

7 ibid., pp. 25–6.

8 ibid., pp. 119–20.

9 ibid., p. 88.

10 ibid., p. 100.

11 ibid., p. 114.

12 ibid., pp. 90–1.

13 ibid., pp. 110–11.

14 ibid., p. 29.

15 ibid., pp. 99–101.

16 Mukotani Rugyendo, *The Contest* in *The Barbed Wire and other plays*, (London: Heinemann Educational Books 1977). See especially the production note, pp. 36–8, from which the information and quotations in this chapter are taken.

17 There has been an experiment proposed by Salihu Bappa in Zaria, Nigeria, to develop a Hausa version of *The Contest*, using the praise-singing/begging art of *Roko* which is still used today in the Hausa farming competitions called *Gaya*.

18 Rugyendo, *The Contest*, p. 41.

19 Isaac Oluwalalaaro Akanji Nasiru, 'Communication and the Nigerian drama in English' (PhD thesis, Ibadan: University of Ibadan 1978).

20 Kaabwe Kasoma, 'Theatre and development', paper presented at the International Workshop on Communication for Social Development, Lusaka, University of Zambia, 1974.

21 Clark, *Ozidi*, p. 32.

22 ibid., p. 48.

3   Transpositions and adaptations in African drama

We need to return to the complex influence of western culture in modern Africa. This has continued since independence: formally through education systems which, despite the rhetoric of manpower needs, continues to sustain a social hierarchy based on clerical and administrative skills (already an 'over-developed' sector, some social critics would argue, of underdeveloped states); informally through urbanization and consumerism. The former is the means of access to the latter. However, what concerns us now is not the undetected influence of what may loosely be called western culture, but the quite deliberate concern of African playwrights to rework plays of other cultures to suit their own societies.

Translation, transposition and adaptation have been endemic in European drama: they are the means by which play-texts have survived the process of history, and have become part of a 'great tradition' (which itself is part and parcel of a particular static view of history). In taking over the European concern to 'rework' the great dramatic works of the past, African playwrights have also taken over this particular historical perspective.

In reworking play-texts any or all of the following changes are made in order to point to its relevance in the playwright's own society:

1   the names of people, places and titles may be changed, as, for example, in Ola Rotimi's *The Gods are not to Blame*, based on Sophocles's *King Oedipus*, where Oedipus becomes Odewale, the Greek city of Thebes becomes Kutuje, and all other names are given Yoruba equivalents;
2   the period or the setting may be changed, as, for example, in the Oshogbo *Everyman* where the late medieval European town of the mid fifteenth century becomes a Yoruba town in the 1960s;

3 the framework, or context, may be changed, as, for example, when Sophocles's third play in his Theban trilogy, *Antigone*, becomes a play done by two political prisoners on Robben Island, South Africa, in *The Island* by Fugard, Kani and Ntshona;

4 the story may be changed: Soyinka introduces the slave leader as an important new character in his reworking of Euripides's *The Bacchae*, which he calls *The Bacchae of Euripides*;

5 the themes may be changed: for example, the inexorability of fate becomes instead the issue of personal culpability in Rotimi's *The Gods are not to Blame*.

Adapting or transposing a play, therefore, may be limited to superficial changes or may involve anything from superficial changes of detail to a radical recasting or rewriting. At one extreme this is nothing more than translation; at the other extreme it is a new play: an original play influenced by or alluding to an earlier work. Yet there is an important difference between the intention of a writer who translates a play, and the intention of a playwright who transposes a play. The translator will attempt to render the original play as accurately as possible in his own language losing as little as possible of its dramatic quality, while the transposer will seek to redefine the original play's dramatic qualities in terms of theatre audiences in his own society.[1]

A playwright who transposes a play from another culture is not, by virtue of this fact, less of a playwright than someone who produces an entirely original piece. 'Originality', which has connotations of excellence, is actually a difficult concept and needs to be carefully defined. For example, Roman comedy, which was based on the earlier Greek comedy, developed the art of comedy in the theatre far beyond the Greek models. Again, some outstanding contemporary European plays are reworkings of plays from foreign or earlier cultures: for example, Edward Bond's *Lear* (in English – from Shakespeare's *King Lear*), Bertolt Brecht's *Coriolan* (in German – from Shakespeare's *Coriolanus*), Jean-Paul Sartre's *The Flies* (in French – from Aeschylus's *Oresteia*), and, from the same Greek trilogy, the American playwright, Eugene O'Neill's *Mourning becomes Electra*, and the English playwright, T. S. Eliot's *The Family Reunion*.

There have also been successful transpositions by African playwrights, such as President Julius Nyerere's Swahili version of Shakespeare's *Julius Caesar*, and Soyinka's *Opera Wonyosi* (transposition of Brecht's *The Threepenny Opera*, which in turn was a transposition of Gay's *The Beggar's Opera* – Soyinka's play–is discussed in a later chapter).

The transpositions which we are going to consider in this chapter are, first, two Yoruba versions (probably the same play) of the play *Everyman* by von Hofmannsthal, who transposed his play from the medieval European play of the same title;[2] second, the Nigerian Ola Rotimi's extremely popular version of Sophocles's *King Oedipus*, *The Gods are not to Blame*; the Fugard, Kani and Ntshona play, *The Island* which is built around a performance of Sophocles's *Antigone*; and third, Soyinka's reworking of Euripides's *The Bacchae*.

This by no means completes the list of published transpositions, or of those successfully presented in performance – like 'Segun Oyekunle's Nigerian Pidgin version of Brecht's *The Good Person of Szechuan* (and a Kenyan Swahili version of the same play).

We will consider the *Everyman* transpositions first, even though the English medieval *Everyman*, translated from a Dutch play *Elkerlijk*, was written in the latter half of the fifteenth century. The play was derived, apparently, from an eighth century work, *Barlaam and Josaphat*, which itself originally came from a Buddhist legend. The English medieval *Everyman* was, therefore, written and performed at least 1800 years *after* the plays of the Greeks: Sophocles (495?–406?BC) and Euripides (c. 480–406?BC).[3] The African transpositions are our own societies' contemporary works. Although the medieval *Everyman* is chronologically a much later play than *King Oedipus*, *Antigone* and *The Bacchae*, it is much 'earlier' than the Greek plays in terms of a concept of a development in drama and theatre. The Greeks express a view of man in society which is more humanist and expansive than that of feudal Europe dominated by Christianity.[4] This is precisely why the rediscovery of Greek intellectualism was so exciting to Renaissance readers and authors, and why ancient Greek and Roman plays were so 'new' and so stimulating to the European dramatists of the sixteenth and seventeenth centuries. Greek humanism, for which her playwrights found an effective form, is also probably what appeals to African intellectuals today.

Everyman

Everyman is within the tradition of the European morality plays.

This tradition developed both before and during the Reformation: that period in European history when the spiritual and secular authority of the Church of Rome was being challenged by devout clerics on the one hand, and pragmatic monarchs of rising nations on the other. The morality plays developed as a tradition of theatre in the wake of the other more important dramatic tradition of the great cycles of the miracle plays, which were sponsored by urban trade and craft guilds and supported by the Catholic Church. These cycles told the story of the creation, the advent, death and resurrection of Jesus Christ, and final judgement.[5] The morality plays were shorter than the miracle cycles, simpler to stage, and presented contemporary characters in an allegorical form. Eventually morality plays in countries which became Protestant through their rulers came to support a Protestant instead of Catholic ethic. The English *Everyman* appeared before Protestantism took hold in England, and it is very much a Catholic morality play. The Protestant moral ethic differed from Catholic morality in that the Protestants believed that man could communicate directly with God, and no longer had to rely on the priesthood through which to approach their creator. A man could therefore follow the dictates of his own conscience. The English *Everyman* has important passages in praise of the priesthood; and the play emphasizes the crucial importance of *good deeds* in obtaining salvation.

The morality plays used *allegory* as the means of dramatizing those moral issues which were the concern of the times. Allegory was a means of making abstract notions concrete and giving them a material form; for example, the doing of good deeds in one's lifetime is allegorically represented as an old woman called, obviously, 'Good Deeds'. If the central character in the play has not done many good deeds during his life then Good Deeds will be portrayed as decrepit and feeble. The central character of the morality play almost always stands for all men, for mankind, for common humanity.

Not only were the characters allegorical, but so too were the ways in which the plots of the plays were constructed. What the plots themselves embodied were the moral concerns that sprang from the teachings of Christ. This was seen in abstract as follows: man was conceived in a state of sin – original sin – and therefore needed to be saved (from his own wicked, human, nature), or, put another way, man's nature was such that he was prey to temptation, and his capacity for sin was matched only by God's boundless mercy. The basic dramatic allegory for this abstract theology was to show a central character – 'Mankind', 'Everyman' – preyed upon by Vice, who was always adroit at devising plans and arranging schemes to deflect Mankind from the path of goodness. He was helped by a variety of cronies, such as Greed, Lust, Avarice: all characters in the play. Fighting to save Mankind's soul were the figures representing goodness: Conscience, Soul, Good Deeds, and so on. These were weakened as Mankind veered from the straight and narrow path – with inevitable implications for his salvation. However, because God's mercy was infinite there was always an opportunity for repentance, sometimes represented as a character and sometimes as a process. The steps to salvation were always allegorically precise.

In *Everyman* the moral dilemma was how to reconcile the acquisition of wealth with salvation: how could a man who had worked hard and prospered be sure of his place in heaven, when Christianity teaches that poverty is a virtue and wealth an obstacle to salvation. The play allegorically charts a way.

God sends Death to summon Everyman to give an account of himself. Everyman, caught up in his wealth and luxury, has forgotten God. This is shown in the absence of any good deeds on his part, characterized as a weak and hopeless old woman. She is weak and hopeless because Everyman has neglected her. When Death summons Everyman and tells him to go on a journey from which there is no return, all his friends and relatives desert him. So do his worldly goods. Only Good Deeds is prepared to accompany him to God's throne to help him give an account of his life; but she is so weak she cannot even stand. However, she leads Everyman to Knowledge (another character) and together they lead him to Confession who teaches him to make an act of contrition. Beauty, Strength, Discretion and Five Wits – all characters – gather round him, but he now begins to weaken on his journey. All desert him in the end, even Knowledge; but it is Good Deeds who has helped him to repentance and helped him find favour with God.

Ẹ̀dá Duro Ladipọ and *Everyman* Obotunde Ijimere

The two versions of *Everyman* are apparently the same play and are derived from a German version of *Everyman* by the Romantic poet, librettist and playwright, Hugo von Hofmannsthal (1874–1929). In the late 1950s and early 1960s Ladipọ was encouraged to write by Ulli Beier, who provided Yoruba writers, playwrights, artists and musicians with the opportunity to explore and develop their creativity in the Mbari Clubs which he helped establish in Oshogbo and Ibadan, two towns in the Yoruba heartlands of Nigeria.

'Ijimere' may be the nom-de-plume for Ulli Beier himself. The literal translation of the name is Obotunde = the monkey is here; Ijimere = baboon. Thus the name is roughly 'Monkey Monkey', and clearly no one would allow himself to be called that. 'Ijimere's' brief 'biography' and photograph appear on the back of the first edition (1966) of *The Imprisonment of Obatala and other plays*, and his 'work' is discussed by Beier in an introduction to this collection of plays. Whoever this is a nom-de-plume for is a shadowy figure who has subsequently proved very elusive, though the three plays in the collection are widely studied and frequently performed. In the end the actual identity of the author is not all that important – the original *Everyman* is itself anonymously authored – and the only reason why we need to discuss the issue is because authorship of what is substantially the same play is claimed by two playwrights.

In the introduction to Ijimere's plays, Beier refers to Ẹ̀dá, Ladipọ's title for his version of *Everyman*, as being Ijimere's play:

He [Ijimere] began to write plays for Ladipọ's company. One of these plays, Ẹ̀dá, has already been performed by Ladipọ with great success.

In this two-page introduction to Ijimere's plays, Ladipọ's name is mentioned twelve times while Ijimere's is only mentioned seven. *Ẹ̀dá*, subtitled *Opera by Duro Ladipọ*, is transcribed in Yoruba from performances and translated into English by Val Ọlayẹmi, and was published by the Institute of African Studies, University of Ibadan in 1970. It is printed as a parallel text in English and in Yoruba. Ladipọ claims the copyright of the Yoruba text, and the Institute of African Studies the copyright of the transcription and translation.

The variations in the two English versions are mainly linguistic, not structural, and as such clearly show the difference between a translation, which aims to render in English the Yoruba text, and an adaptation which aims to create a Nigerian play in English. In discussing the plays we will use the abbreviations DL – Duro

Ladipọ – for the Institute of African Studies publication, and OI – Obotunde Ijimere – for the Heinemann Educational Books edition.

The first scene is in 'God's Palace' (DL), 'Prologue in Heaven' (OI). Olódùmarè is God, Owner-of-the-world. Men and women have their origin in heaven before his throne, and each is permitted to choose his fate, as a gift from Olódùmarè to take into the world. The choice entails a promise to make proper use of the gifts given. Everyman (OI), Èdá (DL), had chosen money, and Olódùmarè had granted him his fate. But Everyman has abused his gift and forgotten God: 'Èdá has grossly misbehaved' (DL), 'Now I am tired of Everyman, / 'For he broke his promise' (OI), and Death, Ikú, is summoned by God and ordered to fetch Everyman to appear before his throne and give an account of himself.

The next scene, 'In Èdá's House' (DL), 'The Play of Everyman. In front of Everyman's house' (OI), begins with Everyman ordering his servants and his Companion (OI), Ìyàndá (DL), to prepare for a party. The Companion is asked to fetch Bisi (OI), Risi (DL), the expensive 'lady-lover' of Everyman, and to give her money to provide her with all she needs. A long list is given in the Ijimere version:

> . . . This money
> Will get her velvet cloth, rekyi rekyi,
> Sarasobia scent, fine pomade, gold and silver,
> Headtie, handkerchiefs, umbrella, shoes,
> Shirt and blouse, iron bed, blanket and
> Bed sheets, pillows and pillow-cases,
> Sleeping-gowns, easy chairs, door blinds,
> Window blinds, mosquito-net, table and
> Table-cloth, carpets, bed curtains,
> Handwatch, looking-glass, powder,
> Sewing-machine, portmanteaux, trunk box,
> Bicycle, gramophone and so many other
> Things a woman could use. [OI, p. 51]

The list, by virtue of its fullness and its length is obviously meant to be comic: that she should need all these things to come to a party!

There is a similar list in Ladipọ's play, but the manner of going through it is different:

Èdá: I am a man for certain.
Tell her to . . . er . . . buy a velvet cloth:

> The cloth which her social club is buying . . . tell her to buy it.
> She is to buy hand-woven cloth and a sewing machine.
> She is to buy a bicycle.

Ìyàndá: Yes.

Ẹdá: She is to buy a gramophone.

Ìyàndá: Yes.

Ẹdá: She is to buy gold [ornaments].

Ìyàndá: Yes.

Ẹdá: She is to buy silver [ornaments] . . . for the ears, for the face. . . .
The shoes she has in mind are as long as this . . . .
Tell her I said she should buy them.
Tell her to buy Sosorobia.

Ìyàndà: Eda, son of Oòduà!

Ẹdá: I am a man for certain! [DL, pp. 38–9, 40–41]

The list is much shorter, but the extravagance of it is built up dramatically and more effectively by the involvement of Ìyàndá and Ẹdá's boasts that begin and end the list. However, in both cases, the list very much reflects the consumer aspirations of the late 1950s in Nigeria: and today it would make Everyman and Bisi seem rather 'bush'. Bisi's wants today would be less modest and much more sophisticated: a car, stereo, video-cassette recorder, air conditioners, trips to London.

The list of Bisi's 'needs', even before Ìyàndá has time to set off, is immediately followed by the appearance of the Poor Neighbour (OI); the Beggar (DL), who begs Everyman for some money, pointing out that he was once Everyman's neighbour and knew better days but ran into debt. Ẹdá insults him, in front of Ìyàndá, and throws him threepence. He tells him:

> That's . . . that's how it is.
> Don't you ever come to me
> When I am enjoying myself.
> I don't like it.
> Whenever you come again I will disgrace you.
> You with puny little eyes! [DL, pp. 46–7]

Ìyàndá, taking his cue from Ẹdá, adds, 'You with narrow-slit eyes!' and they go on abusing him in this vein. Everyman in the Ijimere version is more at pains to explain that money can't be given out for nothing and that once one starts giving out money there is no end:

> . . . But suppose
> All my property was divided equally
> Among all those who are in need –
> Do you think your share would be bigger,
> Than these three pence here?   [OI, p. 53]

'You answered him well,' comments the Companion; ' – let me hurry and invite Bisi to the feast.' 'Don't forget the errand I sent you on,' Èdá tells Ìyàndá. 'I haven't forgotten,' replies Ìyàndá and goes off to Bisi's house. There is a spectacular waste of money on the harlot, but only threepence for the Beggar; and this part of the scene has been deliberately structured to emphasize this irony. It represents, dramatically, Everyman's failure to do a good deed. 'He ill-treated poor people', Olódùmarè said in the first scene (DL, p. 3), and this is a manifestation of it.

Whilst Ìyàndá is away fetching Bisi, the Debtor and his Wife enter, followed by a policeman. In Ladipọ's play, Èdá is shown to be totally without remorse, inhuman:

Èdá: . . . He is still talking.
When he comes out of prison this time
He will then go again.
He will go again and again and again . . .

Wife: Please, have pity on his children!
The children he has. . . .

Èdá: Nonsense!

Wife: Father, for God's sake.

Èdá: Do you hear . . .?

Wife: He will pay back your money.

Èdá: All this does not impress me.

Wife: Ah! Please let it impress you.

Èdá: I'll forget about it all.
Prison it is that . . .
Look man . . . jail, jail!

Wife: Father, in spite of my plea . . . [*The* **Debtor** *and his* **Wife** *start to cry.* . . . **Èdá** *laughs. The* **Policeman** *marches the* **Debtor** *and his* **Wife** *out*]   [DL, pp. 58–9]

Ladipọ's play increasingly emphasizes the arrogance of Èdá, and his boastfulness. His praises have been sung endlessly by his servants and sycophants, and he replies over and over, 'I am a man for certain!'. He even cautions himself against his own temper, as though he were so powerful that nothing can stop him behaving as he wants except he himself: 'Don't be violent. / A violent man can't hold a group together.' He has a heart of stone. Ijimere tends to emphasize more the power of money. His Everyman tells the Debtor and his family:

> Blessed is the day when money was invented!
> Money has power over any other thing:
> There is no house, no land, no wife it cannot buy.
> Money is more powerful than armies,
> It is more powerful than judges and kings.
> Money is the most faithful servant
> To the man who owns it.
> There is nothing it refuses to do.
> There is nothing it cannot do.
> It is money I hold in my hand
> That raises me high above you.
> Had you known how to deal with money
> You would not be on your way to prison now!   [OI, p. 55]

The Debtor gets carted off to prison.

But, strangely enough, Èdá, Everyman, has a premonition of death which he finds entirely inexplicable: 'No one knows when we shall leave this wretched world. / Father, endow us with good gifts.' (DL, p. 61); 'Something spoils my pleasure today: / Something worries my head – / Something like fear.' (OI, p. 56). The Ifa Priest, or Babálawo, enters. Èdá recovers his arrogance and roundly abuses him – but asks him to divine for him, mainly as a joke, but partly, too, in earnest. The Priest throws the palm-nuts and then recites the story of Ogbe who refused to sacrifice when he went hunting. He sheltered, unwittingly, from the rain in the anus of an elephant. The relatives had to offer many sacrifices before Ogbe was finally passed out with the elephant's faeces. The Babálawo is driven off as Bisi and the guests arrive full of praise:

> Èdá, a man of the world.
> How lovely!
> If but one star remains in the sky alone. . . .
> How lovely!
> You are the one we'll vote for.   [DL, pp. 68–9]

and

> Everyman treats money like his slave!
> He sends him to bring food,

> He sends him to bring drink,
> He sends him to bring woman,
> And the slave obeys! [OI, p. 59]

(In this eulogy to Everyman the guests are being unexpectedly frank about their own motives for coming!) But from the start of the party Everyman is distracted. His thoughts, despite himself, are on death, and he finds himself insulting his guests – whom he realizes he has bought anyway. Despite the insults (and because of his money) they try to cheer him up.

Death's drum is heard by Everyman – though not by the others – and it cannot be drowned by the noise of the highlife band. It gets closer and closer. Ikú comes in and calls Everyman from a distance:

> Can you rightly say that you are enjoying worldly pleasures,
> Enjoying the company of your woman,
> When you have forgotten your creator?   [DL, p. 89]

Who is this impudent person? Ikú takes his time before he tells Èdá and the assembled guests that he is

> . . . Death! ! ! [*Noise and confusion. The friends run away*]
> I kill people at any time
> And I cut hearts unexpectedly.   [DL, p. 91]

Everyman begs for time – 'ten, twelve years' – and is finally given one hour by Ikú. Èdá first asks Ìyàndá, the Companion, to come with him, but Ìyàndá wishes him luck and hurries away. He turns to his relatives – blood is thicker than water, after all – but after wishing him luck, too, they also leave.

Everyman's money is next. The staging devices in this part of the allegory are somewhat different in the two plays. In the Ijimere version, Everyman's money-box is dragged in by a servant. Money, Owó, leaps out, beautifully attired and with a grinning mask. Everyman orders him to follow him to Olódùmarè:

Owó: Follow you? That cannot be.

Everyman: You are my property – do as you are told!
   You dwarf!   [OI, p. 71]

Everyman who thought he controlled money finds he is ruled by money, who tells him, tearing away his grinning mask and revealing a fearful face beneath:

> Well now: you'll make your trip,

> Alone, a small and naked fool.
> I'll stay right here – to play with other men.   [OI, p. 72]

Ladipọ's Èdá doesn't recognize Owó when he comes in. When he knows who he is he, too, orders Owó to follow him and is roughly rejected:

> I turned you into a senseless person in your lifetime
> And I made you a wealthy man in your lifetime.
> Today I will show you what I am. [*He climbs on* **Èdá. Èdá** *screams*]
> I will leave you now.
> I will start enjoying life with someone else.
> And you will go your way. [DL, pp. 108–9]

Money was a demon on his back.

Good Deeds staggers in. She is a decrepit old woman who collapses on the stage. Even at this critical point Everyman, who does not recognize who she is, has no time for the weak and the needy. She had come to follow him on his journey, but now decides not to: she falls down and dies. (The Ijimere version does not state that she dies.) Èdá realizes the implications of it, all too late:

> Money, treacherous friend!
> He has made me lead a reckless life
> And he has made me use people badly for my enjoyment.
> Ah! Now Good Deeds lies dead by my side. [DL, p. 111]

The full significance of being found guilty is made explicit in Ijimere's version:

> Woe unto me:
> My promises were broken – my life was wasted
> And to the potsherd heaven shall I be condemned. [OI, p. 72]

Traditional Yoruba belief is in the living world of the ancestors and in reincarnation within the family. The ultimate punishment by Olódùmarè is to be denied rebirth and to be sent to what is metaphorically represented as the heaven of broken pots. This is made explicit with the entrance of Sídíkátù, Èdá's daughter, who is seen to be very pregnant: 'You want to leave me./It is a pity' (DL, p. 113). Death's drum heralds his final entrance. Èdá breaks out in a sweat:

> My daughter, let us pray, let us pray!
> O God, I implore You on Your throne in heaven,
> You, Who own earth and heaven.

Let my daughter be safely delivered of her child.
Through the child let my sins be erased.
Let the child be full of wisdom and intelligence. [DL, pp. 112–13]

Sídíkátù is accusing in the Ijimere version; and it is she who suggests that they pray for his return through her child:

The owner of heaven may forgive you.
You have betrayed his trust,
You have broken your promises –
But let us pray for another chance.
Let us pray that you may return,
Come back to earth and start your life once more.
Let us pray for another beginning. [OI, p. 74]

He prays 'Forgive my breach of promise – / And through her, / grant me a new beginning.' Death, Ikú, strikes Everyman dead.

The third and final scene – 'In the House of the Ifa Priest' (DL, pp. 114–15), 'Epilogue / Sídíkátù is seen with a baby in her arms. She is consulting a Babaláwo' (OI, p. 75) – it is the revelation of the outcome of Èdá's dying prayer. What is the augury for the new-born child? 'This child will be poorer than a rat' (DL, p. 119). But he will have wisdom. Money doesn't prevent anyone from being lame, dumb or stupid. 'Wisdom is the pride of man' (OI, p. 76), that is, wisdom differentiates us from the other orders of creation. And how shall the child be called? Babátúndé, which means Father-is-come-again. Their prayers have been answered. Everyman has not been sent to the heaven of potsherds, but has returned to earth as the child of his daughter:

Priest: . . . if a man has a child,
    In due course, the child can in turn
    Beget his father, certainly!
    From heaven to enjoy life on earth,
    From earth back to heaven;
    From heaven to enjoy life on earth,
    Thus from earth, back to the heavenly realm!
    Therefore, Babátúndé will be the child's name. [DL, pp. 120–21]

The Ijimere version concludes: 'Let the child remember . . . Wisdom is the pride of man'. Ladipo's play celebrates the continuity of life – 'Surely! I understand it! / Babátúndé! Babátúndé!'.

The Oshogbo *Èdá / Everyman* has changed the medieval *Every-man* in its essential meaning. In the European play, Everyman does finally get into heaven, despite his wealth and his pride, through repentance and contrition. It is good deeds which enable him to gain his place in heaven; good deeds are the means to grace. The allegory charts out the procedure, with every correlation fixed. The contemporary Yoruba *Everyman* operates in a cosmogony in which there is no fall of man and original sin, no concept of a final judgement, no end of the world, and no division of souls into 'damned' and 'saved', with a corresponding notion of heaven and hell. The Yoruba believe in the continuity of life, in reincarnation and in the conterminus existence of the worlds of the living, the unborn and the dead, which implies a contradiction of the Christian dogma in some of its most essential aspects. This will inevitably alter the specific morality of the Yoruba play which has become humanist. Ladipọ's play especially is concerned to indict Everyman because he abuses his fellow man, through his arrogance and slavish devotion to money. The medieval *Everyman* accuses Everyman of having forgotten God. Olódùmarè accuses him instead of having forgotten his promise at the moment of his creation. The Christian Everyman is saved, in the end, from his all too human nature (he was conceived in original sin, anyway); Èdá is returned to his human nature, to earth, as his 'salvation' – he is 'saved' from his inhumanity.

In both plays wealth is abused. In the European play wealth is to be tempered by good deeds. The church taught that wealth would make man love the world and forget God, and so fall from a state of grace. In fact, the European morality play slyly teaches almost the opposite: wealth can enable man to perform good deeds which can *help* him to a state of grace. The Yoruba play ends up ironically being much sterner about wealth: it is set in opposition to wisdom. Èdá is born again, destitute but wise. The Christian play teaches Everyman to be humble and contrite (and he can enjoy his wealth); the Yoruba play teaches Everyman to be proud – but of man's capacity for wisdom, not through wealth.

This Yoruba humanism weakens the allegorical structure of its model. In the end, Èdá is personalized through his daughter Sídíkátù; and is born again as her child. The crisis of Èdá's death becomes the crisis of a particular man, who may or may not represent us, and not the crisis of mankind. The Beggar, the Debtor, Ìyàndá are fully rounded characters, and not two-dimensional allegorical figures. Èdá's salvation results from the chance intervention of his daughter – he has not given her a thought as he looks for someone to accompany him. But the

European Everyman follows a formula and a process, step by step, to his salvation.

What is the appeal of the original play to Ladipọ? Obviously, its theatrical possibilities, which are tied up with the theme of *death* in the midst of *life*. This powerful theme is able to cross cultural barriers very easily and compel audiences to seek an answer to the (existential) question of the meaning of life in the moment of death. It was an opportunity, probably, for Ladipọ to set two moral outlooks side by side, by taking the Christian play and interpreting it through the Yoruba world view. In the end, *Èdá* is no longer a Christian play at all.

There is, however, a very popular *Christian* African version of *Everyman*: the Ghanaian play *Odasani* which was originally devised by Efua Sutherland with the Studio Players in Accra.[6] It was subsequently directed by the Ghanaian theatre producer Sandy Arkhurst with the *Kusum Agoromba*, a professional touring company based in the University of Ghana drama studio in the Institute of African Studies, who travel around the country and perform in the *lingua franca*, Akan. Arkhurst devised his production of *Odasani* for Church audiences: the play was performed in all sorts of churches in various towns around Ghana, as a sermon-in-performance with a reverend minister or priest invited to each performance. Thus a late medieval Catholic play has become a predominantly Protestant African play today. Ghana television subsequently screened it several times, in Akan. It was widely reported that people repented of their sins after watching this play.

King Oedipus Sophocles

King Oedipus, in its original Greek form and in its many translations and adaptations over 2400 years, is one of the great plays of world drama. The Greek playwright, Sophocles, was chronologically in the middle of the three great fifth century BC Athenian tragedians, Aeschylus, Sophocles and Euripides, some of whose original plays survived to provide the basis for so much world drama. *King Oedipus* is the first play in what is referred to as a 'trilogy', known as *The Theban Plays*. However, although all three plays deal with consecutive events in the crisis in Oedipus's family, they are not written consecutively or as a trilogy. *Antigone*, the last play in the 'trilogy's chronology, was the first to be presented in performance when the playwright was a young man. *King Oedipus* was performed later in his life; *Oedipus at Colonus*, the middle play, was written at the end of his long life and only performed after his death, in 401 BC.[7]

The playwright's life covers an epoch that was scarred by two major conflicts and saw the eventual decline in the Athenian city–state as the pre-eminent political entity in the eastern Mediterranean. The intellectual and creative energy that had been manifest during the rise of Athenian democracy was still sustained, however, for another hundred years or so, even though Athens's political power was eclipsed by the Macedonian commanders, Philip and then his son Alexander, who were actually northern Greeks. Euripides appears to have been exiled to Macedonia towards the end of his life, and Aristotle was Alexander's tutor.

It is perhaps necessary to add at the outset that although political life was manifest in a very sophisticated form of democracy, and although Greek intellectual life was very high-minded, humanist and rational, the whole society was socially and economically under-pinned by slavery. It is estimated that by the middle of Sophocles's life three-quarters of all the people living in the Athenian state were slaves. Slaves were classed as *instrumentum vocale*, 'speaking tools'. They had no rights whatsoever. They in no way enjoyed the benefits of the Greek citizens' humanist outlook; paradoxically slavery did not seem to affect the development of their rational modes of thought, or, in their drama, of their concepts of personal and individual freedom. All three Athenian tragedians belonged in all likelihood to the upper or patrician class, with a higher social standing than the ordinary citizens, and were the owners of slaves.

Sophocles in his plays often expressed a patrician point of view, which in Athenian society was support for the democratic institutions, a piety and a sense of duty towards the Gods, who were in fact acknowledged formally rather than spiritually by the citizenry. Euripides, who was a younger man than Sophocles at the time of Athenian political decline, was more cynical, and, as we shall see when we discuss his play *The Bacchae*, ironical about the role of the Gods in the affairs of people.

King Oedipus has been constantly re-interpreted by scholars and critics from the time of Sophocles's fellow-Athenian, the philosopher Aristotle. Behind all the interpretations is a play about a man's attempt to escape his awful destiny, prophesied at his birth.

The play's special impact derives, however, from its structure as much as from its theme: as a play it demonstrates the potential of *irony* in drama to convey a deeper meaning, and of the separate but related theatrical device of *dramatic irony* to engage an audience in the unfolding action of the play. *King Oedipus* is, structurally, an extended experiment in the use of irony and of dramatic irony.

Irony, which was mentioned in the schema in Chapter 1 is, quite simply, the appropriateness of something which you don't expect. Irony in dramatic action can be defined as events not working out as one would expect but which are, on reflection, much more appropriate. Events can be said to have worked out ironically for the better or for the worse. Irony in characterization is when characters behave in an unexpected but much more significant way, or in a way which produces in the particular relationship the opposite response intended. Irony in a character's tone is when he or she is saying the opposite of what their sentences are apparently saying. His or her tone is said to be ironical.

Dramatic irony (also mentioned in Chapter 1, and then again in the discussion on *Ozidi*) is when theatre audiences know something crucially relevant to the action on stage, or to the characters, which some of the characters on stage do not know. Its effect in serious drama is to heighten tensions in the audience. They know people are being deceived but they cannot intervene in the action of the drama in order to set matters right.

Dramatic irony can also be used to heighten the comedy in a humorous situation. A standard example of this is the situation in a bedroom when the husband returns unexpectedly from a trip, and the wife's lover, who has sneaked in while he was away, only has enough time to hide under the bed or in the wardrobe. The wife and the audience know that the lover is under the bed; but the husband doesn't. Such situations can be greatly complicated to create farce. In this type of drama there is little or no meaning and the enjoyment of it is derived solely from the outlandish situations which the playwright manages to create. Therefore the same dramatic device may be used both to deepen meaning and also to eliminate it. Sophocles's *King Oedipus* is probably the first play to explore the use of dramatic irony to enhance meaning.

The action of the play is set in the Greek city of Thebes in times mythical even to Sophocles. The house of Cadmus which ruled Thebes was cursed: one crime generated another by way of

revenge and divine punishment; and the latest in the line was King
Laius whose first-born, it was prophesied at his birth, would kill his
father and marry his mother. This cursed baby could not be
destroyed by its parents for they would then be guilty of infanti-
cide; he was cast out with his feet pierced and bound, abandoned
on the side of a mountain, but rescued by a shepherd and
eventually given to the King of Corinth, whose marriage was
childless. He adopted the baby as his son and named him Oedipus,
'Pierced foot'. As a young man Oedipus heard of the curse that he
would kill his father and marry his mother and to avoid it he fled
from the court of the King of Corinth whose son he imagined
himself to be. In his wanderings he killed a stranger who had
abused him; and when he came to Thebes he was able by his native
wit and intelligence to destroy a fabulous beast, the Sphinx, that
had brought a plague upon the city and held the town in thrall.
For this he was rewarded with the throne and the hand of the
recently widowed queen in marriage. Unknowingly, he had killed
his father – the stranger – and now had married his mother. He
lived for many years very successfully as King of Thebes, was
much loved by his people, and had four children by his mother.
The curse from which he had run and which he continued to
dread had long since come to pass. All that remained was that he
should come to know his guilt. Another plague descended upon
Thebes.

The events for the play itself take place during one day; the play
is not about Oedipus committing the crimes but about him discovering who he really is and what he has really done. The
dramatic irony stems from the fact that the audience are aware of
Oedipus's real identity. Thus, when, for example, he curses the
murderer of Laius and pronounces the sentence of excommunica-
tion, the audience are acutely aware that he is cursing himself.

Oedipus's determination to find his true identity makes us
respond to him positively and to be fearful for him. What he has
already done are terrible crimes, sins: killing his father and
marrying his mother. But he did it in total ignorance, ironically in
an attempt to prevent himself from doing it. Our knowledge of his
guilt and his ignorance makes us as an audience aware of conflicting moral interpretations.

The irony in the play – as opposed to the dramatic irony –
increases the complexity of the issues. Everything Oedipus does
during this day of self-discovery he does in good faith, including

the banishment of his 'wife's' brother Creon and the abuse of the old and blind soothsayer, Tiresias, whom he suspects of plotting against him. Tiresias knows who he is, but refuses to answer Oedipus's question concerning the identity of the murderer of Laius until Oedipus loses his temper with him and insults him. He is then stung into saying who Oedipus is, but not in any way which can be understood by Oedipus who regards himself as a stranger in Thebes. Tiresias's wild and improbable accusations can only mean that he is deliberately lying and trying to stir up trouble on the instigation of Creon, who must now be aspiring to the throne. The audience know that Tiresias is not lying, that Creon is not plotting – and that Oedipus is only wrong because he is behaving rationally. It is his rationalism which has deceived him into thinking that he had any free choice. This is one of the bitter ironies of the play.

Queen Jocasta is also completely ignorant of who Oedipus really is. She loves him as a wife; but the more she seeks to reassure her husband and give him confidence in his search for Laius's killer and for his own identity the closer she brings both Oedipus and herself to an awareness of their true relationship; son and mother. She realizes before Oedipus does that her husband is her son. She goes silently into her bedroom and hangs herself. Even her sudden exit is ironically misconstrued by Oedipus:

> The woman, with more than woman's pride, is shamed
> By my low origin. I am the child of fortune,
> The giver of good, and I shall not be shamed.[8]

A little later he too realizes who he is: ironically, Jocasta had indeed been shamed by her discovery of who he is, but not at all in the way he thought. Earlier, in trying to reassure him she told him not to pay any attention to soothsayers:

> . . . For I can tell you
> No man possesses the secret of divination.
> And I have proof. An oracle was given to Laius . . .
> That he should die by the hands of his own child,
> His child and mine. What came of it? Laius,
> It is common knowledge, was killed by outland robbers
> At a place where three roads meet. . . .[9]

She goes on talking about her child that was abandoned on the mountainside to die and about the inaccuracy of prophecy, but Oedipus is no longer listening because something she has said by the way has made him very uneasy – 'My wife, what you have said has troubled me. My mind goes back. . . .' – and he questions Jocasta closely. He once killed a man 'at a place where three roads meet'; could it be that he is Laius's murderer? 'Ah, wretch! Am I unwittingly self-cursed?'[10] – but only as the murderer of Laius, a stranger. A shepherd is sent for who witnessed the murder: if he still maintains Laius was killed by *robbers* as he did originally then Oedipus is absolved from blame for the murder of Laius – 'one is not more than one'. Well, he can't change his story now, Jocasta reassures her husband, 'the whole town heard it'. This shepherd of course knows that Oedipus is the murderer of Laius, and lied originally. Ironically, what he doesn't realize is that Oedipus is also the baby he rescued from death when told to abandon it on the mountainside.

However, Jocasta is convinced that augury is worthless: Laius wasn't killed by his own child; instead, that child died. Jocasta's disregard for the oracles worries the Chorus of Elders who also do not know who their king really is. The Chorus is a key formal element in Greek tragedy of this period. Collectively they express in chants and songs, accompanied by formal dances, the limited understanding and conventional wisdom of what today we would call 'the man in the street'. The Chorus of Theban Elders wish only to live within the framework of the law; but now they are suffering from the plague and they realize that matters must be resolved concerning the murder of Laius all those years ago. Ignoring the Gods seems to them to be the wrong way to go about it:

> Zeus! If thou livest, all-ruling, all-pervading,
> Awake; old oracles are out of mind;
> Apollo's name denied, his glory fading,
> There is no godliness in all mankind.[11]

The audience's attitude towards the oracles is more ambiguous. The Greek audiences of the time were not especially religious, according to comments, for example, made by Thucydides, the Athenian historian who was Sophocles's contemporary. On the other hand there was an accepted divine order which underpinned the political stability of the state. However, there was no doubt that the intelligence, nobility and moral integrity of Oedipus contradicted his fate, and that the fulfilment of his destiny was wholly undeserved in terms of his character. This was particularly so with regard to Oedipus's ability to reason: I cannot be guilty *circumstantially* of something that I was ignorant of doing; that would be superstition. I must be proved guilty.

If Oedipus is proceeding by logical deduction, he cannot logically arrive at the truth on the basis of incorrect evidence. This is crucial to an understanding of Sophocles's play. For example, someone in Corinth tells him he is not his father's son – something instantly denied by his adoptive parents. When he goes to the oracle to double check he does *not* get an answer to the question: Am I son of the King of Corinth? He gets told instead that he will kill his father and marry his mother. His 'parents' lied to him; and the oracle deliberately confuses him by remaining silent. If he behaves logically on the basis of these two pieces of information it must inevitably take him away from the truth rather than nearer to it. If he is destined to kill his father and marry his mother, and if the oracle doesn't deny that the King and Queen of Corinth are his parents, then he had better put as much distance between them and him as possible.

He is thus driven by two wholly praiseworthy characteristics: a determination to discover the truth, no matter what it means personally; and a logical mind. Both qualities, it seems, are contradicted by the Gods in his ordained fate and its awful fulfilment. However, even in the moment of crisis, when everything is made plain, Oedipus does not relinquish these qualities. The Chorus wonder why he didn't commit suicide, rather than inflict upon himself the pain of blindness and its continuing agony. He replies:

> I will not believe that this was not the best
> That could have been done. Teach me no other lesson.
> How could I meet my father beyond the grave
> With seeing eyes; or my unhappy mother,
> Against whom I have committed such heinous sin
> As no mere death could pay for?
> . . .
> No! Hearing neither! Had I any way
> To dam that channel too, I would not rest
> Till I had prisoned up this body of shame
> In total blankness. For the mind to dwell
> Beyond the reach of pain, were peace indeed.[12]

His reasoning determines a harder way forward than suicide (which in his society would have been more honourable), but by following this course he is able to work out his redemption on earth (a similar resolution in essence, though not in form, to Èdá's sins). In this Oedipus shows the true nobility of his soul. This process is handled in the next play in the 'trilogy', *Oedipus at Colonus*, in which Sophocles allows Oedipus's expiation to bring benefits to Athens, rather than to his native Thebes which still sinks down in blood and civil strife. His noble nature is finally 'sanctified', that is, his qualities are reconciled with the intentions of the Gods.

Taking the two plays separately, as they were in fact written and first presented, or together, the meaning of Sophocles's dramatization of the Oedipus story is, ultimately, conservative. He attempts to balance the rational and humanist potential of Oedipus's character against the inexorability of fate, and of the divine order; and in the second play he synthesizes them into support for the contemporary social order in the Athenian state, which itself was disintegrating at the end of an extended and vicious war with her neighbours. *Oedipus at Colonus* does not have the same dramatic impact or significance as *King Oedipus*, which has held a fascination for other playwrights throughout the ages and throughout the world.

The Gods are not to Blame Rotimi

Partly because of the powerful structuring of the ironies of the original, Ola Rotimi's *The Gods are not to Blame*[13] has proved to be one of the most successful modern plays in performance ever since its first production in 1968 by the playwright at the Ori Olokun Cultural Centre in Ile-Ife, Nigeria. Most of the members of the audiences in West Africa would be ignorant of its Greek model and the Greek myth on which it is based. So Rotimi's transposition differs in intention from some European transpositions of this play, which deliberately counter-balance the new version with their audiences' expectations and knowledge of the original. The twentieth-century version by the French playwright Jean Cocteau is an example of this. Rotimi, on the other hand, is required to introduce his audiences to what is for them a new legend, or new story, as an African play; and, as such, his African audiences always receive it most enthusiastically.

A prologue, therefore, begins the play. A narrator sets the scene with an account of the events of the original Greek legend transposed into a rural Yoruba setting. The time in which the action of the Yoruba play takes place is not made specific; but it is clearly neither contemporary nor colonial, and predates white intrusion into Yorubaland.

As the Narrator speaks, what he describes is enacted in mime; and modern stage devices are used to reinforce the meaning, such as spotlights to isolate the shrine of the God Ogun in the surrounding darkness on the stage, and the rhythmic clinking of metal to emphasize his essence as the God of Iron. Dancers and musicians reflect the changes in mood as the Narrator tells the story, from joy at the birth of a child for King Adetusa and Queen Ojuola of Kutuje (Laius and Jocasta of Thebes), to despair on hearing Ogun's (Apollo's) prophecy; back to joy at the birth of a second son (transposing Creon as uncle of Oedipus to his brother). The dancers also represent in chants and dances the wars which the young stranger Odewale helps the people of Kutuje to turn to their advantage.

The Narrator's role is now taken over by Odewale himself, and he tells how he was rewarded by being made King of Kutuje, 'and have taken for wife, / as custom wishes, / Ojuola, the motherly Queen / of the former King / Adetusa.'[14] He introduces the four children which he has had by her, and his second wife Abero, and brings the story up to the time of the action of the play with a description of the present plague, with which the play itself now opens.

The formal chorus of the Greek play has been replaced by individualized townspeople, royal retainers, bodyguards and chiefs, who all act naturalistically (and not, as in the prologue, in formal dances, chants and mime). Odewale is quickly established as a good and caring king, at one with his people despite being an Ijekun man from Ijekun-Yemoja. He is vigorous and purposeful, inspires confidence, and yet is able to command and be obeyed. These are qualities which Rotimi adds to the qualities of reason and the desire to know the truth of the original Oedipus. They increase rather than lessen the injustice of his fate.

This creates the first major problem of Rotimi's play. The traditional Yoruba concept of fate is only superficially the same as the Greek concept as expressed in *King Oedipus*. In fact, as we have seen in our discussion of *Èdá* and *Everyman*, Yorubas traditionally believe that your fate is your own doing: you kneel down and receive it as a gift from Olódùmarè before being born. Furthermore, it is intrinsic to Yoruba cosmology that a person's fate is never irreversible, and it can be changed from evil to good by appropriate sacrifices which the Ifa Oracle at Ile-Ife will, in the last resort, always determine. Finally, unlike the Greek Olympian pantheon (Zeus, Apollo and the rest) whose divinities pursue vendettas against each other and against mortals, the Yoruba gods are not capricious, least of all Ogun – a point deliberately made in almost every Yoruba drama in which Ogun is represented, and made in this play too:

Priest: My master, Ogun is a god with fierce anger, son; one does not call him to witness so freely.[15]

Thus, there is no familial or other reason why Odewale should have been given such a specifically criminal and heinous fate, especially as something separate from his essential nobility and moral integrity.

Sophocles, on the other hand, is able to set the radical aspects of Oedipus's character against his fate specifically because the Greek gods themselves generated conflicting moral claims. This meant that a person had to determine, finally, his own moral responsibility. Thus, the Greek view of fate could be expressed in another way, namely, as the burden of an established moral position (such as being forced to exact revenge) that needed to be redefined. Sophocles's Oedipus was only able to redefine his moral responsibility by embracing his fate and living through its implications. This is somewhat removed from the Yoruba world view which sees all morality vested in the continuity of life and the survival of the race – a destiny which is embodied, especially, in the god Ogun.

Rotimi is clearly unhappy with this lack of correlation between the Greek and Yoruba cosmogonies. To get round it he resorts to an interpretation of the Greek play which has been derived (inaccurately) from Aristotle since the fifteenth century. This interpretation finds a single 'fault' in the character of Oedipus which overrides all his other virtues and causes his 'downfall': his 'pride'. It is a peculiarly Christian interpretation of the Greek play to see Oedipus as *deserving* his punishment from the gods because of his pride. It is a deeply flawed interpretation. Oedipus's fate was sealed before he even became king, and certainly before we the audience witness what might be termed his 'proud' or 'arrogant' behaviour (presumably his treatment of Creon and Tiresias). In fact, Oedipus's 'guilt' was established the day he was born. The curse on the House of Labdacus must not be confused with the Christian concept of original sin which is the condition of all mankind. In the play, Oedipus *discovers* his culpability; his sinful acts had unwittingly been committed long before.

Rotimi retains the notion of the tragic flaw, but specifically substitutes hot-temperedness for pride. Odewale's flaring temper is constantly commented upon:

Baba Fakunle [*The blind seer*]:   Your hot temper, like a disease from birth, is the curse that has brought you trouble.[16]

Odewale: [*Praying to Ogun before his household shrine*] Cool me, Ogun, cool me. The touch of palm-oil is cool to the body. Cool me. The blood is hot. . . .[17]

Alaka [**Odewale's** *sparring partner of his youth in Ijekun*]:   I did not teach you your hot temper, though!

Odewale: No, no, Shango, the thunder lion, taught me that one![18]

Rotimi then introduces as a 'flash-back' the occasion when Odewale killed an old man at Ede who had arrogantly laid claim to the farm which Odewale had bought. They fight by charms. Finally, however, Odewale reaches for a hoe and brandishes it above his head and chants:

This is . . . Ogun
and Ogun says: Flow!
flow . . . let your blood flow
flow . . . flow . . . f-l-o-w. . . .[19]

And he kills the old man, who, of course, is his father. He kills his father in the god's name. Thus, he not only commits patricide, he blasphemes; and the moment he comes to his senses he feels *guilt*. Oedipus feels no *guilt* for killing a man; it is only when he comes to realize who that man might be that he is *horrified*.

This flash-back is meant to be a crucial demonstration of his hot temper: at the end of the play when he has discovered his identity and his crimes he tells his townspeople:

No, no! Do not blame the Gods. Let no one blame the powers. My people, learn from my fall. The powers would have failed if I did not let them use me. They knew my weakness: the weakness of a man easily moved to the defense of his tribe against others. I once slew a man on my farm in Ede. I could have spared him. But he spat on my tribe. He spat on the tribe I thought was my tribe. The man laughed, and laughing, he called me a 'man from the bush tribe of Ijekun'. And I lost my reason.[20]

The validity of this final statement within the context of the whole play is dubious and seems to be somewhat contrived. The whole thrust of the play is in the opposite direction. The gods are indeed the cause of Odewale's downfall, for his particular crimes would not have been committed if there had been no prophecy. He would have grown up in his family, hot-tempered perhaps, but there is nothing in his character to suggest that he could ever commit patricide and incest. Indeed, despite his hot temper his personality is moral, honourable and caring. The prophecy, which had no reason whatsoever to be uttered, proved to be self-fulfilling: as his parents, and then Odewale himself, sought by all means to avoid the curse, they were unknowingly driven into fulfilling it.

Rotimi finds himself trapped both within the story and within the Greek moral order: if the gods, or 'fate', are to blame and not Odewale, then the Yoruba milieu of the play disintegrates. If, on the other hand, Odewale's hot temper and, as he says, tribalism, is to blame and not the Gods, then the story of the prophecy has no rationale.

Rotimi subsequently suggested in a published interview that the play was an allegory of the civil war in Nigeria which was raging when the play was first performed: the gods were the European powers who were, accordingly, not to blame for the conflict; Odewale represented tribalism in Nigeria; and the civil war was caused not by the intervention of the super-powers but by Nigeria's tribalism: 'The powers would have failed if I did not let them use me'.[21] But what is seen at the end of the play is the tragedy of one man, not of Kutuje or of the Yoruba kingdom; and the civil war was fought on a regional basis in which the Yoruba role itself was not clearly defined. There were many tangled issues caught up in the war, and to reduce it to a single cause is trite. Finally, there are no other correlations in the play for the civil war; and there is the problem of the actual thrust of meaning of the original Greek story.

The Island Fugard, Kani and Ntshona

This play, which was realized through improvisation techniques developed by Fugard, Kani and Ntshona, is not really a transposition. The original Greek play *Antigone*, the third of Sophocles's Theban 'trilogy', is more a thematic equivalent than an actual model for the new play, which is about two black prisoners on Robben Island, the notorious detention centre off the coast at Cape Town, for opponents of the apartheid regime in South Africa. The only two actors in the play retain their own first names as the prisoners: John (Kani) and Winston (Ntshona).

Only two things happen in *The Island* by way of a story: John is informed that his sentence has been reduced from ten years to three years and that he only has three months to go; and the two of them perform John's recollection of the trial scene from Sophocles's *Antigone* at a prisoners' 'concert' organized by the warders.

The characterization of the two prisoners is very detailed and maintained throughout the play even in their roles as Antigone (one of Oedipus's daughters) and her tyrant uncle, Creon, in the little play which they perform. However, *The Island* does make considerable use of stylization: Robben Island is suggested by a raised area representing a cell, with two mats, two blankets, two mugs and a bucket only, and an area around it representing the beach in which, at the beginning, John and Winston each keep endlessly loading a wheelbarrow from a hole which each is digging – merely to fill the other! On occasion they mime being beaten up by warders and guards. We don't ever see a warder or a guard, but John's and Winston's acting is so good we can actually believe that a warder is present. The guard, any guard, is referred to metaphorically throughout the play as Hodoshe, the green carrion fly:

> *A whistle is blown. They stop digging and come together, standing side by side as they are handcuffed together and shackled at the ankles. Another whistle. They start to run . . . John mumbling a prayer, Winston muttering a rhythm for their three-legged run.*
>
> *They do not run fast enough. They get beaten . . . Winston receiving a bad blow to the eye and John spraining an ankle. . . .*[22]

Apart from the whistle which is heard, everything else is mimed: handcuffs, the shackles, the beating.

However, for their performance of *Antigone* in the fourth and final scene of the play, some scraps collected off the beach and from the quarry are fashioned into a necklace (from old nails) and a wig (old rope) for Antigone, and into a badge of office and crown for Creon. A prison blanket makes Creon's robe, Antigone's dress. Before their play begins John addresses the audience as the prison governor, warders and 'Hodoshe'.

Just before this play takes place, while they are in their cell, Winston's torment over John's promised relief in three months time encapsulates the horror of political detention on Robben Island. Winston, talking of another prisoner, tells John relentlessly:

> ... Twenty perfect blocks of stone every day. Nobody else can do it like him. He loves stone. That's why they're nice to him. He's forgotten himself. He's forgotten everything . . . why he's here, where he comes from.
>
> That's happening to me, John. I've forgotten why I'm here. . . . Fuck slogans, fuck politics . . . fuck everything, John. Why am I here? I'm jealous of your freedom, John. I also want to count. God also gave me ten fingers, but what do I count? My life? How do I count it, John? One . . . one . . . another day comes . . . one. . . . Help me, John! Another day . . . one . . . one. . . . Help me, brother! one. . . .
> [John *has sunk to the floor, helpless in the face of the other man's torment and pain. Winston almost seems to bend under the weight of life stretching ahead of him on the Island. For a few seconds he lives in silence with his reality, then slowly straightens up. He turns and looks at John. When he speaks again, it is the voice of a man who has come to terms with his fate, massively compassionate*][23]

They perform their little play, *The Trial and Punishment of Antigone*. It is comprised of speeches which John has written out from memory around the basic structure of the scene which he has recalled. He has made Winston learn the speeches of Antigone off-by-heart. In the Greek play, Creon (technically the same person as in *King Oedipus*, though now characterized as a younger man) has refused burial for Antigone's brother (another of Oedipus's children) who has led an attack against Thebes. Antigone attempts to bury him twice and is caught. Creon stands by the law; Antigone tells him that it was he who made the law, and it is an inhuman law which contradicts a greater, divine authority. In John's play, Antigone, played by Winston, tells Creon: 'Guilty against God I will not be for any man on this earth.'[24] The little play ends:

John [*As* **Creon**]: There was a law. The law was broken, the law stipulated its penalty. My hands are tied. Take her from where she stands, straight to the Island! There wall her up in a cell for life, with enough food to acquit ourselves of the taint of her blood.

Winston [*As* **Antigone** *to the audience*]: Brothers and sisters of the land! I go now on my last journey. I must leave the light of day forever, for the

Island, strange and cold, to be lost between life and death. So, to my grave, my everlasting prison, condemned alive to solitary death. [*Tearing off his wig and confronting the audience as* **Winston**, *not* **Antigone**] Gods of our Fathers! My Land! My Home! Time waits no longer. I go now to my living death, because I honoured those things to which honour belongs. [*The two men take off their costumes and then strike their 'set'*]²⁵

The play ends as it began, with the men shackled together doing their three-legged run around the stage, the beach. The ancient Greek play has been made applicable to the situation in South Africa today, and used as a point of reference for an exploration of the character of Winston, especially, who comes to accept his fate.

The Bacchae Euripides

Euripides's play,²⁶ and Soyinka's play based upon it, are both about a Greek god, Dionysus. His later Greek name, ΒΑΚΧΑΙ, in Latin Bacchus, gives us the English words 'bacchanal', meaning either a drunken reveller or a debauched party, and 'bacchanalian', the adjective. The Romans who assimilated many of the Greek gods into their own society tended to emphasize certain characteristics to the exclusion of others. Thus Bacchus was for them the god of wine; and he became known as such to Christianized Europe during the Renaissance which found him difficult to accommodate. In fact, Dionysus, or Bacchus, had been assimilated into Barbarian Europe many many centuries earlier, in various Pagan rites – which Christianity then supplanted.

Dionysus (sometimes spelt Dionysos, as it is in fact in Soyinka's play) was a much more complex figure in his original Greek manifestation because he constituted both a religious and a political influence. He was a god of the people, the common folk, as opposed to the Olympian gods of the established order (Zeus, Apollo and many others, dwelling on Mount Olympus, who reinforced the authority of the state and to whom access was denied save through an elaborately constituted priesthood). His cult swept through Asia Minor and the eastern Mediterranean prior to the period when the Greek city–states were establishing themselves economically and politically in the area, and probably as early as the thirteenth century BC.

He was presented as an earth god, and his votaries proclaimed wine, the fruit of the vine, as sacred to him. His special rites evoked for his followers an earlier mode of existence, closer to nature and its seasons. In this way it became a means of transcending the daily oppressions of those bound either to the land in one form or another, or to other men, living in the cities, as their labourers or slaves, as wars and economic expansion forced peasants off their land and into the armies and the cities. Dionysus's rites reasserted for them earth's productiveness and the unfettered spirit of men and women.

His cult had special appeal for women; and the title of Euripides's play, *The Bacchae*, refers to the female followers of the god. They literally are his followers in the play, for they have followed the god, who appears in the play both as man and as god, from Phrygia (in Asia Minor), spreading his influence, back to the place where the Greek myth asserts he was born: the city of Thebes.

It is indeed the same Thebes of the Oedipus legend; and some of the *dramatis personae* are also the same: Cadmus, the founder of Thebes (who actually appears in this play) and Tiresias, the blind seer, who was a character in *King Oedipus*. The various legends drastically distort the chronology: and it is obvious that Thebes, for the Athenian dramatists, was a mythical city which was the disastrous alternative to their own (idealized) city of Athens.

Dionysus was the 'illegitimate' child of Zeus, foremost of the Olympians and Semele, mortal daughter of Cadmus. Semele's family did not believe she had been visited by Zeus and they accused her of fornication; her issue, Dionysus, was denied as god. Soyinka's Dionysos states his patrimony thus:

> A seed of Zeus was sown in Semele my mother earth, here on this spot. It has burgeoned through the cragged rocks of far Afghanistan, burst the banks of fertile Tmolus, sprung oases through the red-eyed sands of Arabia; flowered in hill and gorge of dark Ethiopia. It pounds in the blood and breasts of my wild-haired women, long companions on this journey home through Phrygia and the isles of Crete. It beats on the walls of Thebes, bringing vengeance on all who deny my holy origin and call my mother – slut.[27]

In both Euripides's play and in Soyinka's version of it, Thebes is now ruled by Pentheus, Cadmus's grandson and Semele's nephew, who is determined to resist the new religious madness that seems to have gripped Thebes and the women especially. The play becomes a conflict between Pentheus and Dionysus. Pentheus represents the nobility sustained by the established order: the law, the army, and of course the 'mysteries': Apollo and his Oracle at Delphi, and other Olympian gods – all mediated by a burgeoning and powerful priesthood in the control of Tiresias, who himself nevertheless recognizes the strength of his new cult and sides with it against Pentheus. Dionysus comes to the people. He represents the force of nature and contradicts man's socialization. Admittedly he is Zeus's progeny; but it is in the same way that Christ is the son of the Judaic god though he is resisted and denied by Judaism.

In the play, Dionysus has taken on the appearance of a man, leading his Bacchantes, his women followers, who realize that he is a god. He is returning to Thebes with the purpose of humbling (humiliating? punishing?) those in his place of conception who had dishonoured him. Pentheus is deceived by Dionysus's seeming mortality; his mistake lies in thinking that he can control him and curtail his worship – 'this madness . . . chaos' – with the forces of the state at his command. However, once what Dionysus and his followers represents has gripped the minds of the people of Thebes his effect on the community is cumulative. An enormous amount of energy is released. Others are swept up, including Pentheus's own aunts and his mother Agauë – all sisters of the dead mother of Dionysus who had labelled her a slut. They have gone up into the mountain, following the Phrygian Bacchantes.

The more repressive Pentheus becomes as he tries to curb this energy, the more violent becomes the reaction against him. The force of Pentheus's own repressive reaction similarly escalates. There is little difference in the intensity of the passion on either side now: a contradictory 'madness', 'chaos', has been created in the upholder of law and order. Pentheus has lost his reason and, deluded, is now easily led by Dionysus to the mountain, to 'witness' the women's revels, to 'spy' upon them, disguised as a worshipper himself.

An awful death awaits him on the mountainside. The Theban Bacchantes, led by his own mother, Agauë, in their state of divine possession mistake him for a young lion. They give chase; capture him; tear him exultantly, limb from limb; and return triumphant into Thebes bearing his gory, severed head aloft, still imagining that they have killed a young lion with their bare hands. Their inflamed imaginations subside, and Agauë perceives that she has actually killed her own son.

The ending of Euripides's play is difficult and complex. The meaning of the text submerges into its particular cultural context: the Athens of Euripides, viewed from his exile in Macedonia. In the absence of detailed stage directions we are left with only the dialogue and the structure of the scene, and even this is faulty, with several lacunae. If we are dependent on a translation from the original Greek we can only hope that the translator has interpreted the tone correctly. With these reservations in mind we can try and discover the meaning of the ending.

Dionysus, who has previously appeared in the play as a man, now appears as a god: impersonal, remote, unyielding. He banishes Agaüe and Cadmus from Thebes, and imposes a long period of suffering and a terrible destiny upon them for their earlier blasphemy and present crimes. Agaüe's reaction to what she has done is one of complete horror, and, like Oedipus, she embraces her punishment and wants emotionally and physically to distance herself from the place in which she committed her atrocities. She tells her father, when the god has withdrawn:

Agaüe: Where can I turn for comfort, homeless and exiled?. . . .
. . . Farewell, my home; farewell the land I know.
Exiled, accursed and wretched, now I go
Forth from this door where first I came a bride.

Cadmus: Go, daughter; find some secret place to hide
Your shame and sorrow.

Agaüe: Father, I weep for you.

Cadmus: I for your suffering, and your sister's too.

Agaüe: There is strange tyranny in the god who sent
Against your house this cruel punishment.

Cadmus: Not strange: our citizens despised his claim,
And you, and they, put him to open shame.

Agaüe: Father, farewell.

Cadmus: Poor child! I cannot tell
How you can fare well; yet I say, Farewell.

Agaüe: I go to lead my sisters by the hand
To share my wretchedness in a foreign land. . . .
. . . Gods, lead me to some place
Where loath'd Cithaeron may not see my face,
Nor I Cithaeron. I have had my fill
Of mountain-ecstasy; now take who will
My holy ivy-wreath, my thyrsus-rod,
All that reminds me how I served this god![28]

Agauë seems to be expressing a horror of the god's mode of intervention in human affairs, as much as a horror at what she has done. The situation is similar to that of *King Oedipus*, but the tone in Euripides's play suggests a completely different attitude: why should we be burdened with the gods? Can we not conduct our affairs without them? In general, and as far as the Olympian gods are concerned, we could. However, Dionysus represents a very different sort of religious impulse, which we have already described as a reassertion of the rhythms of nature, and its response in the human psyche.

This involves the passions, ecstasy, and the breaking-down of inhibitions, manifested in sexuality and intoxication: a celebration. It also has a violent manifestation: in recklessness, in the danger and exhilaration of the hunt, in the killing of the sacrifice. This duality can be symbolized in the inter-relationship in some rites of wine and blood.

The transition from wine to blood in the hallucinations of Agauë and the other women in *The Bacchae*, is reflected in similar transitions in other beliefs and other cultures. The central ritual in the Roman Catholic form of Christianity, for instance, involves the mystical transubstantiation of the holy wine into the blood of Jesus Christ which his priests are required to drink. Christianity, too, was initially a religion of the oppressed, whether they were peasants on the land or a displaced peasantry constituting an impoverished and enslaved urban labour force.

Soyinka himself points out the other very close parallel of the Dionysiac rites: the rituals of the Yoruba god Ogun (the same god who constituted the Yoruba equivalent for Apollo in Rotimi's *The Gods are not to Blame*). Dionysus is a far more significant equation; and Soyinka isolates three striking parallels. First, there is the phallic *thyrsus* of Dionysus, a staff tipped by a pine-cone and twined with ivy and vine leaves, which was carried by his votaries. This is matched by the *opa Ogun*, 'a long willowy pole . . . topped by a frond-bound lump of ore which strains the pole in wilful curves and keeps it vibrant'. Second, the slaughter of a dog as Ogun's sacrifice and 'the mock struggle of the head priest and his acolytes for the carcass, during which it is literally torn limb from limb, inevitably brings to mind the dismemberment of Zagreus, son of Zeus'*; and finally, the parallel between the wine of the

---

* It is not clear what Soyinka is referring to here, for it was Pentheus, not Dionysus (Zagreus is another name) who was dismembered.

grape sacred to Dionysus, and the wine of the palm, also an intoxicant, sacred to Ogun. (Quoted by Soyinka in his introduction to his play *The Bacchae of Euripides*, from his essay 'The fourth stage').[29] The importance of Ogun, symbolically, for Soyinka, is considered in greater detail in the chapter on Soyinka's protest plays.

For Euripides a different contradiction seems to exist in the phenomenon and being of Dionysus to that of the duality both Dionysus and Ogun embody for Soyinka. Man's rationality is directly contradicted by his nature – not an evil nature explained by concepts of the 'fall' of man and 'original sin', as in Christianity, but a nature which is seen to be inevitably co-existent with man's reason and interacting with it, neither of which can be denied. This view is partly expressed today in the rephrasing in psychological terms we were suggesting earlier, namely in the substitution of man's nature by the concept of the 'id', which is that part of the psyche that is the source of primal energy, dictated by 'the pleasure principle'.

Agauë is shocked at the gods, and shocked at her own nature. It is not a matter for rejoicing; rather, it is despair at our puny state of being. Our intellects are capable of perceiving a more equitable and fulfilling destiny than our present history shows, but we seem physically unable to realize it.

Soyinka's conclusion to his play is very different. In the introduction he acknowledges that he finds the ending of Euripides's play unsatisfactory:

The ending especially, the petering off of ecstasy into a suggestion of a prelude to another play. But *The Bacchae* is not an episode in a historical series, and this is not merely because Euripides did not live to write the next instalment. The drama is far too powerful a play of forces in the human condition, far too rounded a rite of the communal psyche to permit such a notion.[30]

In his play, Agave (Agauë) comes to a realization of what she has done; but instead of an enduring revulsion and a sense of alienation from her normal human state, she rapidly comes to terms with her actions during the period of her possession. She resolves to remove the head of her son from the pole before she realizes that it was her own hand which caused his death:

Let no hand but mine be laid on him.
I am his mother. I brought him out to life.
I shall prepare him for death.[31]

She is about to climb the ladder, and then learns from Kadmos (Cadmus) that she has killed him:

Kadmos: You killed him.

Agave: I?

Kadmos: You and your sisters. You were possessed.

Agave: [*A soft sigh*] A-ah. [*She stands stock-still, then turns towards the ladder*] It is time to bring him down.[32]

Tiresias talks of a need for renewal from life-sustaining earth, and he suggests that the sacrifice of Pentheus may fulfil this need:

> O Kadmos, it was a cause beyond madness, this
> Scattering of his flesh to the seven winds, the rain
> Of blood that streamed out endlessly to soak
> Our land.[33]

As Agave is about to lift down the head, the god manifests himself – but not in any way like his coldly divine presence at the end of Euripides's play; it is contained almost entirely in the stage directions:

> [*The theme music of* **Dionysos** *wells up and fills the stage with the god's presence as a powerful red glow shines suddenly as from within the head of* **Pentheus**, *rendering it near luminous. The stage is bathed in it instantly; from every orifice of the impaled head spring red jets, spurting in every direction. Reactions of horror and panic.* **Agave** *screams and flattens herself below the head, hugging the ladder*]

Tiresias: What is it Kadmos? What is it?

Kadmos: Again blood, Tiresias, nothing but blood.

Tiresias: [*Feels his way nearer the fount. A spray hits him and he holds out his hand, catches some of the fluid and sniffs. Tastes it*] No. It's wine.

> [*Slowly, dreamlike, they all move towards the fountain, cup their hands and drink.* **Agave** *raises herself at last to observe them, then tilts her head backwards to let a jet flush full in her face and flush her mouth. . . . The light contracts to a final glow around the heads of* **Pentheus** *and* **Agave**][34]

This is an inversion of the Christian rite of changing the wine into the blood of the sacrifice (God). Here the blood of the sacrifice (Pentheus) is changed by the god into wine. Agave, as Soyinka explains in the introduction

releases the reluctant beneficence of Nature.

I see *The Bacchae*, finally, as a prodigious, barbaric banquet, an insightful manifestation of the universal need of man to match himself against nature.[35]

Soyinka has radically transformed the play. His view of the play necessitates the inclusion of a new character, the Slave Leader, through whom he is able to situate the play more specifically in its historical context, for the purpose of drawing relevant parallels with the processes of history today. Soyinka's play is not written primarily for an African audience; it was commissioned by the National Theatre Company of Britain and presented in London in 1973. Soyinka used the opportunity to address a modern British audience as an African and as a representative of one of their former colonies.

The Slave Leader is significant for this audience as the embodiment of an unfeigned acceptance of the life-renewing forces represented in Dionysus (Bromius, Zagreus, Ogun) by those who are oppressed. In the play, the Slave Leader anticipates the advent of the new god, knows him, and is the first to welcome him:

> Welcome the new god! Thrice welcome the new order!
> [*Hands cupped to his mouth, he yodels*] Evohe-e-e-e!
> Evoh-e-e-e![36]

He turns on the other baffled slaves:

> You hesitant fools! Don't you understand?
> Don't you *know*? We are no longer alone –
> Slaves, helots, the near and distant dispossessed!
> This master race, this much vaunted dragon spawn
> Have met their match. Nature has joined forces with us.[37]

Soyinka, therefore, does not see the continuing popularity of *The Bacchae* as a specifically European phenomenon: '*The Bacchae* belongs to that sparse body of plays which evoke awareness of a particular moment in a people's history, yet imbue that moment with a hovering, eternal presence'.[38] Certainly his own reading of the original text interprets the play as 'a prodigious, barbaric banquet'.

The very first scene builds up to a passionate climax as the Slave Leader chants with lyrical enthusiasm the hymn to Bromius (an earlier name for Dionysus) and builds up the passions and excitement of the crowd of Bacchantes and slaves into something which Soyinka describes in the stage directions as a European pop scene ('without degenerating into that tawdry commercial manipulation of teenage mindlessness') and containing the energy of the black hot-gospellers who become physically possessed. Thus there is a pitch of intensity, which has to be achieved early on in any production of the play, which is rarely indicated in the texts of other plays save in their final climaxes. Soyinka's structuring and writing of the scene is certainly less formal and much more passionate then the parallel opening scene in the Greek model.

It would be difficult, and not especially effective dramatically, to sustain this pitch throughout the play. Once the scale of the phenomenon is established, and the release of energy demonstrated, it is necessary to develop the scale of the repression caused by Pentheus commanding the forces of the state. It is the Slave Leader who gives Pentheus an inkling of the strong political threat contained in the new religion:

> And this is what this day we celebrate
> Our feet at the dance are the feet of men
> Grape-pressing, grain-winnowing, our joy
> Is the great joy of union with mother earth
> And the end of separation between man and man.[39]

Dionysos is arrested by Pentheus and chained up in the dungeons in the palace.

There is another passionate appeal in the form of a dirge-cum-chant – '*Like heavy breathing: In–Out*'[40] – by the slaves and the Bacchantes begging Dionysos to manifest his god-head. Then, suddenly, there is '*Darkness, thunder, flames. Roar of collapsing masonry. From among it all the music of Dionysos*'.[41] He has shaken down his prison and shaken off his chains. Again, but still as an ordinary mortal, Dionysos confronts Pentheus, who now calls forth his army in all its might. Dionysos forestalls the intended attack on his followers, the Theban citizenry upon the mountainside, by hypnotizing Pentheus. He does this through two 'shows', two events in the future, one of which occurred three centuries after the death of Euripides himself, which show the power of the god: Hippoclides's wedding (when Hippoclides finally refuses to marry his wealthy but unspeakably ugly bride and dances naked at his own wedding); the Christian New Testament account of the marriage at Cana in Galilee when Christ (a reincarnation of Dionysos in Soyinka's present version) turned the water into wine. Soyinka is attempting to bring Dionysos into European Christian culture, not as he was 'processed' by the

Renaissance scholars avid for Classical reference, but as a Barbarian earth god.

The transformation of Pentheus's bloody head into a fountain of wine which ends the play is a logical outcome of the response of Soyinka to the play by Euripides, and of the changes which he has made to the structure of it. The land of Thebes, as a sort of Everywhere (or just the west in the twentieth century?) has been blessed by a belated acceptance of the god Bromius, Dionysos, Ogun. For Euripides, the land of Thebes (as a reference to his own war-torn Athens?) was further cursed by an angered god, more difficult to deny than other capricious gods.

It is a paradox. Soyinka's play and Euripides's play are the same play, and yet their conclusions are the opposite of each other. Soyinka's romantic and somewhat reactionary stance (his Slave Leader, for example, seeks revolution through mysticism) is at odds with Euripides's awareness of the dualism in man's nature. Nevertheless, Soyinka intends his play to be the same as Euripides's in its intent.

Ironically, this is the reverse of the situation vis-a-vis Ola Rotimi's transposition of *King Oedipus* by Sophocles. This, too, could be said to be the opposite of the same play. But whereas Soyinka means his play to be faithful to the intention of the original Greek author, Rotimi intends his play to have the opposite meaning of his Greek model. Soyinka ends up pursuing his own play's logic to a different conclusion, and in the process discovers new meanings in the original play. Rotimi transposes everything of the Greek world into some Yoruba parallel, but ends up writing the same play with a greatly reduced meaning either within itself or with reference to the original.

The final irony is that Soyinka's play has never, to my knowledge, been publicly performed either in Nigeria or in the rest of Africa; but Rotimi's play is one of the most successful in the new genre of tragedy in the repertoire of African drama. These ironies exemplify the complexity surrounding the adaptation of plays from a different or earlier culture into the contemporary milieu.

Notes and references

1 A transposer may not even work from the original language of the play which he is transposing. But someone who is forced to use a translation – because he cannot read the language of the

original – will prefer to work from a prosaic but accurate version by the translator, rather than one in which the translator has sacrificed accuracy for some dramatic effect of his own choosing.

2 Hugo von Hofmannsthal (1894–1929) adapted a German version of the medieval *Everyman* (*Jedermann*). Hofmannsthal's *Jedermann* was produced in 1911 by Max Reinhardt at the Salzburg Festival which was a special concern of Hofmannsthal for many years.

It is perhaps relevant to note in the context of the Yoruba transposition based on it that Hofmannsthal's *Jedermann* minimizes the Roman Catholic ambience of the original medieval play (without, however, becoming anti-Catholic) by eliminating the allegorical character Confession. And, as Jethro Bithell points out, one of Hofmannsthal's obsessions was '. . . the unity and continuity of creation; the idea: I am my ancestors . . . This conception of continuity, of course, implies that I am the future as well as the past: I am my descendants, too. . . .' (Jethro Bithell, *Modern German Tragedy, 1880–1950* (London: Methuen 1959), p. 213.

3 An interesting study of the political and economic processes of this period is contained in Perry Anderson, 1974, *Passages from Antiquity to Feudalism* (London: New Left Books 1974, also Verso Editions 1978).

4 A study which explores the Ancient Greek consciousness through the performing arts and the literature of the Greeks is Brian Vickers, *Towards Greek Tragedy: Drama, Myth, Society* (London: Longman 1973).

5 There is a great deal of critical and scholarly literature on the English and European miracle plays and moralities. The established text of the English *Everyman* is A. C. Cawley, *Everyman and Medieval Miracle Plays* (London: Dent 1962). The standard text on the Medieval theatre and its origins is Glynne Wickham, *The Medieval Theatre* (London: Weidenfeld and Nicolson 1974); and an interesting study of the popular forms of theatre during this period is: David Bevington, *From Mankind to Marlowe: growth and structure in the popular drama of Tudor England* (Cambridge, Mass.: Harvard University Press 1962).

6 This production was described to me by Sandy Arkhurst.

7 In connection with the dates of these Greek playwrights, note

Aristotle's own dates, viz. 384–322 BC. He was writing nearly a hundred years after the Athenian tragedians whose work he uses to form the basis of his theory of tragedy.

8 Sophocles (trans. E. F. Watling), *The Theban Plays* (Harmondsworth: Penguin 1947), p. 55.

9 ibid., p. 45.

10 ibid., p. 46.

11 ibid., p. 50.

12 ibid, pp. 63–4.

13 Ola Rotimi, *The Gods are not to Blame* (London: Oxford University Press 1971). According to Michael Crowder, who was the director of the Institute of African Studies at Ife University at the time Ola Rotimi wrote and produced his play there, *The Gods are not to Blame* was the first of a number of transpositions which Rotimi planned to do of the plays in the 'great tradition'. Instead he turned to writing the Nigerian history plays which proved so popular.

14 ibid., p. 7.

15 ibid., p. 35.

16 ibid., p. 29.

17 ibid., p. 39.

18 ibid., p. 44.

19 ibid., p. 49.

20 ibid., pp. 70–71.

21 Bernth Lindfors (ed.), *Dem Say: interviews with eight Nigerian writers* (Austin University of Texas at Austin, occasional publication, African and Afro-American Studies and Research Center 1974).

22 Athol Fugard, *et al.*, *The Island* in *Statements: three plays* (London: Oxford University Press 1974), p. 47.

23 ibid., pp. 71–2.

24 ibid., p. 76.

25 ibid., p. 77.

26 The text of Euripides's play, in Greek, is published by Oxford University Press (London), with an introduction and detailed commentary, in English, by E. R. Dodds. It was first published in this edition in 1944, and revised in 1960. I mention it because the introduction presents a scholarly and balanced analysis of the play.

27 Wole Soyinka, *The Bacchae of Euripides: a communion rite* (London: Eyre Methuen 1973).

28 Translated by Philip Vellacott, in Euripides, *The Bacchae and other plays* (Harmondsworth: Penguin 1954; reissued with a revised text and new introduction, 1972), pp. 243–4, lines 1366–87.

29 Soyinka, *The Bacchae of Euripides*, p. vi; Wole Soyinka, 'The fourth stage', in *Myth, Literature and the African World* (Cambridge: Cambridge University Press 1976). There is a further discussion on this essay by Soyinka in Chapter 6.

30 Soyinka, introduction to *The Bacchae of Euripides*, p. xi.

31 Soyinka, *The Bacchae of Euripides*, p. 95.

32 ibid., p. 96.

33 ibid., p. 97.

34 ibid.

35 Introduction in ibid., pp. xi-xii.

36 ibid., p. 7.

37 ibid.

38 Introduction in ibid., p. vii.

39 ibid., p. 38.

40 ibid., p. 51.

41 ibid., p. 53.

4 Plays about colonialism and the struggle for independence

The content of the plays we are going to consider in this chapter comes from history – events which took place and which are verifiable from written records or the oral tradition – rather than from myth and legend. The plays are a direct reworking of the chosen events into drama, and not a reworking of older plays which have already reworked the source of the story into a dramatic form.

We must briefly establish what we mean by history. First, history is made by people, in both senses of the word 'made': it is people who are the activists and people who are the recorders. Second, history tends to emphasize the movements, the 'big moments', the 'crucial decisions' and the 'personalities', rather than everyday events. Third, and partly because of this emphasis on what is noteworthy, it is a *story*, that is to say it is broken down into units which have a beginning, a middle and an end, and which can be narrated. There is particularity and causality in the segment of history which the narrator (the 'historian') has chosen to tell. Because this is so, history can never be free from interpretation or 'bias'. The truth of history lies in the seeming validity of a particular interpretation of events, and in the sense which it makes of the past when the tale of those events is told.

It is perhaps useful to note again the framework which was used in Chapter 1 to show the way actuality is transformed into drama, in performance:

Actuality – what is to be depicted; which is first understood as a –
Story – involving particularity and causality; which is transformed into a –
Scenario – the story takes dramatic shape, with the scenes particularly ordered; which is mediated by –
Form – the theatre techniques, stylization, language; through

which is realized a –
Performance or
Performances – before an audience; from which the writer can
transcribe a –
Play-text – the play in a final literary form.

For the dramatist history not only provides stories; it also
provides themes which are specific to the dramatist's world view,
such as the struggle for independence. History also provides a
specific content, in terms of the playwright's own society, which
embodies those broad themes. For example, the history of Mau
Mau in Kenya is, for Kenyan dramatists as well as Kenyan
audiences, the embodiment of the struggle for independence.

For some dramatists, history can provide the theme of a 'golden
age' as the content for their plays: periods when certain qualities
appeared to inform the conduct of human affairs which have
subsequently been eclipsed by a mean and ignoble time. This leads
to a romanticization of the past. For some African playwrights the
precolonial period is the 'golden age'; though since it is dependent
on the oral or bardic tradition it tends to be restricted to those
societies who had sufficient opinion of their greatness to keep their
history as such (and not mythologize it).

However, the colonialists first confirmed the greatness of the
indigenous kingdoms, and then obscured it by conquering them,
denigrating their heroes, rejecting their values and belittling their
institutions. The negritude movement was a reassertion of confidence in the past and embodied a need to re-establish the historical
validity of it. Plays informed by the spirit of negritude predominate among the francophone African playwrights, as, for example,
the versions of Chaka by Léopold Sédar Senghor (Sénégal) and
Seydou Badian (Mali), *Les derniers jours de Lat Dior*, by Amadou
Cissé Dia (Sénégal), *Kondo, le requin*, by the Beninois playwright Jean Pliya.[1] There are also examples by anglophone
African playwrights, such as *The Mightier Sword*, by the Ghanaian
playwright Martin Owusu; *Kurunmi* by Ola Rotimi and the play
about the same emponymous Yoruba warrior–king by fellow-
Nigerian Wale Ogunyemi, *The Ijaye War*; *Shehu Umar*, by Ladan
and Lyndersay.

All these historical dramas focus upon a leader: a king or
warrior who is a hero. The drama creates the heroic stature of the
leader. Each play is structured so that the central figure rises

above adversity and all efforts to undermine his authority and position through the inherent nobility of his character. Of course, he may also be destroyed in the process. Often the public figure is contradicted by his private person. Ceremonial scenes which establish his greatness in the public eye alternate with intimate scenes which manifest an inner turmoil; the audience are allowed an insight into the hidden processes which determine his decisions. Such agonizing decisions are often the climax of the drama: the hero is faced with hideous alternatives, and his decisions result in some degree of self-sacrifice. It is through this self-sacrifice, and through a revelation of depths of personal resourcefulness that the negritude hero is established.

Soyinka puts paid to this glorification of the past in his early play *A Dance of the Forests* (which is analysed in Chapter 6). The Court of Mata Kharibu is shown to be as small-minded, corrupt and evil as the present generation; and although Soyinka makes up the events of this actual reign they appear to the audience, in the context of the play as a whole, quite valid. Nobody at the court of Mata Kharibu is heroic.

Thus, central characters in history can become heroes in plays. These heroes are not quite the same as the so-called 'Aristotelian hero', a simplification of Aristotle's theory of tragedy mentioned in the discussion of Rotimi's play *Thè Gods are not to Blame*. This 'hero' is great in all but one respect, and this 'flaw' leads to his tragic 'downfall'.

We will now turn from this more obvious transformation of history into drama, which uses the history of pre-colonialism and the drama of heroism, to the ways in which more recent history has been turned into drama – that history which African audiences have a direct experience of in one way or another: colonialism and the struggle for independence. We will however be returning to the concept of the hero in drama a little later in this chapter when we turn to plays about contemporary heroes of the people.

Nor are we quite finished with Aristotle. There is another aspect of his theory which has some relevance to the issue of 'truth' in the context of turning history into drama. Aristotle describes how certain sequences of events in a tragedy can seem *probable* even though in actuality they may not have happened that way; while other sequences seem quite *improbable*, even though they are what, in fact, happened. Drama has the power to suggest the probability of events which in turn makes the drama seem a true reflection of actuality. This is achieved in the process of making the story, whatever its source, into a scenario. If the source is history, however, the process has a special significance. For history can be deliberately distorted to make it seem to be more like history, and not, as it really is, a dramatic distortion of it. Drama has this power to suggest the probability of events. If what we see on the stage appears to be valid in itself, and valid as history too, we may be convinced that we have been shown the 'truth' of history. And yet this seeming truth can have been achieved by a deliberate intention to falsify it. For example, many people have derived an unfavourable impression of King Richard III of England from Shakespeare's deliberately unfavourable distortion of his character.

On the other hand, the historical material in a drama may be entirely accurate, and yet the audience may feel that what they are looking at is specious and partisan. Or again, a play may intend to correct inaccurate historical analysis, through a wider reference, or new facts, or the correction of a previously unsuspected bias, and yet in the process move farther away from the truth; while another play may acknowledge a deliberate distortion of history and yet, ironically, come nearer to a truth about it. The discussion on the plays in this chapter should indicate some of these paradoxes and contradictions.

The plays are: *Ovonramwen Nogbaisi*, by Ola Rotimi, the author of *The Gods are not to Blame*; *Kinjeketile*, by Ebrahim Hussein, a Tanzanian who writes in English and Swahili; *The Trial of Dedan Kimathi*, by the Kenyans Ngugi wa Thiong'o and Micere Mugo; and the *Black Mamba Plays* (*Black Mamba One*, *Two* and *Three*) by the Zambian playwright Kabwe Kasoma.

Rotimi wants to rescue Oba Ovonramwen Nogbaisi, the last independent ruler of the powerful Benin empire who capitulated to the British in 1897, from 'the biases of colonial history' – yet his hero seems to end up more deeply indicted than before. Hussein announces a deliberate artistic distortion in his recreation of the character of Kinjeketile, the leader of the Maji Maji Uprising in Tanganyika in 1904 – yet his play has an historical and contemporary validity for his Tanzanian audiences today. Ngugi and Mugo declare an overt political intention in restoring Dedan Kimathi as the people's hero of the Mau Mau Revolution, yet its staging is very complex and requires specialized theatre resources. Kasoma's dramatization of Zambia's struggle for independence is according to him non-political, yet the Zambian government banned its performance and publication.

We may be helped initially in understanding these paradoxes by seeing 'historical truth' and 'artistic truth' as alternatives to each other, both legitimate but governed by different critieria. For a start, drama is an art. It is not history. Its principal mode is the creation of illusion, and the seeming reality of this illusion. (There is a very complex interaction of concepts here which need not be the concern of the immediate argument.) History, on the other hand, seeks to pierce the illusion of probability and circumstance in order to reach reality; it is not satisfied with the obvious reasons but seeks the hidden or underlying causes.

A great deal of contemporary political drama does this too, but it is at odds with its principal mode, i.e. the creation on the stage of the illusion of reality, and the final chapter argues that this conflict will develop a new mode of drama altogether.

The dramatist who has turned to recent history for the subject matter, the content, of his play has to be aware that he is working with a history which is well documented, in addition to which his audience already have a view, or views, about the meaning of that period – though the view and the documentation may not necessarily correlate with each other. Furthermore, he is still writing a play; not history. He needs to acknowledge his dramatic intentions. Rotimi, Ngugi and Mugo, and Kasoma all acknowledge their historical or political intentions. Only Hussein acknowledges his artistic intentions.

The four plays exemplify, in one way or another, as well as through comparison with each other, this central dichotomy which the playwright who has turned to history faces between the demands of history and the demands of drama. Through the discussion of the plays we may in fact begin to understand more about the nature of drama.

Ovonramwen Nogbaisi Ola Rotimi

Ola Rotimi's play, performed in 1971 and published in 1974, about the Oba of Benin who surrendered to the British forces of occupation in 1897[2] could be described as 'stagey': the dramatist uses a number of different theatrical devices to convey his meaning. The full meaning of the play, therefore, may be more obvious to an audience at a performance than to the reader of the text.

A composite stage image of suffering is developed as a prologue and then reproduced in a somewhat modified form as an epilogue. In the near darkness on the stage there is a sound of a cock crowing, and then another sound of chains clanking; as the darkness lightens somewhat there is a vision of prisoners moving under the lash. Two voices among the human forms of the prisoners sing a 'wailing duet'. In the scene which immediately follows, the first scene of Act 1, these prisoners are revealed as Oba Ovonramwen's political rivals whose execution he orders. In the epilogue, the prisoners, now only two figures in a brighter stage light, are Benin war lords, sentenced to death by the British Consul-General, now in control of the Benin empire. The stage direction here, however, becomes cryptic:

[*They chant in lament: symbolic representations of the enshacklement of a god–king, the fall of an empire, the end of an era. . . .*][3]

Presumably the 'symbolic representations' means a series of gestures which conveys the meaning of the songs, sung by the two prisoners as they move across the stage. These songs have an English translation for the reader of the text, but in performance they are sung in Edo, one of the languages of the people of Benin City (where the production was first staged). For the members of the audience who do not understand Edo, there may be a problem of meaning, for it will then be the gestures alone of the two prisoners which will convey this complex emotional state indicated in the stage direction. It is important to establish this particular meaning – the enshacklement of a god–king, etc. – in this the final scene of the play, for otherwise the prologue and epilogue together could be taken in an altogether different sense, namely, that the brutality of the British merely replaced the brutality of Ovonramwen. In fact this meaning has already been suggested in Consul-General Moor's death sentence on seven of the Oba's chiefs for the deaths of seven British in the original massacre:

Well now, we all know that your chiefs have killed seven Whitemen. And you know that those Whitemen were my representatives, my chiefs. According to your custom, therefore, seven of your chiefs must now die. That's fair, isn't it?[4]

However, if this isn't the real meaning of the play, and Rotimi's stated intention indicates that it is not, then a great deal of the ultimate meaning of the whole play rests upon unspecified gestures in the stage direction – '. . . symbolic representations of the enshacklement of a god–king, the fall of an empire. . . .' But as a presentation of a crucial moment in the Benin people's history, are we not looking for even more than this in the meaning of the play? If we are looking for reasons why the empire fell, why the god–king failed, then the thrust of meaning throughout the play is ambiguous. We seem to be presented instead with Oba Ovonram-wen's state of mind. In order to understand the significance of this we need now to analyse the structure of the play.

The action of the play, between the prologue and the epilogue, shows Ovonramwen attempting to consolidate his hold upon his empire. He is warned of disaster in his reign by the oracle. He is disobeyed by his war lords who massacre some British. He then suffers total defeat and humiliation at the hands of the British.

In Act 1 we are shown Oba Ovonramwen administering stern justice on rebellious chiefs and disciplining his vassal states. The whites are at his court trying to get a trade concession out of him. He receives a very grave warning from the oracle at Ife that his reign will swim in blood, which profoundly affects him. In Act 2 the whites are shown advancing in a huge caravan, determined to wring trade treaties out of Ovonramwen. They arrogantly decide to press on into Benin City despite being warned by one of the Benin war lords that the Ague Festival is in progress which debars foreigners from entering the city during its seven days duration. The whites are massacred. This action has been taken by the Benin war lords against the advice and instruction of Ovonramwen. Ologbosere, whom Ovonramwen has favoured over more senior war lords and chiefs, leads the others in contradicting Ovonram-wen's advice to proceed with caution. Ovonramwen has told them – as he was told by the oracle:

> Caution is our word, my people. Let the Whiteman rudely prod us further, in spite of caution, then he will know that the way a cat walks is not the way it catches a rat![5]

When he goes out of the room Ologbosere says:

> . . . Now a foreign enemy threatens the whole empire, and the Oba says to us Defenders of the land: 'caution'! You think he truly expects obedience?[6]

They go out and ambush the whites who ignorantly insist on entering the city, and decapitate them.

Ovonramwen is shocked at what his generals have done, as they dance up to him with the heads of the whites on top of swaying poles. Rotimi wants to show that there is no simulation in Ovonramwen's horror and that he is deeply distressed at what has happened. He employs a stage device, already introduced in Act 1, which takes us into Ovonramwen's mind: a crucial phrase used by the Ifa Priest echoes over the amplifiers in the theatre. The stage direction indicates Ovonramwen's reaction:

> [*After a while, he raises a hand: drumming, jubilation subside.*
>   *Voices – that of the* **Ifa Priest**, *chanting, mingled with the agonized group-singing of the prisoners of the prologue. Interspersing these, the dire apocalypse of one of the prisoners is intoned in a languid drawl: 'the whiteman who is stronger than you will soon come and conquer you!'*
>   *The voices echo in over loudspeakers intimating Ovonramwen's thoughts. He begins to sway dizzily. Chiefs rush to him to stay him. Leaning heavily on his supports,* **Ovonramwen** *barely manages to utter, as voices die down:*]

Ovonramwen: Children of our fathers, Benin I fear, has this day swallowed a long pestle; now we shall have to sleep standing upright.[7]

The use of amplifiers ('loudspeakers') to convey the thoughts and inner motivations of Ovonramwen is established towards the end of Act 1. The Ifa Priest had given his warning to Ovonramwen:

> Oba Alaiyeluwa, Ifa has sent me to deliver the word – caution.
> I have delivered the word. Caution.[8]

A little later, Ovonramwen sends out the white emissaries without their trade treaty signed. The stage direction comments:

> [*They depart.*
>   *Ovonramwen paces about in deep thoughts, as the chanting of the* **Ifa Priest** *echoes over loudspeakers on to stage, indicating the focus of those thoughts*][9]

And, at the end of the act, when he raises Ologbosere above the others, he tells him:

> Indeed . . . it sees fire . . . blood . . . bodies . . . without number . . . floating . . . [*His words become faint with emotion*] Floating . . . in the fire . . . and in blood . . . [*His voice is subdued by the now too-familiar chanting of the* **Ifa Priest**, *wafting in through loudspeakers:* **Oba Ovonramwen**'s *fears*][10]

Now, as he is confronted with the severed heads he hears the amplified warning again. It is jumbled up with other fears in the form of amplified snatches of dialogue, warnings, premonitions, echoing around the theatre.

Of course, nobody else on the stage can 'hear' these sounds; and so the audience accepts them as the turmoil in Ovonramwen's thoughts. This stage device, therefore, lets us know the 'truth' about Ovonramwen. But what sort of 'truth'? It is still an illusion. The man on the stage is an actor, not Ovonramwen, and the structure and devising of the scene is all Rotimi's own. In fact, the playwright goes even further in developing the emotional impact of the scene. The din in Ovonramwen's head is set against the harmonious chant of the Benin warriors (sung in the original production by the Edo Cultural Group) which 'thunders in again'. It is actually very difficult for the reader to hold the full stage effect of the music and songs as well as the ethereal sounds of the amplified Ifa Priest's voice in his mind as he reads the text. The songs especially, in the absence of any idea of their rhythms and melodies, are particularly inaccessible to the reader who sees them only as verse on the page and doesn't hear them at all. Thus the reader may get the sense of the scene, but not its emotional impact.

Of course, it is possible that this emotional dimension might obscure the deeper meaning of the play, instead of enhancing it.

The central scene of Act 2 (and of the whole play as well) shows the forces of Benin being defeated by the British. This scene employs yet another type of stage device, namely, what is sometimes referred to as the 'split stage'. Here, one group of men – the British officers – are on one side of the stage in a pool of sharp light, surrounded by darkness, planning their strategies for the assault on Benin; while on another side of the stage, in another pool of light, the Benin war lords plan their defence of their city. The two areas on the stage are lit alternately; the one fading to blackness as the other brightens. Thus, we swiftly move from one short scene to the next, showing plans being laid out and preparations made as the final confrontation edges closer and closer. The effect of this device is to convey the urgency of the operations.

The battle itself is fought using symbolic objects (another stage device) to represent the opposing empires and their armies. In addition, an individual represents the whole force. Ologbosere bears the 'ada', traditionally the symbol of the Benin empire. Consul-General Moor bears the union jack – the British flag – the symbol of that other empire. These two men face each other and fight with their national symbols. Ologbosere is eventually forced to the ground. Then there is a spectacular charge on to the stage.

Ovonramwen allows himself to be led off into hiding. The royal bards sing the 'wailing duet' which occurs again in the epilogue, ending the play. Whilst they are singing this plaintive lament for the end of an epoch, the whites, Moor and his officers ransack the palace and make off with the treasures.

This powerful little scene at the end of the intensely emotional experience of the battle is surely intended to function symbolically, like the rest of the scene, and show a representation of Britain's rapaciousness. However, the indications in the stage direction of furtiveness in their actions – 'they begin to leave furtively' – suggests a sense of guilt which Britain certainly did not feel in conquering the Benin empire. She exulted in her conquest. She had put down the 'heathen', 'sadistic' blacks. What reason did Moor have for leaving 'furtively'? His country was going to plunder far more than ever he and his men could load on to their backs.

It is stage images like this which introduce a degree of ambiguity into the meaning of the play. Rotimi talks of 'correcting the biases of colonial history', and if these biases mean anything they mean the complacency with which Britain contemplated the 'rightness' of her imperial mission and the Christian zeal with which she justified the extension of her trade as an extension of Christian 'civilization' to areas of 'darkness'. Is Rotimi suggesting that the British trade mission and subsequent punitive expedition was perverted by its British officers? It seems unlikely for earlier he indicted the mission itself when he makes the leader of the trade mission, Consul-General Phillips (who was decapitated) declare to his accompanying officers:

> Commerce, Mr Campbell! That is your answer! The conduct of trade in the Colonies demands direct contact with the interior that produces the goods! Meanwhile Overami has placed a Juju on all produce from that interior. I get the complaints, gentlemen. As her Majesty's prime representative in this Protectorate, I also get the blame from London for every blasted minute that passes without an effective enforcement of the 1892 trade treaty with Benin . . . [11]

In the next act, Consul-General Moor prosecutes with vigour and with the arrogance of an outright victor the total surrender of Ovonramwen and his forces. As far as they are concerned, they are obeying their orders from Britain.

If the British were obeying orders, Ovonramwen's chiefs and war lords were not. This is a significant aspect of the play, and another source of ambiguity. In Act 1, Ovonramwen is shown exercising his power over all subsidiary chiefs and title-holders; and indeed they appear to be intimidated on stage by the demonstration of his power. The only dissenting voices are those of the prisoner-chiefs already condemned to death, and, in private, Ovonramwen's court jester, Uzazakpo. It is Uzazakpo who advises Ovonramwen to favour Ologbosere (over his more senior commanders) and it is advice which Ovonramwen takes. The subsequent disobedience of Ologbosere seems inexplicable – even as an excess of devotion, which is what is suggested in the text.

The other war lords seem to obey Ologbosere more as a result of muddled thinking than anything else:

Obayulwana: Too much discussion brings confusion! My brothers-at-arms, is it war we must be ready for, or discussion?[12]

(Eventually this chief commits suicide when sentenced to death by the British). Iyase and Ezomo, the two War Lords senior to Ologbosere, are shadowy figures, until the final Act when they become the mediators between Ovonramwen and the British. They beg the Oba to surrender:

Chief Ezomo: [*Urgently kneels before* **Ovonramwen**] Pray, my lord, do nothing to provoke him again!

Iyase: [*Fervently beseeching*] Benin . . . think of Benin!

Osodin: [*Kneeling*] It is the peace in Benin that matters now!

Iyase: Forget self! Forget status! Let Power die so that Benin may live! Do as he commands . . . for Benin . . . for Benin. . . .[13]

Ezomo betrays Ovonramwen a second time, and reveals his new hiding-place to the British.

Ologbosere, it seems, escapes.

What are we to make of Ovonramwen's relationships with his chiefs? After the opening scene there is no indication of any overt rebellion or coherent dissension among them or towards Ovonramwen. There is no plotting; and, as we have seen, their refusal to obey his advice to proceed with caution seems more a result of confusion than of any articulated opposition to Ovonramwen's policies. We are forced to the conclusion that Oba Ovonramwen Nogbaisi has unlimited powers; but, in the exercise of them, he is weak.

Perhaps he is weak because of his fear of the prediction of the Ifa oracle. Some Nigerian critics, who comment on the basis of their understanding of the nature of the Ifa oracle, contend that in the end the oracle will always be able to suggest appropriate sacrifices, in order to change an unfavourable prediction (as was the case in Duro Ladipọ's play *Ẹ̀dá*). Ovonramwen would have been advised what sacrifices were necessary to avoid the looming catastrophe within his reign. This criticism is also levelled at Rotimi's *The Gods are not to Blame* in which the oracle fails to offer Odewale any way out of his awful destiny. Whether either accusation is valid ethnologically or not, Rotimi's use of the Ifa oracle is certainly self-fulfilling in both plays: once uttered, it causes the subject of the prophecy to act in such a way that the prediction is, ironically, fulfilled. This can reinforce a fatalistic view of the universe.

The Ifa oracle is not, as in *Macbeth*, a temptation to evil, but the source of stability for the community through timely admonishments. Certainly, by the deliberate use of the stage devices we have already noted – indeed almost by their over-use – Rotimi makes it unequivocally clear that this morally positive oracle robs Ovonramwen of the power to act. This is the source of his weakness. Is his dependence, therefore, on the oracle a *mistake* on Ovonramwen's part?

It is possible to see in Rotimi's dramatized version of Ovonramwen's surrender a number of mistakes on the part of the Oba: wrong decisions in a moment of crisis. All or some of the following might be interpreted as mistakes: trusting Uzazakpo, who advised him to make Ologbosere his 'favoured' general; despairing at the oracle's prophecy; not placing his generals specifically under his orders when the crisis first loomed; not 'disciplining' them after they had decapitated the whites; surrendering himself; not committing suicide.

However, Rotimi never makes it clear that Ovonramwen was presented with alternatives at these critical points, let alone any 'correct' alternative. From the brief *Background* which prefaces the text of the play, Rotimi claims to defend Ovonramwen from the 'biases of colonial history', and that he was 'in actuality "a man more sinned against that (sic) he ever sinned".' There are no mistakes, then, on Ovonramwen's part; he was, in fact, the victim of circumstances.

We are left then with the possibility that the real meaning of

Rotimi's play is that Ovonramwen was the victim of fate. We have already seen the stress laid upon the oracle in Acts 1 and 2; and we have had privileged access to Ovonramwen's mind. In Act 3 Ovonramwen's surrender is hedged about by the religious taboos pertaining to his high state. It is also resolutely determined upon by the British, keen to exact vengeance for the massacre of their compatriots. Ovonramwen's attempts to avoid his captors are accompanied by the following chant which is repeated over and over again:

Emwẹn Ovọnramwẹn	It is not for one day.
Emwẹn Ovọnramwẹn	
Ọ nai ghi r'iyẹn n'ọ gha	Nay, it is not for one day alone –
fo vb' otọe	This story of Ovonramwen is a story for ever.[14]

The events pertaining to his flight and capture are linked by songs which sing of the inevitability of calamity and misfortune and the stoical endurance of it. The final song of the epilogue concludes:

Agbọn ma roro iroro	It is well.
Agbọn ma	Let fate laugh on.
Agbọn ma roro iroro.	It is well.[15]

Ola Rotimi would appear to be fatalistic, therefore, in his view of history. The colonial biases of history have been replaced by a fatalistic bias: 'this was the way it was bound to happen'. It is a nostalgic point of view, and runs the risk of becoming self-indulgent: 'what greatness was here overthrown by the march of history!' The unfortunate fact is that Ovonramwen surrendered; he did not die defending the independence of his empire. He appears weak – especially as a result of Rotimi's fatalistic portrait. He is neither statesman, nor politician, nor warrior-king. It is difficult to form anything but a negative impression of him.

Kinjeketile Ebrahim Hussein

Kinjeketile was performed in 1969 and published in 1970. Apart from the time of the action of the play – 1904, 7 years after Ovonramwen surrendered to the British – Hussein's play about the Maji Maji Uprising in Tanganyika[16] is different from *Ovonramwen Nogbaisi* in almost every other way. *Kinjeketile* is straightforward in its theatrical presentation. The action unfolds through a series of short scenes, some narration, and a final series of battles which are partially narrated as it progresses and then climaxes in the firing of guns – including the 'big gun' of the Germans – in a stage blackout. There is an important concluding scene set in the German fort where the rebels have been taken, as prisoners condemned to die.

Everything that does not contribute to the play's core of meaning has been dispensed with. Each scene makes a specific point which builds up into the playwright's argument. Even though the statement which Hussein is attempting to make is complex and difficult, it is presented unequivocally and with clarity.

Hussein appears to be concerned with the two concepts of reason and national liberation, and what they can mean today to a Tanzanian audience. He sees a way in which the two concepts can be shown to interrelate significantly in the Maji Maji Uprising, which a Tanzanian audience would be very familiar with. He goes to the heart of the problem by seeing the failure of that rebellion in terms of a central contradiction in the movement itself: the thing which united the Tanganyikan tribes and gave them the necessary courage to attack their oppressors, also caused their defeat and led them to die in their thousands.

This was the magic water, or holy water, given to them by their god, which would protect them from the German bullets. This divine intervention came through the agent of the god Hongo, Kinjeketile, who was accorded the status of seer or prophet. He gave his people faith in themselves by anointing them with the holy water, the 'maji'. This new-found confidence brought them together and stopped them fighting among themselves. Once unity was achieved, however, Kinjeketile could not very well remove that faith, that confidence, when it came to attacking the Germans. He could not now tell them that the 'maji' would not stop the bullets from killing them. Without the magic water there would be no unity among the oppressed peasants, and their oppression would continue; but once the unity so necessary as a precondition for the anti-colonial struggle was achieved, the 'magic' water then betrayed them. We need to see how Hussein builds up the presentation of this contradiction.

He first establishes in the play the sufferings under the Germans, the disunity among the tribes and the inevitably low level of political consciousness. Hussein does this through the families of the two men who, in the play, become central to the movement,

Kinjeketile himself and Kitunda. Their wives have no food; Kitunda's daughter is taken off in front of him and raped by an Askari; Kitunda himself is beaten up. His wife sobs in frustration and desperation at the neighbours, her husband's fellow-workers:

> Get out! Get out of here, you women you! Two little men were enough to scare the whole lot of you. You have been enslaved body and spirit. Do you still regard yourselves as men? Do you call yourselves Wamatumbi? Oh no, not at all. You are mere women, you! You're forced to dig – yes. Your children are seized – yes. You are 'yes' men. What have you crept in here to do? You hid until those two were gone.[17]

Kitunda himself has tried to organize the opposition, but all it seems to do is to stir up dissension. This is probably because Kitunda himself adopts, instinctively, a much more rational approach than the others. There is a paradox here: the rational man is indeed recognized by the others as the potential leader of the group, yet his rational arguments are used by them to undermine his position. Kitunda is called a coward and an informer by another man, Mkichi, who, vaguely, wants immediate action. Kitunda patiently explains his position:

Kitunda: . . . I see thousands and thousands of our people dying.

Mkichi: But it is better to die than to live like this. We are made to work like beasts in the cotton plantation. We are forced to pay tax. We die of hunger because we cannot work on our shambas. I say death is better than this life.

Kitunda: It's better to live like this than to go to war and lose thousands of our men. And the few who will survive will get the same treatment, or worse, as before. [*A long pause*][18]

Kitunda's voice is the voice of reason; but what he has to say is unpalatable to the others.

As the instances of oppression accumulate, Kinjeketile, Kitunda's fellow-villager, moves in a completely different direction to Kitunda. He withdraws into himself, becomes involved in prayers and rituals in his hut; and then one day (this is in Act 2, scene 1) he emerges from his hut in a trance. He is apparently possessed; and as Kinjeketile's family, as well as Kitunda and his family, watch, horrified, he seems to be being dragged by some hidden force down to the river (off stage) into which he falls. He doesn't resurface; and the wife and the others come back onto the stage. She is inconsolable.

Twenty-four hours later many other villagers are gathered together, and they try to determine what to do – again there is quarrelling among them – and in the midst of their confusion Kinjeketile emerges, coming up from the direction of the river. He is carrying a small pot in his left hand, and a fly whisk in his right. He is still in a trance and utters a powerful incantation to the assembled throng. Kitunda kneels to feel his garment – which he discovers is quite dry – and the rest of the village, imagining that he is kneeling in awe, follow his example. Kinjeketile intones his message from the god Hongo:

> He who partakes of this water
> no harm will befall him.
> No bullet will penetrate his body.
> These are the gifts given us by our ancestors and our spirits.
> Hear from me who comes from Bokelo, the land of our ancestors,
> the message from our forefathers:
> 'Destroy the Red Earth!'
> And these are the instruments.[19]

Kitunda is ordained by Kinjeketile as the one to build up and lead the army.

In this scene the slogan for the war is quickly established: 'Maji! Maji!'. Ordinarily it means 'water'; now in this new context it comes to mean so much more: it means 'freedom'. As Kinjeketile later says: 'A word is born. . . .'

To summarize, then, the development of the argument to this point: the people are oppressed by the colonialists (mainly working through their black stooges) and this oppression and hopelessness leads them to fight among themselves, thus making the possibility of resistance even more remote. Two men are characterized. They are friends and fellow-peasants, yet the one, Kitunda, seeks to organize an opposition to the colonialists as rationally as he can within his limited understanding of the situation, while the other, Kinjeketile, moves deeper into ritual and belief. He goes through an ordeal of water, miraculously emerges dry, and presents the people with the sacred water to immunize them against the weapons of the Germans. He appoints Kitunda to lead the forces. The revolution now begins to gather momentum.

We are near to the middle of the play now; and a crucial scene takes place between Kitunda and Kinjeketile. Kitunda the rationalist has been puzzled by certain aspects of Kinjeketile's divine revelation and subsequent demeanour. In particular, he asks Kinjeketile who Seyyid Said is, because Kinjeketile had spoken in his trance of the people becoming the children of Seyyid Said. He is an Arab, Kinjeketile tells him, the Sultan of Zanzibar. 'You speak some strange Swahili,' Kitunda tells him, ' – like Arabic.'

Kinjeketile: I do?

Kitunda: Yes.

Kinjeketile: Me?

Kitunda: You said that we will be the children of Seyyid Said.

Kinjeketile: I said so? [*He shakes* **Kitunda**] Tell me, please tell me. Tell me all that I said.

Kitunda: You said that we should all unite. After we are united, then we can declare war. And that we will win. You said that the ancestors at Bokelo give us their support. You also said that after our victory, we will be the children of Seyyid Said.

Kinjeketile: After winning the war we will be under Seyyid Said? I said that?

Kitunda: Yes. Are you ill . . .? Your face . . . where are you going?[20]

Kinjeketile is genuinely shocked. The writing of the scene at this point leaves us no room for doubt about his deep sense of shock. He goes frantic at what he now knows he said whilst being possessed:

I've been cheated! They have killed me – no, I have killed myself! It was a dream, yes, I was dreaming!
No, no, no, no! I have been cheated! No! [*He gives a terrible cry and falls down. Blackout*]

Kinjeketile has realized the implications of what he has said, and what his trance may come to mean – though these implications are not yet articulated in the play either for Kitunda, or for the audience.

What is important to note at this point is that Kinjeketile really believed he had been possessed. He had in no way simulated or faked his trance or his ordeal. The play is quite unambiguous here. Kinjeketile's belief in Hongo to this point has been absolute. This is important to Hussein's argument in the play.

Now, however, there are doubts. Kinjeketile refuses to give the order to start the war, even though the Wazaramo tribe is on the point of joining the movement. The men are getting restless. Kinjeketile withdraws into himself and Kitunda's own position as his general becomes difficult.

Eventually he has a confrontation with Kinjeketile. Ironically, there has been a complete reversal of their positions. Kitunda is now arguing in favour of starting the war – 'We have the water now, and we have the people, and what's more, we are united'[21] – and Kinjeketile, like Kitunda in the first scene of the play, is advising Kitunda to wait. Kinjeketile is now the one who is arguing on the basis of reason:

Kinjeketile: No, you are not ready to fight! What you mean is, you are confirmed in the belief that the water and the spirits will fight the war for you. You are depending on the water. Remove the water, and you will have a war – amongst yourselves, tribe against tribe.

Kitunda: But there is no need to think like that because we have got the water. We have been given the water by our spirit Hongo. Hongo is our spirit. I don't see why there should be any doubt.

Kinjeketile: How do you know it was Hongo and not another spirit? If this is Hongo, then why does he say that we will be the children of Seyyid Said after winning the war? Why does he help us? Why get rid of the white man, only to usher in an Arab? If that is the case, it would be better for us to remain just as we are.[22]

Kitunda, formerly the rational one, now feels very unsettled. He accuses Kinjeketile of lying to them and cheating them. He is going straight out to tell the men that the 'maji' was all a fraud. 'Go tell them,' Kinjeketile says, 'and by tomorrow there won't be a single soul out there. And you will be under the white man's rule for ever.'

It is important for Hussein's purpose that Kitunda finds it difficult to rationalize the dilemma. It enables Kinjeketile to repeat the central problem (the stage direction says: '. . . *as if he is talking to a child*') so that Kitunda – and the playwright's audiences today – may grasp it:

If this Seyyid Said could with our consent enslave us body and mind, he would be a far worse enemy than the German. He could rule us without ever setting foot in this country. Let us therefore wait. We will be strong; but not by being strengthened by some dubious aid from the outside. We will be strong because this strength comes from us – our own strength.[23]

Kitunda still doesn't understand. And so it is repeated a third time:

> Look, true, we have been given the water. But the question is, who gave us the water? Was it really Hongo? If it was Hongo why . . . is he selling us, his own people to another master. . . .[24]

Kinjeketile, however, has not given up his belief in God; and he still does not doubt that he was indeed possessed. What exactly is Hussein arguing through his characters at this point? It seems that he is undermining superstition from within, rather than outside of, the margins of religious belief. We don't doubt God, but what do we make of his spirit's guidance? In this way Hussein maintains contact with the ordinary folk who constitute his audiences (the play was originally written and performed in Swahili) who would be quite religious in one way or another. In making out a case for a rational approach to greater political consciousness – which seems to be the ultimate purpose of this argument – Hussein is nevertheless still respecting the fundamental beliefs of his audience.

After Kitunda and Kinjeketile have had this argument, the representative of the Wazaramo is brought in to Kinjeketile. He has a question to ask Kinjeketile. The Wazaramo's guiding spirit, god, is Kolelo. 'Are Hongo and Kolelo one and the same spirit?' If they are different names for the same god then the Wazaramo will join Kinjeketile's and Kitunda's forces. Kinjeketile's tone is indicated as he gives his reply:

Kinjeketile: [*Almost timidly*] Hongo is merely another name for Kolelo.[25]

The audience are aware how difficult it must be for Kinjeketile to make this statement, for they have just seen all too clearly to what extent his faith in Hongo as the god of his prophecy has been undermined. And yet they must have much bigger forces if they are to succeed against the Germans. In telling the representative of the Wazaramo that Hongo is merely another name for Kolelo, Kinjeketile is forced to live in the very eye of contradiction. If he denies the connection the Wazaramo won't join the movement and the revolution will die before it has even got started. On the other hand, what is he saying yes to? Certain death? And the possibility of no ultimate victory? What Kinjeketile is beginning to see is that the religious belief of the people contradicts that which it would promote: their liberation from the yoke of colonialism.

Kitunda has now been undermined by Kinjeketile; and he advises his forces to wait and be patient. However, he tells Kinjeketile in private:

> It's the people. You gave them the water. They believe in its power. They see no reason for waiting any more.[26]

Kinjeketile is beginning to understand things more clearly:

> A man gives birth to a word . . . the word grows bigger and bigger . . . and destroys the man who let it loose. A word born of man grows strong, and ends by enslaving him. . . .[27]

He tells Kitunda:

> Or, let us agree on this. When you lead the people to war you will act and plan as if the water did not exist. Use your own strength. You must not depend on the water, do you hear, you must not depend on the water![28]

Finally, Kinjeketile accedes to the men's demand to start the war immediately.

Act 3 shows the progress of the war. Kitunda provides a link narration, seemingly recounting the struggle after it is all over: 'We wanted payment – to harm as we had been harmed, to kill as we had been killed. . . .' He describes how as more and more of the men were killed by the bullets he came round to Kinjeketile's understanding of the nature of the struggle. We actually see him increasingly alienated from his fellow rebels in scenes in which he tries to persuade them to follow the war strategies which he outlines and not to rely on the water: 'There is a war ahead of us and, by god, I don't want people to die because of some silly beliefs and superstitions.'[29] His plans are eminently sensible: attack the fort from four quarters; one quarter camouflaged with tree branches as they advance; one group attack from the east – '. . . the sun will be behind us, which will dazzle the Germans at the fort'; the whole attack to be co-ordinated by Kitunda, and each group to wait for the signal. But none of these strategies was heeded; and the Germans used their 'big gun'. Kitunda, as narrator, describes the aftermath:

> We lost more than 1200 men from the Second Company. Those of us who survived stumbled about like raving lunatics, some screaming, 'Kinjeketile has betrayed us all!' And although they were crying no tears flowed, no tears. Others were struck into a stupor, and did

nothing. Most of us felt it was no use fighting any more. We fell into a hopeless despair.[30]

The final scene is inside the fort. There Kitunda and the remnants of his rebels find Kinjeketile lying unconscious on the prison floor. The Askari – small irony, this – saves him from being killed by his warriors. The Germans are torturing Kinjeketile, trying to make him confess that the water was a lie. However, he stubbornly refuses to admit it. The German officer even tells him in the other prisoners' hearing:

> Listen, if you agree to tell the people that the water didn't have any medicine, we will let all these people go free.
>
> **Kinjeketile** *looks at his fellow prisoners. He sees* **Kitunda**. *They look at each other for a long time*][31]

Kitunda asks for permission to speak to him alone, and this is agreed. At first Kinjeketile refuses to talk about the failure of the rebellion; but Kitunda insists. There is a final and profoundly ironical reversal of roles between the two men. Kitunda is now totally disbelieving of the power of the water; but Kinjeketile refuses to deny that the water was magic:

Kinjeketile: They want me to say that the water was a lie. Where was the lie?

Kitunda: Was the water true? Did you believe in it?

Kinjeketile: [*Laughs long and bitterly. A pause*] Do you know what they will say tomorrow? The officer will say we were wrong. He will tell our children we were wrong in fighting him. He will tell that to our children, Kitunda. That to fight him is wrong! That to fight for one's country is wrong! And he wants me to help him by retracting all that I said. He wants me to say that the water was a lie. Do you know what that means? The moment I say that, people in the north, south, east and west will stop fighting. They will fall into hopeless despair – they will give up. I will not say that! A word has been born. Our great grand children will hear of it. One day the word will cease to be a dream, it will be a reality.[32]

He refuses to retract; and at last Kitunda understands the significance of the contradiction. They have perceived an understanding through contradiction. Unity is a precondition of the struggle against colonialism. In time, unity which could at first only be achieved through a failing magic can be achieved eventually through a greater understanding of the political forces involved. In the end 'Maji! Maji!' doesn't mean the magic water; it means freedom. Kinjeketile could not compromise on that. The word – freedom – had been born and he would not deny it.

Hussein claims artistic licence as far as his handling of the historical material is concerned. Readers who are interested in the history of the Maji Maji Uprising can consult the historians. The Kinjeketile in the play is Hussein's creation, although he is not denying history in the writing of the play. What he is doing is re-establishing Kinjeketile as a hero of the people, then and now. It is not just the final sacrifice of his life which makes him heroic; it is also his intellect, particularly in one who has no formal schooling, for it is an intellect used on behalf of his people.

What the playwright has done is to make the way Kinjeketile understands the political processes, of which he is a part, accessible to audiences here and now so that they too can achieve a higher level of consciousness. The method for achieving this higher level of political consciousness is through the characterization of Kinjeketile and Kitunda within the precise structuring of the play. They are brought to an understanding of a specific contradiction, and become aware of living through contradiction in general – contradiction being when things start happening, apparently inexplicably, in the opposite way to what is intended; or when things start happening *negatively* as the direct result of a series of positive actions. An understanding of contradiction enables us to perceive the hidden forces operating within a given social system. It enabled Kinjeketile to see the true significance of his actions – which might have been thought to have been negative – as well as the real nature of the forces of colonialism which he and his people were opposing.

Hussein, then, sets out to distort actual history in order to show his audiences what he sees as the more valid wider historical processes: the structure of resistance, if one likes, to colonialism. He wishes to make this presentation accessible to ordinary folk for whom this historical process is by no means complete.

It is very different from Rotimi's intention in writing *Ovonramwen Nogbaisi*. In this play he sets out to correct actual history; but, as some would see it, he ends up distorting it further by an inherently fatalistic approach towards the forces of colonialism and imperialism. Specific comparisons between the two plays can be made – such as between the pairs of central characters, Ovonramwen and his general, Ologbosere, and Kinjeketile and his general, Kitunda; or between the differing impacts each of the crucial battles has on the minds of the vanquished; or between the relative advantages and disadvantages of theatrical inventiveness and theatrical simplification. But these comparisons are not our specific concern at this point.

We need to turn to much more recent history, to Kenya's war of liberation known as Mau Mau, and to Zambia's struggle for independence within the context of the Central African Federation; and to see how each of these crucial events in the lives of the people of those countries has been made the subject-matter of drama.

The Trial of Dedan Kimathi Ngugi and Mugo

We have talked of the growth of political consciousness, or of greater understanding, of the playwright, of the characters in his plays, and of his audiences. It may be useful to mention a phrase, relating to consciousness, of Karl Marx, who said that '. . . It is not the consciousness of men that determines their being, but, on the contrary, their social being that determines their consciousness'.[33] What we understand about life has been fabricated in our minds by the way our social and economic system works. In a given social system, the way we relate to people (for example, manager to labourer, teacher to pupil, husband to wife, lender to borrower, specialist to layman) is an expression of that system and makes us think in certain ways. This leads to an understanding of our lives in a certain way.

We always assume that this 'certain way' is in fact the only way; and if we don't understand things fully it is because we are not sufficiently well educated, or not sufficiently 'bright'. However, very 'bright' and very well-educated people sometimes see that the way we think is only one way; and that in another sort of social system we might well think in another way. For example, Bertolt Brecht always tried to show in his plays our most commonly accepted notions as outlandish and very strange.

With hindsight we all can see that the most cherished notions of previous ages, or different cultures, can be limited *and limiting*. An immediate example, which we noted in the previous chapter, is that the liberal and democratic Athenians of the fifth century BC never thought that slavery was wrong, or that owning slaves contradicted their basic philosophy of personal liberty.[34] In fact it was the slaves who gave them their leisure to think about personal liberty.

In this chapter we are considering plays in which the way colonialism is normally thought about is being challenged by the playwrights. Rotimi sets out to challenge 'the colonial biases of history'; but in *Kinjeketile* we have a much clearer example of how our most deeply-rooted thought processes can be called into question. In that play Hongo is shown as the spirit of god, and nobody disputes this. Once Hongo has revealed his will to Kinjeketile and given him the magic water, there is no need for anyone to doubt any further. If some men are killed by bullets, then it is because they had broken certain taboos. Finally, when men were massacred it was Kinjeketile himself who had betrayed them. But Hussein's Kinjeketile and Kitunda have already begun to doubt Hongo before this final crisis; and they at any rate, in the end, achieve some degree of political consciousness of where their real strength lies: it is in a wider unity in the struggle against colonialism, and in themselves.

It is obvious in this chapter we are not specifically concerned with the accuracy of the historical detail in the plays. I have not summarized any or all of the historical analyses of the particular periods which form the subject-matter of the plays. Nor do I think that this is especially important with regard to plays dealing with an earlier period of colonial history – the British occupation of Benin and the uprising on the German plantation colonies in Tanganyika – because the times have passed; and, with the exception perhaps of the people of Benin City and of descendants of Kinjeketile and his followers – and probably not even these people – no African audience today has any commitment to the precise details of those events. If they have they will go to the history books and not to a play in the theatre. Audiences at a performance are disposed to accept the historical data as the playwright presents them; and to judge the play as a good or bad play. In this particular context, i.e. of a play about colonial history, we may describe a 'good' play as an evening's entertainment which also brings the audience to an understanding of the issues of colonialism, and how it affects their thinking.

When we come to the more recent events which form the subject-matter of *The Trial of Dedan Kimathi* and the *Black Mamba Plays* I would expect the readers of this book to familiarize themselves with the history of the struggle for independence in Kenya and Zambia. The reasons for this are because, in the first place, the nature of the struggle is still relevant; second, because the playwrights are challenging not only the colonial view of that period of history, but also an indigenous post-independence view; and third, because the playwrights are writing primarily for audiences in their own countries for many of whom the struggle for independence is a direct and powerful experience which has shaped their lives.

The playwrights, in fact, give the historical source-work to which they are most indebted, in the introductions to their respective plays: Karari Njama's *Mau Mau from Within* (Ngugi's and Mugo's *The Trial of Dedan Kimathi*); *Zambia Shall Be Free* by Kenneth Kaunda (President of Zambia) (Kasoma's *Black Mamba Plays*).[35] It is interesting that both these source-works are personal testimonies by activists. Much more has been written, of course, about the Mau Mau War and Zambia's struggle for independence; whoever is interested sufficiently in the period can compare the different accounts. He or she will almost certainly then want to write a different play from the ones we are presently going to consider.

What we are now concerned with is the purpose of the play-wrights in writing their plays, and we are immediately concerned with the intentions of Ngugi wa Thiong'o and Micere Githae Mugo in their jointly writing *The Trial of Dedan Kimathi*.

They began writing in 1974. The play was performed in 1975, and published in 1976. The events which form the historical basis for the play occurred almost twenty years earlier. They have prefaced their plays with a frank and unequivocal statement of the nature of their commitment to Kenya, to literature and to the theatre. The starting point of their collaboration in writing this play is a shared hatred of capitalism as the cause of the continuing poverty and despair of the working masses and of the peasants in the third world. This socialist view is then related to the struggle for independence in Kenya which culminated in the Mau Mau War, and which is seen by the authors not only as a war against colonialism and imperialism but also as a class war which is by no means over. The 'independence' won for Kenya in 1960 largely by the efforts of the masses was not synonymous with freedom for those masses.

Kimathi, the leading general of that war becomes the focus of their interest. They travel to Kimathi's home area, and they are deeply moved by the place Kimathi still holds in the people's hearts. This implies that his heroic stature has been officially curtailed:

> We would try to recreate the same great man of courage, of commitment to the people, as had been so graphically described to us by the people . . .

However, in recognizing and depicting Kimathi as the hero of the Kenyan masses, the authors' real focus is the continuing class struggle, exacerbated now by post-independence neo-colonialism:

> It was crucial that all this be put together as one vision, stretching from the pre-colonial wars of resistance against European intrusion and European slavery, through the anti-colonial struggles for independence and democracy to the post-independence struggle against neo-colonialism.

In creating Kimathi as the people's hero, Mugo and Ngugi also make the people themselves heroic. The act of writing the play is part of their overall polemic, just as their understanding of history informs their concept of the function of theatre:

> We believe that good theatre is that which is on the side of the people, that which, without masking mistakes and weaknesses, gives people courage and urges them to higher resolves in their struggle for total liberation. So the challenge was to truly depict the masses (symbolized by Kimathi) in the only historically correct perspective: positively, heroically and as the true makers of history.

The playwrights use Kimathi's 'trial' at Nyeri as a starting point. The core of the action of the play, the story element, concerns a peasant woman who separates a ragged urban youth from fighting a similarly impoverished girl, and then co-opts him in her efforts to get a gun to Kimathi in jail. The youth is not initially aware of the nature of the mission; but his and the girl's eventual understanding of the struggle and commitment to it lead to the climax of the play. This is the firing of a shot in the court-room after Kimathi has had the sentence of death passed on him. The shot symbolizes the continuation of the struggle through the young boy and the girl.

This core of the play – a core of meaning as well as a story-line – has woven around it a cumulative portrait of Dedan Kimathi, developed through four symbolic trials, which are not to be confused with the 'trial' stage by the colonialists in the Nyeri court-house. These four symbolic trials take place in the cell in the jail which itself is symbolic of a state of mind, or of a 'wilderness'.

The play is in three movements, which we are advised to imagine as one single movement, with actions, events, incidents – all the parts of the play, in fact – moving along with great urgency. The four trials of Kimathi occur in the Second Movement.

The First Movement is largely concerned with the establishment of the historical perspective of the present struggle against imperialism, the Mau Mau War; and in particular with this critical phase of the war, Kimathi's arrest and detention in Nyeri. The woman, the boy and the girl – they are simply called Woman, Boy, Girl in the play – are established as representatives of the oppressed, in the specific context of an operation against the so-called terrorists by the British troops in Nyeri. Music, dances and mime at the beginning of the movement, show the coming of the Europeans, slavery, colonialism and the growing struggle against the oppressors.

The Third Movement brings together the portrait of Kimathi and the story of how the Woman brings Boy and Girl into the struggle. It also shows an earlier incident in the mountain camps when Kimathi spared his brother's life. Wambararia, and others, had sneaked out of the camps to treat with the British. The revolutionaries had arrested them and brought them back into the forest for trial. Some now argue for their lives to be spared; others, and this includes Woman, argue for their death, including the death of Wambararia. But Kimathi relents. Wambararia subsequently betrays him. The scene shows not only the circumstances of his betrayal, but also something of the way the revolutionary movement – any revolutionary movement on behalf of the masses – is organized, and emphasizes the criteria which must predominate over all other criteria.

This, the Third Movement, builds up to the climax in the court-room. Kimathi confronts his oppressors with the undying revolution:

Kimathi: But our people will never surrender
Internal and external foes
Will be demolished
And Kenya shall be free!

[*Applause from Africans*]

Judge: Order in Court!

Kimathi: [*Addressing the people*]
So, go!

Organise in your homes
Organise in the mountains
Know that your only
Kindred blood is he
Who is in the struggle
Denounce those who weaken
Our struggle
By creating ethnic divisions
Uproot from you those
Who are selling out to imperialism
Kenyan masses shall be free!

Judge: Kimathi s/o Wachiuri, you are sentenced to die by hanging.
You will be hanged by the rope until you are dead.

Kimathi laughs. Boy and Girl reveal themselves, both holding the
gun, and shout defiantly: 'Not dead!'[36]
    The play has a prologue – called an Opening – in that same
court-house where it ends – or almost ends. For after the shout by
Boy and Girl and the firing of the gun there is a blackout on stage.
After a moment's silence there is a 'thunderous freedom song',
and the lights come up to reveal all the people jubilantly singing –
except for the whites and the soldiers, who have vanished. We are
told that at the opening night of the first production, which was in
the National Theatre, Nairobi, the audience danced down the
aisles with the performers and out on to the street.
    This, in broad outline, is the structure of the play. In coming
into the text more closely we can usefully refer to the theatre
techniques used by Rotimi in *Ovonramwen Nogbaisi*, as well as to
the dramatic method of Hussein in *Kinjeketile*. In a somewhat
schematic sense *The Trial of Dedan Kimathi* combines many of the
techniques of *Ovonramwen Nogbaisi*, as well as some further stage
devices; and some, though not all, of Hussein's methodology. The
most obvious parallel with *Ovonramwen Nogbaisi* is the use of the
amplified voice repeating something said earlier which sticks in a
particular character's mind. In a crucial action in the First Movement between Boy and Woman, which is about political understanding (and this makes the scene very similar in intent to the
crucial scenes in *Kinjeketile*), Woman tells the youth:

What is it you don't understand? The things I talk about are written all
over, written like large signs everywhere. [*Pause*] The day you understand why your father died; the day you ask yourself whether it was
right for him to die so; the day you ask yourself: 'What can I do so that

another shall not be made to die under such grisly circumstances?' – that day, my son, you'll become a man. Just now you are a beast and the girl was right to call you a brute.[37]

At the end of the movement, when the peasant woman seems to have disappeared and Boy is beginning to lose his new-found confidence –

[. . . *a whisper breaks through the air*]

Woman's voice: The day you'll ask yourself. . . . What can I do so that another shall not die under such grisly circumstances . . . that day, my son, you'll become a man.

Boy: The Trial of Dedan Kimathi. I must be there to hear it.[38]

The voice re-echoes again, later, when he is trying to persuade Girl to join him in his new-found purpose, and the same words are repeated:

. . . That day you'll become a man.

[*Boy is mesmerized as if in a trance*]

Girl: What's it?

Boy: Didn't you hear her?

Girl: Who?

Boy: The woman.

Girl: When? Where? Why do you tremble so? [*She asks that resting her hand on his shoulder*]

Boy: No, no, not now, Mama.
But how can I turn
Against her call
And
Live?[39]

This stage device is used for the same purpose as it is in *Ovonramwen Nogbaisi*: it allows us into the mind of a particular character.

However, the effect of the repeated statements in their respective plays is the opposite of each other: Ovonramwen's fatalistic warning by the Yoruba oracle at Ile-Ife, 'Caution!' robs the Oba of the power to act; while Boy's admonition by the peasant woman (representing the masses rather than an establishment priesthood) spurs him on to act. The Oba's confidence is destroyed; the youth's is restored.

The opening dance and mime in *Ovonramwen Nogbaisi* and *The*

Trial of Dedan Kimathi can also be seen – superficially at least – as the same stage device used for a similar purpose: the creation of a composite stage image of suffering. Rotimi's scene is more or less a tableau (repeated again with some variation at the end of the play); but Ngugi and Mugo have a concern to show not just the suffering but its causes and inevitable consequences in terms of the class struggle. In terms of meaning, therefore, Rotimi's scene could be said to be passive or static: suffering is seen as unending; the Kenyan's scene could be seen as dynamic: suffering is replaced by a struggle towards total liberation.

Other elements of stylization in *The Trial of Dedan Kimathi* tend to reinforce this determination of the playwrights to explain the reasons why things happen in a certain way and how they can be changed. Thus, the four trials which Kimathi undergoes are symbolic because they represent 'temptations' to end the struggle; and their apparent reasonableness has to be answered by a deeper analysis.

Kimathi is appealed to first by Shaw Henderson, described as the 'friend and killer of the Africans', who offers to save Kimathi's life if only he will plead guilty. Henderson appears in the jail as Kimathi is remembering, vividly, his childhood along the ridges, and his mother, who has now gone mad. He feels guilty about her, and Henderson's first words to him catch his mood: 'Hey, Dedan, Field Marshal. Guilty visitation?' Henderson represents the liberal colonialist's point of view. Give in, he tells Kimathi. 'You can name your prize. You'll have your life. Only we must end this strife. . . .' Kimathi replies:

My life is our People
Struggling
Fighting
Not like you to maintain
Slavery
Oppression
Exploitation
But
To end slavery, exploitation,
Modern cannibalism. Out. Rat.[40]

In the second trial the offer is more attractive. These 'tempters' now represent British, or European, big business. They appear in the cell as Kimathi is agonizing over how disease and poverty can be wiped out. Again, the first words of the intruders catch the tone of his honest doubt: 'You are right, Dedan. Hunger, disease. Ignorance. Those are the true enemies of your people'. There is an Indian businessman accompanying the European banker, as well as a silent, nodding, African businessman in this delegation. They offer the solution of 'a black man's government. In partnership' – if only he'll confess and plead guilty. Their rationale is summed up by the banker:

> Toilers there will always be. Even in America, England, France, Germany, Switzerland, Sweden, Japan . . . all the civilised world. There are servants and masters . . . sellers of labour and buyers of labour. Masters and servants.[41]

This, for Kimathi, is no better than colonization: 'The religion of enslavement! Like colonialism which makes the colonized sweat and bleed while master comes to harvest'.

In the third trial the stakes are even higher, the offer more tempting. This time the delegation is all African: a businessman, a politician and a priest. The Business Executive asks Kimathi: 'Don't you think we have won the war?' But winning the war means something completely different for these Africans than it does for Kimathi. Freedom for these pragmatists, capitalists, means personal gain: 'Black skins, colonial settlers' hearts. . . . I now understand . . . loans . . . token shares in banks, companies. . . . Grab shops. . . . Grab gems, Transport Buses, land. . . . Grab, Grab, Grab'.[42] The priest is with them. Kimathi asks him: 'Can it be wrong even in the eyes of your God for a people to fight against exploitation?' And after they have gone, he agonizes:

> Who are friends and who enemies?
> Oh, the agony of a lone battle!
> But I will fight on to the end
> Alone. . . .
> Alone, did I say?
> No. Cast out these doubts![43]

The fourth trial is a physical assault on Kimathi, by Shaw Henderson again, but this time in a very different mien. Now he is the Torturer. The audience witness, partially in a blackout on the stage, Kimathi being violently tortured. This trial becomes as much a scourging as a 'temptation'. Despite the pain and degradation, Kimathi refuses to recant and plead guilty.

There are other symbolic groupings on the stage. The courtroom scene occurs three times. It is the same event on the first two occasions, namely Kimathi's first appearance before the white judge which results in an adjournment. The third court scene – the climax of the play – is Kimathi's reappearance in court and pronouncement of the death sentence upon him. Whites and Africans are symbolically divided in the court-room:

> [*In court, blacks and whites sit on separate sides. It is as if a huge gulf lies between them. The air is still and tense . . .*][44]

In the final court-house scene the whites' side now contains, symbolically, the blacks whom we earlier saw as some of Kimathi's 'tempters'. The blacks' side, made up of people in very ragged clothes, consistently supports Kimathi whenever he speaks. The whites are settlers, and they react towards Kimathi with frenzied hate. With Kimathi in chains in the dock, challenging the white judge's right to try him, the scene visually shows how Kimathi brings the oppressors into confrontation with the oppressed.

In another scene, at the beginning of the Third Movement, Woman, Boy and Girl are brought together in a symbolic grouping:

> [*They move a little way off. Both* **Girl** *and* **Boy** *sit at the feet of the* **Woman**. *It should be symbolic: the* **Woman** *now represents all the working mothers talking to their children*][45]

Finally, time itself is symbolically distorted in the play:

The action should on the whole be seen as breaking the barrier between formal and infinite time, so that past and future and present flow into one another.[46]

The reason for this is to link dramatically cause and effect. In a structural sense we could see the dances and the mimes as representing the past; Woman, Boy and Girl as representing the present looking to the future; Dedan Kimathi, through his social vision, is the validation of that future. Without Kimathi there is no future for the likes of the youth and the girl, the modern urban unemployed. We must keep returning to the past in order to understand the future; but this is not to say that the action of the play is cyclic (as the staging techniques in *Ovonramwen Nogbaisi* seem to indicate the action in that play is). The story of the Woman, Boy and Girl moves forward chronologically; Kimathi's court-house trial culminates in the death sentence. These two events are brought together in the one climax: Kimathi's death is nullified by the decisive action of the young people. They have become the makers of history.

The central concern of the playwrights in writing *The Trial of Dedan Kimathi* is much the same as Hussein's in *Kinjeketile*: to come to a wider consciousness, a greater understanding. The peasant woman tells the boy: 'What is it you don't understand? The things I talk about are written all over, written like large signs everywhere . . .'[47] This question of understanding has, as its corollary, the concept of unity. The woman later tells the girl: 'United, our strength becomes the faith that moves mountains'. Kimathi, too, constantly talks of unity:

> But
> Stronger than any machine-gun fire. . . .
> Is our unity and discipline in struggle. . . .[48]

His vision of unity is specific: it is national, Kenyan, not regional or tribal on the one hand, nor pan-Africanist or international socialist on the other:

> Hear me. Kenya is one indivisible whole. The cause we fight for is
> larger than provinces; it shatters ethnic barriers.
> It is a whole people's cause. . . .[49]

This emphasis on the national dimension of the struggle for freedom is important – we saw an undeveloped form of it in Kinjeketile's concern for unity among the different tribes – and it is very much an African perspective.

However, in a curious way there is a deeper and perhaps unconscious structure in the play, which reflects the paradigm of the sacrifice of the god, in this instance epitomized by the Christian Eucharist: the temptation, betrayal, scourging, death and resurrection. Kimathi, like Christ, is judged by his accusers. He has been betrayed by his own fellow-fighters, including Wambararia his brother, as Christ was betrayed by one of his disciples, Judas Iscariot. The temptations which Christ suffered in the wilderness are reflected in the first three of the four trials which Kimathi undergoes: the 'half-way solutions' (which are not solutions at all) to the poverty and oppression of the masses. These 'solutions' are seen by the hero-sufferer to be contradictions of the redemption of his fellow-sufferers, and they need to be resisted. This deep accord with the mass of humanity fundamentally opposes the self-interest of the oppressor: the hero-sufferer, or the new god, becomes a threat and is scourged. Kimathi is tortured in the fourth trial, as Christ was scourged before being led to the cross. Christ's death upon the cross was followed three days later by his resurrection, attested to by his followers. The triumph of Kimathi over his death is the crux of Mugo's and Ngugi's play. They refer, in the preface, to their visit to Kimathi's birth-place and to the attitude of the people there:

He was clearly their beloved son, their respected leader and they talked of him as still being alive. 'Kimathi will never die,' the woman said. 'But of course if you people have killed him, go and show us his grave!' She said this in a strange tone of voice, between defiance and bitterness, and for a minute we all kept quiet.

This worries the authors: 'Why then the sudden hostility when one of us raised the question of Kimathi's death?' They don't answer this question directly; but relate Kimathi to the wider sweep of history which shows '. . . the masses (symbolized by Kimathi) . . . as the true makers of history'. This, they maintain '. . . would be in the spirit of the woman who told us that Kimathi would never die'. In the final climactic moment of the play the judge, having passed sentence, goes out of the court. Boy and Girl stand up and move swiftly to Kimathi. Note what happens next: Girl breaks the bread – reminiscent of the Christian Eucharist, this – inside of which is the gun. Boy and Girl simultaneously hold the gun and shout 'Not dead!'. The next stage direction indicates the way the transition from one state of being to another is to be presented on the stage:

[*Utter commotion as a struggle between opposing forces ensues. A loud shot is heard. Sudden darkness falls, but only for a moment: for soon, the stage gives way to a mighty crowd of workers and peasants at the centre of which are* **Boy** *and* **Girl**, *singing a thunderous freedom song. All the soldiers are gone, except for the* **First Soldier** *who shyly joins in the singing from behind*][50]

The absence of any opposing forces on the stage and the celebratory nature of the song depicts the promised state of total freedom, finally achieved. It is the very essence of the Eucharist, which in Christian parlance means not only the sacrament of holy mass, and in particular the consecrated bread which is symbolically, but in a more general sense, 'thanksgiving'. It is also the 'celebration' with which Soyinka ends his version of Euripides's *The Bacchae* (though, as we saw, not the way Euripides ended his own play): thanksgiving for the bounty of the god – whether it be nature's productiveness and eternal renewal, or eternal life here-after, or total freedom of the oppressed.

Although Kimathi, and Woman, argue against Christianity at various times, the context of their argument is still religious. For example, Woman tells the youth that she was a '. . . bad woman . . . a lost stinking life . . . until I heard the call'. Boy, naturally, asks 'Of Jesus?' To which Woman replies: 'The call of our people. The humiliated, the injured, the insulted, the exploited, the submerged millions of labouring men and women of Kenya'.[51]

Or again, in the third trial in the cell, the black priest tells Kimathi: 'Jesus will never betray you'. Ironically, it is Kimathi who will never betray the cause – who, like Goethe's Faust, holds a belief in man's final triumph over his social and physical limitations:

> . . . I have spoken with the God of my ancestors . . . and not once did he counsel me to barter for my soul. One day . . . I thought I saw a glimpse of Kenya to come: workers joining hands from the Coast to the Lake, making rivers, volcanoes, thunderbolts in the sky, making all these power monsters of nature administer to their needs and desires. Man slave of Nature? Nature slave of man. . . .(pp. 49, 50)

Goethe's Faust was eventually saved. Kimathi's answer to the priest, like Soyinka's Greek god Dionysos to the priest Tiresias, contains a greater sense of religious purpose than that which the 'official' religion has come to embody.

It is important, finally, to work out the precise difference, if we can, between the religious dimension of this play and that of *Kinjeketile*. In the latter we saw that religion was being under-mined from within. Kinjeketile found himself asking if Hongo, their mediating spirit of God, would betray them to the God of the Arabs of Zanzibar, so that they would then exchange the Germans for the Arabs as their masters. In the end, religion is set against reason: Kitunda tells his fighters: 'I don't want people to die because of some silly beliefs and superstitions'. Characters in the play are deliberately made to adopt a religious stance while the thrust of the play as a whole deliberately sets out to undermine any sort of religious approach.

The Trial of Dedan Kimathi is almost exactly the reverse in its use of the religious dimension. The characters adopt an anti-religious stance; and, indeed, the play is consciously structured to express the same meaning as *Kinjeketile*. However, an alternative, and perhaps unconscious, structure at a deeper level moves in a contrary direction as the Christ-like hero struggles against the people's oppressors. Indeed, the people's hero is in danger of being depicted as the people's god.

Furthermore, the play's complicated theatricality (which makes any performance of it dependent upon the technical resources of stage lighting, amplified sound, levels and effects), suggests that its intended audiences are not so much the Kenyan masses, as African intellectuals – whose political consciousness demands an intellectualized framework in which this consciousness can be culturally situated.

Having made this analysis I must stress that Ngugi himself has clearly transcended this rather rhetorical level of political commitment to the masses. The economic and political analysis of Kenyan society in his subsequent novel, *Petals of Blood*, is much more rigorous and disciplined. And after *Petals of Blood* he became involved with a community-based adult education project at Kamiriithu, which collaboration resulted in the play *Ngaahika Ndeenda* which was performed in Gikuyu at Kamirithu to audiences who had walked miles through the bush to see the play. The objective was to entertain them through the process of raising their political consciousness; for this Ngugi was imprisoned for a year.[52]

If a play reflects the people as the makers of history, it must also make that history accessible to them as drama. Otherwise it may just as easily deprive the masses of their history altogether.

Black Mamba Plays Kabwe Kasoma

Kabwe Kasoma is not generally well-known as a playwright outside of Zambia. Like Ebrahim Hussein in Tanzania, he has an overriding commitment to creating local audiences for a theatre which is part of the process of national development. He was a member of the United National Independence Party (UNIP), the Party that has ruled Zambia since independence in 1964, during the struggle to oust colonialism. His interest in theatre springs from his love of the performing arts generally and of acting in particular and from a desire to take theatre to the people as a continuing form of conscientization:

. . . Theatre which engages in art for art's sake is a luxury in Africa. Our theatre must therefore be totally committed to national development. I have always regarded it as a most powerful communication tool in national development plans. I have always seen it as a vehicle for critical appraisal of government plans that are faulty (with all the dangers that this entails for the social health of the dramatists).[53]

Kasoma has written and produced many plays.[54] The three *Black Mamba Plays* together, completed in 1971 and not published except for *Black Mamba Two*, form his major dramatic work so far. The criterion for all his plays, including these three, is the accessibility of what he wants to say to a mass urban or rural audience. He has commented that a people's theatre should be able to be performed anywhere, so that 'the theatre can go to the people rather than expect the people to come to the theatre'. His criteria also embrace the circumstances of traditional performances – stories or dances, songs and meetings – so that the audience is relaxed and engaged in the event: it is their event. In the same Lagos paper, quoted above, he has written:

In the contemporary African theatre of commitment I expect the audience to be provoked not only into making comments on the action on stage, but actually to interrupt the stage action by arguing or disagreeing with the actors. . . .

Opponents of this type of theatre argue that it is chaotic, that the audience's direct participation into the play will tend to derail the players off their line tracks. Very true. But I am thinking of a theatre that allows for and anticipates such interruptions. The play script should contain a large component of improvisation within the context of the message the play intends to portray to the target audience. It is amazing how the quarrel between a government official and the players in a Kitwe show of *The Poisoned Cultural Meat* kept within the intended message.

Kasoma's plays are often sharply critical of government practice and policy; but he often suffers from being seen as the 'man in the middle'. Intellectuals sometimes accuse him of being the mouthpiece of the government and the Party; officials regard him as 'rocking the boat' in his use of theatre as a potentially dangerous political weapon with regard to the masses.

His plays make use of music and dance as reflected in the traditional performances, but also as reflected in the songs and chants that were developed during the struggle for independence. More important is his use of a variety of languages in a single play. He recognizes that any urban audience made up of the Zambian masses will not be linguistically homogeneous, and his urban plays reflect the linguistic mix within the ranks of his audiences. He uses registers of English, the main Zambian languages, and the urban argot; he advises his actors to be attuned to the language preferences of each audience they perform before, and to adjust the language or languages of the play's dialogue accordingly. Certain types of English are used creatively to reinforce the characterization. This use of language, as well as of the actual songs and dances of the struggle for independence is manifest in the *Black Mamba Plays*.

Kasoma tends to make his plays very directly. Each scene must make a point in the overall argument, as well as carry the story forward; and any stage devices used are obvious in themselves and are intended to make the meaning obvious. Indeed, as a dramatist he comes much nearer to the author of *The Contest*, Mukotani Rugyendo, than any other playwright whose work we have considered. Kasoma tells the producer of his plays: whatever works, use it; use the songs, the languages familiar to your own audiences. The primary concern is to communicate with the audience, rather than to perform before them. The texts of the plays, therefore, are somewhat more inaccessible to the reader than most other play-texts, partly because of the different languages used, and partly because of being written for audience engagement.

The history which forms the base of the *Black Mamba Plays* is Kaunda's *Zambia Shall Be Free* and although Kaunda is the central character, the plays are not so much about Kenneth Kaunda as they are an expression of his point of view. Although we see people responding to his leadership, he never really emerges as the hero. He is not shown, for example, as having the charisma the late Mwansa Kapwepwe has, in the play.

There are three plays: *Black Mamba One*, *Black Mamba Two* and *Black Mamba Three*. They are a trilogy, though their publication as a trilogy in Zambia was followed immediately by the text and any future performance of the text, being banned by the government.[55] The only one of the plays published elsewhere (in London) is *Black Mamba Two*. The three plays do not have a uniform style. *Black Mamba One* is a straightforward, sequential drama about Kenneth Kaunda and Simon Kapwepwe as mission boys (Kaunda's father was a reverend; Kapwepwe himself was not of the mission in the same way as Kaunda), youths and young men. There is little elaboration and the story-line is tenuous: the two lads meet through a fist fight; they get their teacher's certificates; they go to Lusaka during the Second World War to find employment as army instructors. They are only employed for a day before being considered undesirables and slung out. After sleeping rough in the market Kapwepwe goes back to the rural areas; Kaunda goes to Southern Rhodesia in search of a mission job which doesn't materialize. This play perhaps reflects more than anything else the limited horizons and non-existent opportunities for even the most intelligent blacks – perhaps especially for the most intelligent – at this colonial period.

It was these increasingly politicized blacks who were described by the colonialists as 'black mambas', for the black mamba was a deadly poisonous snake, common in Central Africa.

Black Mamba Two shows Kaunda organizing strikes and protests with the leader of the African National Congress, Harry Nkumbula. It shows the Party and Congress being established in the rural areas, and organizing strikes on the copper mines. Again the story-line is tenuous, more a series of vignettes: the visit of the District Officer to a village and being confronted by a black ex-serviceman, Chipayeni, who is imprisoned for his insolence; Kaunda involved in establishing Congress in that same village and using Chipayeni to help him; scenes of political activism on the Copperbelt; finally, the arrest of Nkumbula, Kaunda, Kapwepwe, Kalulu and Kamanga – the 'black mambas' – caught at last.

Black Mamba Three is concerned with the later stages of the struggle for independence, during the Central African Federation, and the final achievement of Zambian nationhood. This play, too, is episodic like the others, but it is much more complex. Whereas previously the fight was simply African against the white colonialists, now the fight is both with them and within the movement (showing the breaking-away of Kaunda's ZANC from Nkumbula's ANC and then the formation of UNIP, headed by Kaunda when he comes out of prison). The whites themselves are beginning to divide in their response to African nationalism.

The divisions among the black leadership are reflected in the confusion at the grass roots, which is further exacerbated over the radio by the colonialist propaganda. Political protest becomes violent and eventually a constitutional conference in London is called which grants Zambia independence. The play ends with the celebrations marking independence: the arrival of the President-designate and the Princess Royal; the lowering of the union jack and the raising of the Zambian flag; cheering, anthems, and a fireworks display.

The episodic nature of the plays includes the great sweep of events encompassed, all shown directly upon a stage in front of the audience: Governor, drunks, colonialists, organizers, militants, strikers, families and their live-stock, a lion, the Princess Royal and a fireworks display, news bulletins, crucial executive meetings and scenes in prisons, the Governor scheming with whites, school-boys fighting. All this might easily distract the reader from the very careful structuring of the action in the second and third of the plays.

In *Black Mamba Two*, for instance, the first three scenes have been very carefully organized so that scene 3 is a mirror of scene 1, with scene 2 as a crucial transition. It is worth looking at them closely. In scene 1, the District Officer, Captain Good-fellow, visits the village of Chief Chibesakunda. Goodfellow epitomizes the oppression of the colonial occupation. He is carried into the village on a machila, speaks only through interpreters, collects the head tax making no concessions, humiliates the chief, demands to be supplied with food and shelter. In the process of this degrading ceremony, Goodfellow is challenged by the re-turned ex-soldier, Chipayeni. In the play, Chipayeni is skilfully introduced:

[*A young man in an old King's African Rifles coat, with regimental stripes is seen walking in a leisurely way from his hut to the grain-store as if nothing is happening in the village. He is wearing old army boots and is carrying a stick under his armpit as a sergeant's cane*]

Captain Goodfellow: [*Noticing the cheeky ex-soldier*] Hey look! [*Pointing*] Look there. What does that baboon think he is?

The DO's reaction is to have the chief beaten and to order Chipayeni to be brought in front of him. What happens next is an economical dramatic representation of the historical significance of the returned ex-serviceman in the rise of political consciousness:

[*Every villager is filled with fear for the mad returned ex-soldier. They all watch the Bwana (**Goodfellow**) who is trembling with rage*]

Captain Goodfellow: What a cheap baboon this is! Is that the teaching of the stupid war? I have never been so insulted by a kaffir. What makes you think you have the right to insult me . . . a District Officer?

Chipayeni: I am ready for insult the Gavinala imselufu. Why you finki you are?

Captain Goodfellow: [*Stammering with uncontrollable rage and stamping his foot*] You . . . you . . . you, a nigger, have the cheek to insult the King's representative! You, a stinking baboon, whose tail stump is still showing from late evolution, are insulting the King himself! I cannot judge your case, kaffir. The higher authorities will.

Chipayeni: I am insult even King Joliji imselefu. You white people is all liars. You tell us if we fighting for you, we receiving gifts from King. Dey say if we fight Germans, the King and Gavinala dey give us farms, money, ploughs, clothes and does who education a bit to get good jobs for mines and Gavament. Where is money, farms, and ploughs and mine jobs now?

[*The DO is taken completely unawares.* **Chipayeni** *is speaking the truth, and this increases his anger. He furtively looks around to detect any possible support for the returned soldier. There is none. The crowd is engaged in a general murmur of disapproval*][56]

After this, Chipayeni moves into speaking Bemba, and speaking directly to the other villagers. He criticizes them strongly for complying in their humiliation and for not joining Congress. When Chipayeni's speech is translated for the 'Bwana', he works himself up into a fury:

. . . I will have none of this Congress nonsense in my district and particularly in this village. If you allow any such political baboons as Unkumbula or Kaunda in the village it will be . . . life imprisonment! Do you hear? [*To the* **Clerk**] Tell him.

But the Clerk comes from another part of the country and can only render the DO's words in 'broken Nyanja-Bemba'. Chipayeni is ordered to be beaten, but he refuses to let the Messenger grab him and acts as though he were in charge of a platoon of soldiers. However, he is eventually beaten and tied up to a tree prior to being taken off to jail.

After this exhibition of colonial thuggery, Goodfellow – the irony in his name is deliberate – demands his food which is reluctantly brought to him. The scene ends with the song: 'Whitemen are cunning / They have taken over our country / Sorrow and misery / . . . . / What shall we do?'[57]

This scene functions on a number of levels: levels of language use, of individual characterization, of historical reference, which cover the brutalism of the colonial presence, the compliance of the blacks – from other parts of the country – who form the DO's entourage, the submissiveness of the villagers, and the lone rebellion of Chipayeni, the returned ex-soldier, who is able to expose the system.

This scene would rouse the anger of an audience. It is immediately followed by a transitional scene in which Kaunda confronts a lion which eventually allows him to pass. Like the fabled exploits of Dedan Kimathi, which Boy and Girl repeat, this particular episode has had great significance for many Zambians. Kasoma, in the play, indicates why. As Kaunda outstares the lion he says:

> It might be one of the departed great ones.
> If you are one of those great chiefs;
> If you are Mubanga Chipoya, Kapalakasha;
> If you are Chitapankwa;
> If you are Nkole – Mfumu – let your son pass.
> Let your son go to do your bidding.
> To free this land, the land you left your children,
> From the hands of foreign vultures.[58]

He passes on to Chibesakunda's village, where the next scene, scene 3, takes place. It is several months after the DO's visit and Chipayeni has been released. Kaunda's visit to the village takes the same form as the DO's, yet it is the exact opposite of it in every other way. Kaunda comes in on a bicycle; the people all attend his meeting – voluntarily; Chipayeni is accorded respect, and the example of his service and present opposition to the colonial authority is the peg on which Kaunda hangs his explanations of the situation for the benefit of the villagers' understanding. He shows them a picture of Nkumbula:

> This man Mwaanga Nkumbula, son of the Tonga, is prepared to die for us all. Why is he prepared to die? In order that you and me are free in the land of our birth.[59]

Kaunda asks for subscriptions, which are very low, and those that haven't got the money, give in kind – willingly giving to Kaunda what they had been forced to give the white DO:

Second Villager: I have no money. But here is a hen. You may sell it if you like. But please let me have the ANC card.

> [*Many others who have no money to buy the membership cards pay in kind; they bring hens, eggs, millet in baskets, and beans and groundnuts in pots*][60]

After these three scenes, the action of the play moves to the urban Copperbelt. There is a scene in which Kaunda and Nkumbula get thrown out of a whites-only mines' mess. They get arrested by Constable Hantuba. The scene shifts to the charge office, where the officer commanding Kitwe Division of the Police Force is none other than Captain Goodfellow, who actually, ageless almost, weaves in and out of all three plays in various official roles that prop up the white rule in the territory. It is similar to the characterization of Shaw Henderson in *The Trial of Dedan Kimathi*, but Goodfellow is both more of a caricature and yet much more carefully observed than Shaw Henderson. The way Goodfellow keeps cropping up in different offices, behind the big desk, to which the 'black mambas' are continually dragged, powerfully conveys both the monotony of the struggle and the tenacity of white rule that needs to be undermined. It also enables the playwright to show a hardening of the attitude of the political activists to the white authority, until, in *Black Mamba Three*, in the final scene in which we see Goodfellow, this time as prison warder in the detention camp, he is chased around his office by an outraged Kaunda who is his political prisoner:

Captain Goodfellow: Messenger! [*Enter the* **Messenger** *who quickly stands between them*]

Messenger: Please, my son, Do not hurt the Bwana. Please from me as if from your father. Go back outside to your place. [**Kaunda** *looks at the old* **Messenger**, *and then at the trembling DO*]

Kaunda: I respect the Messenger more than I do you.

[**Kaunda** *goes out.* **Goodfellow** *goes out by another door. The* **Messenger** *is left alone. Gradually he begins to smile. He takes off the messenger's hat and laughs wildly at length. Drumming comes from backstage.* **Messenger** *performs a sexy Luvale dance, old though he is, and dances off the stage*][61]

The writing in this little scene has an unexpected focus: the old Messenger; not Kaunda or Goodfellow. The Messenger saves the whiteman from Kaunda's anger; and Kaunda recognizes the old man's inherent decency, his humanity, in doing so. The Messenger's dignity as a man, beneath his degrading government position, has been established for him by Kaunda's single line. At last the people are beginning to sense their liberation.

All three plays have as their real focus, in fact, the so-called common man, the ordinary folk. In *Black Mamba One*, Kaunda and Kapwepwe, as youths from the rural areas in the town, are the dispossessed peasantry. In the next two plays they are the leaders. Their role and their destiny in the widening struggle makes them special. Even in the first scene in *Black Mamba Two* when we see him, he is established as one 'chosen' by the ancestors. It is Chipayeni and his fellow villagers now who are Kasoma's characterization of the masses. So are the black miners on the Copperbelt who are on strike. This is clearly established by the following stage direction:

The action moves to an African Mine Township at Nkana Mine. Black miners are on strike. Boots and protected clothing lie neglected about the place. The miners while away the hours playing solo or cards, while others lie about drunkenly. Their womenfolk go about their usual domestic chores, chatting, gossiping, and calling to each other or to the children. A group of other miners are listening and dancing to music from a radiogram. Most of them are discussing the politics of the day. Actors playing the parts of the striking miners must improvise their own lines here.[62]

This very public scene shifts to the court where the action brought against ANC declaring the strike illegal is thrown out. There is much rejoicing. It is a climax which the whole strike scene has built up to and it is immediately followed by an intensely private scene which shows Kaunda being arrested in his bed in the middle of the night in front of his family. The scene moves to the charge office where all the other 'black mambas' are. They have been arrested as well. The victory of the previous scene is now replaced by the painful defeat of this scene – which in fact ends this play in the trilogy.

The two scenes are further harmonized, structurally, and made into one unit by the use of the radio news bulletins. After the opening improvisation in the strike scene, the radio voice is heard:

Voice [*From the FBC Radio*]   This is the Federal Broadcasting Corporation, broadcasting from Salisbury. [*All collect round the radio to listen to the latest news, except those who do not understand English*] Here is the news read by Len Miles. The Federal Prime Minister, Sir Roy Welensky has warned. . . .[63]

There follows, as a new bulletin, a summary of the action we are now in the midst of on stage. This, of course, immediately makes the improvisation (of the miners on strike) absolutely clear to the audience. There really was a newsreader in the FBC called Len Miles and Kasoma has caught the tone of the radio news. It is an inspired stage device: first, as we have said, it explains the scene; second, on a purely naturalistic level, the news bulletin was of great importance in the lives of the people; third, it enables the dramatist to situate precisely the action we are about to see; fourth, we are actually shown 'the biases of colonial history' in opera-tion – there is a deliberate example of this in *Black Mamba Three* (which we will be coming to later) – and contradicted by the very actions of the people we are watching; fifth, it can show the people as 'the true makers of history': the news, broadcast by the oppressors has been forced to be about the very people listening.

At the end of the next scene, the arrest of Kaunda and the rest, there is another news-cast, also by Len Miles, announcing their arrest. The colonialists have reasserted themselves; the news is now about them:

. . . The Governor of Northern Rhodesia, Sir Arthur Benson, opened a new wing of hostels at the Oppenheimer College of Social Work this morning.

And here is a late news item: Harry Unkumbula, Kenneth Kaunda, Simon Kapwepwe and Reuben Kamanga, have all been sentenced to two months' imprisonment with hard labour. . . .[64]

This is followed by the singing of the Congress Solidarity Song (which has formed the *leitmotiv* of the whole of *Black Mamba Two*) as the four 'black mambas' as prisoners, with their warders, cross the stage:

. . . They are wearing prisoners' uniforms and they are carrying picks and shovels, rakes and a wheelbarrow. They are dirty all over. . . .[65]

In *Black Mamba Three* the issues which have been raised in *Black Mamba Two* are taken up and developed. The 'common man' is now represented by a most unlikely character: he is a drunkard in the domestic employ of the Governor, Sir Arthur Benson, and his name, ironically, is Pretoria. His actions through-out the play are deliberately contradictory – deliberately, because he stands in the middle, between the Party militants and the other blacks: the stooges, the policemen, government employees, ser-vants and those black politicians anxious to do deals with the more liberal whites.

Pretoria gleans information, as one of the Governor's domes-tics, which he passes on to the Party. At the beginning of the play the Party is still the unified Congress. The focus of the action in the first half of the play is the boycott of the government beerhalls which was called by Congress, and then called off, unilaterally, by Congress leader, Nkumbula, who is increasingly shown as a drunkard, colluding more and more with the whites, in particular with Harry Franklin. Pretoria, a drunkard himself, is opposed to the boycott. He gets beaten up by the Party militants – and then hears his 'death' reported on the radio:

Militant 2:   Punch the idiot! Teach him not to go against Congress orders. [*The militants beat up* **Pretoria**, *shouting 'Freedom! One man one vote!' Presently police arrive on the scene.* **Militants 1** *and* **2** *are arrested as the rest scatter and run away.* **Pretoria** *is lifted by the police from the ground where he lies bleeding . . .*]

He re-enters, after the Congress song, bandaged and limping, and carrying his portable radio:

Pretoria: Well my friends. I learnt my lesson. I am not going to the beerhall today. No one is going. They all fear Congress. And the beer is rotting. The Gavment is very angry for Congress. . . .

The radio news comes on.

Voice: This is the Federal Broadcasting Corporation, broadcasting from Salisbury. Here is the news read by Len Miles. The Northern Rhodesia African National Congress boycott of Municipal beerhalls enters its fourth day today. But many Africans are still patronising the Municipal beerhalls despite the Congress boycott. One African, identified as Pretoria Chidehi, was beaten to death – [**Pretoria** *shows surprise*] – by Congress thugs as he left a Lusaka beerhall . . .

Pretoria: [*turns off his radio and turns to the audience*] You see, my friends, now Gavment is tell lie. My name is Pretoria. And I am very much alive. There is no one drink in beerhall. I am eye-witness. Ha! Now I am know what to believe in newspapers.

Pretoria then informs the audience that he has seen Nkumbula drinking with Harry Franklin in white men's bars: '. . . Why is he drink himself and with whitemen? [*With determination*] I am going to the beerhall myself'.

The militants find him drinking again; but an announcement on the radio by Len Miles informs them that Nkumbula has disso- ciated himself from the boycott. The militants get into an argu- ment with the black police constables and find that they have been left high and dry. This political action had become a fiasco and the issue comes up in the next scene when Congress Executive meets – and Nkumbula arrives with Harry Franklin. This scene, in essence, is the same as the Second and Third Trial scenes in Kimathi's cell: it is the rejection of a sell-out. However, in *The Trial of Dedan Kimathi* the meaning is expressed through one man and in a generalized ideological form. In *Black Mamba Three* the meaning is couched in the particular political circumstances of the moment. Kaunda, Kapwepwe and the others opposing Nkumbula, are trapped in a specific situation – a moment in history – and the issues have to be sorted out in that context.

The split in the ranks of the leadership brings us back to Pretoria and his radio. One minute he is going to join Kaunda's breakaway party, ZANC; the next minute he is thrown into confusion by Nkumbula getting elected to the Legislative Council. We see a drive for membership of ZANC, which has now become an overtly socialist party. Inevitably, the leaders of this party get arrested. There is a sustained middle section of the play which conveys this hiatus in the struggle: the leaders' families wait at home, keeping going through the dull routine, day by day; Kaunda and the others, separated, wait in detention and then in prison also following their daily routine. But the political pressure is building up in the countryside and Kaunda comes out of jail to lead it.

The pace of the play quickens as it moves to the conclusion with the granting of independence. There is a kaleidoscope of actions, reactions, personalities, events, passing across the stage: images, fleetingly, of a recent and familiar past. It is difficult to produce, not because of the need for specialized stage technology such as sophisticated stage lighting and elaborate sets, but because of the scope and quantity of the basic elements of drama: actors, and props and costumes as well; and all needing to be carefully co-ordinated. But done properly, whether it be on a football field on a Sunday afternoon, or in a theatre, the meaning is clear: this was what the people had fought for and achieved.

The play stops at independence, and makes no statement about Zambia's development since independence. It is interesting to compare it in this respect with *The Trial of Dedan Kimathi* which seeks to mount a critique of Kenyan nationhood by suggesting that the struggle of the masses was betrayed by the political and economic arrangements at independence. The struggle for the total independence of the Kenyan masses continues. Kasoma's play, on the other hand, seeks to recapture the optimistic spirit of the times so that his audiences may contrast it with the present frustrations and disillusionment. *Black Mamba Three* is very much a play about an historical moment, Independence, rather than a play about a concept: freedom, independence.

Notes and references

1 I have not dealt with the francophone African plays (see the Introduction) nor have I listed more than those mentioned in the text in the bibliography. Francophone studies of African drama quite naturally concentrate on francophone texts.

See Bakary Traore, *Le théâtre Négro-Africain et ses fonctions sociales* (Paris: Présence Africaine 1958). This is translated into English by Dapo Adelugba, *The Black African Theatre and its social functions* (Ibadan: Ibadan University Press 1972). Robert Cornevin, *Le théâtre en Afrique noire et à Madagascar* (Paris: Le livre Africain 1970). Clive Wake has a short but useful chapter, in English, on theatre in the francophone African states in Martin Banham, *African Theatre Today* (London: Pitman 1976). There is also a collection of papers, *Actes du Colloque sur le théâtre négro-africain* (Paris: Présence Africaine 1971).

2 For relevant historical studies of Benin during this period see: Alan Ryder, *Benin and the Europeans 1485–1897* (London: Longman 1969, paperback 1977), especially Chapter 7; Philip Aigbona Igbafe, *Benin under British Administration* (London: Longman 1979), especially chapters 1 and 2.

3 Ola Rotimi, *Ovonramwen Nogbaisi* (Ibadan: Oxford University Press 1974), p. 79.

4 ibid., p. 60.

5 ibid., p. 34.

6 ibid., pp. 35–6.

7 ibid., p. 37.

8 ibid., p. 16.

9 ibid., p. 20.

10 ibid., p. 23.

11 ibid., p. 31.

12 ibid., p. 36.

13 ibid., p. 53–4.

14 ibid., p. 67.

15 ibid., p. 79.

16 An account from the colonial records of the Maji-Maji Uprising is given in W. O. Henderson, 'German East Africa,

1884–1918', in Vincent Harlowe and E. M. Chilver (eds.), *History of East Africa*, vol. II (London: Oxford University Press 1965). A more detailed account is in John Iliffe, *Tanganyika Under German Rule, 1905–12* (Cambridge: Cambridge University Press 1969).

17 Ebrahim N. Hussein, *Kinjeketile* (Dar es Salaam: Oxford University Press 1970), p. 10.

18 ibid., p. 8.

19 ibid., p. 16.

20 ibid., p. 21.

21 ibid., p. 27.

22 ibid., p. 28.

23 ibid., p. 29.

24 ibid.

25 ibid., p. 32. Hussein, in the introduction to his play-text, describes the religious beliefs of the Wamatumbi. After God (*Mungu*) and the minor gods (*miungu*) there are the spirits (*mizimu* and *pepo*): 'Hongo is a spirit. . . . He possesses Kinjeketile but the course of action he reveals to him, involving possible bloodshed, is above his domain. But as he is also the mediator between man and God, makes Kinjeketile's dilemma all the more intensive, together with the fact that Kinjeketile is in turn mediator between men, Hongo, the *misiumu*, the *miungu* and *Mungu* (God).'

26 ibid., p. 36.

27 ibid.

28 ibid.

29 ibid., p. 46.

30 ibid., pp. 48–9.

31 ibid., p. 51.

32 ibid., p. 53.

33 Karl Marx, preface to *A Contribution to the Critiques of Political Economy*. This is quoted in Raymond Williams, *Marxism and Literature* (London: Oxford University Press 1977), p. 75, in a discussion entitled 'Cultural theory' which greatly extends the discussion on the relationship of history to art (literature and performance).

34 Mention was made of this point in Chapter 3 in this book. The reference, again, is to Perry Anderson, *Passages from Antiquity to Feudalism* (London: Verso Editions, New Left Books 1974), pp. 39–40 particularly.

35 Relevant historical sources for Zambia are: Andrew Roberts, *A History of Zambia* (London: Heinemann Educational Books 1976); David C. Mulford, *Zambia, the Politics of Independence* (London: Oxford University Press 1967).

Relevant historical sources for Kenya and for a discussion on Mau Mau are: Donald L. Barnett and Kariari Njama, *Mau Mau from Within* (New York and London: Modern Readers Paperback 1966); Oginga Odinga, *Not Yet Uhuru* (London: Heinemann Educational Books 1967).

For an analysis of Kenya since independence, see: Colin Leys, *Underdevelopment in Kenya: the political economy of neo-colonialism 1964–71* (London: Heinemann Educational Books 1975).

And for a wider political analysis of Eastern Africa see: John S. Saul, *The State and Revolution in Eastern Africa* (London: Heinemann Educational Books 1979).

36 Ngugi wa Thiong'o and Micere Githae Mugo, *The Trial of Dedan Kimathi* (London: Heinemann Educational Books 1977), pp. 83–4.
37 ibid., p. 19.
38 ibid., p. 22.
39 ibid., p. 43.
40 ibid., pp. 35–6.
41 ibid., p. 40.
42 ibid., p. 47.
43 ibid., p. 51.
44 ibid., p. 23.
45 ibid., p. 59.
46 ibid., p. 2.
47 ibid., p. 19.
48 ibid., p. 69.
49 ibid., p. 46.
50 ibid., p. 84.
51 ibid., p. 19.
52 *Ngaahika Ndeenda* ('I will marry when I feel like it') was produced by and at the Kamiriithu Community Educational and Cultural Centre at Limuru, where Ngugi wa Thiong'o collaborated with Ngugi wa Mirii and other adult educators. The production (and Ngugi's subsequent arrest and imprisonment) have been variously reported, in the *Daily Nation* (Kenya, January 1979) by Miriam Kahiga; in *Africa*, no. 90

(February 1979), in which Magina Magina records an interview with Ngugi shortly after his release; and in *Viva* (December 1978), which is more a report of the Kamiriithu Centre and how it continued after Ngugi's arrest. In *The Weekly Review* (5 January 1979), Margaretta wa Gacheru interviews Ngugi.

At the time of this book's publication I had not been able to see an English translation of the play, either by Ngugi wa Thiong'o or Ngugi wa Mirii, but there is an excellent analysis of the whole project by the latter, viz.: Ngugi wa Mirii, *On the Relevant Literacy Content*, Working Paper no. 340 (University of Nairobi, Kenya: Institute for Development Studies, no date).

53 Quoted from Kabwe Kasoma, 'The theatre of commitment', a paper written for the First International Colloquim/Workshop on the Social Theatre in Africa (Lagos 1978).

54 Some of Kasoma's other plays are: *The Fools Marry, The Long Arm of the Law, Distortion, Lobengula, Mankenda, Katongo Chala*.

For a discussion of some of the early works see my article: Michael Etherton, 'The dilemma of the popular playwright: the work of Kabwe Kasoma and V. E. Musinga', in Eldred Jones (ed.), *African Literature Today, no. 8: Drama in Africa* (London: Heinemann Educational Books 1976).

55 It is difficult to know why the plays were banned. It may be that the play offended some members of the government or the Party. It is, I suppose, difficult to write a play about people who are still very much centre stage in real life. There is, I understand, a suggestion that the ban may be lifted.

56 Kabwe Kasoma, *Black Mamba Two*, in Michael Etherton (ed.), *African Plays for Playing*, vol. 2 (London: Heinemann Educational Books 1975), pp. 40–41.

57 ibid., p. 45.

58 ibid.

59 ibid., pp. 51–2.

60 ibid., p. 54.

61 Kabwe Kasoma, *Black Mamba Three*.

62 Kasoma, *Black Mamba Two*, p. 58.

63 ibid., p. 58.

64 ibid., p. 65.

65 ibid., p. 66.

5   The art theatre:
three Ghanaian plays

The term *art theatre* implies a category of theatre which is differentiated from *popular theatre*. Both terms are highly generalized and within each category there are conflicting definitions, even apart from an opposition between the two categories. For instance, in post-industrial societies of late capitalism the art theatre can refer to the subsidized but still essentially commercial 'establishment' theatre (of the opera, the ballet, the 'classical' theatre – all performing the 'great works' of the culture) as well as to the *avant garde* theatre which attacks the establishment and its theatres, and even the artistic pretensions of those theatres. Similarly, *popular theatre* can simultaneously describe a debased commercial theatre, which panders to the lowest tastes of the mass of the people, and a theatre which attempts to inspire people to a collective and radical reassessment of their society.

Broadly speaking, the *art theatre* as a category approaches theatre from the side of the artistic product, and focuses on the process of creativity; *popular theatre* as a category approaches theatre from the side of the audience and focuses on the process of consumption. In the end they are not exclusive categories. They can be seen to exist primarily in opposition to each other in a dialectical relationship in which actors (playwrights) and audiences strive to find a synthesis between the process of creativity and the process of consumption. The two terms in opposition can show the changing relationship between theatre and society; and I would emphasize again the need to see the work of playwrights not as isolated works of art – as 'things' – but as part of a creative process which stretches through time as well as through the act of creation. Even the survival of 'great works' from previous ages and cultures in the canon of contemporary African drama is evidence of an assumed view of history, of art and of social development.

In the rapidly changing societies in Africa hardly anyone is concerned with art for art's sake (which might be considered the 'extreme' form of the art theatre). Everyone has some attitude towards social development and those who are writing plays consciously mirror the ways in which a new society is established. The mirroring of society's development can be taken by play-wrights in two quite contrary directions: either in the direction of idealism (the new nation–state as reflected in its rhetoric) or in the direction of *naturalism* (the mirroring of the failures and disgraces of the new nation–state). For some playwrights the ideal for society lies in the past: a 'golden age' that pre-dated colonialism and western intrusion, which provides the blue-print for the future. For others the ideal lies in a future predicated by the present: if the present is inadequate, the future will be too.

Some of the plays which have already been discussed are texts of, and productions for, the art theatre in Africa, such as John Pepper Clark's *Ozidi*, Rotimi's *The Gods are not to Blame*, and Ngugi's and Mugo's *The Trial of Dedan Kimathi*. In these plays the stories were taken from, respectively, legend, another play and recent history. In the art theatre plays we are now going to consider each playwright intends to work entirely from his or her imagination, creating a fictionalized story as the base for the play. There is no qualitative difference between plays which are worked entirely out of the imagination, and plays whose content is derived consciously from another source. Wole Soyinka, for instance, sometimes takes an actual incident around which he builds a play of his own devising (for example, *Death and the King's Horseman*),[1] sometimes reworks a play from another culture (for example, *The Bacchae of Euripides*), and sometimes creates a play entirely out of his own imagination and experience (for example, *Madmen and Specialists*). Each is assessed as a valid creation of the playwright.

The three Ghanaian plays which we are going to analyse in this chapter are *Amavi* by Jacob Hevi, *The Marriage of Anansewa* by Efua Sutherland and *Anowa* by Ama Ata Aidoo. Sutherland and Aidoo are well-established creative writers; and they are also national figures. Sutherland has been an activist in the theatre since the time of Kwame Nkrumah, when she was involved in establishing a drama and theatre of and for the people in the newly independent Ghanaian nation. She has been playwright and theatre director, the founder of Ghana's most notable ex-perimental theatre groups such as the Ghana Experimental

Theatre and *Kusum Agoromba*, and the creator of imaginative community theatre places like *Kodzidan* (Story-house) in Ekumfi-Atwia, and the Ghana Drama Studio in Accra.[2] She continually refers her theatre experiments back to the ordinary folk by mounting productions in Ghanaian languages, by encouraging the establishment of professional companies and getting drama students to work with these actors, and by researching community-based dramatic forms. Despite this extensive involvement in what might be called popular theatre in Ghana, I hope that my analysis of *The Marriage of Anansewa* will indicate why I would categorize it as a product of the art theatre in Ghana: the emphasis on artistic dramatic form seems to override all other considerations.

Ama Ata Aidoo is primarily a writer, not just of plays, but of prose fiction and poetry. She too is a politically committed intellectual, and is concerned that Ghanaian society develops in a way that will most benefit the masses.

Hevi is virtually unknown. His one published play, *Amavi*, reflects the work of someone who has found an ideal form for expressing something which he urgently wants to say. All three plays, in fact, have an artistic achievement which stems from the relationship of what the playwrights want to say with the unique dramatic way they find for saying it. We need to come now to a discussion of what is meant by form in drama – identified in our schema – and what the terms *stylization* and *naturalism* mean.

Hevi's *Amavi* and Aidoo's *Anowa* constitute in each case a personal statement of something deeply felt. Sutherland however has distanced herself in *The Marriage of Anansewa* from what the play might communicate to an audience. It is an established folk-tale, or at least in the tradition of the Ananse stories.[3] Her commitment is not so much to the specific story as to making Ananse and his exploits contemporary – relevant to the modern Ghanaian world – and in the process to establish a modern African theatre form on ancient traditional foundations. The form, therefore, is perhaps more important to Sutherland than the story or even actuality. Amavi and Anowa, whose names give the titles to their respective plays, are both young peasant women whose lives end tragically. Each playwright is able to say through their chosen character something about the lot of women in peasant African society. Their commitment is to their respective visions of society; and they need to find a way of conveying the *meaning* of their social vision. Sutherland, on the other hand, starts with a form – the Ananse story-telling tradition from the Akan culture – and this in the end becomes her only 'commitment' in the play.

Form, in the theatre, is often constituted as a continuum from extreme stylization at one end to minimum, or seemingly non-existent, stylization at the other end (where naturalism is often placed). Stylization in the theatre might best be described as stage conventions to achieve certain theatrical effects. These conventions may be used in a way which makes their conventional use obvious, or which deliberately obscures it. Stage conventions are the devices and techniques which are understood by playwrights and audiences in common to mean specific things.

The main conventions could be summarized as (1) effecting the distortion of time; (2) completing the action of the drama; (3) using the stage space (visual transformations); (4) using speech, music, song and dance (aural transformations). Let us consider these a little more closely.

1   There are certain devices used to distort time. The passing of time is shown by dividing a play into scenes, and one scene is differentiated from another by the use of stage curtains or the elimination of stage lighting to effect a 'black-out' in the theatre. Time is also speeded up or slowed down by *pacing* the dialogue and the action. Pacing is a technical production term[4] referring to the way in which the action of the play is developed towards a crisis in such a way as to generate and sustain the interest and excitement of the audience.

2   Plays are especially 'shaped' – which is not to be confused with pacing – so that the action moves towards a climax or series of climaxes which resolve the issues of the drama, positively or negatively and make the play complete. Matters are rarely so resolved in our actual lives. The resolution of certain issues is the start of something else; and what seems good may rapidly turn out to be much less than satisfactory. In some modern European plays – the most notable one is *Waiting for Godot* by Beckett – the focus of the play has been on the very absence of any climax and accompanying resolution. The playwrights actually use the audience's expectation of crisis and climax to get over their message of its unreality. But on the whole people don't like plays to end unresolved. It is akin to having no moral position in the drama.

3   Well-equipped stages in small or large theatres can create an

infinite number of illusions of spacial reality. The stage can become a mountainside, a busy street, a vast hall or a tiny bedroom; and the stage space can be transformed from one milieu to another in a matter of seconds. Furthermore, people can appear to fly through the air, or disappear in plain sight; nature can be distorted, and a dream world created. Thus, an inner state of mind can be given physical reality on stage, as can an outwardly normal and recognizable place. The conventions which govern the use of stage space range from the use of perspective, through the use of *flats, drops, flies, traps, rostra* – all terms for the basic *scenery* structures – to the use of stage lighting, lasers and computers.

4 Speech, music, song and dance have been established as the conventional modes of performance long before the building of theatres. Actors are able to *project* their voices so that even a confidential whisper on the stage can be heard by a thousand people in the auditorium; and actors dance and sing with each other in formal ways, completely distinct from the behaviour found in ordinary life. But the audience understand the significance of the dance or the chant, or of actors singing to each other, because there is a mutual understanding of the conventions.

The interesting thing is that the more familiar one is with a stage convention, the less it is realized to be such. Indeed, a person does not register the use of a stage convention if thoroughly familiar with it. It is only if you come upon a performance as a complete outsider that you will consider what you are seeing as strange or bizarre. For instance, if you have grown up to appreciate western opera in which the entire drama is sung from beginning to end with the accompaniment of a large orchestra, you do not register it as strange that people should sing conversations to each other; nor do you realize, consciously, all the intricate rules relating to musical composition which the composer of that opera has mastered. The conventions and the rules are acquired unconsciously, in much the same way as the conventions of language are acquired in every-day speech. It is the same with most stage conventions.

It is the community, in fact, which establishes the conventions of theatre and performance: not only the playwrights, directors and actors, but also the audiences and the critics. It is a process equally applicable to small-scale local communities, as with the Tiv *Kwagh hir* puppet theatre,[5] and to large-scale communities. It is probably true to say that, on the whole, theatre in Africa in the

1960s and 1970s was 'conventionalized' by university communities where a great deal of experimentation with theatrical form took place, carrying forward with it a largely university-trained audience. Within the scope of this experimentation two forms were understood to be in opposition: 'highly stylized' drama which related to traditional performance modes, and 'naturalistic' drama which was considered to relate to western theatrical form.

This opposition could be said to be reflected in the three plays we are considering in this chapter. *The Marriage of Anansewa* is a deliberate exploration of a whole range of non-naturalistic conventions derived from the traditional performing arts of the Akan; *Amavi*, on the other hand, is contained entirely within a naturalistic mode of drama. *Anowa*, however, could be said to transcend 'formalism', in that the play reveals a mastery of dramatic form rather than being subservient to it. In fact, our choosing to discuss these three plays in this chapter in this way is itself 'formalistic'; and we have to be careful that we ourselves are not dominated in our discussion of the plays by the formula:

Anansewa = extensive stylization
Amavi   = extensive naturalism
Anowa   = synthesis of naturalistic and non-naturalistic techniques

because this will distort the meaning and significance of each play. Each play is obviously much more than a barren exercise in form, and probably none is consciously written to correct or contradict the form of another play – though Sutherland may have had this in mind when she wrote the *Anansegoro* (plays based on the Ananse stories). Nevertheless, the search for an appropriate dramatic form is a search for meaning and for the critic terms like 'naturalism', 'non-naturalism' and 'stylization' are conceptual tools which provide a way of talking about meaning in art.

Naturalism is especially interesting because it developed, historically, as a movement in European art at a time when industrialization had isolated the mass of the population from their traditional cultures and had cut them off from art.[6] Politically, naturalism was an attempt to force the middle class to face the realities of their society and its morality by making the characters and the scenarios reflect the causes of the sordid poverty and squalor in the lives of ordinary working men and women. Artistically, naturalism attempted to 'mirror' life, in literature and then on the stage, by, for example, making the characters use the vocabularies they would if they were actual people, and by the creation on stage of the milieu of poverty. The work of the French novelist, Émile Zola (1840–1902), and the German playwright, Gerhart Hauptmann (1862–1946), were key figures in the development of naturalism as a literary movement. The two major European dramatists of the nineteenth century, the Norwegian, Henrik Ibsen (1828–1906), and the Swede, Johan August Strindberg (1849–1912), were both involved with naturalism in their play-writing, but they each laid emphasis on the hypocrisy – particularly with regard to sex and personal relationships – of the ruling middle-class, rather than making the poor and the destitute the subject of their plays. Furthermore, both Ibsen and Strindberg were influenced by, and in turn reshaped, other literary and artistic movements.

Initially, naturalism was an attempt to break away from 'art' (artifice), 'style' (stylization), 'form' (formalism) which was seen as the essential artificiality and unreality of bourgeois art. 'Art', 'style' and 'form' were seen as barriers to an understanding of the modern world; and the new fiction and drama were to depict the contemporary world directly. However, it would be wrong to see this naturalism in nineteenth century European drama as being *without* form and having *no* stylization. The necessary distortion of time was still there, and achieved through the same conventions. So too was the working towards a climax, and the stage conventions covering speech projection, characterization and pacing. Even the naturalistic stage settings (perhaps even with a real coal fire in the kitchen stove!) had the 'fourth wall' – where the audience were sitting – 'unnaturally' missing. Indeed, the stage settings still had to be arranged so that everybody in the theatre could see and hear. So, in the end, naturalism became just another type of stylization; its virtue lay not so much in the development of a new form in drama *per se* as in the fact that through this form it actually gave drama a new type of content which was politically relevant to the time.

Radical political perspectives in the arts in Europe, especially in the theatre at the end of the century, were taken over by essentially non-naturalistic movements like 'expressionism' and 'surrealism' of the twentieth century. Paradoxically, the aridity of the naturalistic conventions as form without substance was revealed by the imposition of 'social realism' on the art of the 1930s and the 1940s in the Soviet Union. In the 1950s there was something of a revival of naturalism in Britain in the so-called 'kitchen-sink drama' of the 'angry young men' (primarily the playwright John Osborne).

Naturalism is, however, an important element in the development of a great deal of twentieth century third world drama, and in particular of African drama. In almost every instance it is a formal response to the imposition of dramatic forms by a colonizing power, and is an attempt to show the contemporary experience exactly as it is for the formerly colonized intellectuals. In this sense, naturalism is also a reaction to the traditional – for example, African – culture, which itself is no longer seen as being an adequate reflection or explanation of the forces operating in people's lives. In fact this is very similar to the European experience in the eighteenth and nineteenth centuries when the peasantry were forced off the land and into the factories, and in the process deprived of the validity of their traditional cultural forms. So naturalism in Africa is a reaction on two fronts: politically and artistically to the substance and forms of colonialism; and culturally, but *not* politically, to the traditional performing arts. It is because of this seeming contradiction that African drama critics and politically conscious intellectuals are ambiguous in their response to naturalistic African drama. On the one hand, for example, drama students will spend hours discussing the exact form of relationships and social behaviour in a particular naturalistic improvisation which they are developing – body posture, gestures, clothing, tone of voice – yet those same students will write essays in defence of the use of non-naturalistic indigenous forms of drama (for example, some Yoruba folk opera) that flatly contradicts the precise view of the contemporary world they had previously responded to so unaffectedly. Furthermore, both university and non-university audiences respond to plays that present instantly recognizable characters and situations in straightforward scenarios without music, dances or songs. These may be comic and satirical (such as the shows of 'Baba Sala') or tragic (such as Sofola's *Wedlock of the Gods*, or Sarif Easmon's *The New Patriots*). The response is quite genuine and such plays usually produce heated discussions among members of the audience about the accuracy of what is being shown on stage – where 'accuracy' corresponds with their own experiences and insights. These same people also enjoy the traditional shows – the masquerades and festivals, the professional entertainers – even though they are, in their own terms, clearly 'inaccurate'. Their comments and criticisms relate instead to the art of the performance and how well or how badly it was done.

One crucial problem is that while modern audiences find the content of the traditional shows increasingly irrelevant to the modern world as they know it, they nevertheless want to cling to the conventional wisdom or 'message' derived from that content. Some African playwrights are profoundly aware of this as a problem; and the inadequacy of traditional morality is a recurring theme in their plays, which are written, as it were, in counter-point to their audience's expectations. Some of the plays of 'Yemi Ajibade, Soyinka, Hussein and Chifunyise are structured in such a way as to show the inadequacy of the traditional morality as expressed in the traditional performances. Sometimes, a naturalistic play about the contemporary experience of social and moral breakdown supports in the end, paradoxically, the conventional moral view: Sofola's *Wedlock of the Gods*, Sutherland's *Edufa*, Musinga's *The Tragedy of Mr No-Balance* all end in a way which seems to contradict the development of the play to that point. On the other hand, and very occasionally, a play like Maddy's *Gbana Gbendu* will recreate a totally non-naturalistic presentation of a traditional performance in order to undermine its traditional wisdom and established moral implications. Such plays, however, as we shall see in the case of *Amavi* and *Anowa*, are too *avant-garde* for the audiences at present attracted to African theatre.

In summary, therefore, the art theatre at its most significantly creative level explores the dynamic relationship between having something to say (depicting reality) and finding a dramatically appropriate way of saying it (the form). This involves *stylization*, which can be considered as a continuum between a highly 'conventionalized' performance and a performance which seemingly uses only few conventions. Such a continuum must always relate to the particular theatre culture, the particular society and to particular audiences. The theatre in societies in the third world experiencing rapid social change tends to move in the direction of naturalism which is against performance conventions, apparently, whether they be traditional or western. This is as much a development in the political content of drama as it is in the dramatic form. Nevertheless, although we talk of a relationship between content and form, they are part of the same work of art; and the separation is only as a means of analysing the creative process.

Amavi Jacob Hevi

Amavi is a play about a peasant woman of that name. At the end of the play there is an image of the destitute Amavi, and the stage direction indicates how that image is to be created. Amavi is sitting outside her father's house which is 'gradually crumbling'. She is wearing the cloth she was given many years before; it is 'faded, threadbare'. She is crouched over a little fire, staring at it. 'A priest and teacher pass by . . .'; they are probably the same priest and teacher whose linguistic observations on Ewe patronymics began the play. They are observers of the peasant community, educated and therefore somewhat distanced from the illiterate farmers. The teacher comments that Amavi has drudged all her life hoping for a future. Her mother and father are now dead; and her sons, growing adolescents, are away in Agota with their father who threw her out. They have no understanding of their mother's predicament. 'Life', concludes the teacher, 'is a chance game.' A farmer joins them – he is obviously a peasant and, by the way he is dressed, going to his farm. In a little speech which closes the play, made haltingly because of his sense of desperation at seeing Amavi destitute, he says that many are like her. 'Man' is individualized in 'his' suffering – 'but they are men, not man' – and they are differentiated in their capacity to endure. Amavi is a great woman because she has endured all the decisions made for her – by her father, then by her husband – hoping to find love and hope through acceptance of the status quo.

Thus the play reaches its conclusion. Nothing has been resolved, and we are left with the sense of life going on for Amavi's husband and the usurping young wife Sewa, and for Amavi's sons; with the image, in the passing priest, teacher and farmer, of life passing by Amavi herself. This is very far removed from the revenge drama which *Ozidi* exemplified (and transcended). Amavi has been wronged by Sewa and her husband; and the scene in which she is cast out is written in such a way that the audience cannot help but feel totally involved in her tragedy and outraged at the treatment she receives. Yet nothing is done to avenge her, neither by her father who dies, apparently, shortly after her return, nor by her friend Kofiga, who was full of promises but who drinks too much, nor by the other villagers who have their own problems. This is deliberate: the play is written to emphasize the harsh lot of a peasant woman in contemporary African society.

Amavi is complete in itself, though matters remain unresolved for Amavi herself, with her parents having died in certain unhappiness, leaving her unfulfilled and despairing. In this sense, the play's ending could be said to be unsatisfactory: there is no tragic resolution, even, with Amavi dying so that Kokutse can realize the error of his judgement, or some variation of this. Yet the play itself is 'complete'. How can we explain this seeming paradox? How can an ending which is unsatisfactory make a play 'complete'? And what exactly do we mean by 'complete'? We need, first of all, to see exactly what happens in the play.

The play begins with Amavi's betrothal to Kokutse. This is arranged by Amavi's father, Agbeka, and opposed by Amavi's mother, Abrakpoe, and by Amavi herself, who has no say in the matter. The careful way in which the relationship between Agbeka and Abrakpoe, as husband and wife, is presented indicates that we should look at it closely. The subservient role which is ascribed to women in marriage in this community seems to conflict with Abrakpoe's nature. She is particularly stubborn with regard to her only child, her beautiful daughter, Amavi. She refuses, initially, to accept the marriage proposal arranged by her husband and the family of the young man, Kokutse. However, she appears to be powerless to do anything about it, other than to resist it and ignore all the arrangements. This stirs up her husband's anger and she is forced to give reasons for her objections.

'But should people not start working before they marry?' she asks her husband, implying that Kokutse is not 'working'. He is a young peasant farmer who is going to take his new wife off to a place remote to them to start a new cacao farm. It is clear that what Abrakpoe means by 'working' is 'earning'. Agbeka replies:

> Yes, yes; you women. . . . You always want somebody else to work for you. You never want to work for anyone . . . . You want your daughter to marry a white man's worker. You want her to ride a 'tonning car'. This is how you women ruin your daughters. So, you are ashamed to have a farmer as your son-in-law. You must be ashamed of me too, then.[7]

Abrakpoe is lost for a reply. Having weakened her position morally, Agbeka tells her to take over sole responsibility for Amavi. Of course, Abrakpoe cannot; all she can do is accept the status quo.

'She is your daughter,' she tells him, conceding defeat. 'Whatever you want to do with her, she is at your disposal.'[8]

Agbeka accepts his victory with a reply which is repeated almost exactly by Kokutse years later when he throws Amavi out of his house:

> You women. I anticipate your tricks. You think a man is a fool. If you think a crab's eye is wood, touch it and see.[9]

With that, Amavi's future is decided; and it is only a matter of days before she is out of her home in Avegbe Tonu and struggling up the slopes of Agota to her husband's new farm. It is on this farm many years later and after a life of drudgery that her husband Kokutse shouts at her:

> Though my hair is not yet grey I know you women. I know your evil machinations. You women! Hear this once and for all: if you play with me you will be sorry. You will see it all in the flicker of a second like a picture on a cinema screen.[10]

and moments later he says:

> Look! Do you think a crab's eye is wood? [*Knocking his breast*] I am a man; the master of my own house. From this very moment I do not want to see you under my roof.[11]

So Amavi is driven out of her only other home, with her husband using the same metaphor – the image of man observing women's 'machinations' with an apparently unseeing eye. Amavi, like most peasant women, is the victim of the traditional arrangements between man and woman, and, like her mother before her, she accepts it – because she cannot perceive or articulate any viable alternative.

However, the additional metaphorical embellishment which Kokutse uses – 'You will see it all in the flicker of a second like a picture on a cinema screen' – makes him unequivocally a peasant farmer in the modern world and aware of it. We have been told that as his farm begins to yield he spends more and more time in the town; and that he and his second wife often speak to each other in English. The farmer-husband, just because he is a man, can experience something more than the common rural ground. The dramatist, therefore, is consciously creating in the character of Amavi someone who would rebel against the status quo – because her youth and beauty give her some grounds for hope for a better future for herself – but who has no means within either her imagination or experience to articulate her rebellion. Ironically, the man's experience of a somewhat wider world makes him more dissatisfied with his plodding rural wife. The paradox is that Amavi's youthful beauty, which is the source of her hope for the future, betrays her: it is too soon used up in the hard life of a farmer's wife, and her attraction for her husband disappears. A younger, a more 'modern' woman is sought.

The complex relationship between beauty, love and hard work is developed by Ama Ata Aidoo, as we shall see later, in her play *Anowa*. In *Amavi*, the notion of ageing is tied up with the loss of beauty and hope. Don't aim too high, Agbeka tells his daughter just before her marriage and he cites the terrible example of a beggar woman in the village who married a German and was abandoned by him, albeit reluctantly, when the European World War broke out. On the contrary, Agbeka claims, the marriage to a cacao farmer could turn out to be successful and profitable.

We don't see the wedding, but its aftermath and the young couple's departure for Agota. The scene focuses on the family's and the villagers' ambivalent feelings about the young couple's future. Hope, together with a casual optimism, is always on the edge of despair; and there is an awareness that the happiness of childhood will be swallowed up rapidly in the drudgery of adulthood. Amavi's unhappiness is commented upon by the other married women in the village. Why didn't she refuse?

Second Woman: My friend, could you have refused it against your father's will?

First Woman: Of course, I should have known that. This is how our fathers force the yoke onto our necks.[12]

Later, this same woman comments to all who are present:

Do you think it is easy to marry a beginner in farming? We women are unfortunate by nature.[13]

Abrakpoe's advice to her daughter is bleak:

If anything happens there will be no one to help you. Therefore, obey him. That place is a wilderness. You have heard all that your father has told you. If you leave your husband and come back to your father, he will simply not take any notice of you.[14]

Agbeka's advice to his son-in-law is more conventional, but nevertheless also has a tone of desperation, of someone realizing that he is unable to affect the outcome of events or the development of the relationship.

The lorry to take them towards Agota, named 'Is-this-the-sort-of-people-they-are?', hoots for them off-stage and gives an urgency to the scene. Agbeka bustles around, Abrakpoe is passive. In the same way, her daughter allows her own husband to hurry her along. The village women gaze on the scene knowingly. The tone of the scene is summed up in the person of Kofiga, the young man who is everybody's friend and who seems to resist any thought of the future except to mock it. Later, and in this sense specifically, he comes to have an increasingly important role in the play.

The journey to the bit of land Kokutse's father acquired at Agota is long and wearying; but Kokutse cares for his new wife and tries to encourage her, even though there is nothing he can do about the fact that she has to walk for many miles carrying her loads. He is conscious of needing friendship and help from the 'foreigners', and he waits patiently for someone to come by who will take them to the Chief of Agota. When he sees how exhausted Amavi is he comments, desperately, 'It has come to a critical point now.' When they eventually arrive at their lands and the derelict shack high up the mountain slopes, Amavi discovers a snake where she is supposed to sleep; and even after Kokutse has killed it she refuses to go in and lie down. Kokutse comments morosely, after he has at last got her to sleep:

Is that I, Kokutse, coming to start a farm? Failure! Curse of nature! Ancestors forbid – oh, my case alone, I know; but sombody's daughter! [*Right thumb in his mouth*] Eh! My heart will totter to report what happens in this strange wilderness. A taste of life's bitterness. [. . . *He dozes . . .*] When . . . I'm so sleepy too.[15]

He works hard; but he is unimaginative. He lacks the wit and the warmth of his friend Kofiga, who eventually comes to farm in Agota as well, and seems to do better than Kokutse, with much less effort.

There is a charming scene, scene 6, in the middle of the play, which marks the best moment of the relationship between Amavi and Kokutse. Amavi dresses a wound on her husband's leg – his cutlass slipped while he was clearing the ground – and they comfort each other. Then we see Amavi very pregnant and tired, and needing to lie down. Kokutse comes home and discovers a cold hearth and a dirty kitchen. Where can Amavi have gone, he wonders. A baby's cry is heard from the inner room. He runs inside:

God! Only God! God help me! [*He comes out of the room with a small bottle of Heineken schnapps and a small glass. He is very excited. He pours some schnapps into the glass, about to pour it into his mouth*] Oh! Yes, I have to give some to the mother first. [*He dashes into the room and comes out soon*] Truly, I know there is God! Oh God, thanks, thanks, thanks a lot!*¹⁶

Then there is a long citation to his ancestors, which culminates in fervent hope for the future, tinged with insecurity:

Give us wealth and possessions. And give us safe return home. If anyone says he will not live nor let us also live, change his mind. If anyone plays to effect our separation by sowing confusion between us, confound him. . . .¹⁷

Kofiga arrives at this moment; and there is rejoicing. But it is Kofiga rather than Amavi's husband who marvels at her strength and powers of endurance. As he leaves husband, wife and baby, Kofiga ends the scene with a warning to Kokutse:

The greater the attachment, the more frivolous and unreasonable the cause of separation. . . . I am happy that you are both happy. . . . Before I came here, I knew more about the women of Agota than the natives themselves. They can turn you upside down; and they can turn your head against your wife at any time! Kokutse, listen well. The day you allow any woman of Agota to influence you, you are doomed.¹⁸

The scene has worked up to this point. The relationship is insecure, if for no other reason than a farmer's inability to control his destiny; and the counter-balancing of rejoicing with scepticism shows how tenuous relationships are in the peasant's world.

Hevi sets the next scene back in Avegbe Tonu. It takes place two years after the previous scene and shows Amavi's first visit home to her parents. Once again, rejoicing at the rather qualified success of Amavi's last five years is tempered by scepticism:

Abrakpoe: [*In a low voice*] Has he sent you anything?

Agbeka: There you go again. You women! Always with palms open for something. You never give yourselves. Anyway, have you searched through her luggage?

Abrakpoe: For my part, I have still to see whether this marriage is a success. Is she not using the kente you gave her to carry her first child?¹⁹

The village women, too, wonder why she is wearing such faded clothes. One comments: 'I think she is used to cottage life; she is now used to the dirty part of the work'. And another adds, 'But she has turned so virile!'

That is the end of her beauty. Life must go on.

Kokutse does only moderately well over the years; Kofiga does much better, though neither can ever move out of their peasant class. Amavi has other children; and when she visits her parents again, an old woman of Agota starts calling on Kokutse and begins to undermine the relationship. Kokutse begins to go into Agota town for cacao meetings and meets local women, including the old woman's niece, Sewa. A new and bigger cottage is built by Kokutse and Amavi. And when it is completed, Kokutse brings Sewa back to it as his second wife:

Amavi: Eh! Kodsoto, who is this . . .?

Kokutse: [*In a rough voice*] She is my wife.

   Amavi *turns away and continues her work as if nothing has happened. The children . . . keep on staring at their father and the lady. . . .*][20]

Kokutse's character has changed. He is determined to have his own way – just like Amavi's father – and, like him, he now leans heavily upon the authoritarian role which is traditionally allowed the man as husband and father. Amavi is suddenly made totally insecure. She is as she was when she first arrived in Agota all those years ago, except that now she has lost her beauty and her hope, and her husband is no longer the caring, if ineffectual, ingenuous young man he was. He has retreated into the stereotype of the husband–wife relationship, and as the dominant husband, has forced his wife into it as well.

From this point the scene begins to build up to a climax. The pace quickens and we should see how Hevi has contrived it, for it happens very quickly indeed. After Kokutse has ordered Amavi to move out of his room and into the spare room (and ordered Sewa to move into his room) there is the following stage direction:

[**Amavi** *gazes at him for some time. Musicians play furiously. Time passes. People go into the house, tense and angry. As the music ends,* **Kokutse** *comes out of his house ready for work in a new smock. A sack dangles from his shoulder. There are some seedlings of cacao and oranges in it.* **Sewa** *comes out of the house too dragging her feet on the ground.*][21]

There is an exchange between Sewa and Kokutse in which they are especially nice to each other, and Kokutse himself even tries to be witty, the only time in the whole play. Again, a few words in the stage directions indicate the tone of the scene:

Sewa: [*With a clumsy smile*] Brother Kokutse.

Kokutse: Sewa, what is the matter? [*He swats an insect on his calf with the flat of his cutlass*]

Sewa: [*With simulated coyness, wriggling herself*] I would like to pay a visit to my aunt. It is a long time since I saw her.

Kokutse: Yes, yes, Torogbani the divineress. It is high time I visited her myself, too. You may go. But don't bring back any bad augury, hein?[22]

This last joke is as artificial as is Sewa's simulated coyness; Kokutse is not used to making jokes. But it is more than a bad joke, for it turns out that 'bad augury' is exactly what Sewa is going to her aunt for. The artificiality in this relationship is as clearly established in this little vignette as was the sincerity in the relationship between Amavi and Kokutse in the earlier scene in which he had cut his leg. The contrast is deliberate.

Even more deliberate is the contrast between Kokutse's attitude towards the new wife and his attitude now towards Amavi, revealed in a slightly longer vignette which immediately follows the exchange with Sewa without a break. Kokutse bangs his toe against his ancestors' stone. He goes into his room to get schnapps to placate the ancestors, and as he is about to do so Amavi comes by and spills some water on the stone by accident. She is unaware of what she has done, but Kokutse uses it as an excuse to berate her. She starts to ask her husband to instruct his new wife to help her, because she is not feeling well. To which Kokutse replies 'You are never healthy' – an outrageous accusation to her of all people.

He builds himself up into a rage and in an effort to justify his anger with her he retreats into superstition and all but accuses her of witchcraft:

The ancestors are always guarding my footsteps. I, Aflamato's Kokutse, have not come to this wilderness empty-handed. If you don't know it know it today. I can hear things; I can see things. How dare you pour water on that stone . . . With all this space, that is the only place you choose to pass with your water.[23]

He disappears in the direction of his farm. Kofiga enters at this moment; he has been drinking and is as jovial and extrovert as ever. He yells into Sewa's room to wake her up.

Kofiga: . . . What a wife! I am told she is a schoolgirl.

Amavi: But what do you think? They even speak the white man's language sometimes.[24]

Kofiga tries to reassure Amavi:

> Amavi, don't fear any overthrow. What! Under the very eyes of the youths of Avegbe. That is impossible. If you see any sign, cry 'Ootoo. . . .' We will be here at once.[25]

The stage direction says: *He dances off*. Kokutse comes back on to the stage and demands to know what Kofiga is doing in his compound. There was a moment in the past, when Amavi was away and before he married Sewa, when Kokutse begged Kofiga to stay the night with him and help him ward off the evil spirits which he felt were plaguing him. Kofiga did not understand him – whether deliberately or not is not quite clear – and sent over his young daughter the next day to cook for him. Hevi seems to be creating a contradiction in Kofiga's character: he is always around, but, metaphorically speaking, he always keeps his distance. On this previous occasion there was a failure of the friendship. Now, in this present crisis for Amavi there is a suspicion that Kofiga's reassurances may only be rhetorical.

Amavi tries to rouse Sewa –

> [*The door gradually opens, revealing Sewa's clouded, sleepy face*] Who is troubling me here?

– and, ironically, at that moment Sewa's medicine-men arrive to put love potions around the house. Sewa directs them where to put the potions; Amavi watches, concealed, and when they have gone she accuses her of witchcraft, uproots and destroys all of them and says she is going to tell Kokutse. However, when he returns, Sewa gets in first and uses all the evidence to accuse Amavi of witchcraft.

This is the device of dramatic irony. The audience know that Amavi is innocent and that Sewa is lying and coolly calculating; because they are outside the action they can't warn Kokutse and tell him the truth. As Amavi tries to tell her husband the truth he beats her; Sewa runs into her room. Amavi, on her knees, complains:

> Is this what I deserve for all that I have done for you? Now that we are both jaded and tired from plodding all these years? . . . That is why I did not want to marry a farmer. I foresaw all this, but my father forced me into it. It is my own fault. It is my own fault.[26]

Sewa is made to throw Amavi's few belongings out of the house. Amavi gathers up into her arms her terrified youngest child and sets off in the darkness down the steep slope to the main road.

A great deal has been made of the precipitous nature of the slope up to their lands throughout the play: it now is the cause of the death of Amavi's youngest child, for Amavi slips on her way down and crushes the child in her fall. We do not see this happening however. We only learn about it in the next scene.

The next scene, the penultimate scene, is in Avegbe Tonu. This scene and the final scene of the play are actually a 'tailing-off' from the climax. This sort of ending is sometimes called an anti-climax; though this same word is often used pejoratively to mean an ending which the writer didn't intend: a *failed* climax. However, here it is deliberate, and naturally follows the climax which the play has successfully built up to. Amavi returns home. It is, ultimately, after all these years, a failure of her marriage: a loss of hope, an affirmation, finally, of the non-existent future, which people knew all along.

Her father, Agbeka, now an old man and a widower, is made to acknowledge his original mistake in marrying her off to a farmer:

> Amavi, you are right: I threw you away. Suppose something had happened to you in the dark? What on earth would have Kokutse have told me? All right! All is in the hands of God. [*Drooping his head*] Amavino told me this. I am sorry she is no more. She is not here to hit this bald top of mine to stop me seeing Kokutse's face anymore. [*Suddenly raising his head*] Look friends, go to your houses. I do not want any judgement in this matter. It serves me right.[27]

This is where the play began, in Agbeka's house, with Agbeka justifying the marriage which he had arranged for his daughter in good faith. Scene 10, which is really an epilogue to balance the prologue (scene 1), contains the image with which we began the analysis of this play: an old woman covered in a faded, worn cloth, humped on a stool, a priest, a teacher and then a farmer, gazing at her, remembering who she was.

Who is to blame? Agbeka now blames himself for insisting on the marriage when his wife warned him against it and his daughter held back her tears in mute opposition. Amavi herself takes the blame for agreeing to marry a peasant who had not yet begun his own farm. And yet the dramatist has been at pains to point out that initially there was nothing wrong with Kokutse, except that he was a young illiterate who still had to prove himself by making a farm out of the bush. The villagers, in a rather perfunctory way, blame the 'witches of Agota', 'the women of Agota'; and superficially the divineress Torogbani and her niece Sewa are the immediate cause of the destruction of the marriage. But it is Sewa's guile, rather than her love potions which Amavi throws away, which cause the rift. More significantly, it is Kokutse's own uncertainty and lack of confidence which allow Torogbani and Sewa to gain a hold over him. He is not an evil man; just lacking in imagination. He works extremely hard and has an enormous amount of energy; but it never brings its rewards. Amavi also works very hard over the years and although she was beautiful as a young woman, she too is lacking in imagination. Both are measured against Kofiga who has some wit and intelligence and who does as well as anyone could within the narrow confines of a peasant-farmer's world. The way he copes with the restricted horizons of this world is to drink. He tells Amavi:

. . . I for one, I am only concerned with what I can get today and leave some for my children tomorrow. For the rest Kofiga is satisfied, in and out, as long as he gets his calabash of palm-wine every morning. . . .[28]

Kokutse and Amavi each feel they ought to have a wider future, Kokutse because of his capacity for work, Amavi because of her beauty. But neither beauty nor strength is sufficient to lift either of them out of the drudgery which is the lot of every peasant. It is their hope which is ultimately to blame for the breakdown of their marriage. This is the central, bleak contradiction of the play: their hope for a better life undermines their present life. The realization of this contradiction makes the play seem complete. This realization is achieved by the way the play is structured, by the way in which its *form* enhances its meaning. Hevi's form for this play is *naturalism*.

First of all there is an attention to minute detail, for example the limp sack with the cacao and orange seedlings in it, a great deal of which could hardly be consciously noticed by the audience. However, it does build up the verisimilitude of each of the scenes.

Second, Hevi tries to show things as they really are, rather than as we always hope they will be. Ironically he uses a number of the set themes of some contemporary African drama: the romantic rural milieu; the beautiful daughter of the village; the journey into unknown territory; the overbearing father who marries the daughter off to someone against her will; witches, medicine and magic; the young second wife after the husband's money; the death of a child and retribution for the harsh father.

In each case, however, the cliché is transformed from the fantasy wish-fulfilment, which it nearly always is, into a rather unpleasant reality.

The central theme of the play is that in fact the rural life is far from bucolic and is certainly not a 'golden age'. The world of the peasant today is shown to be hard and restricting, with very little chance of escape from it, especially for women. Amavi's beauty is, as we have seen, her disadvantage. Agbeka is not different from any other father in those circumstances and he genuinely thinks that he is doing the right thing for his daughter. Neither mother nor daughter can suggest any real alternative to the marriage he proposes. The young couple receive help and co-operation from the chief and the people in Agota. The use of magic is peripheral to, and not the cause of, the crisis. It has no validity in itself, except in so far as it is an excuse for Kokutse's lack of confidence in himself. Sewa is depicted as lazy and not particularly attractive. Rather than being evil she simply takes advantage of her youth and her urban experience. The death of Amavi's child is not a focus of the play, but merely by the way. Far from being an ennobling sacrifice, through which people learn their true natures, it is felt by everyone to be embarrassing and sordid. Agbeka accepts culpability, but can do little about it. He is too old, and dies shortly afterwards. Indeed, no one derives any satisfaction from his being proved wrong about his daughter's marriage.

Naturalism is, initially, an attempt to overturn what is stale and worn-out in dramatic content and theatre practice in order to approach reality. In this sense, then, *Amavi* can be said to be a naturalistic play: Hevi has tried to get to the truth beyond the cliché-ed situations we have found in so many third-rate plays. Nevertheless, as our analysis has shown, the play is still heavily structured.

For example, time, in the play, is drastically condensed. The action of the play spans over fourteen years; and the events which would actually take place over a few days are condensed into a few minutes within a single scene by (*a*) using musicians to play to indicate the passage of time; (*b*) the use of a multiple set; (*c*) getting the actors to change the scene in full view of the audience; (*d*) substituting specially aged props and costumes for their pristine counterparts during the course of the play, such as

Agbeka's deck-chair and Amavi's kente; and (*e*) showing the development of a scene through a few key images.

Another example of the complex structuring of the action of *Amavi* is the constant orientation towards the central point that is being made, namely that for farmers there is little to hope for, and for their peasant wives no future at all. This is a general point, which is made in various ways by both the main characters and the onlookers. The play is also developed towards a particularized climax: the precise way in which Amavi is ousted from her husband's home after helping him build up the farm over a dozen years. And it is developed towards the conclusion that this outcome was to be expected. Doubts are expressed and warnings made and these are carefully set against the hopes and aspirations which everyone would like to have.

The ending seems an inevitable outcome, not so much of events, as of a world in which a particular social category of people are trapped. It is because of this seeming inevitability that we are able to sustain the bleakness of it. It is painful to see Amavi as she is at the end of the play; but as a mirror of contemporary reality it seems to have some truth in it. The action does seem to us, the audience, to be complete. We may not want to look at the play unfolding; but once we are drawn into its depiction of reality, we follow it through to the end.

The Marriage of Anansewa Efua Sutherland

If the number of performances are anything to go by we certainly do want to look at *The Marriage of Anansewa*; and in this play everything works out perfectly. Anansewa is finally married off to the Chief-Who-Is-Chief, whom she loves and who will care for her the most; Kweku Ananse, her father, whose schemes lead to the match, has managed to wriggle out of a tight corner and is himself probably going to marry Christie – 'Rare helper, your thanks await you' – and the Story-teller and players sing a concluding song, 'Is love's power so strong? / Let's relate in love / That we may thrive'. This song is an answer to the song the players sing at the very beginning of the play: 'Life is a struggle / Citizens, / Life is a pain / In this world. . . .' The play's ending is very close to the ending in the English story-telling tradition, 'and they all lived happily ever after'. In the European fairy-tale things start badly, get worse, and end up very well.

It is far removed from the desolate conclusion of *Amavi*: Amavi's life proved that love was a dubious thing and that there never was any happily-ever-after to live for. Efua Sutherland is herself a socially committed playwright, keen to seen Ghanaian drama depicting Ghanaian social reality and cultural identity. Is she suggesting that in the contemporary African world of coups, military take-overs, national bankruptcy, corruption and intrigue, love will conquer all? Or is she offering stylish entertainment that resists any obvious 'message' or inhibiting social analysis? Is it perhaps that her concern for cultural identity and an up-dating of ancient Akan performance traditions outweighs her concern to depict a reality which might be somehow alienating? Perhaps none of these approaches is valid and we need to look at the play in a completely different way.

We can abandon the central tenet of naturalism, verisimilitude, in favour of drama as caricature: an exaggeration of the foibles of people in order to criticize excesses in human behaviour. Satire is the essence of this type of drama. *The Marriage of Anansewa*, which comes to the conclusion that love will help us find a way, may have an ironical tone; and perhaps Sutherland is being satirical today about Kweku Ananse, who is the trickster of the Akan story-telling traditions. We need to look at the playwright's introduction, character list and stage directions in order to see what tone the playwright has adopted; and what deeper meaning that tone might suggest.

Sutherland explains in the foreword that she had developed a system of traditional theatre which she has called *Anansegoro*, based on the Akan story-telling art, *Anansesɛm*. In describing the central character of these stories, Ananse, she observes that the audience's main response to him and to his exploits is laughter and sarcastic comments. She concludes:

That Ananse is, artistically, a medium for society to criticise itself can be seen in the expression 'Exterminate Ananse, and society will be ruined'.[29]

Then she describes the way in which she had developed two other traditional performance elements: the story-teller, and the musical performances which are called *Mboguo*. It is traditional for the story-teller to up-date his stories as he tells them, giving them contemporary relevance; and in this way he adopts a conscious tone in the telling of the story. *Mboguo* are initiated either by the story-teller or by members of the audience as an integral part not only of the telling of the story but of the content itself and often in counterpoint to it:

Contributed *Mboguo* may be reflective of a mood or aimed at quickening the pace of the performance or inspiring the general assembly.[30]

Anansesɛm is a community art and since this is the main element which Sutherland wishes to transfer to contemporary theatre she attempts to define exactly how it is communal: the audience come prepared to be 'hoaxed' – she translates the word from Akan – to be 'taken in' by the story, to become attuned as a member of the audience listening to the story, to the elaborate joke that is being told. Thus entertainment for the audiences of *Anansesɛm* is part of a rather gentle satirical process; and Ananse himself represents the audience.

But how could this traditional participation in the satire, this deliberate response to the irony, be put on the contemporary stage? Sutherland maintains it was the most difficult of the problems which she encountered in her adaptations. Her solution was to create a pool of players, an audience-within-an-audience, (which we have seen in Rugyendo's *The Contest* and will see again in Oyekunle's *Katakata for Sufferhead*) who will bring the players and the real audience together by directing the attention of the latter and encouraging their response. This point is emphasized in the character list:

Players: All performers in the play, grouped together as a unified pool of music-makers, dancers, actors, *and as a participating audience* [the playwright's emphasis]. . . .
When necessary, actors simply detach themselves at convenient times to dress, returning when their roles are over.[31]

There is also a Property Man, who fulfils the role of stage manager, but in full view of the audience rather than behind the scenes as is more normal. He can act, and be the prompt. In other words he can deliberately destroy the illusion that the audience are spying on a slice of life, which they are unable to change or interrupt. (In *Amavi*, for instance, there is no way the audience can tell Kokutse that he is being misled by Sewa. If somebody did stop the play, what would the actors do with the rest of the scene, or even the rest of the play?)

The play has been produced in Akan and in English; and this

text is presumably the outcome of experimentation in performance of 'hoaxing' the contemporary Ghanaian theatre audiences – that is, of finding an ironical tone that holds precise meaning and is accepted by the audience for what it is. What is the irony in *The Marriage of Anansewa*? How does it 'hoax' the audience?

At the beginning of the story we find Ananse complaining about his poverty. He is battered by life's cares and woes. He is unable to find the fees to enable his only daughter Anansewa to continue her course at EP's Secretarial School, or to pay the instalments on her typewriter. Where is the money to come from so that he can lift himself out of the mire of poverty and acquire the consumer durables and social perquisites which are the mark of a successful Ghanaian? He has a plan, and without telling his daughter what it is – though it directly concerns her – he sets about putting it into operation, and getting her to help him.

He dictates four letters for his daughter to type, to four different chiefs, all given flowery appellations, promising each of them 'the object of your interest' and hoping they will do the proper thing. The letters are posted in a great rush (emphasized by the *Mboguo* which is sung at this point); and as soon as the letters are posted and the process cannot be reversed, Ananse gives his daughter the fees for her course and tells her that the four letters to the four chiefs were each offering her in marriage.

The 'hoaxing' of the audience has begun; Ananse must be joking. How can he promise one daughter to four chiefs? This is carrying the business of arranged marriages to farcical limits. How could all the chiefs be so gullible? Have they ever seen Anansewa? Yes, Ananse has recently travelled the length and breadth of the country showing her photographs to the chosen chiefs. Surely Anansewa will refuse to comply with this madness? Of course, she refuses. But Ananse has put his daughter in an intolerable position: if she won't comply she must give him back the fees in her hand, and she can try to find the fees herself. And anyway, surely she isn't going to object to being married to the Chief-Who-Is-Chief, 'the finely built, glowing black, large-eyed, handsome as anything, courageous and famous Chief-Who-Is-Chief?' She begins to have second thoughts. But how could she hope for such a match? Well, where does she think the fees in her hand have come from? She is won over to his scheme – and then remembers the other three letters which she typed:

Ananse: Listen, my one and only daughter, what I have done is that I have organised around you a most lively competition.

Anansewa: But aren't you afraid?

Ananse: [*Nasally*] Who said I wasn't afraid?[32]

Ananse is tired out with all his efforts. 'Ananse certainly needs a rest after spinning such a web,' says the Story-teller; and the Players as members of the audience, the stage direction tells us, 'roar with laughter'. There is another *Mboguo*; and the Players, still as members of the audience, move out of the action to sing a 'spontaneous' *Mboguo*. The Story-teller then questions the legality of what Ananse has done so far and he asks the audience: 'If negotiations have only reached this stage, is there any law binding him to give his daughter in marriage to any of those four chiefs?' And the Players answer, 'There is no such law'.[33]

To emphasize this point, an *Mboguo*, with an appropriate dramatization involving a young man and his wayward girl-friend, illustrates that nothing is legal until the boy has brought the girl's parents the customary head-drink. The Story-teller's comments are the end of the song:

As I was saying, it is possible to profit from the gifts his daughter's suitors bring, and not be bound by any obligation at all. What craftiness. Also, he has been careful to explain what his daughter Anansewa stands to gain from his design, but nobody has heard him making any direct hints about what he personally will gain. . . .[34]

But, he adds after a moment's reflection, the scheme is full of snares.

A postman comes on to the acting area, having detached himself from the body of Players and donned an appropriate uniform, with a letter for George K. Ananse – who is still resting from his earlier exertions. We are now back in the story. The first of the gifts have arrived from Chief Togbe Klu. Ananse is jubilant and on this note the first act ends.

The *Mboguo, Odum's Child*, by which the Story-teller introduces the second act, tells of the rich little girl who led such a protected life she wasn't at all prepared for the rigours of marriage. Ananse is now showing signs of affluence. Messengers from another of the chiefs arrive and give him more money. This gift is so generous Ananse is able to go to church on Sunday and make a spectacular public donation and on Monday the tradesmen arrive, Carpenter, Mason and Painter, to make alterations to his house. Ananse leads them around, smoking his cigar:

> Top priority is this leaking roof. That's you, Carpenter, so listen carefully; particularly in that corner there. Do your best to make us waterproof. Now, which is Mason? Yes, you with the trowel, of course. I'm ordering new floors in the bedrooms. You'll see in a minute what a shocking state they're in. Ah, you're the Painter. Total painting. In all the rooms.[35]

The tradesmen realize they are going to be able to take him for a ride and they arrange to take their time. *Mboguo* work songs punctuate this scene.

Ananse begins to enjoy his wealth; but he also begins to worry that it will be short-lived. 'I must not permit events to take me by surprise,' he tells the Property Man – who, at this moment 'manipulates a large toy electric fan beside him'. More money arrives but nothing further from the Chief-Who-Is-Chief. Ananse is worried; but then his Messenger finally arrives (described in the character list as 'the image of a high-grade diplomat') who informs Ananse that the customary head-drink for the lady will be placed on the table in two weeks time.

However, on the heels of this high-grade diplomat comes a telegram from Chief Sapa: he too is coming to conduct the head-drink ceremony in two weeks time. Ananse falls into a deep reverie and the Property Man places a spider-web screen in front of him. Ananse in the stories is traditionally the spider; and his trickster schemes are imaged in the webs the spider spins. The Story-teller and the Players try to draw him out of his reverie with a mocking song. But he has a headache and rouses himself sufficient only to tell the Property Man to phone Miss Christina Yamoah at the Institute for Prospective Brides. The stage direction describes the end of the act:

> *The Players sing loudly again. Ananse stuffs his ears with his fingers with irritation and takes to flight. Property Man mimes telephoning vigorously. The song ends with his act.*[36]

When Act 3 opens we are once again within the story. There are two new characters, drawn from the ranks of the Players: Ananse's mother, Aya, and his aunt, Ekuwa. Ananse, it seems, has decided to have an outdooring ceremony[37] for Anansewa – five years too late, as her grandmother points out. What is up? Is this a further 'hoaxing' of the audience? Christie – 'Miss Christina Yamoah, a fashionable woman' – has also arrived and has involved herself in the outdooring ceremony. As Aya comments pointedly: 'The way I see it, she is leaning her ladder on my grandchild in order to climb to my son'.[38] There follows an elaborate enactment of Anansewa's outdooring ceremony, with Christie trying to up-stage everybody. It culminates in Aya's present to her grand-daughter. This takes the form of a prayer:

> . . . yet this same empty hand will succeed in placing a gift in your bowl. What this hand is offering is this prayer of mine. May the man who comes to take you from our hands to his home be. . . .[39]

But Ananse forestalls us hearing her prayer by encouraging all the girls to burst forth into song – and at the same time stops the story from becoming sincere and thus changing its tone from irony to sentimentality.

Another telegram arrives; more complications; Ananse's head aches and Christie is ordered to get rid of the girls who are celebrating Anansewa's outdooring. Christie unwittingly announces further complications herself: a telegram from the Chief of the Mines – 'I had no idea we have now turned our attention to the Mines people. I was thinking our attention was strongly concentrated on the Chief-Who-Is-Chief.'[40] Ananse is visibly irritated. Christie evidently hasn't yet caught up with his schemes.

In a long and somewhat convoluted exchange, Ananse persuades Anansewa that she must 'die', and once she has agreed to his new scheme to get rid of three of the four chiefs who are coming hot-foot to claim her as their bride, he leads her behind his spider-web screen. The pace of the story quickens momentarily. Christie is sent to summon a taxi to take Ananse's mother and aunt post-haste back to the village. Ananse lies to them that his enemies have set fire to his cacao farm. However, once they are safely out of the way, the Story-teller takes over again for further comments and another digression:

> I wish I could have one eye looking on Nanka as the taxi arrives there with these two respectable ladies. They will already be wailing while they are landing, or if they have chosen to be furious instead, they will be clamorous with insults. . . .
>
> But, friends, the branches of this story of the Marriage of Anansewa have multiplied. Here comes one of them.[41]

And we see the affair between Christie and Ananse beginning to flourish. The final act, act four, begins with a dirge. It seems that Anansewa has died. The stage direction clearly indicates the tone:

> *Two women rush on to the stage with a half-dirging, half-weeping act. It is difficult to determine if they are pretending or serious . . .*[42]

The Players sing a song – 'How could it happen? / They called in Dispenser Hammond' – and the Story-teller informs the audience 'I can't laugh enough. Listen, Ananse is lying, he really is, and so relax'.[43]

The Story-teller then tells the audience what has happened, how Ananse went through the whole charade of discovering and bewailing the 'death' of his daughter, and how in his 'grief' he wouldn't let anyone near the body. Christie is obviously his accomplice. Half in song and half in speech, the Story-teller tries to figure out how Ananse's new scheme is going to work. If she is dead he gets out of his obligations to the four chiefs, of course, or at least to the three that neither he nor his daughter is interested in. But if she is dead she will have to be buried. . . . As he finished speaking, the Property Man, Ananse and Christie stealthily arrange the 'death' chamber behind the spider-web screens. Christie then reads out the arrangements for the reception of the chiefs' various messengers. 'Make your voice quiver a little more,' Ananse tells her, 'so that you'll be in practice'.[44] Just before Anansewa assumes her role as a corpse, Ananse makes a little speech to the Players and the audience:

> I know that not all my ways can be considered straight. But, before God, I'm not motivated by bad thoughts at this moment. I have a deep fatherly concern for this only child of mine. If the world were not what it is, I would not gamble with such a priceless possession. So what I plead is this: may grace be granted so that from among the four chiefs who desire to marry my child, the one will reveal himself who will love her and take good care of her when I give her to him.[45]

The stage direction – 'He is indeed weary' – indicates the tone which has become less ironical and rather more 'serious'.

Anansewa is laid out, Ananse takes up his mourning position, and the first messengers are ushered in by Christie. They are from the mines. It turns out that this chief's councillors had opposed the match, 'and she would have gone there to get hated,' comments Ananse, after they have gone convinced that she is truly dead. 'Very well, I have untied that part of the knot.'

The next messengers, from the Chief of Sapaase, arrive: two women, one of whom comments to the 'corpse':

> I was campaigning for you so that I could get a beautiful baby from your womb to carry on my back, and display my pride for the purpose of putting to shame a certain bitchy, ugly somebody who is there in Sapaase Palace.[46]

They too are convinced; and Anansewa is well out of that match.

The messengers arrive from Togbe Klu. This chief, fortunately, has become both businessman – Anansewa was to help him run his businesses – and spiritualist, and he is prepared to leave matters in God's hands; so Ananse has got his daughter safely out of that commitment, though the prospect of Anansewa's partnership in Togbe Klu's businesses seems not such a bad proposition at all. What if Chief-Who-Is-Chief doesn't come up with anything better? But he does: his messengers arrive with tokens and expressions of true love and devotion and a terrible sense of bereavement.

Ananse goes into a trance, which is well-sustained, theatrically, by his resources as an actor, and with the help of musicians, singers, Christie and the Property Man. It is a theatrical *tour-de-force*; and in the midst of it, Anansewa is 'roused' from the 'dead' – 'Father, I could hear Chief-Who-Is-Chief calling me!' 'He was indeed calling you,' Ananse replies. 'His love has won a great victory for us all.' Amazement all around, jubilation, happiness, at the perfect outcome of events.

The audience knows it was all an act. The Story-teller bursts out laughing, 'That's Kweku, all right.' Ananse, still in the story, orders him to '. . . manage the guest's departure for me, to end this whole event right now.'

'I understand you too well,' says the Story-teller. 'In that case, friends, we will end this *Anansegoro* right here.' He has moved right outside the story. 'Whether you have found it interesting or not, do take parts of it away, leaving parts of it with me. We are shaking hands for departure.'

The stage direction indicates that the Players, Anansewa, Christie and the Property Man are still within the story, shaking hands with each other, as they sing the last song, 'Is love's power so strong? / Let's relate in love/ That we may thrive. . . .'

In describing the story of *The Marriage of Anansewa* we have been forced to describe the story process as well, what might best be described as the style in which the story is told. We have been forced into doing this because of the playwright's persistence in taking us (readers or audience) in and out of the story itself, in order to develop an ironical tone. There is no doubt about the theatrical qualities of the play with its sophisticated performance devices, inventiveness and skilful integration of music and speech. Efua Sutherland is a playwright of considerable ability and experience; she tests her art always in performance. Our analysis has shown the play's style; but have we yet got to its meaning?

Ananse is not to be taken seriously except as a satirical reflection of the hopes and fears of 'ordinary people' who are hoping to get on in this world. 'This world' is very much the contemporary world of Ghana: the world of cars, electric fans, refrigerators, of EP's Secretarial School, the Institute for Prospective Brides, casual tradesmen and socializing Christianity. It is easy for the intellectuals and the people with established wealth to be patronizing about those struggling to make their way up the social ladder; and there is something of this patrician class in Anansewa's characterization. When her father lists the items of material success which he lacks at the moment she asks him:

> So, father, do you desire all those things? Haven't you condemned many of them often and often? You have pooh-poohed them, haven't you?[47]

Yes . . . but, and his mind again wanders down the avenues of social success. Anansewa comments: 'He's forgotten I'm here. This absentmindedness of father's is most trying.' Her vocabulary – 'condemned', 'pooh-poohed', 'absent-mindedness' in a 'father' who is 'trying' – is not the vocabulary of the peasant or urban worker, but of one who has got beyond such trivial concerns as electric fans and handsome church donations. She is going to marry the man she loves, not some 'old chief'; and she quickly realizes that she does love the style and ultimate affluence of the Chief-Who-Is-Chief.

By the time Aya, Ekuwa and Christie arrive on the scene, Ananse's ménage has become decidedly middle class. Ananse's mother's disdain for Christie is the disdain of the patrician for the *nouveau riche*. At the end of the play Anansewa marries wealth; and by inference so does Miss Christina Yamoah. Ananse pleaded poverty initially, but halfway through the play we discover that he has a cacao farm back in the village for his enemies to set fire to (should they so decide). We seem very far away from the cacao farm of Kokutse which Amavi spent her beauty and her youth trying to clear. In that play, the more urbanized Sewa could only aspire to Kokutse's peasant holding, which necessitated, even, the ousting of Kokutse's first wife. In the case of Ananse's 'Sewa, the young aspirant of EP's Secretarial School aspires to the very highest in the land; and nothing pollutes the purity of their love, which overcomes all obstacles.

Perhaps these two Ghanaian plays, each about a father arranging a marriage for his daughter, and concerned to get the best for her, cannot properly be compared with each other. The credibility of *The Marriage of Anansewa* obviously does not lie in its approximation to the reality of the daily lives of people in a specific social stratum, but rather in its essential meaning. This concerns general observations about human behaviour, exaggerated for the purposes of satire and comedy. But what is being satirized in the play? If anything it is a patrician satire on the behaviour of the plebeians. Are Ananse's greed and his tricks the object of criticism? On both counts he forestalls criticism of himself in passages which we have already noted: he only wants a moderate degree of material success and his lies and schemes are only for Anansewa's benefit (though he of course makes something out of it). He is neither nasty nor really corrupt. His scheming is akin to upper class 'pranks'.

Are the four chiefs, then, the object of the satire? The motives of one are wholly praiseworthy, and those of the other three are certainly legitimate and understandable. The women? Apart from the somewhat patrician behaviour of grandmother and granddaughter (and this may not even be deliberate on the part of the writer), and over-enthusiasm on the part of Christie, the women's characters actually epitomize moderation and understanding. The Story-teller is, as we would expect, public and convivial, and the rest of the Players are more actors and animators than characters in a satire (except, perhaps, the tradesmen, and they are stereotypes rather than caricatures). In fact, it is hard to find any specific satire or finely-honed criticism of a particular society.

Perhaps, ultimately, the meaning is only on the surface: Ananse schemes, keeps his options open, sails close to the wind, and finally gets his daughter well-matched, to their mutual benefit. Perhaps the dramatic sophistication of the play is more important than any 'contrived' profundity: tight control in the writing, a precise ironical tone, well-regulated comedy and excitement, embellishment and inventiveness – in short, high art.

However, when a play succeeds as well as this play does, in terms of its dramatic experimentation, a curious thing tends to happen. Audiences feel there must be a deeper meaning. If it cannot be perceived directly, either through naturalism or as comedy or satire, then perhaps the meaning lies deeply hidden, in symbolism or in allegory. This search for meaning gives rise to interpretations of the play that reveal a 'hidden' meaning.

One such interpretation of this play which is persistent in Ghana[48] is that it is an allegorical representation of Ghana's policy of non-alignment in its relations with other nations following independence. Anansewa is Ghana; Ananse the national leader; the four chiefs the representatives of the international community. The central conceit is therefore the imaging of non-alignment in Ananse's schemes to marry his daughter to the one who loves her the most. The point is that it is legal and appropriate to get as much aid as possible from other nations by holding out promises of alliances (trade agreements, perhaps) but withholding actual commitment until the donor's motives have been tested and proven.

The allegory breaks down when one attempts to make the correlations more explicitly historical. Is Ananse supposed to be Nkrumah? Or does Ananse represent something abstract like the 'Spirit of the Ghanaian People' (with the outdooring of Anansewa an allegory of independence itself)? Does Anansewa, with her patrician confidence, represent all the peoples of Ghana, or just the social group who actually inherited the fruits of independence? Which nations do the various chiefs actually represent, especially the Chief-Who-Is-Chief? Does the latter represent pan-Africanism as expressed in the OAU? And does the central metaphor actually work historically? In fact, since independence, Ghana has given far more, in terms of her natural resources, to foreign interests than ever she gained from them in aid and trade. Although the play is set in the contemporary world, nothing of the impoverishment of the Ghanaian economy, through deals made by successive regimes with the wealthy nations, is even hinted at. This would be a major element in any detailed allegory along the lines suggested. Finally, is it sensible, in the real international situation of economic exploitation and opposing ideologies, to think that true love will enable the nation to survive, let alone to thrive? The allegory is only on the surface, and again, meaning tends to disintegrate upon close analysis.

It would seem that we are left with a double irony with regard to this play. First, its indisputable artistic achievement suggests a depth of meaning. Yet while striving, quite successfully, for an original African form for modern Ghanaian theatre, there is a lack of real meaning in the play, particularly when compared with other Ghanaian plays, like *Amavi*, which is stylistically and formally much less innovative. Furthermore, *The Marriage of Anansewa* is much more successful and widely read than plays with a more profound meaning for African audiences.

This highlights a problem of the development of the art theatre in Africa which we previously noted, namely, that audiences want a theatre to be very effective, highly professional, stylish, just as traditional performances in small-scale societies once were, and occasionally still are, highly artistic. They also want a theatre which is about their own immediate experiences. However, an achievement in one direction does not guarantee an achievement in another direction; indeed, it might even hinder it.

It is often very difficult, then, for a dramatist to work out his priorities. Hevi, it seems, has found neither audience nor readership, in or out of Ghana. Perhaps, since we have no further plays from him published, he now distrusts his vision of his society, which proves on analysis to be profound. Efua Sutherland, on the other hand, is widely acclaimed for her theatre artistry and dramatic ability. She has written and produced many more *Anansegoro* than just *The Marriage of Anansewa* (apart from all her other less popular and more serious plays). Thus does the art theatre tend to develop, reflecting the preferences of its audiences.

We must now look at the third play, *Anowa*, which shows the problem to be even more acute than this.

Anowa Ama Ata Aidoo

The play *Anowa* is set in what is now Ghana a hundred years ago, in about 1870. It tells the story of an exceptional woman who had an inquiring and wilful mind, as well as insights and an understanding well beyond that of her peers. Neighbours said that she should have been apprenticed to the priestesses of the local Cult; but since she was the only child of her parents, they hoped for a normal married life for her and a continuation of the family.

Against her mother's wishes she wilfully marries Kofi Ako, the young man of her own choice, and walks out of her parents' home swearing never to return.

Anowa and Kofi Ako begin trading between the coast and the hinterland. Initially, they experience and share many hardships; but they endure everything with good humour, lots of energy and love for each other. The trade prospers and Kofi Ako soon finds himself able to afford slaves so as to further expand the business. Anowa bitterly opposes this move and takes an absolute stand against slavery, which she sees as buying men and making them do the work that they themselves should do. Kofi finds her objections odd and ignores them. From this point their relationship begins to deteriorate. Anowa refuses to share in his ever-accumulating wealth, and lives a pauper in their big house at Oguaa. Husband and wife no longer understand each other or find any way to resolve the differences between them. Kofi Ako eventually resolves to divorce her and send her back to her parents in Yebi. She refuses to leave, and wants to find out the reason why she is to be divorced. She suddenly realizes that Kofi is impotent; that he has been told that she has made him impotent; but that she knows it is the purchasing of slaves which has devoured his manhood. Kofi realizes that the embarrassed slaves and elders in the house have overheard their quarrel. He goes out and shoots himself. Anowa drowns herself.

The crucial issue in the marriage is whether or not Kofi Ako should purchase slaves for himself, and also for Anowa. Kofi's decision occurs almost exactly in the middle of the play. We need to look closely at the structure of the play to see how Aidoo prepares her audience for this moment, and how she chooses to present the argument between the two protagonists, which is worked out in their subsequent lives and deaths.

Aidoo makes use of a framing device: an old man with wisdom who anticipates change, and a cantankerous old woman who represents the status quo. They are referred to together as 'the Mouth-that-Eats-Pepe-and-Salt'. They reflect the range of opinions and prejudices of the community in which the action of the play takes place. Their characterization refers back a hundred years to the historical period in which the events of the play are set but, in addition, their characterization also embraces the present time. Their wisdom, or lack of it, has a contemporary tone and substance. The speech of the old man, which opens the play, has the same wry tone that Clark's Story-teller in *Ozidi* adopts. What the old man is saying could be paraphrased as follows: although our country, this state of Abura, is pretty well perfect in every way, there are one or two things which we might just hint at . . . a justifiable pragmatism . . . help from the whiteman against our kinsmen from the north . . . our participation in the slave trade. . . . Some of us benefited from the exploitation of our resources by the whiteman: who can blame them? In the end, they are still of us. . . .

The old man's speech is more convoluted but all the accusations are there, and the tone is ironical. The old woman comes on to the stage to add her voice to the introduction. Unlike the old man she is direct in what she says but she is less aware than he is. She introduces Anowa and Kofi Ako as young people courting; but the old man sums up their whole lives, and fixes their experience historically. Thus, the old man seems to be speaking to the audience outside of the story, whereas the old woman speaks from within it. For the old woman Kofi and Anowa are not yet married and she gives her views on the headstrong girl and her mother Badua; but the old man is staring into the future to the issue that will come to dominate and undermine the relationship.

The old man and the old woman appear at the end of each of what the playwright terms the three phases of the drama, and these alternative perspectives in their characterization are sustained throughout. This framing device is crucial to the establishment of the full meaning of the play.

The particular staging required, which is carefully described by Aidoo in the production notes and in the stage directions, is also important in establishing meaning. Aidoo insists on two stages: an 'upper' or main stage, and a 'lower' stage between the main stage and the audience. The use of two separate areas for the acting, marked off both by varying height and depth, enables the actors to present different actions which are taking place at the same time but in different places without a break. As the action of the play moves from the upper stage to the lower stage and *vice versa*, the audience knows that they are seeing parallel events which are happening miles apart. More important, however, is the fact that the main stage, the upper stage represents Anowa's two homes (her parents' home at Yebi, and Kofi's home at Oguaa) while the lower stage represents the domain of the wayfarer, the person without roots and without a home, the slave. Anowa says 'I am a wayfarer, with no belongings either here or there'. For Kofi Ako the term 'wayfarer' is the polite word for a slave. He tells Anowa: 'But a wayfarer belongs to other people!' 'Oh no, not always,' Anowa replies. 'One can belong to oneself without belonging to a place.' The main stage is nearly always set as one or other house, with their various chairs, utensils, possessions. The lower stage has nothing.

Aidoo's suggestions for the staging of the play suggest either a proscenium arch theatre or a thrust stage. However, it is possible to create the two distinct areas required both in theatre-in-the-round and on a traverse stage. The significance of the journeying will be heightened, even, by having the lower level close to or among the audience.

The play divides into two halves: before the decision to buy slaves and after that decision. However, it is arranged into three acts, which Aidoo calls phases. 'Phase' is a good description for each of the sections: Phase 1 is a hopeful phase; Phase 2 is a crisis phase; Phase 3 is a phase of despair.

Phase 1 introduces the characters, which include not only Anowa and Kofi, and the Mouth-that-Eats-Pepe-and-Salt, but also Anowa's parents, Osam, her father, and Badua, her mother. The relationship between Osam and Badua is different from the relationship between Amavi's parents, Agbeka and Abrakpoe. In Akan society, which is matrilineal, it is for the mother's side of the family to arrange the marriage. Osam is passive over the issue of Anowa's marriage. First Anowa refuses all the suitors; then she comes up with the choice of a man who is not acceptable to Badua – ' . . . this fool, this good-for-nothing cassava-man, this watery male of all watery males . . .' though Osam feels that he comes from a good clan, except he is going to say nothing about the matter. Badua tells Anowa: '. . . marriage is like a piece of cloth . . . and like cloth, its beauty passes with wear and tear.'[49] This image is given substance in *Amavi*: Amavi wears the same piece of fading kente throughout the years of her marriage. And even though members of the family have adopted contrary positions in the two plays, the hopes and fears for the daughter's marriage are very much the same. Despite the opposition from her mother, Anowa is optimistic about the future and positive about the world she is going out to embrace.

Phase 2 describes the transition from high hopes to despair. It covers an extended period of time which is contracted into a continuous experience. It begins with a journey by Kofi and Anowa, just after they are married, made without slaves. It is one journey to symbolize many, and it culminates in Kofi Ako's decision to purchase slaves. He fails to comprehend Anowa's deep-rooted opposition to slavery. There is an interlude on the upper – main – stage, in Badua's and Osam's house in Yebi, with the parents discussing the reports of Kofi's trading successes, without their comprehending what is happening to the relationship. Then there is another journey, which mirrors the first composite journey; but this time it is with a caravan of slaves to do all the hard work.

There are other formal elements in the shaping of this phase. Anowa's laughter, which had been unaffected and an expression of her genuine happiness on the first journey, has become hard, grating, ironical on the latter journey.

Phase 3 is an exploration of despair. It begins with an ironical manifestation of Kofi's wealth, in a scene in which he is borne in a procession on the backs of slaves (ironical, because he said he would never have slaves to carry him), and ends with his suicide. It begins with a demonstration of Anowa's self-imposed poverty, and with an account of her childhood trauma when she first learned about slavery, and ends, too, with her suicide. The other people in this phase are mainly their young slaves, who are paradoxically shown to have an existential freedom which is now denied Kofi and Anowa. They are owned by the latter; they witness the tragedy of their lives and yet they remain untouched by it.

This, then, is the structure of the play. Basically, it shows the lives of the two protagonists to be purposeful and their relationship totally fulfilling up to the point that they decide to buy slaves. From that point, although ironically fame and fortune come to them, their lives become meaningless. They cease to be able to communicate with each other, and they sink into despair.

What, therefore, is Ama Ata Aidoo trying to say about slavery? What is she trying to say about the central character, Anowa, whom she makes such a bitter opponent of her husband's decision to purchase slaves? We need to look closely at the text.

The first thing to note is that Anowa and Kofi Ako, as characters, and in their relationship with each other, are created within their milieu. They have no Western education – how could they over a hundred years ago? – and no other formal education outside the parameters of their small farming and trading society.

Anowa is considered different only to the point of being apprenticed to the cult as a dancer-priestess. There are adequate reasons
within the society to explain her character: she is exceptionally
beautiful; an only child, spoilt by her mother; wilful, and with a
high opinion of herself. And she has 'the hot eyes and nimble feet
of one born to dance for the gods'. She is not exceptional, at least
at the beginning of the play, beyond the comprehension of her
society.

Kofi Ako, on the other hand, is ordinary to the point of being at
fault – at least as far as his future mother-in-law is concerned. The
only thing the villagers can't understand is why Anowa chose
someone so ordinary as Kofi Ako. But it is specifically pointed out
that this is not the first time in that society that a couple have
disobeyed their parents and married for love. Even if they don't
see themselves belonging to Yebi, Kofi and Anowa do at least see
themselves as being part of the society of the area, as they begin to
travel together and trade between the hinterland and the coast.

This trade, of course, is suddenly increasing at this time because
of the economic expansion of European imperialism during the
process of industrialization in the nineteenth century. Kofi and
Anowa are ignorant of this historical perspective and are able, like
the rest of the villagers, to articulate the trade and their success in
it only in terms of their own social perceptions.

The social containment of Anowa, especially, and also of Kofi
Ako, is central to Aidoo's concept of the issue of slavery. When
Kofi first broaches the subject to Anowa on the journey, he speaks
about slavery from within a society that engages in it:

Kofi: I think that the time has come for us to think of looking for one or
two men to help us.

Anowa: What men?

Kofi: I hear they are not expensive. . . . I am not buying these men to
come and carry me. They are coming to help us in our work. . . . What
is wrong with buying one or two people to help us? They are cheap. . . .
Everyone does it . . . does not everyone do it? . . . Anowa, who told
you that buying men is wrong? . . .[50]

Kofi then makes a significant statement: 'I like you and the way
you are different. But, Anowa, sometimes, you are too different.'
Anowa replies:

I shall not feel happy with slaves around . . . Kofi, no man made a slave
of his friend and came to much himself. It is wrong. It is evil.[51]

Kofi is truly mystified by her vehemence. 'Where did you get these ideas from?' he asks her. Anowa replies: 'Are there never things one can think out for oneself?' To which Kofi rejoins, 'I know you think you are the wise one of the two of us'. But Anowa is not meaning to be clever. How could Anowa know better than their forefathers? The old woman, of the Mouth-that-Eats-Pepe-and-Salt, asks this at the end of the phase:

> She thinks our forefathers should have waited for her to be born so she could have upbraided them for their misdeeds and shown them what actions of men are virtuous.

To which the old man replies:

> . . . it is not too much to think that the heavens might show something to children of a latter day which was hidden from them of old.[52]

The old woman is 'flabbergasted' at his reply.

Two things emerge from this. First, that slavery is the norm of that society and is unquestioned, and that in questioning it Anowa steps out of her society and becomes 'too different'. Second, a woman must acknowledge and accept the superior wisdom of the man. Aidoo ties the issue of slavery to another issue she is concerned with in the play: the position of women in society (not especially African society, either), and in particular, the issue of the very intelligent woman in male-dominated society. The link between these two issues is sustained in the next part of the phase, the discussion back in Yebi between Osam and Badua:

Badua: [*Bitterly*] . . . Have you heard from the blowing winds how their trade with the white men is growing? And how they are buying men and women?

Osam: Yes, and also how unhappy she is about those slaves, and how they quarrel from morning to night.

Badua: . . . she should have waited for me to tell her how to marry a man. . . .

Osam: Hmm.

Badua: A good woman does not have a brain or a mouth.[53]

This observation is flatly contradicted by Badua's own character. She seems to be nothing but mouth, even though she only has conventional observations to make with it.

Another discussion between Anowa and Kofi Ako takes place on the later journey, when all the hard work is being done by the slaves. Although the discussion is about slaves it concerns Anowa's own life. 'How can a human being rest all the time? I cannot. . . . I shall not know what to do with myself as each day breaks.' What role will she have in the house? And in the relationship?

Kofi asks, 'So what you want to be is my mother-wife?' To which Anowa replies, 'Yes, or your friend or your sister.' To Kofi she has become a strange woman – 'Too strange' – but the oracles which he has consulted consistently show her to be innocent of any evil intent. As the discussion develops it is obvious that Anowa herself has no sense of having special powers. She does not regard herself as a prophet or seer. In fact, in an earlier discussion between them she had rejected charms and magical potions to protect the two of them, '. . . we only need a bead or two,' Kofi had said. Her response shows her to be rational and humble:

> But a shrine has to be worshipped however small its size. And a kind god angered is a thousand times more evil than a mean god unknown. To have a little something to eat and a rag on our back is not a matter to approach a god about.[54]

Her attitude towards the religion is very similar to Hussein's characterization of Kinjeketile: the character's rationalism tackles superstition from within the framework of the religion, simply because it would be impossible for either character to step outside it (in the way their creators are able to do so today).

All Anowa feels is that she doesn't belong anywhere. She is a wayfarer:

> A wayfarer is a traveller. Therefore to call someone a wayfarer is a painless way of saying he does not belong. That he has no home, no family, no village, no stool of his own; has no feast days, no holidays, no state, no territory.[55]

She is restless because she is intelligent. She is uneducated, and yet she is rational, with an understanding too advanced for a static society. All her society can do is understand her as a priestess, or a prophetess or a witch. Indeed, how many women have been branded witch by a society unable to cope with their intelligence and rationalism? Anowa is able to comprehend the absolute evil of slavery in a way that her husband, contained within the social system, cannot. She is also able to comprehend the true significance of the relationship between a man and a woman, a husband and a wife.

This present discussion again links the issue of slavery with relationships between men and women. 'How can having bonded men be evil?' Kofi asks her. 'After all, the slaves are treated well by us.' Anowa replies: 'And if they fare well among us, it is not so among all peoples. And even here who knows what strange happenings go on behind closed doors?' A proper husband would beat the nonsense out of her head, but Kofi cannot lay a hand on her. He still loves her too much:

> Shamelessly, you rake up the dirt of life. You bare our wounds. You are too fond of looking for the common pain and the general wrong. . . . But please, bring your mind home. . . . Be happy in being my wife and maybe we shall have our own children. Be my glorious wife, Anowa, and the contented mother of my children.[56]

She gives a harsh grating laugh in reply to this earnest appeal. Their 'overflowing wealth' is founded on their owning slaves. She utterly rejects slavery; and so, logically, she must reject the fruits of slavery. Even the fact that their marriage is childless matters less; it is the owning of slaves that is the evil in their lives. Kofi Ako's simple sincerity is false.

Phase 2 has explored the crisis. At any point then the process might have been reversed, if Anowa could have found a way to show Kofi Ako that slavery was an absolute evil. In Phase 3 nothing can be changed and there is only their deepening isolation and cumulative despair. Anowa is now obsessed with the trauma of her childhood when she first learned about slavery. She had questioned her grandmother, who had travelled a great deal, about the white man's world and she deduces from the answers that black man had sold black man into the white man's slavery:

> What happened to those who were taken away?
> Do people hear from them?
> How are they?
> Shut up child.
> It is too late child.
> Sleep well, child.
> All good men and women try to forget;
> They have forgotten![57]

Obviously the grandmother hadn't forgotten; and, since then, neither has Anowa. The conversation with her grandmother was followed by the terrible nightmare which she describes. In her dream she was the mother of all her people, men, women and children pouring out of holes in her body. The boiling sea threw up giant lobsters who turned into people with lobster heads and claws, and who fell upon the people she was giving birth to, grinding them to dust on mountains of stone. (The grandmother had described white men as boiled or roasted lobsters.) 'But there was never a cry or a murmur,' Anowa continues; 'only a bursting, as of a ripe tomato or a swollen pod. And everything went on and on and on.'[58] She adds, ending her soliloquy, that any time there is mention of a slave, 'I see a woman who is me and a bursting as of a ripe tomato or a swollen pod'. Slavery is slavery, whether it be whites carrying off blacks across the ocean or blacks purchasing a few other blacks to help them in their work. The image is of fecundity and waste.

Her monologue gives way to a scene in which one of Kofi's young slaves, a girl who is the image of Anowa when she was a girl, banters with another lad, also a slave, while they are supposedly cleaning Kofi's reception chamber. The discussion is partly about Anowa and Kofi – Kofi has insisted that the young slaves should call them 'mother' and 'father' – and partly about themselves. The boy asks the girl what she would do if she was in Anowa's ('mother's') position. Anowa enters unnoticed at this moment and eavesdrops on her reply, in which the girl sees Anowa's wealth as the way to 'freedom'.

> O if I were her, and she were me
> Jewels on my hair, my finger and my knee
> In my ears the dangles, on my wrists the bangles
> My sandals will be jewelled, my hair will be dressed;
> My perfumes will be milled, my talcums of the best.
> On my soups I will be keen
> No fish-heads to be seen
> O for her to be me
> So that I could be free![59]

Anowa, on her own again, comments that the girl was right, and quotes the proverb: 'The string of orphan beads might look better on the wrist of the leopard but it is the antelope who has lost his mother.'[60] The person who has caused hardship might look better wearing the badge of hardship, but he or she is not the one actually suffering the hardship. Anowa might make herself look like a slave, but she still shares Kofi's culpability in owning the slaves. Or, as the girl is really saying: why doesn't she change places with me? I who was a slave will have no scruples enslaving others. Anowa, who is so rational, realizes that she is totally isolated in her objection to slavery. She sees the fanning of Kofi Ako's gilded chair by the little twin slaves, Panyin-na-Kakra, as something insane. She imagines how their mother must have suffered during her pregnancy:

> Then the hour of the breaking of the amnion, when the space between her life and her death wore thin like a needy woman's hair thread. O the stench of old blood gone hot. . . . Did she go through all that and with her rest at the end postponed so they [*Pointing at the boys*] will come and fan an empty chair? To fan an empty chair?[61]

We can appreciate the logic and humanity of her observations, but her own society cannot. It is painful for us to see her isolated and branded as a witch. But it is not just Anowa's society, the 'Gold Coast' of the 1880s, which resists reason and humanity. Contemporary society does so as well. Aidoo has clearly articulated a contradiction which exists as much today as it did a hundred years ago: how can we enjoy the wealth which we haven't laboured for? In Anowa's society the particular question is: How can we enjoy the wealth made for us by slaves? In contemporary African society 'international capitalism', 'the multinational corporations' can be substituted for slavery – indeed, they are the actual outcome of the economic processes of a hundred years ago which swept up Kofi Ako and Anowa – and the question can be asked: How can we enjoy a wealth which means the certain impoverishment of others? Aidoo's play, *Anowa*, does not answer this question, either in general or in the particular. What it does do is to show how isolated one can become who is committed to asking the question. The irony of the play is that reason and understanding is a cruel affliction; it is especially cruel if it is found in a woman.

The old man gives the final comment:

> They used to say around here that Anowa behaved as though she were a heroine in a story. Some of us wish she had been happier and that her life had not had so much of the familiar human scent in it. She was true to herself. . . .[62]

Anowa is a traditional tale, a legend of the Akan. Aidoo has returned to the folk story to find what might be meaningful in it for contemporary society. She brings to the story, as she considers it again, issues which she sees as crucial for any thinking African today: exploitation of men, of women; concepts of personal responsibility, in general, and of the intellectual in particular. Can the old tale particularize any of these issues? And once she has found meaning she can then try to reach the form that will give that meaning substance. It is the very opposite to Sutherland's approach to the oral tradition.

Anowa must surely be one of the most profound African plays to have been written so far. And yet it is not popular, in my experience, even among students, especially men, who insist that Anowa herself is a witch and needs to be slapped by her husband. Ama Ata Aidoo's reputation as a dramatist rests upon her earlier and much less complex play, *Dilemma of a Ghost*, which is about a young professional Ghanaian who returns from the United States with a Black American wife. She is a child of slaves say the women of the community and they intend to shun her.

Ghanaian theatre is lively and diverse; its scope is certainly not contained in the three plays that have been analysed. Any comprehensive discussion on the art theatre in Ghana would have to include the work of the late Joe de Graft,[63] as well as the younger publishing playwrights like Martin Owusu and Asiedu Yirenkyi. The three plays, however, do suggest one thing which is typical of a great deal of the art theatre in Ghana. This is a concern to explore the problems of marriage and the nature of the family; and it is the closest and most intimate relationships which are considered. Unlike much Nigerian drama, it is private and domestic, rather than public and of the main street. It is true the three plays here deal with villagers and townsfolk, but the audience is taken right inside the home to see the family at its most private. The presence of prying neighbours tends to reinforce rather than mitigate the private nature of the drama. This doesn't mean that the issues themselves are only domestic. *Anowa* and *Amavi* are very much concerned with issues of class and state. However, these big themes begin from a crisis in the family, and are then worked out in highly personal terms.

Domestic drama is obviously less private the lower down the social scale it is situated. A peasant's world is less private than a banker's: there is less to hide and fewer rooms to retreat into. This is the same for the Moslem world as for the non-Moslem world; and everyone, no matter what his social status, desires privacy. People will make as many private corners for themselves as they can, depending of course on their temperament. Kokutse doesn't have a gilded chair in a reception chamber, but he does have his own bedroom that he can move his wife out of, and Anowa and Kofi Ako can still be overheard in the big house at Oguaa.

In the comparison of the three plays – each of which starts with the efforts of the parents to secure their only daughter's future – we are able to observe a profound analysis, collectively, of marriage. What the comparison has also shown is that artistic success and depth of meaning are not necessarily related, and that an intellectual drama can develop only so far as its audiences and its critics will let it.

Notes and references

1 Soyinka's *Death and the King's Horseman* is based on an actual incident in Oyo in 1946 which formed the basis for a play by Duro Ladipo, *Oba Waja*. The publishers, Heinemann Educational Books, have had the manuscript for years, along with *Oba Ko So* and *Oba Moro*, but they have never had permission to publish them. (*Oba Ko So* is published by the Institute of African Studies, University of Ibadan.)

2 It is surprising that there is no biographical account of Efua Sutherland and her contribution to the development of theatre in Ghana. She has been one of the most active and imaginative theatre practitioners in independent Africa, and the scope of her work is considerable.

3 *Anowa* is derived from Fanti folk-lore. Anowa was the proud one who insisted on choosing her own husband. — *Ama Ata Aidoo*

4 For working definitions of technical theatre terms see the glossary at the beginning of the book.

5 Hagher's account of *Kwagh hir* (Zaria: PhD 1981) shows these indigenous performances to be as 'conventionalized' as western opera, and as secular.

6 The following studies deal with European naturalism: Roy Pascal, *From Naturalism to Expressionism: German literature and society 1880–1918* (London: Weidenfeld and Nicolson 1973). This concentrates – obviously – on Germany. John A. Henderson, *The First Avant-Garde (1887–1894): sources of French theatre* (London: Harrap 1971), deals with France. Lilian R. Furst and Peter N. Skrine, *Naturalism* (London: Methuen and Co. 1971), is a general introduction to naturalism as a critical concept.

7 Jacob Hevi, *Amavi* in *African Plays for Playing*, vol. 1 (London: Heinemann Educational Books 1975), p. 57.

8 ibid.

9 ibid.

10 ibid., p. 83.

11 ibid., p. 88.

12 ibid., p. 59.

13 ibid., p. 60.

14 ibid., p. 61.

15 ibid., p. 68.

16 ibid., p. 70.

17 ibid.

18 ibid., p. 74.

19 ibid., p. 76.

20 ibid., p. 81.

21 ibid., p. 82.

22 ibid.

23 ibid., p. 83.

24 ibid., p. 85.

25 ibid.

26 ibid., 87–8.

27 ibid., p. 91.

28 ibid., p. 84.

29 Efua Sutherland, *The Marriage of Anansewa* (London: Longman 1975), p.v.

30 ibid., p. vi.

31 ibid., p. ix.

32 ibid., p. 14.

33 ibid., p. 17.

34 ibid., p. 19.

35 ibid., p. 26.

36 ibid., p. 34.

37 In Ghana the 'outdooring' ceremony sometimes refers to the naming of the new baby. Here, however, Sutherland is referring to the puberty rites or ceremonies at which a young woman is beautifully dressed and taken around the community to announce that she has reached a marriageable age. It is common throughout Akan societies in Ghana.

38 Sutherland, *The Marriage of Anansewa*, p. 37.

39 ibid., p. 42.

40 ibid., p. 44.

41 ibid., p. 56.
42 ibid., p. 59.
43 ibid., p. 60.
44 ibid., p. 66.
45 ibid., p. 67.
46 ibid., p. 70.
47 ibid., p. 5.
48 I heard this interpretation from the Ghanaian playwright Asiedu Yirenkyi.
49 Ama Ata Aidoo, *Anowa* (London: Longman 1970), p. 17.
50 ibid., pp. 29–30.
51 ibid., p. 30.
52 ibid., p. 41.
53 ibid., p. 32.
54 ibid., p. 25.
55 ibid., p. 37.
56 ibid., pp. 38–9.
57 ibid., p. 46.
58 ibid., p. 46.
59 ibid., p. 50.
60 ibid., p. 51.
61 ibid., pp. 51–2.
62 ibid., pp. 64.
63 Many Ghanaian theatre practitioners acknowledge Joe de Graft as their mentor. As a playwright he explored a number of theatre styles; and, as a teacher, he encouraged his students to experiment. He was a superb actor and director, but he never suffocated younger and greener talent. His untimely death in November, 1978 was a great shock to Ghanaians.

6 The art theatre: Soyinka's protest plays

Nigerian drama has been dominated by Wole Soyinka[1] who has been one of the sternest and most unrelenting critics of his country. Yet although he has influenced Nigerian playwrights in many other ways, a great deal of contemporary drama in Nigeria has tended to be uncritical, in any coherent analytical sense, of the society or of the body politic. It is surprising because many intellectuals have been critical of the imbalance in the social structure and of the direction in which the country is moving; and Nigeria has been a relatively open society, allowing many forms of cultural development, including some highly critical presentations and publications.

Where the drama has been critical, in the theatre, on the television and on the radio, the criticism has been of people. Types are satirized – they may even be class types – but invariably they are the architects of their own misfortunes and the cause of their downfall. This may reflect the satire in the performance traditions of Nigeria and their inherently conservative function of preserving the status quo by timely public criticism of the excesses of the traditional elite. Soyinka's work is partly in this tradition; but it transcends it. His satire and parody are directed against society itself and its power structures. His criticism is bound up with his metaphysics, and, in his terms, goes well beyond an attack on any particular system. Instead, it reaches towards an understanding of the fundamental basis of man's existence. This chapter will look at Soyinka's work as a critique of society which develops out of metaphysical considerations.

The central problem in the relationship between the art theatre and a protest drama is partly a problem of the relationship between content and form. As we shall see in a later chapter, political theatre for the third world probably requires a new form and not merely new content in either the existing western or traditional dramatic forms. The scale of the problem varies depending on the expectations of particular audiences. There is a greater range of possible solutions if the audience have no previous experience of formal theatre, whereas plays for the art theatre audience are less free to be innovative. In Nigeria, especially in the south, there is an art theatre audience, built up by the elaborate productions of Dexter Lyndersay and Ola Rotimi over the years, to name but two of the most popular Nigerian theatre directors. Soyinka, too, directs his own plays in performance, and his productions are for this fairly well established art theatre audience.

This is a good place to start a discussion of Soyinka's work, for it brings into focus a number of paradoxes, both within his work and between him and the society with which he interacts. Soyinka is unquestionably Africa's leading playwright, but the African audiences for his major philosophical plays are very small indeed. He addresses himself to the reflection of an African sensibility and the creation of an African drama, but his plays have non-Africans amongst their most ardent admirers. His left-wing African critics accuse him of a reactionary sensibility and intellect; yet his political activities, for which he has suffered imprisonment and exile, seem to stem from a deep concern for the common man seen as mercilessly exploited by tyrants, bureaucrats and opportunists. He has been consistently and passionately pan-Africanist in his public life;[2] and yet he is often regarded elsewhere in Africa – and even in Nigeria – as narrowly Yoruba in his intellectual affinities.

He is probably more deeply aware of the contradictions in his life and work than even his most ardent critics, for he consciously embraces the contradiction of destruction and creativity in the figure which is central to his philosophy – Ogun, the god of iron. Another contradiction is his simultaneous commitment to continuity and desire for change. His commitment to continuity emerges out of his metaphysical analysis; while his deep-moving sensibility provokes a desire for change. Indeed the holding in tension of his metaphysics and his sensibility is that which generates his art. In fact, these are notions related not only to his plays but also to his audiences (and go some way to explaining his relationship to an African theatre audience).

First of all, he is very specific about the role of the African audience in a live theatre performance: the members of the audience are part of the space of the performance and therefore metaphysically part of the conflict taking place. This conflict is itself symbolic of a primal conflict in the origin of the race. The audience participate in this much deeper metaphysical sense throughout the 'ritual' – which is the word Soyinka uses for the drama in performance – because they are an integral part of the space in which the performance of the conflict takes place; and he refers to the audience as a 'chorus' who give the protagonist strength in 'the symbolic struggle with the chthonic presences'.

Soyinka therefore sees the use of the stage space (that is the space used by the actors during a performance) as *affective*, not merely effective, because it *affects* the audience in certain emotional and physical ways. Therefore the use of the stage space moves from being metaphorical, as in Aidoo's *Anowa*, to being metaphysical: the stage space becomes 'the dangerous area of transformation', with 'area' being used in a specifically spatial sense. This metaphysical awareness on the part of the audience is, for Soyinka, most clearly seen in those performances of 'ritual' theatre where a fundamental anxiety manifests itself in members of the audience over whether or not the protagonist will survive confrontation with the forces of chaos which now exist in the arena or performance space.

This leads Soyinka on to a consideration of the tragic impulse, of tragedy, as it applies to drama. He contends that Europeans, or westerners, tend to see the tragic impulse as being encapsulated by a given world order at a given time and in relation to a particular individual. The African mind, on the other hand, has a tragic understanding which 'transcends the causes of individual disjunction and recognizes them as reflections of a far greater disharmony in the communal psyche'.[3] 'Tragic understanding', therefore, lies in the complex awareness of the audience that human existence, which is contained within a tenuous and uncompromising physical environment, is concerned with the survival of the community and not specifically with the survival of any one individual. The audience remains aware of this even when it has moved away from a society in which the mere question of survival is paramount, and moved towards a more complex and seemingly more secure, 'developed', society. This audience may sympathize with the individual whose conflict and tragic experience they witness, but their presence in the 'arena of conflict', in the theatre, makes them profoundly aware of the communal significance of the conflict, beyond its significance for the individual. The drama is tragic because the protagonist reveals to the audience the chaos before creation. This is why, Soyinka maintains, much of this tragic ritual drama is concerned with a re-enactment of the origin of the race.

Soyinka's essays in his important theoretical text, *Myth, Literature and the African World*, suggest that it is not through ethics or the moral codes of religions or through political dogmas, that this central conflict – man's struggle with chaos – is resolved. It is the communal will, expressed in the theatre by the audience, 'willing through' the central actor to bridge the chaos, which provides this deeper understanding of man's essential being. This communal will reflects the human condition and is quite amoral; it is itself a manifestation of the harsh, irreducible laws of the physical world.

This 'oneness' of actor and audience in the performance space, and the 'oneness' of the actor with nature – amoral and destructive as it is creative – is the metaphysical framework for much of Soyinka's work. We will seek to relate it to the social protest which is another element in the work. We will consider three plays: *Madmen and Specialists*, written at the end of the Nigerian civil war: *A Dance of the Forests*, written over ten years before, for the Nigerian independence celebrations; and *Opera Wonyosi*, produced at the beginning of 1978 while the military still held power in Nigeria and after the coronation of Bokasa as the Emperor (briefly) of the Central African Empire (also short-lived). *Madmen and Specialists*, which comes roughly half-way chronologically between *A Dance of the Forests* and *Opera Wonyosi*, serves as the principal reference point for a discussion of Soyinka's work in the context of this chapter, which is why I have chosen to deal with it first.

Madmen and Specialists

Madmen and Specialists was probably conceived while Soyinka was in prison during the Nigerian civil war. It was first staged, in America, ten months after his release, in August 1970. Soyinka records his abuse in prison in *The Man Died*. We note these facts not because they explain the content of the play, but because they indicate the personal experience that has been assimilated into his sensibility – which, in turn, has shaped the play.

Soyinka has experienced emotions beyond despair, and has constituted these objectively as a profound self-awareness, and a cynicism which is tempered by a resolve to live in the very eye of contradiction. He has then attempted, in the play, to create characters and situations in which these emotions can be bodied forth.

The central character in the play is the Old Man. He is the one who is most deeply aware of the scale and magnitude of the crisis which humanity in general and his society in particular has entered, in the aftermath of the war which forms the play's background. He is constantly referred to as Old Man; in fact he is the father of the other central character in the play, Bero, a doctor, and of Bero's sister, Si Bero. When war broke out Bero went off to the war front in the army medical corps while his sister stayed behind to tend the surgery. She persuades two old women, Iya Agba and Iya Mate, to teach her all about the earth's cures for sickness. These two women are more than cult herbalists: they are earth mothers, whose function within the play we will discuss later.

Later, the Old Man himself went off to the war front, as the accounts of horror and destruction multiplied, seemingly in search of some deeper meaning to life, and 'armed' only with – according to his friend the village pastor – with a determination to legalize cannibalism. We hear from his son, Bero, that he served up human flesh to the war leaders, but only told them what it was after they had eaten. He had been given the job behind the lines of rehabilitating the war victims:

> help the wounded re-adjust to the pieces and remnants of their bodies. Physically. Teach them to make baskets if they still had fingers, to use their mouths to ply needles if they had none, or use it to sing if their vocal cords had not been shot away.[4]

But instead, the Old Man had taught them about their exploitation. In particular, he had disabused their minds of the healing powers of religion or belief.

The central target of his attack is organized religion which is cynically used by those in authority to maintain and consolidate their power. 'Good' (faith, hope and charity) is used for 'evil' (controlling lives, mutilating bodies and abusing minds). To the Old Man it has now gone beyond the 'ends justifying the means'; control has become an end in itself and justifies the 'meanness'. This to the war leaders is plainly subversive; and it is the last straw when he leads them into breaking the taboo on eating human flesh, though it is something which the other lower ranks in the army are forced to do because of the shortage of food. He is imprisoned and put in the charge of his son, Bero, who has moved from the medical corps to army intelligence, and has become the senior man in that unit. Bero, with calculating cruelty, puts four of his father's former 'patients', four war-deformed beggars, whose thinking the Old Man has illuminated, as his gaolers; brings him back to the village under cover of darkness; and locks him up in his former surgery.

It seems that before the war Bero effectively combined modern medicine and traditional cures, and had used his sister and his father in the curing of patients in the village. He was regarded as a very good man. It is the war that has turned Bero from one who cured people to one who abuses them. Ironically it was his father who gave that transformation the *coup de grâce*. He was shocked, Bero tells his sister, when his father first tricked him into eating human flesh, and he vomited it up.

Afterwards I said why not? What is one flesh from another? So I tried again, just to be sure of myself. It was the first step to power you understand. Power in its purest sense. The end of inhibitions. The conquest of the weakness of your too human flesh with all its sentiment. . . .[5]

Bero in the play is the embodiment of the aberrant exercise of the will, and the one whose passion for control and social order can eventually lead to cosmic disorder. In the end Bero shoots his father dead.

During the course of Bero's interrogation of his father, the latter asks Bero why he hesitates to kill him. He is deliberately tempting him to further excesses in the perverse exercise of his power. The Old Man tells him:

Once you begin there is no stopping. You say, ah, this is the last step, the highest step, but there is always one more step. For those who want to step beyond, there is always one further step.[6]

Bero comments: 'Nothing more is needed'; to which the Old Man replies:

Oh yes there is. I am the last proof of the human in you. The last shadow. Shadows are tough things to be rid of . . . How does one prove he was never born of man? Of course you could kill me. . . .[7]

At the end of the play Bero does kill him, though again he is tricked into the breaking of this taboo by the Old Man: he appears to Bero to have gone mad and to be about to kill the Cripple. We need to look carefully at this act of murder.

It may seem odd to deal with the end of the play first; but in fact the act of Bero killing his father is the one event which the whole play has led up to. It involves not only the death of the Old Man but also, simultaneously, the burning down of Si Bero's store, filled with nature's remedies and cures, by the earth mothers who helped her collect it together. Both the death of the Old Man and the burning of the store are generated by the same impulse: a willing sacrifice, to curtail, or at least set a limit to, Bero's capacity for evil.

Because we are considering the play in the abstract, and not immediately after a performance of it, we cannot experience the impact of this climax – or indeed of the whole play – which in performance manages to transcend the literal meanings of the words. The play does indeed make the stage space into that 'dangerous area of transformation', and the audience are aware, beyond the meaning of the words, of some ritual archetype deeply rooted in their collective experience. An analysis of the text tends to make us wholly dependent on the words; but it is the nature of this double sacrifice which we must endeavour to comprehend.

The Old Man's parody of 'operating' on the Cripple, which provokes Bero, is done deliberately in order to distract Bero's attention from the earth mothers who have come to set fire to Bero's house so as to destroy all the herbs, cures and medicines contained therein that the earth has yielded to Si Bero through their knowledge. The text is quite specific in its stage directions:

> (*She* [**Iya Agba**] *raises the pot* [of glowing charcoals] *suddenly to throw the embers into the store.* **Bero** *steps out at that moment, gun in hand, bearing down on* **Iya Agba**)

Old Man: (*His voice has risen to a frenzy*) Practise, Practise, Practise . . . on the cyst in the system. . . .

> (*Bero is checked in stride by the voice. He now hesitates between the two distractions*)[8]

The Old Man rants on, entering fully into the role play of parody, the game he and the mendicants have so often played before. The Cripple asks a question; and within the parody he must be silenced. Playing the game the other mendicants 'torture' him, and then throw him on to the table for an 'operation'. The Old Man is shouting 'Fire! Riot! Hot-line! Armageddon!' He has snatched up his son's surgery operating gear: he is now specifically parodying his son in an ironic conflation of Bero's former (positive) role as a doctor, and present (negative) role as army intelligence supervisor: the specialist. Again the stage directions are explicit:

> (*They heave him* [*the* **Cripple**] *on to the table and hold him down while the* **Old Man** *rips the shirt open to bare the Cripple's chest.* **Bero** *rushes in and takes in the scene, raises his pistol and aims at the* **Old Man**)[9]

The Old Man flings the final ironic taunt at his son, whilst still remaining totally within the parody:

Old Man: Let us taste just what makes a heretic tick.

Note the choice of the words 'taste' and 'heretic'; and the specific stage direction which follows:

> (*He raises the scalpel in a motion for incision.* **Bero** *fires. The* **Old Man** *spins, falls face upwards on the table as the* **Cripple** *slides to the ground from under him. A momentary freeze on stage*)[10]

The Old Man has taken the Cripple's place on the operating table. He is, as far as Bero is concerned, the 'heretic'; but he is now really dead, killed by his real and manic son. Within the play the mendicants' and the Old Man's parodying role-playing has been superseded by reality.

At this moment of distraction, Iya Agba sets fire to the store. The Old Man's deliberate distraction of his gun-carrying son enabled the Old Women to destroy the goodness he would have abused. They are sacrificing the 'goodness' which they have collected over a life-time; the Old Man has sacrificed his life.

We can now see how the rest of the play fits into Soyinka's pattern of meaning. There is no doubt that Bero would have abused his sister's collection and the Old Women's knowledge. We are given a specific example of his doing so. Si Bero has collected, by accident, some highly poisonous berries. Bero steals these from her store and cynically gives them to his father:

Bero: Just now I came through that room of herbs, I saw something I recognised.

Old Man: Something to sap the mind? Or destroy it altogether?

Bero: Depends on the dose. I brought you some. (*He brings some berries from his pocket and drops them gently over the* **Old Man**'s *head.*) If you ever get tired and you feel you need a night-cap like a certain Greek you were so fond of quoting, just soak a handful of them in water.[11]

(The Greek referred to was the Ancient Athenian philosopher Socrates who was forced by the state authorities to commit suicide by drinking hemlock.)

A discussion has taken place with regard to these berries during the scene in which the audience first encounter the Old Women, the earth mothers. Iya Agba explains to Si Bero that the berries come from the poisonous twin of a very special plant. She comments that the farmers are foolish to burn the soil where they find it growing. 'Poison has its uses too,' she says. 'You can cure with poison if you use it right. Or kill.' When Bero later gives his father the berries, the latter comments: 'You've used it before, haven't you? Or something similar. I saw your victims afterwards.' At the end of this scene, when Bero storms out of the surgery, the Old Man comments to himself: 'I would have told him what's happening in the future. A faithful woman picking herbs for a smoke-screen on abuse.' The 'faithful woman' is his daughter, Si Bero.

The moment he finishes speaking the scene changes without a break – the stage direction is precise – to the Old Women's hut. 'Abuse! Abuse!' Iya Agba is screaming. 'What do we do? Close our eyes and see nothing?' She resolves to destroy the herb store, which action, as we have seen, forms the climax and ending of the play.

Who are these two women, Iya Agba and Iya Mate? We referred to them initially as earth mothers, and it seems that their persons and roles have a greater significance than simply as herbalists or cultists who teach the younger Si Bero their knowledge of the physical world. In fact, their approach to their work is metaphysical, in that their knowledge of the earth's secrets is related to the primal causes of existence. Their powers of observation and deduction are such that they seem to peer into the depths of human behaviour. They do not prophesy, and they are not witches; but they do have great insight.

At first they share Si Bero's eager anticipation for the return home of the brother and the father. However, from the moment Bero returns Iya Agba begins to have some doubts. Of him she says: 'I hope it's a good seed. That was two lives we poured into her hands. Two long lives spent pecking at secrets, grain by grain.' More than two, replies Iya Mate. 'What she took from us began with others we no longer call by name.'

The first confrontation between Bero and Iya Agba has potential for violence. Bero goes up to their hut 'holstering a revolver', as the stage direction says. He is verbally aggressive towards Iya Agba and threatening. 'Your mind has run farther than the truth,' she tells him. 'I see it searching, going round and round in darkness. Truth is always too simple for a desperate mind.' When Bero tells her that she and her cult are proscribed and banned she replies, 'You'll proscribe earth itself?' And if he bans earth, what will he walk on? 'Even on the road to damnation a man must rest his foot somewhere.' Bero storms away from her and goes towards his house; but he is arrested by the singing of the mendicants from his surgery. They build up to a parody of 'When the Saints Go Marching In':

> Before I bid this earth adieu
>
> . . . .
>
> I want my dues from that damned quorum
> Before I bid this earth adieu.[12]

When the Old Women finally come to Si Bero with the pot of glowing embers to burn her store down, Iya Agba sums up their position:

> What is used for evil is also put to use. Have I not sat with the knowledge of abuse these many days and kept the eyes of my mind open? . . . Rain falls and seasons turn. Night comes and goes – do you think they wait for the likes of you?[13]

These earth mothers are profoundly aware of the 'metaphysics of the irreducible' – a phrase which Soyinka uses later in *Myth Literature and the African World*, and means by it 'knowledge of birth and death as the human cycle; the wind as a moving, felling, cleansing, destroying, winnowing force; the duality of the knife as blood-letter and creative implement; earth and sun as life sustaining verities, and so on'. Morality fits into this basic framework; and the highest moral order is that which 'guarantees a parallel continuity of the species'.

The earth mothers represent this highest moral order in the play; but it is only, it seems, as a point of reference. They stand aside from the terrible conflicts generated by man as predator and exploiter of his fellow human beings. These conflicts can, as in the case of Bero himself, carry man 'farther than the truth' – and therefore out of the sphere of the earth mothers' moral order. It is, therefore, left to the Old Man, ironically Bero's own father, to take it upon himself to challenge his son; and he chooses to do so through the mouths of those who have been most abused by Bero's society: the war wounded, racked by poverty, maimed and reduced to beggary. It is as Bero's challengers that Soyinka creates the characters of the four mendicants.

The creation of the characters of the mendicants reflects Soyinka's sensibility at its most complex; and through them are made manifest his resources as a playwright. First, he creates the mendicants as the people who are most abused by the system which Bero upholds and develops. They are, as we have said, war victims: young men mutilated by armed conflict. The system, or the state, making a gesture in the general direction of humanitarianism, has felt obliged to 'rehabilitate' the war disabled; and has intended to teach them to use what's left of their mangled bodies and disturbed minds, and to convince them of the state's good intentions. It is, as we have seen, the Old Man who was given this task. Instead of teaching them passivity and acceptance, however, he has taught them to use their minds and has unmasked the system of authority in ways which they can understand. This has made him a heretic. Bero tells his sister: 'Can you picture a more treacherous deed than to place a working mind in a mangled body?' To pay the Old Man back for his 'impertinence', his son makes four of his former patients act as his gaolers.

The four are Aafaa, who suffers from chorea or St Vitus's Dance; the Blindman; the Cripple (neither of whom has any other name); and Goyi, who has an iron rod contraption in place of a spine. Each of the mendicants has a distinct character. Aafaa's nervous disease, which we gather came on during the war, is linked with his wider education than the others, and greater aspirations and neuroticism. He is the most voluble of the four, though not always their spokesman. Cripple is the dreamer; the one who has not yet given up hope. He says he collaborates with the Old Man's son, the specialist, in the faint hope that Bero will be able to make him walk again. The Blindman is the most aesthetic of the four, and the most aware. He knows before any of the others what the Old Man is driving at. Goyi is the least intelligent member of the quartet and the one whose body is most mutilated.

It is Aafaa who expresses the first of a number of crucial contradictions which they are obliged to live through and eventually articulate: they owe their new awareness to the Old Man, but are obliged to do Bero's bidding against him. When Aafaa rebels and says he at least is not 'under orders' from Bero, Bero strikes him across the face with his swagger-stick. Aafaa says to Bero: 'You think we spent all that time with your old man without learning a thing or two?' And during the course of the play all the mendicants refer, quite sincerely, to the 'sweet times' with the Old Man, and to 'the best song' he ever wrote for them. They recall his words and what he taught them. As they embark on their final parody, with its tragic ending, they all say that it is just like 'old times'. However, they appear to have no loyalty to the Old Man, whether or not out of fear of Bero we cannot say; nor does the Old Man demand any loyalty from them. When Bero instructs them to tell his sister who made them 'insane', Aafaa readily obliges on behalf of the others and says it was the Old Man. But it is a parody of a confession. It sounds like a recitation of what they have been made to say, and so it rebounds upon Bero himself were he more sensitive to their mocking tone.

The mendicants avidly watch Bero trying to break his father's spirit by distorting, misinterpreting and finally denying the latter's simple requests: for his watch and his spectacles, a pencil and paper, and his pipe. Aafaa has his watch and glasses and, led by Aafaa, the mendicants eat the Old Man's food themselves – while justifying their actions in the cynical terms the Old Man has taught them. Goyi accuses Aafaa of being a 'parrot', which Aafaa denies: 'I am a good pupil. The Old Man himself admits it. The quickest of the underdogs, he always said.' And he stuffs his mouth with the Old Man's food. Goyi's reply actually sums up this basic contradiction in their lives: 'First the Old Man tells us we are the underdogs, then his blasted son makes us his watchdogs!'

However, there is no deeper understanding yet; merely a retreat into cynicism. 'Makes life a little more interesting,' Aafaa tells Goyi.

This is linked to another contradiction, which again is first articulated by Aafaa. This time he confronts the Old Man about their present situation: 'I don't see you saving yourself in the situation you're in. (*More to himself*) Or us.' Despite their vocal cynicism and cynical actions, the mendicants are disgusted with the Old Man for accepting a cigarette from Bero, when he has asked for his pipe. Aafaa suddenly encapsulates their dichotomy: 'We may be on opposites of the camp,' he tells the Old Man, 'but I like to see a man stand up for himself.'

'Why?' asks the Old Man.

'So I can beat him down,' Aafaa guffaws. There is a pause; then the Old Man persists: 'You were disgusted?'

'More than,' Aafaa replies. The tone direction given in the text for this answer is: '(*Soberly*)'. Aafaa's reply and his indicated tone of voice is significant. Despite their cynicism and despite the fact that they are now his gaolers, the mendicants want to continue believing in the Old Man.

However, when he shows them the barely-smoked cigarette and then throws it on the ground in front of them, they scramble for it wildly. The principled behaviour which they were looking for in him is cast aside as far as they themselves are concerned in favour of a good smoke. They are too impoverished to have principles. The contradiction, therefore, is that though they can recognize honour, decency and principles – and indeed crave them – they can never achieve them in their own personalities. This gives rise to a special sort of self-disgust which they are obliged to live with perpetually, and which the Old Man has objectified for them. It is summed up in a song which the Old Man composed for them when they were his patients (and not his gaolers) and were visited by the head of state and his wife in the rehabilitation centre. It was called *The Song on the Visit of the First Lady to the Home for the De-balled*. ('De-balled' is a deliberate corruption of 'disabled', with obvious sexual connotations.) The song is about how the grotesquely ugly wife of the country's leader gazes complacently at the mutilated young men who are staring at her with disgust. Her look seems to say that ugly as she is she can still have sex and they can't. She can have principles – or at least, in her case, the semblance of them – and they cannot. More specifically, as 'First Lady', she represents the state that has reduced them to their present position, and her sympathy is something she can afford.

The mendicants love the song; and they sing it again, now, in the surgery, in memory of the 'sweet times'. That, too, is part of the contradiction.

A third contradiction is expressed through the new religion which the Old Man has taught his patients: the doctrine of As. It is not a new religion at all, however, but an attack on organized religion as such. Soyinka subsequently writes about religion in general terms in *Myth, Literature and the African World*, in the essay 'the ritual archetype':

Economics and power have always played a large part in championing the new deities throughout human history. The struggle for authority in early human society with the prize of material advantages, social prestige and the establishment of an elite has been nowhere so intensely marked as in the function of religion, perpetuating itself in repressive orthodoxies, countered by equally determined schisms.[14]

This is almost exactly the realization Aafaa arrives at, at the end of the play. His attack is on the priesthood; and is expressed in the form of a parody of the Gospel according to St John:

In the beginning was the Priesthood, and the Priesthood was one. Then came schism after schism by a parcel of schismatic ticks in the One Body of the Priesthood, the political priesthood went right, the spiritual priesthood went left, or vice versa. . . .

However the split in fact made no difference, Aafaa goes on to say. As he has now come to realize, the schisms were all part and parcel of the same system of domination. Indeed, the very divisions served to bring man into a more complete subjugation. Man retreats further and further into himself. However, at this juncture, he starts tackling his problems without the help of the priesthood. This is the moment for the priesthood, the system, to reassert itself. . . . AS something else. In the re-emergence of belief *as* something 'new', there is paradoxically the unending and unchanging domination of man by man.

The mendicants' repeated chant – 'As – Was – Is – Now – As Ever Shall Be' – parodies part of the Christian church liturgy:

Glory be to the Father,
And to the Son,
And to the Holy Spirit:
As it was in the beginning,
Is now,
And ever shall be,
World without end.   Amen.

At one point they also include the last line 'World without . . .', but they deliberately omit 'end', suggesting that in Christian theology at least the world is outside of, or irrelevant to, this religious system.

'As' – the word representing God – has further resonances. In Norse mythology, 'As' was the name for any of the Norse gods, such as Thor or Odin, who inhabited Asgard, the home of the gods. It comes from the Icelandic word 'ass' meaning a god, but it was obviously the interchangeability of specific gods under the title

As that particularly appealed to Soyinka. For the main emphasis in Soyinka's use of the word As in this play is the insight gained from switching the conjunction 'as' ('like') into a noun (the *process* of transformation into a parallel existence). Let us stop worshipping God as Jehovah, as Christ (in his various schismatic transformations!), as Allah, as Siva, and so on; and let us start acknowledging the transformation process itself: As. As is older than any of the religions and their priesthoods, and is each one's inner dynamic.

Furthermore, As *today* is all the other parts of the system as well: political and economic orthodoxy, science, the law, the judiciary, the arts. As is, in fact, hegemony: the development of the institutions of the state specifically to keep the elite in power, to perpetuate the power-base of the ruling class. 'As' was, 'As' is, 'As' will always be. . . . The Old Man tells the mendicants that they are the cysts in the system –

> . . . and are part of the material for re-formulating the mind of a man into the necessity of the moment's political As, the moment's scientific As, metaphysic As, sociologic As, economic recreative ethical As. . . .[15]

They are going to be used by Bero and his colleagues to experiment on, to practise upon, in order to gain absolute control of their minds. The Old Man tells them that there is no point in saying to Bero and his manipulators, look, we are all human beings, all prey to the same human weaknesses and limitations, and you are man like me; because they will reply that they are 'chosen, restored, re-designated and re-destined', and they are going to practise on all those who undermine the system.

The paradox lies in the doctrine of As seeming to be the new religion of the Old Man and his patients, when it is in fact the religion of Bero himself and the revelation of his continuing exploitation of them. The mendicants and the Old Man live this contradiction out through the role play and constant recourse to parody. They assume the roles of those in command right from the start of the play. In the name of 'As' they 'torture' each other, 'appeal' against the 'torture', are 'tried' then 'executed', and so on. They parody even their own poverty and servility; they parody confession. They parody politicians, whites and neo-colonialists (as in Blindman's superb rendering of a 'refined' public speaker preying on the racial prejudices of his audience – 'I hope I didn't do too badly.' 'No,' replies the Old Man, 'it was quite good really.' 'It was just like old times,' Blindman adds).

The events move towards a crisis, and understanding grows. The Old Man, and then Aafaa, parody the priests; and then, finally, they parody Bero himself, the specialist: 'Practise, Practise, Practise,' they all chant, tempting Bero, gun in hand, to kill his father, as the father parodies his son killing the questioning and hopeful Cripple.

Ironically, throughout the play Bero persists in thinking that 'As' is a new religion of the poor, and therefore a threat to him and his order in society, rather than the true face of his own credo, the awareness of which by the exploited is ultimately much more of a threat.

What has happened in the end? The Old Man has forced his son to kill him – Bero's final impious act for which there is no redress. The Old Man has finally put himself beyond the reach of his son's meanness. However, the Old Man did not do it for that reason, but to distract Bero from shooting the earth mothers. His action ensures that they destroy the herbs that Bero was planning to use himself. The Old Man's action is in effect a sacrifice on behalf of the mendicants: a following-through of self-awareness, and an assertion of the principle of common humanity. He makes the understanding which he has given them substantial. Bero is defiled; and he is cheated of that earth-bound goodness which he sought to bend to his will. The mendicants mockingly chant at him and his ineffectual sister the Old Man's credo which is really his own:

> Bi o ti wa
> . . . .
> As-Was-Is-Now . . .

And the final stage direction: (*The song stops in mid-word and the lights snap out simultaneously*).[16]

A Dance of the Forests

Performed in 1960 for the independence celebrations of Nigeria, and as a direct comment on it, *A Dance of the Forests* is Soyinka's first major play. Within the play, the gathering of the tribes for a great feast, symbolic of Nigeria's independence celebrations, requires the presence of illustrious ancestors from the past. The

Forest Head – who is the Supreme Being – is petitioned; but sends instead two accusers from the past, and so transforms the celebration into a crisis. This leads to 'tortured self-awareness', at least for some of the living.

In the same way, Soyinka's play, as part of the independence celebrations presents, instead of a piece of complacent rhetoric, an apocalyptic vision of a dread future which can only be avoided by self-sacrifice as a result of what he calls 'self-apprehension'. He can have felt no satisfaction whatsoever when he came to write *Madmen and Specialists* ten years later that the 'fanged and bloody future', which he had predicted for the new nation–state of Nigeria, had come to pass in the Nigerian civil war.

In *A Dance of the Forests*, Demoke, the carver, would seek to make the society something better through the profound self-apprehension he achieves during the course of the play. In *Madmen and Specialists*, as we have already seen, the Old Man is trying to torture self-awareness out of the souls of the mendicants, which process in the end leads him to sacrifice his life. However, in the earlier play the awareness is essentially metaphysical, while in the later play the awareness tends to be more social. The metaphysical analysis is not as emphasized. In both plays 'self-apprehension' goes well beyond political awareness, and is unavoidable if there is to be genuine social reform.

There were two other major plays written between *A Dance of the Forests* and *Madmen and Specialists*: *Kongi's Harvest* and *The Road*. In *Kongi's Harvest* an attempted revolutionary act, on the basis of a rite and as a result of a metaphysical analysis, has a negative result. In *The Road* the metaphysical experience of the Professor and Murano is set in deliberate contrast to the political experience of say Tokyo Kid and the other political thugs. Both these plays have proved very popular with audiences and readers. A number of very detailed analyses have been made of them by literary critics and by theatre specialists.

We have already made reference to *Myth, Literature and the African World*. It is, for readers of Soyinka's plays, a source-work on his philosophical, poetic and critical precepts: it is a sort of 'poetic manifesto'. Throughout the four essays which constitute the book runs the theme of the search for 'oneness', or 'wholeness', which the playwright sees the individual achieving only by daring to bridge the abyss of primal chaos, and triumphing by an exercise of the Will. The theme is embodied in the being of the god of iron, Ogun, for Soyinka the central god of the Yoruba pantheon. Ogun alone experienced and explored the primordial chaos 'which he conquered, then bridged, with the aid of the artefacts of his science'. His science was the mastering of iron-ore and the artefacts were the sword and the plough.

Soyinka develops his analysis of Ogun:

Only Ogun experienced the process of being literally torn asunder in cosmic winds, of rescuing himself from the precarious edge of total dissolution by harnessing the untouched part of himself, the will. This is the unique essentiality of Ogun in Yoruba metaphysics: as embodiment of the social, communal will invested in the protagonist of its choice. It is as a paradigm of this experience of dissolution and re-integration that the actor in the ritual archetype can be understood.[17]

In 'The fourth stage', which was written before the other essays in *Myth, Literature and the African World*, there is an earlier analysis of Ogun:

Ogun is the embodiment of Will, and the Will is the paradoxical truth of destructiveness and creativeness in acting man.[18]

He goes on to comment, with perhaps a reference to his own experiences:

Only one who has himself undergone the experience of disintegration, whose spirit has been tested and whose psychic resources laid under stress by forces most inimical to individual assertion, only he can understand and be the force of fusion between the two contradictions.[19]

Ogun is frequently referred to in these essays as the artist, the 'artistic spirit', 'the essence of creativity'. He is also referred to specifically as 'the first actor'. When the actor, the artist, finds himself at the edge of physical and emotional endurance, on the point of disintegration, then

. . . transitional memory takes over and intimations rack him of that intense parallel of his progress through the gulf of transition, of the dissolution of his self and his struggle and triumph over subsumation through the agency of Will.[20]

All these elements of analysis – the dissolution of self, the search for oneness, the exercise of will, the retrieval of self, Ogun as 'the first actor' and the embodiment of contradiction – all are brought together in the concept of the artist's sensibility:

The resulting sensibility is also the sensibility of the artist, and he is a profound artist only to the degree to which he comprehends and expresses this principle of destruction, and re-creation.[21]

As we have seen in *Madmen and Specialists*, Soyinka's own sensibility even goes beyond this basic contradiction, to living through other, specifically social, contradictions, in social conditions where 'oneness' can hardly seem a valid objective. This growing sensibility would seem, therefore, to carry Soyinka away from his metaphysical engagement. However, we need to understand his metaphysics in order to grasp the meaning of *A Dance of the Forests*, and also to comprehend the fountain-head of his poetic inspiration.

There is one other element in the analysis in *Myth, Literature and the African World* which we need to consider before moving on to a consideration of *A Dance of the Forests*: music, and its metaphysical significance. Music, dance and masquerade are crucial to nearly all Soyinka's plays, and especially to *A Dance of the Forests*. Music, he writes, 'is the intensive language of transition.' And as the 'language of transition' it lies at the heart of his metaphysics. It is the actual means of communication to the audience both of the disintegration and the retrieval of self; it actually translates the actor and audience to that state of awareness of the journey through the abyss.

Music's link with Yoruba tragedy, through myth, produces 'weird disruptive melodies' which can unearth 'cosmic uncertainties which pervade human existence', can reveal 'the magnitude and power of creation',[22] and can create the experience of the chasm, the yawning abyss, the chthonic realm.

In this metaphysical sense, music is most apparent and effective in a much later play, *Death and the King's Horseman* (1975), both within the play and between the play itself in performance and its audiences. Within the play it is the means by which Elesin Oba, the King's Horseman, is supposed to commit his ritual suicide in honour of the dead Oba and so restore harmony to the community which the death of the Oba has set at risk. Between the play and its audiences, music shows the far greater disharmony caused by his failure to commit suicide, and carries the audience through a far more profound crisis. The music fulfils a similar crucial function in *A Dance of the Forests*, to which we must now turn.[23]

The play opens in a clearing in the forest. Two ancestors are rising from the earth, breaking its soil surface: a dead man in a rusty warrior's outfit and a dead woman who still carries the pregnancy that died with her. The three town dwellers, Demoke, Rola and Adenebi, and a fourth 'town dweller', Obaneji (who is in fact Forest Head himself in disguise), pass by the ancestors one by one, uncomprehending who they are. The dead pair ask each one in turn to 'take my case', by which each means his separate cause. They are at this point, therefore, seen by the living merely as petitioners, though they are the accusers of those three town dwellers whose former lives, eight centuries before, were viciously intertwined with the lives and deaths of the dead pair. No one will take up either cause, and the dead pair wander off into another part of the forest; while the town dwellers, including the disguised Forest Head, come together, explaining to each other, superficially, why they have escaped from the town and the celebrations and come into the forest. However, the disguised Forest Head forces each one of them to reveal not only their true motives for their escape into the forest but to admit to their guilt. Rola is the first. She is forced to admit to being the notorious courtesan, Madame Tortoise, responsible for the deaths of two men. Demoke the carver, the artist, the servant of Ogun, admits to the murder of his apprentice, Oremole. Only Adenebi, the councillor, who took bribes and was responsible for sixty-five deaths as a result of distorting vehicle regulations, refuses until the very end of the play actually to acknowledge his guilt.

Whilst the Forest Head, as Obaneji, is teasing out admissions of guilt from Demoke, Rola and Adenebi, leading them all the while deeper and deeper into the forest, two other groups are trying to sort out the celebrations, the preparations for which appear to have gone drastically wrong. The activities of the various beings in these two groups, who are all in the forest, alternate with the wandering deeper into the forest of the other six (the dead pair, the town dwellers and the Forest Head himself). One of these groups are the elders from the town, including the father of Demoke, who have called this great Feast to celebrate the Gathering of the Tribes, and who now are desperate to drive back into the forest the ancestors they asked for. They use a band of beaters, a masquerader with his acolyte, a divining elder (Agboreko) and finally an amazing lorry which belches out oil fumes and smoke in copious quantities. The other group are non-humans. They comprise (1) the two gods Eshuoro and Ogun, and (2) all the forest spirits, including Murete and Forest Head's own activist, Aroni, the Lame One. Aroni is in fact organizing Forest Head's own metaphysical Welcoming for the Dead, which is intended as the experience of 'self-apprehension', and perhaps transition through the abyss, for the three town dwellers.

This welcoming also embraces an immediate crisis involving a bitter conflict between the gods Eshuoro and Ogun, for Ogun's servant, Demoke, who as an artist and carver worships the god of iron, has carved a gigantic totem out of the tree sacred to Eshuoro. Worse, it is Eshuoro's worshipper, Oremole, whom Demoke has murdered in the process of carving the totem. Demoke suffers from vertigo. Oremole, his assistant did not, and so climbed higher up the tree than his master, and in the privacy of those heights taunted Demoke, who reached up and caused him to fall to his death.

Eshuoro is therefore in pursuit of Demoke. He is determined to attend Forest Head's Welcoming for the Dead – in order to subvert it, and to gain his own ends. He is not interested in 'torturing self-awareness' out of Demoke, but in immediate and vengeful justice for the murder of Oremole, and the desecration of his sacred tree. Ogun, however, is equally determined to protect his servant Demoke. For Forest Head, the Supreme Being, this conflict too is part of the process of transition through the abyss, and the person being increasingly focused upon is the artist, the actor, Demoke. His impending crisis goes far beyond notions of (1) divine justice, (2) revenge, (3) social and political order. The limitations of each of these as, separately, the key to 'self-apprehension' will become clear as the structure of the second part of the play, the dance itself, is revealed.

The movement deeper and deeper into the forest metaphorically reflects the subsequent movement of the dance: there is a penetration to deeper levels of meaning. Present at the beginning of the second part of the play are the spaces of the three parallel worlds of the living, the ancestors and the unborn. These worlds are conceived as spaces, conterminous with each other, a translation of *time* into spatial terms. It is somewhat confusing, therefore, to speak of the 'past', the 'present' and the 'future' as a linear time scale. One has to imagine them as spatial worlds, and the movement between them is this crucial realm of transition, which Soyinka calls the fourth stage, which is also conceived of as a space.

Eshuoro, whom we meet now for the first time, occupies all three spaces simultaneously. So does Ogun. However, their immediate concern is in the world of the living; and in a long harangue, which actually serves as a prologue to the dance, Eshuoro proclaims himself to be the embodiment of 'the fear in men's lives'. As an extension of this, he is to be seen as the agent of revenge, blind justice, an eye for an eye and a tooth for a tooth: inflexible. He rushes off after his long speech crying for revenge on Demoke.

The forest spirits are assembled to Welcome the Dead. The Forest Crier indicates that lives in the present were also lives in the past; and as they wait for the proceedings to begin Forest Head tells Aroni about leading the three town dwellers to this moment: 'It was their latent violence which frightened me. I did not know what I would do if it involved me.' But now these violent living appear so tame, after having been confronted with their true natures and confessed to their crimes, that even at this early point in the rite they could be sent home. 'But they forget too easily,' comments Forest Head.

Crime – guilt – confession – pardon – expiation: this may be a process for morality, but for Soyinka it stops short of full self-apprehension, the full awareness of being. Those who have the capacity for action, and a sensibility which perceives the inner contradictions in all existence, especially the creative artist, must go further. They must dare the fourth space, that 'luminous area of transition'.

The performance space becomes the arena for this time-warp: Aroni calls forth the past, and the twelfth-century court of Mata Kharibu appears. Demoke and Rola are in their former lives: the Court Poet and Madame Tortoise. They are not forced to act out their former lives: this is that time. We, the audience, perceive an inter-meshing of relationships and a series of actions and decisions which now seem to have peculiar significance. Madame Tortoise, Mata Kharibu's queen, whom he has abducted from a neighbouring king, has forced a war to be fought by Kharibu's armies against the kingdom of her former husband to recover her trousseau. Madame Tortoise is vain, capricious and vindictive. The Court Poet is forced to climb on to the roof of the palace to fetch her canary. Mata Kharibu himself, together with his sycophantic court, is bent on imperialist aggression.

However, one warrior, a captain of his army, reasons out the war's futility and teaches his men to reason too. After a futile effort to get him to recant, the warrior is given to a slave-dealer to be sold into slavery, together with his men. Madame Tortoise offers him the opportunity of overthrowing Kharibu himself, but his antagonism towards her precludes such opportunism. His wife breaks into the throne room to beg the court for mercy. She is pregnant. Madame Tortoise orders the warrior's castration before he is sold into slavery. The wife commits suicide.

The captain and his pregnant wife are, of course, the dead pair. They now have separate petitions for the world of the living, for their special horror has been their separate, but equally deprived, states in the world of the ancestors. The woman who died with the unborn child in her womb has been further disquieted in the world of the unborn to which her foetus belongs.

At the end of this re-creation of the past, Eshuoro and then Ogun arrive in the arena of performance. Eshuoro comments disparagingly on the Dead Man's decision and actions as a living warrior. Ogun taunts and finally clashes with Eshuoro. They are separated by Forest Head who comments that soon he won't know them apart from humans – 'so closely have their habits grown on you'. The attempt by the two gods to transpose Demoke's murder of Oremole onto a mythic plane that will reflect their rival archetypal powers is resisted by Forest Head, who nevertheless acknowledges that this mythic dimension is an integral part of the process. 'Do not deny that all goes as you planned it,' Forest Head tells Eshuoro, and adds to himself, 'but only because it is my wish.'

We now enter the moment of transition. The space is carefully described in the stage directions:

> (*Back-scene lights up gradually to reveal a dark, wet, atmosphere, dripping moisture, and soft, moist soil. A palm-tree sways at a low angle, broken but still alive. Seemingly lightning-reduced stumps. Rotting wood all over the ground. . . . First there is a total stillness, emphasized by the sound of moisture dripping to the ground*)[24]

Forest Head first of all questions the Dead Woman through his masked Questioner, who condemns her for committing suicide. She knows only hate. Then the Dead Man is brought for questioning. He, too, seeks redress for his endless restlessness. This time it is Forest Head who turns the Dead Man's accusation upon him:

> . . . Mulieru, I knew you
> In the days of pillaging, in the days

Of sudden slaughter, and the parting
Of child and brother. I knew you
In the days of grand destroying
And you a part of the waste. . . .[25]

The Dead Man, Mulieru, is certainly not blameless. When he was
a soldier he was part of the destruction; when he was castrated and
sold into slavery as a eunuch he was well-fed and fat. The
Questioner takes up the accusation, and, referring to Madame
Tortoise's offer to the condemned warrior to overthrow Kharibu,
asks:

What did he prove, from the first when,
Power at his grasp, he easily
Surrendered his manhood?[26]

We discover that the masked Questioner is none other than
Eshuoro, who has subverted the role. Forest Head contends that
things will proceed as planned.

Then he does something significant: he dismisses 'for the time
being' the Dead Man and his petition: 'Let the one whose
incompletion denies him rest be patient till the Forest has chor-
used the Future through the lips of the earth-beings.' And the
stage direction adds: (*At this, the Dead Man makes a dumb
distressed protest, but Aroni leads him off*).[27] We never see him
again. Who exactly is he, and how does he fit into the overall
structure of the play? In the court of Mata Kharibu he is the one
who thinks. His protest against the futile war, and against Mata
Kharibu's rule, is a highly intellectualized stance. He is engaged in
verbal altercation by two other intellectuals in the court: the
Physician and the Court Historian. The Physician is well-
intentioned but limited by his lack of perception and lack of
imagination. The warrior easily gets the better of him in the
argument. The Court Historian – Adenebi – is different. His intellectualism is perverse: it is exercised without responsibility and
justifies what cannot be justified. His rhetoric and his verbal
dexterity are corrupting. However, there is also a certain stubborn
arrogance on the part of the warrior himself in his own intellectual
position. He is prepared to sacrifice his wife and unborn child, and
even the men under his command, for it. Ultimately his intellectualism robs him of the power to act.

The Dead Man may be said to represent Soyinka's view of the

limitations of political awareness. It is a position which Soyinka's real protagonist in the play, Demoke, must completely transcend if he is to change anything in the future. The Dead Man has served his purpose. He has embodied a position which had to be stated so that it could be transcended. Now he can be dispensed with in the play.

Not so the Dead Woman and her unborn child. She is relieved of her burden of the unborn child so that 'the tongue of the unborn, stilled for generations, be loosened'. At the same time the three town dwellers are masked and are now incorporated into the dance as forest spirits. This is the transition into the world of the unborn, the space of the future, where all the resources of the earth are wantonly plundered by man, as the words and the masquerade convey; while the Figure in Red, a bloody destiny, plays with the Dead Woman's Half Child – the future – and wins. Because of man's greed and avarice the future will be bloody.

Then comes chaos: the rivers run red, the winds cease, the sun is darkened at noon, the volcanoes – energy within the earth – cease. 'Whose hand is this,' asks Forest Head, 'that reaches from the grave?' The ants have joined the masquerade: they are suffering humanity:

> Down the axis of the world, from
> The whirlwind to the frozen drifts,
> We are the ever legion of the world,
> Smitten, for – 'the good to come'.[28]

But there is no 'good to come'. The Ant Leader curses the future: after the scourge of silent suffering, there will be blind retaliation, like the sting in the tail of the scorpion. A bloody destiny. Again the Figure in Red appeals for the Half Child: a bloody destiny is claiming the future.

Forest Head orders the unmasking of the three town dwellers so that they may see the final enactment of the future with their natural eyes, and not with the eyes of the forest spirits.

The rite now embraces the collective mask of the Three Triplets, who join the dance one after the other. They embody the hideous future that the Ant Leader pronounced. The First Triplet is a manifestation of that 'good to come', for which numberless, nameless human beings have died. But it is hideous, grotesque, headless and no 'good' end at all. It is followed in by the Second Triplet: the Greater Cause that lies like a mirage, beyond all immediate ends. It, too, is grotesque: a huge, drooling head only, the complement of the headless First Triplet. The First and Second Triplets are linked to the world of the living by a comment of Forest Head. The triplets, 'perversions' as he calls them, are born when 'weak, pitiable criminals . . . acquire power over one another, and their instincts are fulfilled a thousandfold, an hundred thousandfold.'

There is a Third Triplet, 'fanged and bloody'. 'I am posterity. Can no one see on what milk I have been nourished?' For the third time the Figure in Red, the embodiment of a bloody destiny, appeals for possession of the future, for the Half Child. We now discover that the Figure in Red is Eshuoro in another disguise, another god-concealing mask. The Half Child struggles to move towards its mother, the future seeking to escape from a blindly vengeful god, uncaring of humanity.

At this point it is perhaps necessary to explain the 'round of "ampe"' which is danced over and over again by the Triplets and the Interpreter (who proves to be one of Eshuoro's minions in disguise). Oyin Ogunba describes 'ampe' thus:

The 'ampe' dance is a Yoruba children's dance ('ampe' means 'Do as I do, we are the same') in which two children face each other, jump and make the same hand and foot movement uttering in unison the sound 'pe pe pe pe pe pe shampe!' and stretching corresponding feet to indicate perfect agreement.[29]

The reader has to try and carry in his imagination the sound of the music, the movement of the dances and the visual spectacle of the masks. The scene has built up to this passionate pitch from the absolute stillness of the dripping scene which marked its beginning.

As the dance moves to its climax, Ogun has intervened, standing behind the mother and drawing the Half Child towards her. The frenzied 'ampe' distracts the Half Child, disarms him, then the first two Triplets catch him up and toss him to the Third Triplet. The Half Child is tossed back and forth as in a furious and lethal game. Demoke tries to save the Half Child – he intervenes to rescue the future from this chaotic and bloody disintegration – and finally, through the help of Ogun, gains possession of it. Demoke would give it back to the mother, but Eshuoro blocks the way. Both Eshuoro and Ogun appeal to the Forest Head for a judgement. He refuses, and in a short speech he expresses the fundamental contradiction between the Creator's omnipotence and man's free-will: '. . . to intervene is to be guilty of contradiction and yet to remain altogether unfelt is to make my long-rumoured ineffectuality complete. . . .' He seeks to 'torture self-awareness' from their souls' in the hope that new beginnings may indeed reflect some change. If Demoke really means to take the world of the unborn, the future, out of Eshuoro's hands, and return it to the human world of the living, he will have to pay a heavy sacrifice. He gives the Half Child to its mother; and the last phase of the dance begins.

A sacrificial basket is strapped to his head by Eshuoro's jester, and he is forced to climb to the top of his totem. This fear of heights – in European Romanticism often expressed in the symbol of a tower or mountain – is the fear of the abyss. Demoke's fall, when Eshuoro sets fire to the tree, is the final moment of transition for him. He is caught by Ogun as he falls. It was Ogun who first dared the abyss; and it is his worshipper's knowledge of his bridging of it by an exercise of the will that has led him to act and to exert his own will. Ogun, who is the embodiment of contradiction, gently lays him down, and the implements of iron that signify Ogun's dual contradictory nature, the gun and the cutlass, he carefully lays by Demoke's side.

Through Demoke's act of will – his sacrifice – humankind edges forward, perhaps, from the blind vindictiveness and revenge of Mata Kharibu's kingdom, embodied in the god-head Eshuoro – the 'fear in men's lives'. It is not to be by way of what Soyinka sees as barren intellectualism (the role and nature of the Dead Man) which is presented with its inevitable opposite in the person of Adenebi and his corrupting cleverness. Instead, it is by way of confronting and embracing the contradiction embodied in the man of action, the creative artist: creativity and destruction. Demoke creates the totem; he kills Oremole his assistant. To exercise the will is to act. Demoke acts: first, by carving the totem (acting under divine inspiration); second, by killing young Oremole (acting in passion); third, by intervening to save the Half Child (an act of compassion); fourth, by giving the Half Child to the mother and fifth, as a willing sacrifice, as in a rite of passage which will carry the burden of his people across the void. 'Willing' is used in two senses: Demoke has *agreed* (is willing) to be the sacrifice; and he is also compelling (willing) his spirit through the darkness.

Opera Wonyosi

Opera Wonyosi was first performed at the University of Ife's convocation ceremony on 16 December 1977. The title plays on the meanings of the word 'opera' in Yoruba and English. Accented thus: òpèrá, it means in Yoruba 'The fool buys. . . .' In English it refers to a very elaborate and expensive form of theatre in which every word is sung to the accompaniment of a large orchestra. Wonyosi was a very expensive type of lace (it cost about $1000 a metre!) for which there was a craze at this time in Nigerian high society. In a prefatory note to the manuscript of the play which circulated after its production, Soyinka writes: '*Opera Wonyosi* has been written at a high period of Nigeria's social decadence, the like of which will probably never again be experienced. . . .'

His play is modelled on two European plays: Bertolt Brecht's *Die Dreigroschenöper* (*The Threepenny Opera*) (1928), which itself was a twentieth century version of a play composed exactly two hundred years before – John Gay's *The Beggar's Opera* (1728).[30] Both titles, like Soyinka's, are ironical; and reflect the fact that both the plays were critical of their societies. Gay satirized the Whig ascendancy in London, which was dominated by Sir Robert Walpole, the First Minister of the Cabinet who advised the German-born King of England, George I; Brecht satirized the excesses of the Weimar Republic in Germany, which was set up after the defeat of Germany in the First World War and before Adolf Hitler's rise to power.

Neither satire was revolutionary. Gay certainly did not seek the dissolution of the aristocracy – or of the emergent bourgeoisie. His satire was directed against individuals and his play aimed at personal reform. Brecht, however, did intend a more fundamental political impact when presenting his play. Using Gay's story of double-dealing and betrayal amongst the criminals and urban destitute, Brecht's play attempts a class analysis and is an indictment of capitalism and the late bourgeois world. Ironically, his play has proved very popular with audiences of the very class he is seeking to undermine through his satire. Like Gay's play, which had phenomenal success on London stages for over a century, Brecht's *Threepenny Opera* made his reputation as a playwright in Europe and the play has been translated into a number of European languages and frequently revived in the west since 1928.

Part of the reason for the success of both these plays is the music. Gay's play was a new art form when it first appeared: a 'ballad opera'. That is to say, the play was not a full opera in which every word was sung – indeed, another aspect of its satire was its attack on the fashionable Italian opera of the time – but a play interspersed with songs. The words of the songs were related to the play – they were usually ironical and focused the criticism of people or society – but the tunes were the familiar and popular ballad tunes of the time. Some of these ballads were genuine folk ballads; but most were songs recently composed and currently popular in London in the 1720s. The tunes, therefore, were very melodious, variously haunting or lively, while the songs themselves were witty and satirical. The art form of the ballad opera has remained popular since Gay introduced it – it is now known in North America and Britain as the 'musical', though musicals tend to be sentimental rather than satirical.

The music for Brecht's play was composed by Kurt Weill, then a young composer and friend of Brecht, who, like Brecht, later had to flee his homeland Germany when Hitler came to power.[31] Weill composed his music jointly with Brecht who wrote the sharp acerbic words of the songs. He used jazz and some popular music, whilst striving for a more profound – and social – meaning through the music. The songs of *The Threepenny Opera* have had a profound appeal for audiences. The opening song, 'Mack the Knife', later popularized by Louis Armstrong's rendering of it, is well known in its own right, and Soyinka uses it as the opening song for *Opera Wonyosi*, with words adapted to the Nigerian situation.

All three operas are set in the underworld of criminals, pimps, prostitutes and beggars, and the conflict is between two underworld characters for more power and a wider sphere of operations. One of the men is known as the King of the Beggars. He has turned the begging of the deformed and distressed into a profitable and well-run business. His power comes from the cynical manipulation of the processes of the law: he both protects criminals and betrays them, and he 'protects' the beggars – or has them beaten up. In Soyinka's play this man is Chief Anikura; in Brecht's and Gay's plays he is called Peachum. The other man is a big-time robber: in Gay's play a highway robber; in all three plays the leader of a gang of robbers, known as Captain MacHeath, Mack the Knife, Mackie.

In Brecht's play, and after him in Soyinka's play, both these men struggle for supremacy within the unbroken continuum of the criminal, professional and business worlds for a monopoly of the pickings. Brecht laboriously tried to show that, under capitalism, there is no difference between the morality of legal business practice and of crime. Capitalism itself is state crime. 'What,' asks one of the characters in *The Threepenny Opera*, 'is robbing a bank compared with founding a bank?' Soyinka is less concerned to *prove* this link than simply to demonstrate it in a more general indictment of greed, materialism and exploitation, in a system in which 'socialists' are as culpable as 'capitalists'.

In the story, MacHeath marries the daughter of Chief Anikura, Polly. This brings Anikura into direct conflict with MacHeath, not simply because of the abduction of his daughter, or for her sake, but because it puts the secrets of his business into MacHeath's hands and so allows him to gain control of it. Anikura gets MacHeath accused and arrested – twice. The first time he is released by the machinations of Polly, who has taken over MacHeath's criminal operations, turned them into legal big business and now runs the gang as a limited liability company. She corrupts the judiciary. In response, Anikura corrupts the very law-makers themselves, who overthrow the ruling of the judiciary and have MacHeath rearrested and condemned to death by firing squad. Mackie is saved at the very last moment by an imperial pardon – imperial, because all the action of the play takes place in the Nigerian Quarter in Bangui during the run-up to Bokasa's coronation in the short-lived Central African Empire. It turns out that his pardon was partly engineered by Anikura himself. Polly has become the brains behind MacHeath's enterprises, whose scale of operations is now vastly increased by being amalgamated with the multinationals. She and her father are now members of that comprador class which leeches society and of which, in real life, Emperor Bokasa was the apotheosis.

Opera Wonyosi is – not necessarily by intent – a satirical inversion of *Madmen and Specialists*. It shows how peace, and oil wealth (which succeeded the Nigerian civil war) can mutilate the population, emotionally and physically, just as much as the war did. War and trade are part of the same process, and are inseparable from each other. The Old Man, who sought to enlighten the maimed of the war about the nature of exploitation, has become the totally cynical Chief Anikura, 'King' of beggars within a society in which everyone begs. The mendicants who struggled forward to self-awareness, have become the people they parodied: the professionals. Now, the politicians, the lawyers, the professors, play the role of beggars; and by begging, in the gutter, learn how to beg and grovel for high office. There is a deeper irony here, for those parodying the beggars are the ones who made the real beggars. Bero, the specialist, and his sister, have in this play become husband and wife, with their roles reversed. Polly, Anikura's daughter, is the aggressor, bent on acquiring economic wealth and power by any means. She is also an example of what Si Bero, pliant and uselessly good, in *Madmen and Specialists*, could so easily become. As Polly's parents comment: 'She's such a sensitive child you don't want to mention blood to her.' MacHeath's execution (which doesn't happen, in fact) is a pseudo-sacrifice; and a demonstration of how sacrifice can be degraded into a cheap public spectacle appealing to not the noblest but the basest instincts in man.

The only people in *Madmen and Specialists* who are not represented are the earth mothers and, indeed, what is absent altogether from the satire is the metaphysical dimension. This has some significance when we come to consider how Soyinka's criticism of his society has developed. But before we can do this we need to see how the very specific satire is used to develop a criticism of Soyinka's society. For this play is not about man or society, the African or African society. It is a critique that is specific to time and place: Nigeria at the end of the 1970s.

The structure of *Opera Wonyosi* is sequential and quite simple. The play is given a theatrical 'frame' by Dee-Jay, the disc-jockey or master of ceremonies. He introduces the play, and indicates (1) its musical form; (2) its begging theme – '. . . that's what the whole nation is doing – begging for a slice of the action'; (3) its topicality and (4) its satirical targets – 'I'm yet to decide whether such a way-out opera should be named after the beggars, the army, the bandits, the police, the cash-madams, the students, the trade-unionists, the alhajis and hajias, the aladura, the academics, the holy patriarchs and unholy heresiarchs. . . .'

Dee-Jay also functions as a narrator, providing a link between the scenes; and at the climax of the play it is he who reads out Bokasa's proclamation announcing the amnesty for criminals, which enables MacHeath to escape the firing squad. Each scene contains one or two songs which serve to widen the relevance of the events in that scene and to extend the satire.

The first scene is set in Anikura's place which is known as 'Home from home for the homeless', in the Nigerian Quarter in Bangui. His business is a sort of beggars' union, or rather, a beggars' protection society: if they don't let him 'protect' them they get beaten up or handed over to the police. He is helped in running the business by his wife, known as De Madam. There are various types of begging outfit. Anikura exhibits these to a new recruit to the business: 'the Cheerful Cripple: Victim of Modern Road Traffic'; 'War casualty'; Tapha-Psychotic; Victim of Modern Industry. It is not the beggars who are being satirized, but the system which creates these types of mental and physical deformity and a song about the 'Cement Bonanza' in Nigeria in 1977 makes the satire specific by referring to the scandal when hundreds of cargo ships waited outside Lagos harbour for months to off-load a ludicrously large order by the army for cement. The song's title is: 'Big man chop cement; cement chop small man'.

The structure of the song emphasizes the irony. There are three verses, in which the labourers unloading the cement round-the-clock sing of their luck at getting what seems like good pay and overtime. The refrain, however, expresses the labourers' later realization that the cement fumes have given them Fibrositis and drastically shortened their lives:

And the overtime pay comes to mere chicken feed
When the cement tycoon has filled out his greed.

The song is sung by Anikura's beggars. Like the songs in Brecht's play, the songs in *Opera Wonyosi* are not meant to be sung naturalistically. Instead, the play stops, the people come on to the stage, and the song is sung as a 'number' at a pop concert. The message of the song is therefore addressed directly to the audience. It is a comment on the situations within the play, and a focusing of the satire. In the cement song the satire is attacking two levels of greed: the knowing and culpable greed of the cement tycoon, and the ignorant greed, on a much more limited scale, of the labourer.

Ahmed, destitute and therefore a new recruit to the business, is given his outfit, then we are given the first development in the story. Polly, the only child of Chief Anikura and De Madam, is not to be found at home and her parents very much fear that she has run off and married Captain MacHeath. A second number is sung, this time by the Chief and De Madam: 'The song of ngh-ngh-ngh'.

This is the sound one makes which, together with a shake of the head, means 'never!', 'not at all!'. Again like Brecht's and Weill's songs, this links the words of the song to a physical gesture, so that the song is 'acted' through as well as sung through. 'The song of ngh-ngh-ngh' comments that anyone's daughter will marry as wealthy a man as she can. This is contradictory – deliberately – to the familiar theme of many African plays in which the beautiful daughter is being forced to marry a wealthy old man, when the only man she wants to marry is the young guy she loves but who is terribly poor. No, says the song, ngh-ngh-ngh. For the daughters of today true love is finished and anyway, everybody is a thief and only the big men get away with it:

We know it's the big fish the net's sure to miss
While your small-time bandit earns lead perforations!

Having taken their time to sing this song, De Madam and Anikura then rush off to search for Polly.

Polly has indeed run off with Mackie, the Captain, and the second scene shows her wedding, in the stables of the Polo Club. This place is transformed into a reception room by a vast array of consumer durables, stolen for the occasion of the wedding by Mack's gang. Mack and Polly seek the glamour of the good life. Mack is determined to whip his gang of crooks into shape and to give them more class. However, the whole scene is a debasement of this expensive life-style, and both Mack and Polly reveal during the course of the scene that they can be just as coarse and unscrupulous as any other crook when the occasion demands. Style is merely a thin covering over the avarice. Mack comments disparagingly of one of his gang: 'He eats caviar with a knife. With a blood-stained knife!' We have an image of the society and it refers to everyone: refinement is only bought with the blood of others.

The prophet Jerubabel comes in, and by means of spurious analogies he is able to justify his being there to bless the marriage. The whole company then sing a 'hymn' to the happy couple which expresses the hope that Mack will never end up as the main attraction at the Bar Beach show – a reference to the public executions which regularly took place at this time at Bar Beach in Lagos. (On the whole only small-time crooks were shot.)

The Commissioner of Police joins the wedding party. In the play he is variously called Tiger Brown (his name in Brecht's play) or Smith. Soyinka reserves a special loathing for this character. He is

totally venal and completely corrupt; and in his train the whole
police force is committed to corruption. In fact it has become so
hot for him back home in Nigeria that he has been loaned
indefinitely to Bokasa and the Central African Empire. He is also
very stupid. Mack and Smith/Brown have a bond which supposedly goes back to when they were both soldiers in the civil war.
They sing a song, which is heavily ironical, about their spirit of
camaraderie: 'Khaki is a man's best friend'. Again, the structure of
the song reflects its irony. The four verses sing of patriotism, glory,
power, while the refrain or chorus sings of the reality of the civil
war and comments that while the nation is one, the soldier's bodies
are definitely not:

We know who won and who got undone
No thought of keeping his body one
It's scattered from Bendel to Bonny Town.

The song satirizes the rhetoric of the Nigerian civil war: neither
side was really fighting for an ideal but for possession of the oil.
What has it got to do with the wedding which is taking place? On
one level it reflects the materialism which lies beneath occasions
such as weddings: marriage and war are business propositions and
the reality is often different from the high-flown rhetoric. The
scene has shown us, therefore, the exact nature of the relationship
between Polly and MacHeath, and of the relationship between
MacHeath and the Commissioner of Police. The 'innocent and
sensitive' young girl has married the master crook for what she can
get out of it; and the most wanted criminal consorts with the Chief
of Police!

In the next scene, which is by way of an interlude, Dee-Jay
introduces us to Emperor Bokasa himself. It must be remembered
that the play was written while this grotesque head of state was still
in power, and this scene was no doubt intended as a vicious attack
on a ruling African leader, whom Soyinka totally despises. Bokasa
is created as a parody, but with the sense that the real Bokasa is
already a parody of himself. He marches onto the stage with his
squad and initially behaves like a sergeant-major. Then he addresses the audience, not as in a public address, but as though he was
standing outside his society and commenting on himself with
brutal frankness, boasting of his viciousness. Then he transforms
his speech into a dance in which his squad mimes trampling people
to death. Bokasa finally joins in, with immense energy and

enjoyment, yelling at the band: 'Give me that Lagosian lynch-mob rallying rhythm!'

Brown – or Smith – Bokasa's (Nigerian) Chief of Police has been summoned by Bokasa to watch this display; and his amused presence throughout the 'imperial stomp' reflects the collusion with Bokasa of at least some members of Nigerian society and the Nigerian body politic. At the end of the stomp the story is moved on a little, for Brown is given specific instructions to avoid any riots or disturbances by the poor during his coronation.

The next scene, set once again in Anikura's establishment, reveals Brown carrying out his instructions from Bokasa. He hopes to sort out Anikura and lock up his beggars for the duration. A hint has been dropped in Brown's ear by MacHeath that Anikura was planning something. Anikura turns the tables on this dumb Chief of Police: unless MacHeath is arrested immediately, thousands and thousands of the poor will march in front of the royal chariot and be filmed on television. The threat of the poor disrupting Boky's coronation is Anikura's ploy to force Brown to arrest MacHeath. Such a demonstration is not intended by Anikura to benefit the poor whom he controls.

A song at this point reflects the cheapness of life for ordinary Nigerians. It is called 'Who killed Nio-Niga?'. Soyinka has based it on a famous syncopated marching song: 'Who killed Cock Robin?'. In the play, the song is highly schematic. A beggar sings the first verse, 'Who killed Nio-Niga / I, said Sir Bigger. . . .'; the second verse, 'Who caught Nio-Niga / I, said Chief Freelance. . . .' is sung by Tiger Brown; the third verse, 'Who heard Nio-Niga/I, said Professor . . .' by Anikura; the fourth verse, 'Who sold Nio-Niga/I, said Ma Trader. . . .' is sung by De Madam; the fifth verse, 'Who carved Nio-Niga / I, said Doc Morgans. . . .' by another Beggar, and so on. When it comes to the last verse, 'Who'll solve Case Niga?' the song abruptly stops, and there is silence, while everyone who has characterized a verse goes earnestly about his business. The stage direction describes it thus:

['**Bigger**' *puffs his cigar smugly,* '**Army**' *salutes,* '**Police**' *drills,* '**Doc**' *sheathes his stethoscope.*]

The chorus, which throughout the song has sung of the callous lack of interest of people, now finally turns its criticism on the audience in the theatre:

Poor Nio-Niga is a-rotting on the Route A2
And a stream of cars passing – including you
And a long stream of cars of the New Republic.

The next scene, 5, takes place back in the Polo Club stables, now Mack's headquarters, and converted into a Board Room by clearing the wedding table, around which are seated Polly, Mack and members of the gang: 'The solemnity of the scene suggests a parody of a Board meeting'. Polly has just tipped off her husband that her father is about to have him arrested. During the course of the scene, Polly takes over as Boss of the gang, now called the Firm, and asserts her authority physically over the gang with the help of a heavy ledger. She proposes that the criminal operations become respectable by affiliating with a new multinational corporation with special holdings in developing countries. Shares have already been bought by Polly for various people in high position in Bangui as an investment against any future charges of corruption.

At the same time, Polly dresses Mack in Wonyosi – the amazingly expensive lace – and the rest of the gang in slightly less expensive blue lace. On the stage, therefore, before the audience's eyes, the gang of crooks is transformed into a group of Nigerian businessmen. Brown comes in to arrest Mack, who is nevertheless able to make his escape in his Wonyosi outfit. Polly and Brown spar with each other, verbally, over the size of the bribe to get Mack off once he is arrested, and then Polly sings a song about her transformation into a tough business lady.

The song is accompanied by a dance, performed by a chorus of women, who first sing of the 'attack trade' which was carried on by Nigerian women across enemy lines during the war. In the second chorus they mime, with the help of Brown's officers who feign being shot and dying, the process of trading in the midst of death. The stage direction describes the dance: '(. . . The women march over them, stop to empty their pockets, take off their watches and carry on business throughout the chorus . . .)'. This song and mime-dance ends the first half of the play; and Soyinka extends the irony by having the women immediately emerge in the interval among the audience selling to its members those wares which they have just 'robbed' from the 'corpses'.

In the first scene of the second half of the play Mack, who is still on the run and not yet arrested, visits the brothel of his favourite harlot, Sukie. De Madam anticipates his visit there and so lays her trap to get him arrested. This involves bribing Sukie. The action is deliberately contrived and artificially arranged. In counterpoint to the deals and arrangements is the shadowy figure of Jenny Leveller who scrubs the steps of the brothel and refuses to take bribes. She sings a powerful song about how, one day, she will take revenge on society. (Compare this, in passing, with the Leader of the Ants in *A Dance of the Forests*.) The essence of her role and the theme of her song both come from Brecht's play, though the character there is integral to the plot. In Soyinka's play, Jenny Leveller is only an incidental part of the scene, but stands as an angry comment on it and on the whole of society.

Scene 7 is in the prison. Mack has been arrested. He tries to bribe, with his Wonyosi outfit, his gaoler, a fellow-countryman named Dogo, who in the end insists on hard cash together with the suit. Brown, then Polly, visit Mack; then Mack's other wife, Lucy, the daughter of the Prison Governor, forces her way in, and Mack has to do some fast talking as the rival wives press their claims for his person. In the end it is Polly who organizes his escape, though not through bribes at the lower end of the social scale but by a stay of execution signed by the Deputy Chief Justice himself. Polly extracts from Mack a promise that he will become 'respectable': 'No treacherous women, no dangerous adventures. Let's go legitimate like the bigger crooks.' 'It's the easy life for me', which is a song about self-interest at all levels, closes the scene.

So Mack gets let off, on a technical point relating to secret societies. The next scene is back in Anikura's establishment, where the Chief is determining on new ways of getting MacHeath arrested. He has managed to lure to his place someone who holds real power in the state, Colonel Moses, who advises Bokasa on all his decrees and who is also on loan from the Nigerian army-government. The satire changes at this point from lampoon and parody to something much more serious, direct and personally specific. Colonel Moses is not caricatured. He is soft-spoken and exudes authority rather than violent aggression. Everybody instinctively defers to him and the beggars positively grovel.

Anikura's proposition that he slightly bend the laws he has made so that the ruling of the judiciary can be overturned in MacHeath's case, meets with a frigid reception. Moses rises to go. However, at this point and quite by accident, his true nature is revealed: he is an actual sadist who gains sexual pleasure from beating people. He prowls the streets at night to find victims among the poor whom he can beat for his pleasure. Anikura now has him in his grasp.

It has been revealed during the course of the scene that many of Anikura's 'beggars' are in fact, professors, lawyers, doctors, agriculturalists and so on, who are learning in Anikura's establishment how to beg for high office. A powerful image has been established on the stage of these elites, dressed like beggars, licking the shoes of the army in the person of this sadistic Moses. Now it seems possible to frame Colonel Moses, at least in Bangui with its paranoid and violent Emperor; and the beggar–professionals plan how to get him hooked. The Nigerian army itself is to be accused of being a secret society on the basis of the army's repeated verdict that those involved in civil riots and civilian murders were '*unknown* soldiers'.

The play has now become a direct attack upon the army, mounted, paradoxically, through an extremely reticent figure, whose characterization lacks any extravagance on stage, and who is therefore in marked contrast to the frenzy and excesses of the other characters. Soyinka has withheld parody from the portrayal of Moses. Why? Perhaps he feels that we can scorn and ridicule the corruption, the begging for high position, and the idiocies of Bokasa, but when we come to the army in Nigeria, its malignant nature, while it ruled, existed beyond satire and parody.

As far as the story is concerned, Anikura's case against Moses is not especially convincing – even though Moses himself is convinced by it, and he goes off to have MacHeath rearrested.

The final scene is Mack's execution by firing squad. The frenzy and parody return to the stage with a speeded-up version of the music for the song 'Who killed Nio-Niga?' and everybody cheering the crowning of Bokasa, while his goon squad hunt out troublemakers. The coronation is made synonymous with the public executions, staged as part of the festivities. The passion of the crowd for grotesque public slaughter knows no bounds, and the public fall over each other in order to get good seats. Dee-Jay acts as a roving news-reporter, and allows everyone he interviews to condemn themselves out of their own mouths. Those connected with the condemned MacHeath all adopt suitable public poses: Polly is in tears, and De Madam is threatening to take her home; the whores of Mack's favourite brothel have been converted to the CSU (Christian Scripture Union) and do a chorus-line dance to the hymn 'Just a closer walk with thee'. The various religions claim Mackie till they hear he has no money, then they give up. Mack's last request is to be allowed to sing a song: 'Mackie's farewell'. In it he attacks both Bokasa and the mindless, sycophantic public.

Then Bokasa's courier arrives, granting an amnesty not to political detainees but to criminals – the final parody of the play.

Anikura steps forward – steps out of the play, in fact – and gives a concluding speech in which, perhaps with the voice of the playwright, he warns against the easy solutions, like the Emperor's courier arriving with a pardon, to society's problems. He warns the audience against radicals and socialists:

> Beware certain well-tuned voices
> That clamour loudest: 'Justice-for-all'
> A ragged coat does not virtue make
> – Here I stand as your prime example –

He warns them against Highway robbers and their more respectable counterparts, the business tycoons:

> Nor is the predator a champion of rights,
> A brave Robin Hood equalizing the loot. . . .
> In proof my son-in-law is more than ample.

Instead, we have to look and see who is really benefiting in the society – 'Who really accumulates and exercises / Power over others?'. In the end it is power, not money, that counts, Anikura's final statement is unequivocal:

> I tell you –
> Power is delicious. (*Turns sharply*) Heel!

This last word is the command of the master to his trained dog to follow close by his heels. The beggars, like dogs, shuffle towards him and cringe by his feet. Then there is a massive procession, headed by Bokasa in his chariot drawn by slaves, behind whom everybody falls in rank order, to the tune that opened the play, *Mack the Knife*.

Anikura's final statement – 'Power is delicious' – takes us to the heart of *Opera Wonyosi*, and also sets the play apart from Brecht's *The Threepenny Opera*. Anyone who seeks to control the lives of other people is, for Soyinka, suspect, no matter where he is on the political spectrum. The attack in *Opera Wonyosi* is not on a particular economic system, though there is a fairly obvious attack on the link between the business world and the criminal world in capitalist Nigeria, which Soyinka does not attempt to gainsay. It is there because of the oil wealth which engendered the headlong pursuit of material possessions on an unprecedented scale.

However, Soyinka wishes to go beyond this, to try to determine what actually drives a man, or a woman, to go on acquiring wealth when they already have more than they could ever consume. He concludes that, in the end, money means power, rather than possessions. And power, unlike wealth which is limited and limiting in its possibilities, knows no constraints.

For Soyinka, the exercise of power over others corresponds with man's base instincts. In his plays he returns to this theme over and over again. We have seen in *A Dance of the Forests*, Forest Head, referring to humankind as weak, pitiable criminals, saying to the three Triplets:

You perversions are born when they acquire power over one another, and their instincts are fulfilled a thousandfold, a hundred thousandfold.

In *Madmen and Specialists* Bero tells his sister 'It was the first step to power you understand. Power in its purest sense.' He later tells his father: 'I do not need illusions. I control lives.' And Anikura, finally, states it bluntly: 'Power is delicious.'

Soyinka's obsession with the seemingly inevitable abuse of power suggests that perhaps instinctively he has some affinities with anarchism. Anarchists seek to abolish the state and to replace it with free association and voluntary co-operation of individuals and groups. However, in Africa, and in other parts of the third world, the integrity of the nation–state is the most basic principle of political life. It is the corner-stone of the OAU's charter. State boundaries are defended against aggression by neighbouring states, to the extent of bringing in non-African powers; and within the state, forces that would divide it are passionately resisted. The nation–state is perceived as a positive entity, for it transcends narrow tribalism and ethnocentricity, and it guarantees some sort of survival in the modern world.

It is, therefore, to be expected that although Soyinka attacks power structures, he does not specifically attack the nation–state, either in the abstract or in, for him, its concretization as Nigeria. Right from Nigeria's inception, when he himself was a young playwright at the beginning of his career, he has espoused liberation yet been intensely critical of post-independence rhetoric. He has held in creative tension the liberation ethos of Nigeria as a nation and its restricting reality. At the beginning of the chapter we suggested that his search for 'oneness' (generated by his Yoruba metaphysics) and his passionate response to suffering and injustice (shaping his profound sensibility) are held in opposition within him and that it is this very opposition which generates his art. The other, political, opposition, between the awareness of liberation and the experience of abuse, both embodied in the new nation–state, only reinforces that dichotomy. His plays are protest plays. They are also works of art.

Notes and references

1 A great deal has been written about Soyinka's work, by Nigerians and non-Nigerians. An early study by Eldred Duro-sinmi Jones, *The Writing of Wole Soyinka* (London: Heinemann Educational Books 1973), remains valid for the work discussed, as does Gerald Moore, *Wole Soyinka* (London: Evans 1971). James Gibbs is compiling a cumulative bibliography on Soyinka, and the scope of this is discussed in James Gibbs, 'Wole Soyinka: bio-bibliography', *Africana Library Journal*, vol. 3 no. 1. Some of the most interesting critical commentary appears as articles and papers and Gibbs has recently collected some of these into an anthology: James Gibbs (ed.), *Critical Perspectives on Wole Soyinka* (Washington: Three Continents Press 1980).

However, students should always refer back to Soyinka's own work of criticism and philosophy: Wole Soyinka, *Myth, Literature and the African World* (Cambridge: Cambridge University Press 1976).

2 See, for example, Soyinka's campaign against Idi Amin, the former ruler of Uganda, which he organized through the columns of *Transition* (Accra). Soyinka was editor through nos. 45–50, and then changed its name to *Ch'Indaba*. For the attack on Amin see, for example, *Transition* no. 49 (July–September 1975).

3 Wole Soyinka, *Myth, Literature and the African World* (Cambridge: Cambridge University Press 1976), p. 46.

4 Wole Soyinka, *Madmen and Specialists* (London: Methuen 1971), p. 37.

5 ibid., p. 36.

6 ibid., p. 49.

7 ibid.

8 ibid., p. 76.

9 ibid., p. 77.

10 ibid.

11 ibid., p. 61.

12 ibid., p. 60.

13 ibid., p. 75.

14 Soyinka, 'The ritual archetype', in *Myth, Literature and the African World*, p. 12.

15 Soyinka, *Madmen and Specialists*, pp. 71–2.

16 ibid., p. 77.

17 Soyinka, 'The ritual archetype', p. 30.

18 Soyinka, 'The fourth stage', in *Myth, Literature and the African World*, p. 30.

19 ibid., p. 150.

20 ibid., p. 149.

21 ibid., p. 150.

22 ibid., p. 148.

23 I am using the first edition of the play, Wole Soyinka, *A Dance of the Forests* (London and Ibadan: Oxford University Press 1963). All page numbers refer to this edition. There are some minor changes in later editions, particularly with regard to the ending.

24 ibid., p. 68.

25 ibid., p. 70.

26 ibid., p. 71.

27 ibid., p. 72.

28 ibid., p. 78.

29 Oyin Ogunba, *The Movement of Transition* (Ibadan: Ibadan University Press 1975), p. 92.

30 The best text of Gay's *The Beggar's Opera* is in the edition in the Regents Restoration Drama Series, edited by Edgar V. Roberts (London: Edward Arnold 1969).

An English translation of Brecht's play is Ralph Manheim and John Willett (eds.) 1979, *Bertolt Brecht: collected plays Vol. 2, Part 2*, New York: Vintage Books, and London, Eyre Methuen. Another translation, by Desmond I. Vesey and Eric Bentley, is in Bertolt Brecht, *Plays Vol. I* (London: Methuen 1960). While I was writing this book Soyinka's *Opera Wonyosi* was not yet published, and I worked from a production copy privately circulated from Ife by Soyinka at the time that the play was produced. It is now published by Rex Collings (London, 1981).

31 There is a lengthy biography of Kurt Weill: Ronald Sanders, *The*

Days Grow Short: the Life and Music of Kurt Weill (London: Weidenfeld & Nicolson 1980). Perhaps a more interesting publication, in terms of a composer-dramatist collaboration to produce socialist songs, is Eric Bentley, *Songs of Bertolt Brecht and Hans Eisler* (New York: Oak Publications 1967). It is a collection of songs in German and in English together with Eisler's musical score.

7 The art theatre: political plays

Mokai Ajibade; *The Chattering and the Song Osofisan*

Two Nigerians who are influenced by Wole Soyinka and, in their separate ways, critical of Nigeria are Yemi Ajibade and Femi Osofisan. Ajibade is, perhaps, better known for his play *Parcel Post*, which was professionally staged in London – it is set in London among Nigerian expatriates – than for his plays written in and about Nigeria. Osofisan is a well-established literary figure on the left and his plays are very popular among students. The influence of Soyinka is seen right away in each playwright's seriousness of dramatic purpose. This is manifest in the content of their plays and in their approach to the craft of playwriting. Both explore a number of dramatic forms and effectively combine wit and comedy with their seriously intended social criticism.

Ajibade's play *Mokai*[1] (which is the one we are going to consider) reveals a close observation of people, but in symbolic rather than naturalistic roles and relationships, and it reflects a deeply rooted pessimism about their increasing ability to co-exist. Osofisan has structured *The Chattering and the Song*[2] (the play of his we are going to consider) to demonstrate a critique of the Nigerian social formation, but through a group of highly individualized intellectuals. Both plays depict a movement in society towards revolution, as well as the attempts by the established order in society to contain and neutralize this revolutionary tendency. At critical moments both plays are concerned with the claims of the traditional beliefs upon the minds of the people. These beliefs are seen as potentially positive, but in the present time distorted. Both plays, therefore, look back, while at the same time looking forward to the future, as Soyinka's do.

Ajibade focuses his play on the Cult from Akilagun. This is not specific. It is neither one of a number of cults or secret societies nor a particular one, but rather 'cultism' in essence. It could also be seen as a metaphysical embodiment of ultimate reality, a potential moral force, a linking of earth with man, and an expression in its masquerades and sacrifices of wholeness. But the Cult itself has been corrupted in the modern world and is now no better than Christianity, portrayed in the play as a revivalist sect. Nor is it any better than the state, which is depicted as opposing military forces or factions. The Cult conflicts with Christianity, and then both are subjugated to the will of the military state, which itself is being destroyed by internal conflict.

The action of the play takes place on a symbolic level; and the central character, the eponymous hero, Mokai, is also symbolically conceived. He has been born into the Cult. His mother, Iyaja, was a special Cult member – an earth mother, in fact – with unique powers and gifts. As a young woman with her new baby she lived with the Old Wizard, referred to by both during the course of the play, in the 'little cottage on the edge of the Savannah'. A tornado then swept it away, and Mokai became separated from his mother. When we first meet him in the play, as an adult, he is ignorant of anything other than the memory of the 'little cottage on the edge of the Savannah', but is searching for his mother. In his quest he is caught, ironically, by the Cult as a 'stranger' whom they intend to sacrifice in their masquerade. However, he displays a superior physical and moral strength, and so Cult members seek to possess him within the Cult. He escapes, and continues with his search. The Pastor of the Christian sect at Olifie, together with his flock, recognize a spiritual quality in him – he is given the title 'The Meek One of the Lord' – and they seek to exploit him, the Pastor spiritually, and the young women of the flock sexually. Mokai accepts whatever role is given him by others. Iyaja, a Christian now in the Pastor's flock, fails to recognize him as her son, but is able to recognize him as a strong character who reminds her of her Cult past. The Cult members, who are pursuing Mokai, then clash with the Christians over 'owning' him.

This is interrupted by gunshots and the manifestation of a military presence. There is a brief scene in which an officer, obviously on the run, tries to rob Mokai of his bundle of clothes; it is later reported that they have in fact changed clothes. Mokai is captured by RATS (Revolutionary Association of Tough Soldiers) who have staged a coup, then captured again, in a counter ambush by the reactionary military forces who assert that he is General Baado, the head of state. Throughout all this Mokai is beaten and assaulted. He must, to serve the military's purpose, be put back into shape. This task is entrusted to Professor Tomwuruwuru who quite unequivocally symbolizes the comprador Nigerian petty bourgeoisie.

The military, in reasserting their authority over the coup faction, make the Cult members and the Christians swear an oath of allegiance and form spurious organizations like the Lord's Brigade and the Farmers' Brigade, and so on. Towards the end of the play, Mokai's own personality emerges through his 'reconstituted' character as General Baado; but as a moral force it is now powerless. Iyaja realizes, too late, that he is her son but Mokai never knows her to be his mother. Before the end of the play he has divested himself of his uniform and probably makes his escape, though Iyaja and the Cult members mourn his apparent death.

If Mokai, as man in the new African nation–state, is searching for his identity, then it is also true to say that within the state sects, factions and affiliations are searching for Mokai – but so that each can reconstitute him in their own image.

If Soyinka embodies in his protagonists the duality of creation and destruction, Ajibade's Mokai embodies at one and the same time a moral stance and an amoral compliance. This duality is manifest whenever he *acts*: seeking his mother; escaping from sacrifice; exchanging clothing. His actions tend to reveal in others hypocrisy and self-deceit.

Osofisan's play occupies a space less redolent with symbolic meaning than either Soyinka's 'fourth stage' or Ajibade's 'clearing in the bush'. It is set in a middle-class house belonging to the play's main character, a playwright and song-writer called Sontri. He is involved in protest against the bourgeoisie, to which class he and the other characters in the play nonetheless belong. Sontri is a member of the subversive and outlawed 'Farmers' Movement', which aims at the government's overthrow. The play takes place on the eve of Sontri's wedding to Yajin.

The critical action of the play is presented as a rehearsal of a play devised by Yajin for the eve of her wedding which concerns the confrontation in 1885 between the rebel Latoye and 'the famous Alafin Abiodun'. Another character, Mokan, who was at university with them and formerly Yajin's fiancé, turns out at the end of this rehearsal to be a member of the secret police. He has used the rehearsal as an excuse to arrest Sontri and Yajin for subversive activities. Metaphorically, the play-within-a-play is the rehearsal for the revolution. During the rehearsal, in which the characters are improvising their parts, there is a long speech by Leje, the character playing the rebel Latoye, about how the wealthy have used religion to secure themselves in power:

> For centuries you have shielded yourselves with the gods. Slowly you painted them in your colour, dressed them in your own cloak of terror, injustice and bloodlust. . . .[3]

This is very close to the Old Man's doctrine of As in *Madmen and Specialists*. Leje, who makes this speech as Latoye, is an interesting character. In the epilogue to the play he turns out to be none other than the secret head of the Farmers' Movement. His role as a drunken friend of Mokan in the play itself is a deliberate mask; his role as Latoye in the play-within-a-play is a fine irony, particularly as Mokan, the member of the secret police, has no idea who he really is. Leje continues Latoye's speech by saying that the gods of the Yoruba pantheon are governed by crucial checks and balances:

> To each of the gods, Edumare gave power and fragility, so that none of them shall be a tyrant over the others, and none a slave.[4]

But rulers like Abiodun have distorted their essential being. What is being criticized, therefore, by the rebel is not belief in the gods, but the hegemonic use of them by power-hungry rulers – a criticism, of course, very similar to Soyinka's Old Man's and also to Mokai's. Osofisan's play is, however, less rooted in Yoruba metaphysics than either Soyinka's or Ajibade's.

There is role-reversal in the play-within-a-play, with the exception of Leje, whose true identity is not known anyway by the wedding party. Sontri and Yajin play Abiodun and Olori, the reactionary rulers. Mokan plays the role of Aresa, a palace guard in revolt against Abiodun's authority. When he arrests Sontri and Yajin, Mokan is quite specific that it is not the play, or the rehearsal of it, which has indicted them; it only formed the occasion for the arrest which has been planned for some time. The play is only metaphorically a rehearsal for the revolution.

In the same way, the weaverbirds, with their chatterings and songs which give the play its title, are another metaphor for the coming revolution. As Sontri says after he has been arrested: 'There's nothing you can do to stop the birds from singing. Mokan, the revolution is already on the wing, you cannot halt it.' In an earlier encounter with Funlola, Yajin's artist friend, Sontri accuses her of chasing the weaverbirds away from the trees. He builds his attack on Funlola into a criticism of the professional middle class, whom he sees her as representing, while the weaverbirds represent the masses whom the former would drive out of their sight and hearing.

In the epilogue to the play Leje confides to Funlola that he is the leader of the Farmers' Movement and has her join the Movement. She, like Sontri, is an artist (like Demoke in *A Dance of the Forests*). Together they return to the child's game of the riddles which Sontri and Yajin played at the beginning of the play. This game – 'Iwori Otura: the bigger riddle begins . . .' – posits the contradictory relationships in the physical, or natural world, and shows these contradictions being resolved into new oppositions. In fact, the Marxist dialectic. Metaphor succeeds metaphor in the game, and the two players take the parts of, for example, hare, tortoise, frog, fish. Through this metaphorical behaviour, Osofisan perhaps hopes to show the dialectical relationship between characters, and how, through their oppositions one to each other, they resolve their beings into new phases of the struggle. The play begins and ends with the same game; the players are different; the struggle goes on.

Mokai and *The Chattering and the Song* have one particular political perspective in common, which should be briefly considered. It concerns the relationship of man to his labour. Mokai, in an attempt to transcend the role of the corrupt head of state, General Baado, keeps on insisting that 'the Nation must labour', but he is unable to translate his words into actions or to inspire others to do what he cannot do. Similarly, *The Chattering and the Song* ends (even though Osofisan tells us in the stage direction: 'The play does NOT end') with the Farmers' Anthem, and the audience are encouraged to join in the chanting. The words of this Anthem reflect Mokai's repeated injunction exactly:

When everyone's a farmer
We'll grow enough food
In the land
No insurrection
When all are fed
Less exploitation
You eat all you need

When everyone's a farmer
We'll wipe out the pests
In the land
No more injustice
Labour's for all
No more oppression
All hands to hoe

When everyone's a farmer
We'll burn out the weeds
In our lives
No alienation
Working on the farm
But brothers and sisters
Sharing everything[5]

The refrain, sung between these verses, begins 'So clear the forest / Turn up the soil. . . .' However, there is no evidence in the text that any of the characters actually do any farming, either on a large or small scale. Nor is it likely that the audiences for this English-language play will themselves farm, even though they may agree with the sentiments.

The position is a rhetorical one. It is like Mokai's 'The Nation must labour!', except that in Ajibade's play the awareness of this ideal as mere rhetoric is cause for further despair in Mokai. It is interesting to note, in relationship to this, that hardly any of Soyinka's characters, to date, ever labour. They are variously artists or politicians or in business. Sometimes they are market people, traders; or if they are working class they are either laid-off or layabouts. If they are peasants, it is not their farming labours which are the concern of the playwright – with the exception of Makuri, his son Igwezu and the Blind Beggar in his very early play *The Swamp Dwellers*.

Soyinka seems much more concerned with what people do in their time out of work than in the way they earn their livelihood. There is nothing especially significant in this, except in one respect. For although it can be argued that work, labour, is generally unrewarding for peasants and the proletariat and that few want to be entertained in their leisure by a representation of the monotony of their working lives, nevertheless the implication that man is profoundly alienated by his working life is of crucial importance. Soyinka chooses to concentrate on those moments in people's lives when meaning can be discovered, but these moments are invariably time out of the ordinary routine of mundane labour. Yet, paradoxically, it is in man's relationship to labour that meaning must be found – as both Ajibade and Osofisan partly realize in their exhortations to labour. Man's alienation from his work, and the exploitation of his labour, is actually a significant cause of many of his social traumas. Ajibade's character says 'The Nation must labour!'; Osofisan gets his audience and actors to sing 'When everyone's a farmer . . . / No more injustice / Labour's for all. . . .': but if these playwrights are trying to show their audiences *how* Nigerians are alienated from their working lives, then these rhetorical positions in themselves do not succeed.

One other play which we will consider in the context of protest theatre in Nigeria is 'Segun Oyekunle's *Katakata for Sufferhead*. There is a crucial element – apart from the social criticism – which links it with the plays we have been discussing. This is the use of *role-play*. In all of the plays, in one way or another, the characters engage in role-play, that is to say, they assume other roles beyond their basic characterization. This can be by 'acting' in a play-within-the-play (as in *The Chattering and the Song*); or, like Eshuoro in *A Dance of the Forests*, by disguising themselves as someone else. They can be forced to become someone other than themselves (for example Mokai as General Baado); or deliberately parody the behaviour of people of a higher social status (the mendicants in *Madmen and Specialists*). They may play games, like Sontri and Yajin, and then Leje and Funlola, in the child's riddle game; or become their alter egos (some of the beggars in *Opera Wonyosi*, who turn out to be highly-placed members of the professionals). What happens when characters engage in role-play within the drama? Let us consider an example from *The Chattering and the Song*.

Sontri plays the role of Abiodun; and any actor who plays the part of Sontri will have to convince us that Sontri is 'real', so that when Sontri plays the part of Abiodun we still think of him as Sontri. This is straightforward. But it can also be the other way around: the initially-established character, which the actor makes us accept as 'reality', turns out in the end actually to be someone else. Think of Leje. Throughout the play we think of Leje in the same way as the rest of the characters do: as Mokan's friend, then as Mokan's collaborator. But in the epilogue he is unmasked – or he unmasks himself – and actually turns out to be the revolutionary leader. Furthermore, when he played the role of the rebel in the rehearsal of Yajin's play, he was in fact playing an assumed role close to the reality of his own role.

The playwright and the actors are in a position to manipulate physical images to reflect the protagonist's search for his 'true self', or his 'identity'. They can peel off the layers of illusion, discovering new deceptions and new 'masks', until the audience see before them images of the characters' *inner* and *non-apparent* selves. This is sometimes described as a deeper *psychological* reality of the characters' personalities. We will return briefly to this a little later in this chapter, in a reference to Athol Fugard's plays.

We need, however, to look at this critically. It is possible to argue that characterization which creates the illusion of reality is a 'fixed' or static sort of characterization and that this in turn can reflect a fixed or static view of society. The depth of meaning a play may achieve may be limited if the playwright is pre-eminently concerned with 'fixed' characters as the 'reality' within his play, characters who may indulge in the 'illusion' or fantasy of role-play, but who nevertheless remain the same. Let us try and explain why.

Some thinkers see the history of man as reflecting a continuous process of becoming, rather than a cyclic one. This historical process can also be personalized: we are always about to become something other than what we are, which was different from what we were, and we are prepared to struggle towards our chosen goals. The classic example of this is the slave who dreams of being free, and who wasn't a slave when he was born. In the same way, we collectively remember our past and struggle towards our future: there will no longer be slavery. All history is seen, therefore, as a progression and people are constantly transcending the limitations of their societies by means of oppositions, which are resolved into new oppositions. This is a dialectical view of history.

Drama can help us explore this dialectical historical process; for its visual and aural images, so concrete and at once apparent, can reflect the process metaphorically. But instead of the 'illusionistic' theatre, instead of individual characters indulging in a search for their 'true' selves in the illusions and fantasies of role-play, *all* aspects of the characterization are depicted in a state of flux. Our characters and our consciousness are formed by our social circumstances. Viewed dialectically, the search for identity cannot be divorced from the social context in which it is being formulated. For, on the one hand, the central character is being modified continuously by political and economic pressures, and on the other hand, the truth about him lies only in the extent to which he is able to change the future.

How does this affect our view of Soyinka's drama? First, Soyinka's protagonists 'discover meaning' in their lives, which concerns the search for self and has metaphysical implications for their societies. The 'oneness' of the protagonist, which he finally achieves, usually in the moment of sacrifice, parallels the restoration of equilibrium in the society. However, in order to achieve this 'oneness' the protagonist has to be a very specific sort of person: he is the one who *acts*; who is able to exercise his will; the creative artist; someone who embodies and comprehends the contradiction of creativity and destruction. Thus, the characterization of Soyinka's protagonist is always determined right from the start and when the protagonist has achieved understanding, identified himself, it has not and does not change his character in essence. Achieving understanding is dependent on character, rather than character being determined by (social) understanding. Second, none of the protagonists actively engages with the society to change it. Their understanding, and each one's sacrifice, is always by way of *an example* to society: a ritual demonstration of its readjustment; a restoration of its equilibrium *by example*.

His theory reinforces this restorative function of the drama. He talks of the 'origin of the race', and the 'chthonic realm'. The latter is, for him, the contemplation of the extinction of the race: it is chaos and the return of primordial darkness. The purpose of his drama, therefore, is the purpose of each of his protagonists: to ensure the survival of the race. For small-scale societies this is the essence of morality:

Where society lives in a close inter-relation with Nature, regulates its existence by natural phenomena within the observable processes of continuity – ebb and tide, waxing and waning of the moon, rain and drought, planting and harvest – the highest moral order is seen as that which guarantees the parallel continuity of the species.[6]

This is essentially a cyclic view of human society.

Bertolt Brecht, whose influence on some African theatre we

have already seen, constructed his plays in such a way that audiences were able to think how the social order, and therefore people, may be changed for the better. This was not a rhetorical position ('Workers arise! Throw off your chains!'); nor was it even a moralistic one ('It is evil for the rich to exploit the poor.'); but an analysis, in a dramatic form, of the social formation informed by a dialectical view of history. At the core of Brecht's dramatic method was his approach to characterization. Not only did he reject the idea that the playwright and the actors must convince audiences that the characters were 'real' and fixed – which we have termed 'illusionistic' theatre – but that characters could discover a 'true' self inside themselves and apart from society. For him, what characters and audiences both needed to discover during the course of a performance was how and why they were unable to achieve what they wanted to, and how and why happiness escaped them. Brecht is often wrongly represented as pursuing social conformity and opposing 'individuality'. In fact, he recognized and admired each individual's claim to happiness through ever-widening horizons of knowledge and experience; and each person's desire to be productive and to contribute to the betterment of human existence. What he doesn't accept are any illusory 'short-cuts' to happiness and achievement, either through religious belief, magic, mysticism or even metaphysics; people have to come to understand the dialectical processes in order to change history.

He saw the 'illusionistic' theatre as a theatre which deliberately or unconsciously keeps the social connections obscure, pursuing as it does individualistic solutions for the benefit of individuals. He developed in its place a theatre which he called 'epic theatre', in which the actors do everything in their power to prevent the audience from imagining they are playing 'fixed' or predetermined characters which they must believe are 'real'. He suggests a number of technical ways in which actors and directors might do this; but the way he creates his characters initially, in the writing, is the significant development: the plays are structured so as to show them capable of highly ambivalent behaviour which leads us to question their actions, and so see that these are often socially determined and contradictory. The contradictions in their behaviour enable us to see the contradictions in the society. For example, in his play *The Good Woman of Szechuan*, the central character is a young exploited prostitute who is forced, in order to survive, to assume the role of an aggressive male cousin. This role-play is not fantasy but two aspects of the central characterization: although she is poor and a prostitute, she is naturally generous to her fellow poor; but she is also capable of survival, and can be ruthless and exploit the very people she wants to help. The question we find ourselves asking is why it is that the poor are forced to exploit each other in order to survive.

Linked with this process of characterization is Brecht's concern to show his audience things which we have come to accept as commonplace and unremarkable – people, actions, relationships – in a new and strange light. By suddenly being able to notice that which previously had escaped our attention, and by seeing standard practice as anything but normal, we have taken the first step towards realizing that the social order is not immutable. The world *can* be changed, and people can change as they change it.

This preamble to a consideration of *Katakata for Sufferhead*[7] is not meant to suggest that it is specifically influenced by Brecht's work. Nor is it specifically influenced by Soyinka's work, and it is interesting to note that it was written before *Opera Wonyosi* – but after Oyekunle had worked with others on a group improvisation of another Nigerian version of Brecht's *The Threepenny Opera*, which preceded Soyinka's own transposition.

Katakata for Sufferhead Segun Oyekunle

Oyekunle's play concerns a young school-leaver, Lateef, who is a 'JJC' – a Johnny-Just-Come, which is a common Nigerian term for someone who has just arrived from the village into town (or at the university or polytechnic). Lateef has just arrived in town. He is also an 'applicant' – another Nigerian term this time for someone who is searching for a job. However, jobs are impossible to come by. Lateef sponges off his friend Femi for a while until Femi has had enough of him and manages, by a trick, to get him out of his room. Lateef has no money, no food and nowhere to go. He refuses to go back to his village and admit defeat. After all, he has a school-leaver's certificate, Grade 1:

> Is this what I have spent five years for in a secondary school? Would it not have been better if I had not gone to school at all? My age-mates who did not go to school at least own farms of their own now. The

powers-that-be say we should go back to farm. Is farming all that easy? Where is the training? The experience? The capital to start with?. . . . Loans in this country are for the highly placed to buy cars and build houses to hire out at high rates to us poor. They are getting richer and we are getting poorer. . . .

Lateef's despairing comments show how his determination not to go back to his village is bound up with his awareness that the likes of him cannot get loans to do what the government tells school-leavers to do, i.e. to farm. Lateef is the voice of both reason and disillusionment.

After he has been pushed out of his friend's house he roams the streets and finally is befriended by two young men, Jac Moro and Toronto, who sleep in front of the Quoxa Cinema and 'guard' it for a tiny weekly 'wage' from the manager. Jac and Toronto get to see all the films. Lateef is allowed to share their mat and sleep on the pavement between them and he is greatly affected by their friendly attitude towards him:

What is all this? With a certificate and yet no hope whatsoever in this world. See me here housed by layabouts. They are even more secure than I am.

Starving hungry, he goes into a local restaurant, into the 'VIP section', and eats a meal which he cannot pay for. He is arrested, of course; taken by the police to the magistrate; and because he cannot pay a bribe, or a 'fine', is sentenced to a term in prison.

Oyekunle actually sets his play in the prison; and he begins the play with Lateef's arrival in the cell: a JJC to the prison, just as he was a JJC in the town. The action of the play involves him telling his tale to the other inmates in the cell: Jangidi (nine years in jail, out of a sentence of thirteen years for taking ₦20 out of public funds) who is the 'boss' of the cell; Ndem (eight years of an indefinite term for using his position as a ₦120 per month store-keeper to try and establish a little business on the side); Darudapo (six years for an unstated crime); Okolo (five years, detention without trial, for having a quarrel with the daughter of a very influential man); and Buhari (also five years without trial for being seduced, as a servant, by the young wife of his master, an ageing and impotent Alhaji). The point is that they are like Lateef: thrown into jail to rot over the years for trivial offences and for their economic inability to bribe their way out of the clutches of the police and the law. In jail they have established their own hierarchy, and they call the prison their 'white college' – 'Dis college na di proper school wey you go learn plenty-plenty: de ting wey no dey hinside book, di ting wey no professor fit lecture you . . . [. . . which no professor is able to tell you]'.

Lateef, as JJC, is 'tried' again, this time by the 'white college'. He tells his story, and it is acted out with comments and interspersions by the inmates of the cell. At the end he is again found 'guilty', not of forging his certificate, which is what he imagines the other prisoners are accusing him of, but of being too poor and vulnerable to stay out of trouble. His 'sentence' is to be in charge of the shit bucket and to keep the mosquitoes from disturbing Jangidi at night: he has been assigned his place at the bottom of the pecking order in the cell.

Why has Oyekunle structured his play in this way? The play seems to function on two levels; a naturalistic level and a symbolic level. Prisons in towns all over Nigeria are probably like the prison in which the play is set; and the prisoners, certainly, typical examples. This is the level of naturalism. The plight of Lateef, as 'JJC' in town, as 'applicant', and then as 'bird' (a convict) was increasingly common at the time the play was written, particularly in the south of the country, and also for southerners in the north, and was likely to get worse. The play goes further than most other Nigerian plays in integrating the sense of social injustice and despair into the actual structure of the play, without losing the elements of wit and satire. The play is not just about one character, Lateef, and his desperate situation; it is about a whole world: the urban proletariat, forced to deviate, in small ways, from the 'straight and narrow' because of an initially exploited position, and then inevitably caught out. Their crimes are petty when compared with the corruption and criminal behaviour of the great and famous; and they rot in some obscure Nigerian jail.

This carries the play on to the symbolic level. The jail is, for these prisoners, and in the play itself, the symbol of Nigeria. Lateef, referring to the two layabouts outside the cinema, Jac Moro and Toronto says:

Their life is not better than ours here. . . . Em, well, except for their freedom.

To which Ndem replies:

Freedom shit! When without it you dey eat tree time dem for day [three times a day].

There is a greater lack of 'freedom' outside the jail, if one is talking about getting enough food to eat to keep alive. It is not that 'freedom' and a 'just society' do not exist; they do. But not for these people. They can't see how it could possibly exist for them, or how the existing order might be changed for the better. This is the central concern of the play. Two incidents indicate the writer's view of people at this level being unable to develop adequate political awareness.

The first is when Ndem is made to play the part of Lateef's friend Femi, with whom Lateef stays until he is pushed out of his house. Ndem is happy to play this role in the beginning; but when it comes to the trick to get rid of Lateef, he declines to play the role any longer:

Ndem: Wait. (*To* **Lateef**) You say Femi commot you by tulass?*

Lateef: Yes.

Ndem: And you no sabi anybody where you fit go?

Lateef: Nobody.

Ndem: Femi no be better person. I no like am so I no go do am again.

Jangidi: You must to continue as you done start am.

Ndem: I say I no fit.

Jangidi: You say you no fit? Oright. De time before when you dey feed nine mout dem with your sixty naira: so, if stranger just come land for your house so, wetin you go do?

Ndem: Ah! Na to chase am commot one time!

Jangidi: OK. Show us you go commot your stranger.

And Ndem does. He acts the role of Femi with great commitment and feeling: he remains hard-hearted and unflinching even when Lateef breaks down and cries. The point that Oyekunle is trying to make in this well constructed little scene is that Ndem is by nature good and would always like to behave generously, but that economic circumstances do not permit him to do so. Put another way, the play at this point is saying, don't judge your neighbour harshly, but the system.

The other example comes a little later in Lateef's story when he is staying with the layabouts outside the cinema. The characters of Jac Moro and Toronto are played by the 'birds', Okolo and Buhari, respectively. There is now an apparently lengthy digres-

---

* 'You say Femi got rid of you by a trick?' 'sabi' = 'know'; 'fit' = 'can'; 'wetin' = 'what'.

sion as Buhari and Okolo get into their role-playing and start
enjoying acting the parts of layabouts. But it is not a digression at
all. It is an analysis of the people's inability to transcend the
limitations of their understanding of the social forces at work in
their lives. Jac Moro, played by Okolo, lives almost entirely in the
fantasy world of the Kung Fu cinema and Nigerian affluence.
Toronto, played by Buhari, is much more of a realist and acts as a
foil to show up the limitations of Jac's thinking. Jac doesn't want
anything to disturb his little world, and he warns Lateef, whom he
describes as 'bookman', against upsetting the situation:

> Make you no start revolution for here. Or else I go retire and dismiss
> you with immediate effect.

Toronto scorns him and tells Lateef:

> He don't know his right. I tell him make we told Manager to increase
> our salary wit one-one naira. But he na so so fear fear! Na Progress-
> Enemy-Numba-One he be, dis one. . . .

Jac Moro's voice is that of the passivity of the exploited. He is
sustained by his fantasies, one of which is Kung Fu, and another is
winning the lottery. And if he suddenly came into money, what
would he do? He is quite specific: he would do exactly what the
wealthy do at present: stay in a hotel suite, have private doctors,
engage in the import–export business, fix price controls in his
favour, bribe the police, and drive around in the owner's corner of
his pleasure car acknowledging the approval of the crowd.

The scene is brilliantly constructed, for it must be remembered
that it is two convicts who are playing the roles of two layabouts in
front of the cinema who themselves are parodying the elite. Yet it
is all out of Okolo's and Buhari's own imaginations. Buhari as
Toronto as the Asian medical doctor is conducting an examination
on Okolo playing Jac 'de Tousanaire' (a 'thousand-aire' is not
quite a millionaire); and on two occasions he returns us to the
reality of the prison cell. The first is when he is 'examining' 'de
Tousanaire's' mouth and he tells him 'your mout dey smell, like
dog wey chop shit' which brings Okolo back to himself to respond
to his prison-mate Buhari with like insult. The second is a bit later
when Buhari (as the doctor), while giving him the physical
examination, tries to pull down Okolo's trousers. Partly in role
and partly out of it Buhari tells him that, as Okolo, he needs to
cure the yaws and jiggers in his crotch if he wants, as Jac 'de

Tousanaire' to pick up smart girls. Okolo replies derisively: 'Once money dey, Nigerian chics no go care. Abi I lie? [Do I lie?]' To which the others all reply: 'No – O!' And he adds, as Jac 'de Tousanaire': 'I go carry dem plenty for one time. Na one of dem go commot my shirt, na anoder go hold my emperor make I piss.' [I will have plenty of girl-friends all together. One of them will hold up my shirt and another will hold my cock when I want to piss.]

There is a direct line drawn by the playwright between the squalid physical conditions of the prisoners in the cell, the squalid behaviour of the rich, and the overriding obsession with money. The connection is made more specific by the compliance of Jac Moro in his poverty. And it must be remembered that Okolo has created the character out of his own imagination on the mere suggestion of Lateef in the telling of his story. Okolo is inside the prison; Jac is outside the prison: they both lack 'freedom', just as Lateef's condition outside the prison is no more 'free' than his condition inside it. The transition from the former to the latter is almost inevitable given their social and economic condition. The prison is variously the 'white college' where the prisoner is 'educated', the 'court', where the prisoner is 'tried' again, the 'theatre' where the prisoner's story is re-enacted, and, in fact, the microcosm of society, with its hierarchies, 'arrangements' and connections. Ndem is the only one who has tried to escape, and only because his wife had been having an affair with the Warder and produced a couple of children by him. His attempt is considered by the others as lunatic – because what can you possibly escape to?

The play ends with all the 'birds' filing out to do hard labour. And what, in the end, is the difference between this and peasant farming?

Up to this point the discussion has been on protest plays by Nigerians who are critical of their society's direction and progress since independence. In terms of the African continent, however, this is an advanced political position, for in South Africa (and in Namibia) the black populations still remain unliberated from the yoke of white supremacy. Racism is at one and the same time both easier to protest about through drama and theatre (because its injustices are obvious) and harder (because naked aggression and brutality, and the sense of outrage, are difficult to recreate on the stage). For this reason, therefore, it is perhaps useful in the context of this chapter to comment on one of the most important protest plays to have come out of South Africa. *Survival*, which was staged in South Africa just prior to the Black Consciousness Movement's violent eruptions in 1976, is seen by its creators not only as a protest play for the people of South Africa, but also as a created work of art. It has subsequently toured North America.

The play is relevant here in another respect too. Those Nigerians who are concerned with the development of criticism of their society through the art of drama, through the art theatre, are also deeply committed to the liberation of South Africa; they see the need for Nigeria, as a nation, to play an economic, political and, if need be, military part in that struggle.

Survival Workshop '71 Theatre Company

Survival[8] is a black South African urban play devised by the fully professional Workshop '71 Theatre Company. It was first performed around the black and coloured urban areas of Cape Town and then in Soweto in 1976. The production was forcibly closed down by a gang of soldiers who beat up the cast and the staff of the YMCA where it was being staged in Soweto. Robert 'Mshengu' Kavanagh writes in an introduction to the text of the play:

In the Cape the play was seen in the black townships of Langa and Gugulethu and in the various so-called Coloured townships (under the auspices of the Black Community Programmes) after June 1976 and before violence spread to the Cape. It was thus seen by thousands of school students and adults at a very sensitive time. It is possible to argue that at that stage the play performed an effective political function. . . .[9]

However, Kavanagh feels that the political function of the play was later obviated by events spearheaded by the Black Consciousness Movement in 1976.

The play's genesis was by group improvisation; its subject-matter and its subsequent demise within South Africa reflect the conditions under which blacks normally live in South Africa. Both group improvisation and *apartheid* need to be briefly summarized before we can fully understand the play, for this company of actors find a need to combine their own harsh experience in South Africa with their art as actors.

In group improvisation the actor ceases to be the means by which a playwright realizes his vision on the stage – in a sense, a technician with little or no autonomy – and becomes the joint creator of the work. The play which is realized by a group of actors is either something which reflects the actors' personal experiences or something which they wish to say collectively or a combination of both. Instead of representing somebody else's ideas they are representing their own collectively. This is an approach to theatre which is being tried increasingly in many parts of the world, as well as in Africa; and it is usually regarded as part of the technique of the theatre of social commitment. In fact this is misleading, for a group improvisation may result in a play which can be devoid of political commitment in all but the most generalized sense, and can simply use the techniques of creative group work in order to realize a more intense and compelling form of acting (such as the 'Poor Theatre' of Jerzy Grotowski, or the experiments of the British theatre director, Peter Brook). On the other hand, there is no reason, obviously, why the work of individual playwrights cannot reflect very strong and coherent social commitment (Brecht, of course; and now, especially, Edward Bond). Nevertheless, it is true to say that group improvisation can sometimes uniquely produce new and compelling theatrical forms for the new experiences of the late twentieth century – like the irresponsibility of scientists, the hidden dangers of super-technology, urban guerrilla warfare, racism.

The problem of turning these contemporary issues into drama and theatre is often seen as the problem of 'finding solutions'. It is probably more appropriate to aim at raising consciousness among the people than to 'find solutions' – as though they existed already, waiting to be discovered. In fact, a solution to one problem will in all probability create a new problem of its own. In fact, 'problems' and 'solutions' are a less satisfactory way of looking at the dynamics of society than oppositions which become resolved into new situations which in turn create fresh oppositions. For example, in *Katakata for Sufferhead*, getting out of jail is hardly a 'solution' to Lateef's predicament – or for any of the other 'birds', as Ndem himself found out when he tried to escape. The situations which severally put them inside the prison still remain in the world beyond the walls of the jail. What the play shows, instead, is that they come to a greater understanding of their society inside the 'white college' than they did when they were outside.

Racism in Southern Africa is an especially intractable issue to present through drama, both within South Africa and elsewhere in Africa. Within South Africa *apartheid* makes racism 'respectable' among the white populations, to the extent that if you are white and consider 'separate development' with its belief in the genetic inferiority of the black race wrong and an evil, you are labelled peculiar and dangerous. If you are black you experience the stark brutality of the police state which *apartheid* legitimizes. If you live outside South Africa you find it very difficult to come to terms with the fact that such an immoral system can exist in the present time. The objectives for any serious play on *apartheid* are different, therefore, depending on the audience for whom it is intended, whether white or black within South Africa, or an audience outside the country. A black audience within South Africa knows much better the true nature of *apartheid* than white South Africans for the most part could possibly understand, and the message one might wish to communicate to blacks would be different to the message black South African actors would have for whites.

Yet this is only part of the problem. How can the reality, the meaning of wasted lives, be represented on the stage? It is a sense of desolation more than mere words can seemingly sustain. On the other hand, because the actors have to act it night after night through the weeks of performances, they need to be distanced from the actual suffering they or their fellow-actors have actually experienced. This is apparently a contradiction: intense engagement and emotional distancing at one and the same time. How do the actors achieve it? In the introduction Kavanagh describes the process by which *Survival* was made:

The play was made in two and a half months of intensive workshops. . . . The group began with nothing except the idea of doing something on prison . . . with explorations to evoke as many experiences of and insights into prison life as possible. Three of the five [four actors and a director] had had first hand experience of jail. . . . These explorations were in dance, mime, drawing, colouring, rhythm, singing, chanting – and tried out with slow motion, reversed motion, zoom lens and tableau effects. . . . Writing, improvisation, tape-recording and group discussion were the basic means of evolving dialogue, editing and recording it. . . .

The process was exhausting but essential because not only did it provide the group with the play, *but also the means to act it*. . . . [emphasis added][10]

The 'means to act it' implies not only the acting skills and physical fitness necessary to sustain vigorous movement, concentration and a cumulative intensity over two hours, but also a particular sensibility. This is reflected in unexpected things almost working against the actual words of the play, like understatement, contradictory gestures, silences. In *Katakata for Sufferhead*, neither the playwright nor the actors who first staged the play had to my knowledge been in jail. Nor are the intended audiences for that play prison audiences in Nigeria. There is, inevitably, a sense among audiences and actors of being removed to some extent from direct experience, which, in the end, doesn't seem to matter. *Katakata* now exists as a play-text. Another Nigerian – or African – director and actors can tackle the play-text and perhaps come up with a more compelling performance than the first. But in the case of *Survival* one has the feeling that any other production, even by other black South Africans, would lack the deep sincerity and unique dramatic experience of the first production by the four actors, Dan Maredi, Seth Sibanda, Themba Ntinga, Fana Kekana, and their director, Mshengu. This is actually implied by Kavanagh – who is in fact Mshengu – in the introduction when he writes about a subsequent production:

In 1978 it was revived in South Africa when 'pirate' performances were given by a new cast, directed by Peter Sephuma. This version, *though considered by the original cast to be a 'diluted' travesty of the original*, was ultimately banned in South Africa. [emphasis added][11]

This raises another question: what is the actor's responsibility to the work which he is presenting? Does he enact it word for word? Or does he communicate his own sense of the work, through his own sensibility and understanding? The question is particularly pressing in the South African context. For playwright–directors like Gibson Kente, whose work we noted in Chapter 1, the question is answered in the way the group is organized: it is a commercial company playing to audiences in the black townships. The actors are there to entertain their audiences. It is interesting to note, however, that performances of Kente's company apparently became more politicized following the success in the townships of the more overtly political groups of the art theatre, especially Workshop '71 Theatre Company.

For Athold Fugard (either with or without his two actors, John Kani and Winston Ntshona) the situation is somewhat different again. Fugard himself clearly sees an actor's first responsibility neither to a company nor to violent protest and change, but to a psychological integrity. Commitment to a particular group of actors and to radical change are there, of course, but they are not the actor's *first* responsibility. This results in the intense focus on personal relationships and a sustained analysis of character which we see in most of his plays. True, these relationships and characters are formed by the society; but for Fugard they actually exist beyond it, in and of themselves. In *The Island*, for example, which we considered in Chapter 3, it is 'Winston's' *character (not*, it must be stressed, the character of the actor playing the part, who is also called Winston) which enables him to endure the bitterness of seeing 'John' get out of the prison; it is their relationship to each other during this testing time which is the focus of the play, rather than the nature of the society which put them on Robben Island. Although this is explored as well, it is *not* the focus of the play. 'Winston's' final speech of endurance at the end of the play is uniquely his and throughout the play 'John' acts as a foil to him in the painful acceptance of his fate. The psychology of someone facing incarceration for the rest of his life is the link with Sophocles's *Antigone*, rather than a specifically political parallel. There is, of course, a reality which is discovered through this approach; but the Workshop '71 Theatre Company appear to see their responsibility as actors primarily in a political rather than a psychological context – even though their method of working and the resulting theatrical forms are sometimes remarkably similar to Fugard's Port Elizabeth group.

The difference is perhaps best summed up by the way *Survival* ends. After the scene which shows the four prisoners staging their hunger-strike, there is the following stage direction: [Very quietly the actors discuss the hunger-strike. Quietly and gently. *The acting is over*] [emphasis added]. There follows a conversation which expresses the hopes of their own lives in juxtaposition to their (possible) premature deaths in terms of the situations which they have just presented *as actors*:

Themba: If I were really to be in a hunger-strike, I would want them to bury me on a faraway island, no people, bleak, where everything is wild.

Dan: Four clever children . . . I would like to see them grow up. I've always promised them they can be what they like. To die before I can keep that promise. . . .

Seth: So much to leave behind. I want a house and a family.

Fana: I can see her – you know, Lindi – I can see her coming towards me to tell me it'll soon be time. She usually plaits her hair. Now it's fluffed out. Time to have our baby. The two of us wanted to travel – especially where the sea is.

Seth: I want to be buried near Blood River.[12]

These are personal details from the actors' own lives. Dan then comments:

> In a real hunger-strike they would have force-fed us. One or two of us would have died. Then they would have brought us better food and we would have won our battle. . . . only a small battle.[13]

The four actors drift into song; and then into some final group – or, as they call it, ensemble – work. This is not acting in a formal sense. Instead it is very much akin to music-making, to singing or playing drums together, in a bus, on the back of a lorry, around a camp-fire: there is a certain structuring of the collective emotional experience of the group, but it is still an improvisation and, especially, a response to the moment.

People who have never been involved in dramatic improvisations often wonder if the dialogue or even the situations can be the same for each performance. Even in the most undirected improvisation (that is, where there is no director and no leader emerges within the group) a 'text' can eventually be realized, a 'stabilized' performance which is substantially the same each time the play is performed. The published text of *Survival* is the final 'stabilized' form of the play (arrived at in the manner described in the introduction). But the ending is rather different from other improvisations, and from the improvisation in most of the rest of this play. What is being expressed are the sentiments and experiences of the actors Dan Maredi, Seth Sibanda, Themba Ntinga, Fana Kekana. They are not the sentiments and experiences of other actors who might choose to present the play. If such actors follow this ending then surely they are misrepresenting the spirit of the original actors' conclusion to *their* play. Instead, the play would now need the personal response of the new actors; and in the process of doing this these actors would have to make their play their own. What might the play become if the actors were not black South Africans?

It should perhaps be noted that Kavanagh seems to provide an illogical note on the staging of the play in terms of what he has previously said about the play's political function historically within South Africa:

How the play is staged depends on the audience. *If it is ideologically in sympathy with the play's meanings, it can be considerably cut.* The beginning of both halves can go and the various other sections which are obviously aimed at another sort of audience. . . . [emphasis added][14]

He implies that the core of the play to be retained are the four 'reports'. What, therefore, seems to be dispensable are those very parts of the improvisation which break through the more formal acting in order to communicate more directly and powerfully with the audience. Any director or actors who omitted this element would surely make the production another '"diluted" travesty' of the work of the original cast.

If the dramatic method by which *Survival* was created is in any way different from the way Fugard created *The Island*, for example, or *Sizwe Bansi is Dead*, then it is precisely in the way an actor finally ceases to act, and presents his or her most personal emotions, but still in the context of the play. To do this there must be an atmosphere of trust which the rest of the play manages to establish at each performance, between actors and audience. With *Survival*, which attempts to communicate the black South African experience of *apartheid* to blacks and whites more urgently and passionately than hitherto, we seem to have moved away from acting in a formal sense but paradoxically heightened the actor's performance.

It is with an understanding of this particularized use of group improvisation in the South African situation that we can try to reach the full meaning of the play – which unfortunately exists for us readers only as a written text.

Survival is set in prison which, like the prison in *Katakata for Sufferhead*, is an image of the outside world. It presents the experiences of four people in what are called the 'four reports' of the play: first, Vusi Mabandla's (called 'Fana's Report' after the actor who plays Vusi, Fana Kekana); then Slaksa Mphahlele's (called 'Dan's Report' after Dan Maredi who plays Slaksa); then Leroi Williams's (called 'Themba's Report' after Themba Ntinga who plays Leroi); and finally Edward Nkosi's (known, oddly, as 'Edward's Report', but played by the actor Seth Sibanda, who also plays the part of Habbakuk Ngwenya, a character appearing in 'Fana's Report'). Although the action of the play is continuous, except for a break in the middle, these four reports could be said to correspond to four scenes or acts. In fact, the terminology of the play's structure is more than a little confusing, partly because the reports are named after the actors rather than the characters they play, and partly because the person/character giving the report is not always the focus of that scene. Thus, for example, 'Fana's Report' is not about the character Vusi who gives it, but about Habbakuk. In the circumstances the table outlining the play's structure is probably helpful.

Survival: the play's structure

Introduction to the characters (Prologue)		
'*Fana's* Report' (scene 1)	by Vusi (played by *Fana*)	about Habbakuk (played by Seth)
'*Dan's* Report' (scene 2)	by Slaksa (played by *Dan*)	about Slaksa (other actors to play non-prisoners)
Actors as prisoners (Interlude/Prologue to second half)		
'*Themba's* Report' (scene 3)	by Leroi (played by *Themba*)	about Edward, Vusi and Leroi
'*Edward's* Report' (scene 4)	by Edward (played by *Seth*)	about the hunger-strike
Actors as themselves (Epilogue)		

[Actual names of the actors are in italics.]

From this the play would seem to be episodic, a collection of experiences. Nevertheless, it contains a well-structured story, which is as follows.

Three men in a jail cell, Vusi, Leroi and Slaksa, are joined by a 'new recruit', Habbakuk, an innocent like the 'JJC', Lateef, in *Katakata for Sufferhead*. Habbakuk is quickly schooled by the others in the ways of the prison and, in the process, in the corrupt ways of the legal world outside. Like Lateef, he is 're-tried' by his cell-mates. However, Habbakuk continues to protest at the system and is finally removed from the cell. His place is taken in the cell by a much more sinister and brutal figure, Edward Nkosi. One of the inmates, Slaksa, has had his sentence reduced and is released from prison, after serving five years. Has the situation changed whilst he was inside? Slaksa finds that it has not changed at all; and he offers himself up for re-arrest. He returns to the cell. Edward Nkosi, Vusi and Leroi all describe how they have become criminals. Edward and Vusi have both killed people. They detail the circumstances and explain their actions. Each is prepared to admit to a desire to kill the oppressor and to accept in themselves a violent initiative. They refuse to accept blame for their actions.* The four in the cell then resolve to go on a hunger-strike. Vusi breaks the strike. Edward and Leroi threaten to kill him but Slaksa dissuades them. There is a final climactic moment indicated in the following stage direction:

> . . . The ritual of rejection. Each prisoner takes a plate and tips the contents on the ground. He clutches his stomach in pain – hunger and beatings – and falls to the ground. Vusi too rejects the food. For a short while there is silence. . . . Then there is the quiet sound of tears. One by one they cry.[15]

That is the end of the *story*; the *play* continues, as has already been described, with the actors discussing out of role the story they have just acted and how it affects their own lives.

There is, therefore, in *Survival* a very detailed structuring of experience. Improvisation is not as open-ended as one would imagine. What appears effortless and spontaneous in performance is almost always the result of (1) intellectual understanding and trust among members of the group, achieved through exercises and discussion; (2) physical experimentation in role of which there has been intense group criticism; (3) an ordering of actions and events, using a whole range of stage conventions and acting techniques. In this play the ordering of actions is complex, for the form of a story (a sequential narrative) intersects with the alternative and sometimes contradictory form of various 'reports' by individual characters (telling the same events from different points of view).

Characterization is central to this structure: and the more formal characterization (characters like Vusi, Slaksa, etc.) intersects with the characterization of the actors' own *personae* (Fana Kekana, Dan Maredi, etc.). Within the formal characterization there is a deliberate organization of contrasts. For example, there is a clear

---

*Actually they use the word 'responsibility' instead of 'blame' – '**All** [*Together*]: We refuse to accept responsibility for our crimes.' – but it seems they *are* accepting responsibility; they are refusing to be *blamed* for them.

and deliberate contrast between Habbakuk, the innocent, and Edward Nkosi, the brutal 'thug'. With deliberate irony, they are both played by the same actor. Habbakuk's naive and honest resistance to the prison regime finally gets him removed from the cell for punishment. The others expect him back. When the actor playing Habbakuk does return the others assume that he is 'Habbakuk'; but he is now 'Edward Nkosi', a silent, sinister figure who 'chops Slaksa down with a swift brutal blow'. The play focuses on Edward from this point, and Habbakuk is no longer seen. Whereas Habbakuk's innocent spirit can be easily silenced by the white regime, Edward's violence ultimately cannot be contained. He leads the hunger-strike.

There is, however, a much more significant dimension to the characterization, namely their eventual achievement of political understanding. Slaksa's growing awareness is presented first. It is on the immediately obvious level, namely that nothing in South Africa changes over the years as a result of international pressure against *apartheid*, and the tinkering with the system is merely 'cosmetic'. In the second half of the play the tone changes when the lives of the other three inmates of the cell are scrutinized. The political awareness of Leroi, Vusi and Edward is the result of a much more complex analysis relating to the crime in all their lives. These men are not terrorists or political detainees, it must be remembered, but common criminals. Each is differentiated; and in the final climax, the hunger-strike, Vusi, who is black middle-class, though a murderer like Edward, is contrasted with Edward and Leroi. When the others threaten to kill Vusi for breaking the strike Slaksa says:

> Leroi you began our strike. You're young but you're heroic. You've got the guts we need. Now listen to the head. Don't beat him up. He's not a traitor. He tried. This time the pressure was too much for him. He was weak. Give him your strength and he too will be heroic.[16]

Vusi rejoins the strike. There is a special political awareness being developed here, for the audience directly: those who desire to join the struggle but who are weak (the vast majority of us in fact) need to be encouraged and sustained by the more heroic. Slaksa's intervention on Vusi's behalf is tangential to the rest of the scene. Both Edward and Vusi, different as they are in temperament, describe in similar terms how they come to recognize their actions for what they are. Edward, for example, is involved in a car crash.

He rescues the black driver from the burning car but allows the white occupants to burn to death. The accident is acted out and there is the following stylized exchange between an 'onlooker' at the scene of the crash and Edward, who is actually addressing the audience in a different time-dimension:

Onlooker: There are people in the car. They'll burn to death.

Edward Nkosi: (*To audience*) I stood and watched the flames rise into the air.

Onlooker: (*To Edward Nkosi*) Why didn't you see them?

Edward Nkosi: (*To audience*) I can't say I didn't see them.

Onlooker: (*To Edward Nkosi*) Why didn't you pull them out while there was still time?

Edward Nkosi: (*To audience*) I can't say why I didn't pull them out in time. Why did I save the black driver and leave the white passengers?[17]

Edward subsequently beats one of his mother's elderly boy-friends to death.

Vusi describes how he tried to get his dying father to the hospital. He drove his father's car without a licence and was stopped by a black policeman and his white superior. In the ensuing argument Vusi strikes the black cop:

Vusi: (*To audience*) In the heat of the fight I had forgotten even that he [**Vusi's** *father*] was there. He was dead. The traffic cop, too. He was dead. On the way to the police station I kept shouting: 'I didn't mean to kill him! I didn't mean to kill him!' Then I thought of father and stopped shouting.[18]

It is Leroi who sums up the nature of their awareness:

Suddenly at obstinate moments, these circumstances come together and trap a human being so tightly that for one moment the parts become a whole. . . .[19]

In the circumstances violence becomes acceptable. There is no blame attached to it. The logic of racialism in South Africa is succinctly expressed at the end of the play when the actors have moved out of role:

Themba: You know, that's what survival means. . . . I wonder how many of those who hate us now, won't one day wish they too could be black. . . .[20]

and he continues a little later:

A people survive by grimly holding on. But at the same time they achieve what their oppressors cannot help envying them for. The strength lies with the people, who carry with them in their lives the justification for the struggle – the victory that is survival.[21]

The will to survive *as a people*, rather than as racially inferior individuals, is the first stage of political awareness. This is as much a moral survival as a physical one: a determination not to blame oneself for the actions one feels compelled to do. No guilt. The play ends with a passionate song about a future beyond survival as the actors march through the audience and out of the theatre with clenched fists raised.

Music – in *Survival*, songs without backing or a band, sung in the style of a 'barbershop quartet' – is also part of the structuring of the play. The songs make a comment on the actions of the characters and they sum up the mood at a particular moment. They have the effect of distancing the audience from the action while drawing them into the mood or emotions of the play. The use of music in *Survival* differs in some ways from the use of music in *Opera Wonyosi* where it is primarily the means whereby the satire of the play is turned upon the audience. It differs more markedly from the use of music in *The Marriage of Anansewa* where it is the means by which the audience actually become involved in the staging of the performance.

A comparison might be made, finally, between *Survival*, *Opera Wonyosi* and *Katakata for Sufferhead*, in the direct relationship which each play depicts between criminality and the existing social system. In *Opera Wonyosi* Soyinka shows that the behaviour of the powerful and the rich is as criminal as the underworld with whom they are inextricably bound up. In *Katakata for Sufferhead*, Oyekunle shows the criminality of the prison inmates to be so petty by comparison with the practices of the up-holders of the Rule of Law as to amount to their complete innocence. In *Survival*, however, the system – racism and *apartheid* – is shown to generate and justify violent crime for which the criminals will not accept the blame. All are unpalatable analyses for the majority of the present art theatre audiences in Africa.

Notes and references

1 Yemi Ajibade, *Mokai* is not published yet.

2 Femi Osofisan, *The Chattering and the Song* (Ibadan: Ibadan University Press 1977).
3 ibid., p. 45.
4 ibid., p. 45.
5 ibid., p. 56.
6 Wole Soyinka, *Myth, Literature and the African World* (Cambridge: Cambridge University Press 1976), p. 52.
7 Segun Oyekunle, *Katakata for Sufferhead*, is not published yet. It was first produced in Zaria in 1978, directed by Tony Humphries.
8 *Survival* is published in Robert Kavanagh (ed.), *South African People's Plays* (London: Heinemann Educational Books 1981).
9 ibid., p. 126.
10 ibid., p. 127.
11 ibid., p. 126.
12 ibid., p. 168.
13 ibid., p. 169.
14 ibid., p. 128.
15 ibid., p. 168.
16 ibid.
17 ibid., p. 164.
18 ibid., p. 160.
19 ibid.
20 ibid., p. 169.
21 ibid., p. 170.

8 Theatre and development

Consider this: One of the tribes in Zambia, the Chewa, has a spectacular dance which celebrates rites of passage. The dance is called *Nyau* and the masquerade is performed on the occasion of a funeral. In one of the villages in this area there was a man who was able to dance *Nyau* so well that all the people from the surrounding communities acknowledged his pre-eminence in the art of the dance; and because the dance celebrated death as a transition from this world to the next, the man was much in demand to perform the dance at funerals. His local fame reached the ears of the ministry of culture in the capital, Lusaka, and talent scouts were sent out to assess whether he could be brought into the National Dance Troupe. Without question he was a natural 'star', and he was soon in Lusaka dancing with the Troupe. Within a year he was performing not only at the International Airport for visiting heads of state, but also in the distant capitals of the world when the National Dance Troupe went on foreign tours, in order to promote the culture of Zambia. His international acclaim was noted by his family and his fellow villagers.

A much-loved fellow back in the village died in tragic circumstances, and a small delegation of fellow peasants came to the capital to ask the internationally famous dancer of *Nyau* if he would come and dance the masquerade at the deceased's funeral. Of course he would come. He remembered the fellow with affection; they had been age-mates. He obtained permission through the ministry's bureaucracy for a short leave of absence, and set off for the village.

Back in the village the dancer marvelled to himself how he could have danced in such heat and dirt without really noticing it. How long ago it all seemed. How could the dance have ever been considered as an art in the midst of the emotional and physical chaos of a funeral? Prepared in his costume, behind a hut, and waiting to dart out in the sacred mask, he pondered on his good fortune that had taken him so far away from this 'bush' life, and which had singled him out to be the one to preserve for all time the only truly great thing about his people's culture, *Nyau*.

The dance began and for a while he was totally absorbed in demonstrating to his fellow-villagers his heightened technique and unassailable virtuosity. He was the star of the occasion. Gradually, however, he became aware of the fact that the villagers were no longer watching him. They seemed to be gazing intently behind him. He turned his head, and was amazed to see a second *Nyau* dancer, dancing behind him, almost as his shadow. He missed the beat and lost his step; but nobody seemed to notice. The second dancer smiled encouragingly at him. Then he realized that the drummers, the musicians, were playing for this other dancer and not for him. He had become irrelevant to the masquerade.

In anger he left the arena and sought out one of the village elders. 'It's all right, my son,' he was told. 'You were dancing *Nyau* incorrectly; and we could not afford to let our illustrious son who has died miss the way to the other side.'

The dancer pondered this new reality in his life for some time. Then he went in search of a length of rope, and hanged himself from a nearby thorn tree.

This is a story, obviously. The form of it indicates that it is. But is it real? Or is it fiction? In fact, it is a summary,[1] in narrative form, of a play by the very popular Zambian playwright, Stephen Chifunyise, whose work we will be considering in this chapter. This play is fictional. However, it is considered by many of the Zambian intellectual middle-class not to be so, for there was a famous dancer of *Vimbuza*, Wilikilifi Ludaka (Mkandawire)[2] who had been the star of the National Dance Troupe, and who recently died. Chifunyise maintains that the play is not about Mkandawire at all. Rather, he insists, it is about a deeper reality which he sees in his society, namely, the contradiction that those who would preserve the traditional culture are actually destroying it. The National Dance Troupe, in Chifunyise's play, co-opts the village dancer. In doing so it encourages his own individualism through elitist performances and international tours, and ignores the community which alone is capable of giving the dance and the masquerade any meaning. The dance, and not the people, are given contemporary value.

It is not clear if Chifunyise sees this contradiction specifically as part of an analysis of how the dominant elitist art, in most contemporary third world societies, usurps the popular culture, but such an analysis is implied in the way he has developed the scenario of his play. The play is intended to show, I think, the complex problem of cultural development in the modern African nation–state, and how certain cultural policies ironically achieve the exact opposite of what was intended. Such a view assumes that intellectuals, cultural planners, playwrights and theatre directors actually want to do the 'right thing' – where the 'right thing' is usually seen as retrieving the culture of the people after it has been ravaged by the long years of colonialism and settlerism. The problem is that these people lack a sufficient understanding of what might be called cultural dynamics.

Another view is the opposite of this. It sees the outcome of national cultural policy as being exactly what is intended by the society's rulers. The people's culture, and in particular those arts of the rural masses which have actually managed to survive colonialism, are used to reinforce the dominance of the new elites. This is done, for example, by making the people's dances and masquerades, which hitherto had had a social function inseparable from its aesthetic, into an art form which now mirrors and encourages individualism. In general, this is achieved both through the content of artistic work – as, for example, in those plays which show individuals achieving success – as well as through a commercialization of the means of artistic production, as, for example, when we 'buy' and 'book' a seat in advance to see a performance of a 'successful' show. Individualism is indicated by such attributes as personal success, high status, and the individual ability to appreciate 'great art'. The hope of acquiring these attributes is inculcated in those masses who, by the very nature of the system, can never attain either success, or high status, or access to 'great art'.

Whichever analysis we use to show how the people are deprived of their art and culture – whether through an inadequate understanding of cultural dynamics or through the deliberate policies of the ruling elite – we find ourselves talking about art in the context of economic and political forces in the society. Indeed, if we are thinking of the whole population in a society, it does not seem possible to talk about the development of theatre and drama in that society without analysing the nature of its economic and political development. Paradoxically, there seem to be hidden pressures to talk about African drama and theatre in absolute terms and as something separate from their societies.

This may be because emphasis is laid, through the educational system, on the study of published play-texts, and on the formal 'artistic' productions of them in performances. These are, in short, the most elitist aspects of the new drama – for who can read the play-texts? And who can go to the theatre in which the expensive production is staged? The established but unwritten plays in vernaculars or in Pidgin; the travelling theatre troupes and concert parties; the unsophisticated performances in remote villages by literacy teachers; the chaotic productions by junior clerks in church halls in provincial towns: none of these are considered worthy of being studied. Any dramatic activity which is not centred on a written text with literary pretensions is not considered worth studying. I have consistently tried to challenge this attitude; to assert that the study of drama is primarily a study of its function in society. Such a study does not exclude the content of the drama, whether this is available in a specifically literary form or not. Indeed, many African playwrights have been concerned to relate their art to their societies much more directly, either to reflect social change, or, more significantly, actually to advocate radical change through the content of their plays.

Some of these plays, which we have analysed, have argued for the revolution. The most notable examples are Ngugi's and Mugo's *The Trial of Dedan Kimathi* and Femi Osofisan's *The Chattering and the Song*. Rugyendo's play *The Contest* has presented the case for a Socialist African state. A great many of the plays have instanced and analysed social evils, past and present (*Anowa* by Ama Ata Aidoo, and *Katakata for Sufferhead* by Oyekunle). Some of these have been protest plays by being satirical and even directly critical of contemporary regimes – Soyinka's plays are the most powerful examples.

There is, therefore, a desire by contemporary African playwrights to participate in social change through their art and perhaps by direct political intervention as well. Some of these playwrights are, no doubt, mere rhetoricians of revolution; but others do care about the oppressed in society and in their lives they are prepared to become involved in dangerous political activity. However, in their plays, the socially critical element is generally restricted to the content. The form of the drama remains untouched. This is, broadly speaking, a dramatic form which has been inherited from the Athenian elites of Ancient Greece through the mediation of western European dramatic art: a play forms a whole, it has a beginning, a middle and an end, and is, in an artistic sense, complete. Furthermore, the means of production of the new dramatic art, which can be summarized as university or government patronage for shows in expensive theatres with elaborately technical stages, and resulting in international publication of play-texts and internationally toured productions of successful plays, is generally accepted and remains largely unchallenged.

This theatre, and even its 'revolutionary' drama, remains inaccessible to the mass of people. The socially committed theatre contributes to the process of social change only insofar as the intellectuals themselves acquire political consciousness.

There is a further point which needs to be borne in mind alongside this. The alternative theatre, which is largely unwritten – the popular touring companies and improvised urban shows discussed in the first chapter – is indeed very often about nothing at all; and though it may start by having significant social meaning for the peasants and proletariat, its mode of organization soon begins to contradict the development of this socially critical approach. We saw this in the particular case of the Yoruba travelling theatre of Hubert Ogunde.

Taken together, these two observations – namely (1) an intellectual drama which barely touches the mass of the people though it professes to be concerned with them, and (2) a theatre of the people which in every instant seems quickly to become debased – raises the crucial problem of African drama and theatre in an acute form. If uneducated and illiterate peasants could, in former times, produce an art of performance in their dances, songs, story-telling traditions, masquerades and festivals, which intellectuals today regard as worthy of study, why is it that now, at this present moment of social development, it is only these intellectuals who can produce a drama and theatre which is similarly worthy of study? In the intellectual's own terms it would seem that the peasants have *stopped* producing an art of performance of any worth, that is, an art which conveys an understanding of their present conditions.

This chapter addresses itself to this question in the process of trying to analyse examples of theatre being used in the development processes. However, when we start talking about theatre and development, we need to be aware of a number of potential confusions in the use of the terminology: 'revolutionary theatre', 'popular theatre', 'development', which have ambiguous and sometimes contradictory meanings, and need to be sorted out before we can turn to the examples.

In discussing 'development' let us talk specifically and concretely of development in rural, peasant-farming areas, and how this affects the communities actually living there. We have to ask: development for whom? For the peasant farmers? Very often increased productivity in agricultural output by peasant farmers in a particular area brings little benefit to the peasant community as a whole. Often it accelerates those forces which in fact cause the disintegration of the community: the growing affluence of a few farmers, the impoverishment of many, the departure from the land and the flight to the towns, particularly by the young adults. The provision of a clinic or a primary school or a road never seems to solve the central problem which is the loss of hope in the future of the community by the rural youth.

Even as foreign aid, agricultural schemes, services and facilities are being made available to rural communities, the central institutions of the state – the bureaucracy, the education system, the judiciary, the religions and their priesthoods, and the decision-making institutions at national, provincial and local levels – through modern communication media, especially radio – are undermining the community's own ethos. Three examples might explain this process.

First, land which was previously owned communally now passes into private ownership. It is a process which is ratified by the legislature and the courts. Thus, even as peasants are being urged to stay on the land and become more productive by various agencies of the government, their land is being sold to representatives of multi-national organizations through the government and private speculators from underneath them.

The second example concerns the encouragement given to farmers by a development agency on behalf of the government, who are implementing a cash crop scheme in a particular area, to switch from self-subsistence to cash crops. They offer the farmers technical advice and the use of mechanized resources – including perhaps a large-scale irrigation project. Agricultural Extension Officers, the radio, and even development films, are used to coerce the peasants into making the change. Later, the poorer farmers discover that the money which they receive for their cash crop (cotton, for example), is not enough to pay for the food for their families which they haven't grown. They are worse off than before.

The third example concerns the adult literacy campaigns which are often set up in rural areas. Mass literacy can be a step towards political consciousness and a means of forgoing stronger community bonds to challenge the dominant and highly literate social systems. However, by the time a mass literacy campaign is put into operation the values of the dominant urban class have very often already been transferred to the rural areas (through improved means of communications) and literacy is presented instead as a means of gaining access on an individual and competitive basis to the sources of development money, or at least to a job in the towns. Literacy, therefore, is seen as a means of becoming a land-owner. For the vast majority, however, this 'hope' is futile.

Thus, development for the masses in the rural areas often means, in actuality, development for a few in the rural areas, and ultimately a further development of the urban areas. And drama, in the context of these development programmes, is like any other communication medium: it is objectively neutral. Drama will reinforce the ultimate aims of the development programme in which it is being used. Theatre will not, *ipso facto*, transform that development programme either into what its superficial rhetoric declares it to be, or into something else. However, live theatre differs significantly from film, television and radio in being a medium of live, or present, communication. More than any other medium it can allow an immediate dialogue to take place. Listeners can themselves become speakers.

Theatre – the live performance in the centre of a village – can have a powerful effect on its present rural audience, which means that its use must be very carefully considered. Apart from being a means of establishing a dialogue between actors and audience during the actual performance of a play, with a view to defining the issues within the play (and within the community) more clearly, theatre is also powerful as a more conventional one-way medium of communication – as, for example, a revolutionary-inspired play for a community conscious of its increasing poverty and discrimination. Even this second use of the medium of live theatre is highly problematic.

It may be appropriate to set the term 'revolutionary' aside when talking about theatre for and by the people. In one sense the word is used in a very general way to cover anything which argues for rapid social change, and it often simply becomes a catch-phrase. In another sense – and especially when 'revolutionary' is used in connection with theatre, or culture generally – it can mean the transformation of art without actually accomplishing any corresponding social transformation. In fact, no theatre can actually make the revolution. It is even doubtful if 'revolutionary theatre' can be construed as the 'rehearsal' for the revolution. A revolutionary theatre may in fact never mean anything more than a theatre of the rhetoric of revolution.

It is much more useful to focus on the terms *'people's* drama' (or theatre) and *'popular* drama' (or theatre), and to differentiate between the two.

A very useful definition which differentiated between a people's theatre and a popular theatre was produced by a group of Latin American theatre activists at a seminar in Berlin in 1980:[3]

We distinguished between the 'people's culture', with its positive and negative aspects, and the 'popular culture'. The people's culture, a mixture of the values from the people and those from the dominant class, has developed in its various forms. By people's culture we mean the culture that exists and manifests itself in a spontaneous and natural way through music, customs, values, etc. It is a culture dominated and absorbed by the ruling culture, and which has been able to impose across time values foreign to the popular interests and favourable to the ruling class. By popular culture we mean the culture that preserves, rescues and incorporates elements whose content is eminently popular, that is to say the culture which strengthens ethnic and class consciousness.

This definition is born out of the Latin American experience. The use of 'popular' in the context of African theatre needs to be clarified, for here it is actually used in a number of contradictory ways, indicated in the following list. Although the various activities can be seen as a series of stages, roughly chronological in this formulation, in the process of returning the art of drama and theatre to the people, nevertheless these stages can and do exist side by side even within the same area:

1 *The traditional performances*, which are being 'preserved' by arts councils, ministries of culture and tourism, ballet troupes and national dance companies, etc.
2 *The concert parties, folk operas and popular travelling theatres*, mainly urban and wholly commercial, and undermined alike by commercial failure and commercial success.

3   '*Taking theatre to the people*', performances of plays by intellectuals (playwrights, students, adult educators) which are subsidized and toured to remote areas. These may be plays already scripted, or plays developed in workshops in the rural areas.

4   *Folk theatre and development*, combining drama (a modern innovation characterized by spoken dialogue, improvisation and role-play) and the so-called 'folk media', of the particular area (for example, songs, dances, masquerades, shadow puppets and so on) into a theatrical performance used to communicate the objectives of a particular development project. The term folk media has now been added to the list of other media of communication, such as radio and film, by United Nations agencies.

5   *Theatre and self-help*. Although this springs from (4) there is a greater emphasis on people in the target community becoming involved in determining development objectives which can be realized through self-help schemes.

6   *Drama as a means of achieving political consciousness*. Theatre becomes part of a wider process of raising political consciousness.

Of these distinct uses of the term popular theatre, the first, second, fourth and fifth all fall directly into the Latin Americans' definition of a people's theatre; while only the last actually falls into their definition of popular theatre. The third is problematic since it may not necessarily involve anything of the people's culture and yet still help to awaken their political consciousness – though not necessarily if it presents a fully-formed class analysis to the people merely on a take-it-or-leave-it basis.

In the remainder of this chapter we will consider examples of drama and theatre which at least aspire to raising the consciousness of the masses, even if they don't always succeed. But to do so we must look even more closely at the word 'popular' and its conflicting meanings in the African context.

The use of 'popular' to describe the urbanized folk operas and plays of the burgeoning African cities refers to a theatre made by creative artists who are economically and socially at one with the masses – at least when they start their professional theatre work and, like Ogunde in Nigeria, first form their theatre companies. Theirs is not a revolutionary theatre, though it is often highly political. Popular here means having a broad appeal within the society.[4]

There is a closely related meaning of popular with which the live travelling theatres and concert parties are often confused: popular also refers to the 'best seller', to 'pulp' magazines, to films which are 'smash hits' or 'box-office draws'; and, above all, to pop (music). In this context, popular means modern. It indicates a technologizing of the means of production of art in order to supply the high consumption of the markets (mainly the young adults) which this technology itself has created. This art is essentially non-live; it is a commercialization of art and a mass-production of culture. Popular, in this sense suggests a debasement of art. In the African context specifically there are further adverse connotations of the word, which suggest a dilution or corruption of the traditional culture and a copying of western cultural modes as these are reflected in, for example, western pop music, *Kung Fu* films, fashions in clothes and in individual physical appearances.

It is necessary to see popular here as referring to an economic process which is essentially on two levels: (1) the spread of a single, world-wide pop culture, as an economic activity, and facilitated by modern technology, the hardware of which is also part of the consumption; and (2) the creation of local pop cultures, which, because of an initial lack of technical resources often begin as a reaction to the world pop culture, but which then tend to become absorbed by it, reflecting it, and contributing to its local economic growth.

Some African intellectuals do not see this type of popular urban culture in the way it is often seen in the West, that is, first of all, as an expression of rebelliousness in the youth, and, second, as a commercialization – and 'neutralizing' – of this rebelliousness. Instead, they view it as an unfortunate continuation of colonialism, an external control of young minds through an alien culture, and as such a negation of the revolutionary spirit which inspired the struggle for independence.

There is an immediate clash of perceptions here, for it is clear that, for example, the Nigerian, Hubert Ogunde, and the South African, Credo Mutwa, whose (live) theatre performances are considered, erroneously, to be part of this urban pop culture, reject absolutely any charge of undermining the traditional culture or the ideals of the struggle for independence. In fact, as we saw in Chapter 1, the very commercialism, which seemingly gives the group its initial autonomy, eventually undermines its ability to provide the mass urban audiences with a continuing and developing analysis of their social conditions from their point of view.

If we accept the Latin Americans' crucial distinction between a people's culture and a popular culture, then the notion of pop as applied to the shows of Ogunde, Mutwa, and the others, is clearly part of the people's culture, for this theatre is initially a spontaneous and natural expression of individual creative artists drawn from among the people, which is subsequently undermined by the values of the dominant culture, particularly by the way in which the theatre companies come to be organized.

The traditional performing arts, which are predominantly rural, just as the pop theatre is predominantly urban, are also a part of this definition of a people's culture: the scenario from Chifunyise's play about the *Nyau* dancer suggests one way at least in which the dominant culture of contemporary elites co-opts and undermines this grass-roots performance art of the people – which, as we have noted, not only survived colonialism, but in unnoticed corners even managed to flourish as a critical comment upon it.

There is another use of the word popular in the context of African theatre. In East Africa, popular, in the context of theatre, was inherited from Bertolt Brecht. However, what Brecht had to say about Europe's populations in 1938 doubtless inspired the Latin Americans in the late 1970s, in the formulation of their definition of *popular theatre* in the third world. In an essay on *The Popular and the Realistic** Brecht maintains that the people (in German *Volk*), to which his use of the word 'popular' (*Volkstumlich*) refers, are no longer to be described as quaint or 'folksy'; nor as a group or class whose time-honoured customs and traditions have now reinforced their inferior social status. 'Our conception of "popular",' he suggests, 'refers to the people who are not only fully involved in the process of development but are actually taking it over, forcing it, deciding it.'

Brecht then manages to link both tradition and revolution in the concept of 'popular', which he defines as '. . . taking over [the people's] own forms of expression and enriching them . . . representing the most progressive section of the people in such a way that it can take over the leadership. . . . Linking with tradition and carrying it further. . . .'

Brecht goes on to reiterate that the people are to take over the culture. The initiative in art, and in the culture generally, is to be taken away from the bourgeoisie who now lead society and given

* In John Willett (ed.), *Brecht on Theatre* (London: Eyre Methuen 1964), pp. 107–12.

to the masses who will soon lead it. The people, in this revolutionary sense of constituting a conscious opposition to the bourgeoisie,
are both the subject-matter *and the target audiences* of Brecht's
drama. Ultimately, they are the makers of their own revolutionary
drama.

Brecht and his fellow radicals arrived at a double equation:

1   All art/cultural movements* which oppose bourgeois art = the
truth about society.

2   Popular = *by* the oppressed, *about* the oppressed and *for*
them.

Together they express the concept of the revolution in society
being reflected in the art of the people. The African writers of the
negritude movement in the 1940s and 1950s saw their own highly
literary art as a reflection of their struggle for liberation in Africa,
and as the African peoples seized their independence in the
colonial territories, so they seized it also in their art. In some cases
these negritude intellectuals did themselves assume political power
– the most notable example is Léopold Sédar Senghor in Senegal –
but, ironically, in the last ten years, the negritude movement has
been reinterpreted as anti-revolutionary and intellectually elitist in
the present African political spectrum in the arts.

The influence of Brecht's ideas was greatest in East Africa
probably because his work was a major component of the theatre
studies in the universities of Dar es Salaam, Tanzania, and of
Zambia, in the 1960s and 1970s. What Brecht had to say about the
supreme importance of the people for whom the popular theatre
was intended was matched by the national philosophies of Zambian Humanism and Nyerere's Scientific Socialism in Tanzania
that followed in the wake of independence in those two countries.

It also reflected the intense desire among young writers to
explode the pretensions of the enduring legacy of the white
colonial theatre, and find wider eager audiences among the people
for the plays they wanted to write and perform. A campaign for
taking theatre out of the University and colonial theatres, in
Zambia, and performing plays among the people, was perhaps
best summed up by Kabwe Kasoma's slogan: 'Bring theatre to the
people, not people to the theatre!'

Ugandan and Tanzanian students had already been doing this in
a variety of interesting ways. A significant feature of the various

*For example, Naturalism, Realism, Surrealism, Expressionism.

*for
the
masses.*

programmes for 'bringing theatre to the people', and thereby seemingly creating a 'popular' theatre, was that it involved intellectuals – students and writers – in performing for the masses. It meant travelling deep into the rural areas; it meant performing in dirty and dilapidated halls or on playing fields, in village clearings or in urban bars; it meant audiences of 3000, or audiences of less than a hundred – though large or small, none had any preconceptions of drama. The mere fact of performing in such circumstances, of deliberately turning one's back on the convenience and artistic challenge of the comfortable theatres, was regarded as 'revolutionary' in the 1960s, irrespective of the *content* of the plays performed. The aim was to shape the content, whatever it was, in such a way that the new mass audiences would understand it.

It is interesting to note that at the same time as this essentially artistic revolution in theatre was going on in East Africa, there was another sort of popular drama taking place in Mozambique, where FRELIMO forces were pressing down from the north to liberate the country from the Portuguese. FRELIMO used drama in the villages which they had liberated to awaken the peasants to their new responsibilities in their communities, on the one hand, and towards struggle for total liberation on the other. This was 'popular' theatre which was assisting a social and political revolution, rather than an artistic one.[5]

'Taking theatre to the people' *I Resign* and *The District Governor Goes to a Village*; two plays by Stephen Chifunyise and *Big Berrin* by Yulisa Amadu Maddy[6]

The two plays by Chifunyise, which are immensely popular among rural and urban audiences in Zambia, expose the actual values of the dominant culture rather than those expressed by the rhetoric. Maddy's play, which was very popular in Freetown, Sierra Leone, was banned by the government and Maddy himself was imprisoned. Chifunyise is concerned primarily with the impoverishment of the people in the rural areas in Zambia; Maddy is more concerned with urban poverty. Both playwrights address audiences who seem unable to understand the nature of the social forces which have enmeshed them, or to devise ways of challenging the coercive values of their societies.

In the play *Katongo Chala* by Kabwe Kasoma, whose *Black Mamba* plays we discussed in Chapter 4, the father of the eponymous hero, who is himself a peasant bound to the land, knows that his son must get off the land and into one of the towns.[7]

> All the young men today are working in offices in towns and sending back lots of money to their parents because they have read a lot of books and are big people in government. Are you going to rot here in this village?

In the real world of Zambia, and not in the world of the play, the government exhorts the young men to go back to the lands even as it attracts them into the towns. In *Shimakamba's Dog*, a play by Chifunyise on a similar theme to *Katongo Chala*, there is not just a comment that people 'rot here in this village. . . .'; we actually see on stage two young men rotting. The play charts their social and moral disintegration in the village situation. It describes a conflict in the village between two peasants who succeed in making their sons antagonistic to each other, mirroring and perpetuating their own animosity. The one man's son attempts to run away to the city with the other's daughter, but the young couple fail in their bid for economic independence and freedom. They return to the village, humilated. The two young men, husband and brother of the girl, are both going insane. They are rotting before they are 20 years old.

Taken together, these two plays by different Zambian authors show that the poor in the society have little hope, though they imagine that the world lies open before them. The town destroys the poor man's character; the village destroys the poor man's mind. Where in actuality are the ideals of the struggle for independence and the fruits of freedom? Although Chifunyise's and Kasoma's plays are nearly always intended for – and given – performance among the people in the town and the country, they are actually an attempt to address party cadres on the so-called common man's behalf. In examining two of Chifunyise's most popular plays we will try to see how the *structuring* of the play reflects this aim.

Both *The District Governor Goes to a Village* and *I Resign* are intended by Chifunyise as plays which avoid literary pretensions. All his plays tend to be short, and are usually focused on a single issue, the complexity of which is none the less clearly reflected. The structure of *I Resign* is particularly interesting in the way it translates a genuine political commitment among certain party cadres to real social change in the face of the prevailing 'double-speak' into drama.[8]

Most of the action of the play takes place in the office of the white managing director of a British-owned Zambian company. There is a short scene in the middle in the personnel manager's office. The play focuses on Mr Leeds who is the managing director of this construction company; but it is structured to reflect the point of view of Mr Banda (a very common Zambian name), the Zambian general manager in the company who is seen as a stooge by the rest of the management. We spend most of the time with Mr Leeds in his office, and we are able to witness him relating to all sorts of different people, both face-to-face and over the telephone. We are privy to his private views; we become conscious of the true significance of things which he says publicly and actually see the manipulation of people and businesses for personal, sectional and foreign interests. His character is not so much an exaggeration as an amalgamation of attitudes of which the playwright is critical.

At the beginning of the play, Leeds confers over the phone with a fellow British businessman. He is confident and apparently successful; and his first 'fault', which is only hinted at, is that his economic allegiance is not to the country in which his company is operating – Zambia – but to Britain. He refers to the need to '. . . help the ailing economy . . . jobs for the boys of course. . . .' His second 'fault', which is also only hinted at, is that he is about to engage in a deceit; he is going to go through the form of consulting Banda, the general manager, when in fact everything is already decided. But if we have not been listening too carefully we may ourselves be deceived by Mr Leeds's tone of voice; he is polite and considerate to everyone with whom he has some dealings. In fact, he seems a very 'nice' man, and not at all a caricature of a corrupt and racist managing director, an imperialist and neo-colonialist, all of which he is later called by Mr Banda.

The initial discussion with Mr Banda also begins in a polite and rather formal way. The rival economic arguments are succinctly stated: the machine which Mr Leeds is planning to buy from Britain will replace 115 workers in the company. Leeds says this is 'very economic'; Banda says that the money to buy the machine has come from the profits which have been achieved by the hard work of the 115 workers, who, as a reward for their hard work, are to be made jobless. Leeds counters this argument and maintains that the machine will increase the profits of the company for the benefit of the workers who remain. Banda rejects this:

If we replace Zambian workers with a British machine we are . . . completely supporting the British workers while the Zambian worker goes jobless.

Now we have been prepared for this point in the private telephone conversation between Leeds and his friend ('. . . yes . . . jobs for the boys. . . .'). Leeds justifies himself: Zambian workers are lazy and unreliable. We can't run away from a programme of educating workers towards greater productivity, counters Banda.

Leeds shifts his ground: with the machine we could build more houses more quickly, which the Zambian government is crying out for. We can't evade our national responsibility in this respect. . . . Banda answers this by accusing Leeds of bringing British technicians to work this machine. . . .

Tempers flare, and the argument becomes personal. Leeds tells Banda that the latter is only employed because the company makes a profit; Leeds is not going to allow Banda to 'turn this company into some Father Christmas-owned business where we keep Zambian workers on just because they must be employed'. Leeds raises his voice; refuses to listen to Banda any longer, and the latter goes out.

The arguments over profits versus workers remained unresolved; the audience remain with Mr Leeds. What is he going to do next? The company accountant, Mr Phiri (a Zambian) and the engineering adviser, Mr Zulu (also a Zambian) then come in to see Leeds. The first thing we discover from these two is that the company is already hiring technicians from Britain and France, and that Zulu himself is jetting back and forth to Europe to interview them. So Banda's hunch was right; and the audience receive this piece of information before they have time to forget Banda's last words before he stormed out. The three men then go on to speak about Banda, their general manager. They joke about him, about humanism and about Zambianization. They exhibit an aggressive elitism. When Leeds suggests that Banda should be transferred to the London office of the company it is Zulu who scorns this suggestion:

To the London office. . . . Surely·you do not mean the London office. Who in the London office is prepared to work with people of Mr Banda's type? Besides what post will you give him? General manager for the London office? (*All laugh*)

Besides, Zulu adds, 'he may even decide to go with all his extended family!' And they all laugh again.

The audience, however, do not share their laughter. They have seen nothing in Mr Banda's behaviour to suggest that he was unintelligent or 'bush', as his fellow Zambian executives now imply. In fact, they have observed the opposite. And the fact that the company has already hired foreign technicians has proved their own deceitfulness.

The next scene shows us the dismissal of the workers. It is very briefly done. The Zambian personnel officer is merely carrying out orders. The first worker who is sacked is desperate, and goes off to find the general manager, Banda. The second worker gets violent with the personnel officer. Banda himself comes in at this point. We learn this is supposed to be Banda's responsibility and yet it has been done without his knowledge or authority. We follow him to Leeds's office.

This time there is no formality and politeness. The offer to go to London is swept aside (contrary to what Zulu predicted) and Banda threatens Leeds with trouble, saying he is resigning. Leeds starts to panic. He prepares for flight and makes concessions with the workers. Yet even at this crisis moment he is arranging payment for the machine, or some other fiddle. The workers are now militantly marching to Leeds's office, and it appears that both Leeds and his supportive Zambian management have lost control of the situation. Banda takes charge. He makes a speech to the workers (and to the audience) interpreting humanism (Zambia's official ideology) in the context of industrial action. The play ends with Banda sitting down across the table from Leeds; but this time in a position of strength. He appears to have established that the company in fact belongs to the workers, and not to its British parent-company.

The play first of all posed some questions – Who do the so-called foreign companies belong to? Who ought they belong to? What should the relationship be between workers and manage-ment in the Zambian context? – which it then tried to answer through the process of play-making, that is, characterization, the story, conflict, and so on. Furthermore, Chifunyise tries to answer the questions from the point of view of the Zambian worker who is unskilled, or at best semi-skilled, and who suffers from the selfish attitudes generated on the Zambian copper-mines by owners, management and labour 'aristocracy' alike. Of course a small privileged work-force will be lukewarm in its defence of the rights of a large, unskilled work-force who are experiencing wage labour relations for the first time. Chifunyise's play also seems to be suggesting that the doctrine of humanism propounded by Zambia's President Kaunda is used and ignored by government officials as and when it suits them. The playwright concretizes the philosophy of humanism, at least in respect of labour relations, in the form of a play. It is for this reason, possibly, that Chifunyise has made Banda a wholly praiseworthy figure: a party militant, but rational and clear-sighted. He succeeds in his endeavours. On the whole, though, Chifunyise's plays are dubious about any possible good materializing for those at the bottom of the social heap in the present economic arrangements between the developed and supposedly developing nations.

The District Governor Goes to a Village shows Chifunyise's pessimism. This play has been widely and repeatedly performed around the rural areas of Zambia by the university's Chikwakwa Theatre of travelling student–actors. It is always performed in the language of the district to which it is being taken. The actor playing the character of the district governor who cannot speak and will not learn the language of the district over whom he is the governor, is made to utter his lines in English. (If particular audiences have no English whatsoever, then one of the actors outside the play altogether will translate what the governor says, before the regional secretary, who is a character within the play, *mis*translates the governor's words.)

The play's plot is deceptively simple. A group of villagers in a remote and 'backward' village are interrupted in their beer-drinking by the arrival of the district governor, a Zambian of course, and also a powerful party man. He has come to inspect the village and to 'develop' or 'up-grade' it according to party policy. He is accompanied by the regional secretary, who is a local party man because he is primarily an opportunist. This regional secretary quickly establishes himself as the most corrupt person of them all. Before the governor arrives, he rehearses the villagers in meaningless slogans of 'suspendence!' (a corruption of 'independence') and 'Buyuntanshi!' (a word in the governor's own language for 'development' – the secretary deliberately does not let them shout any word that would actually mean development to them). 'This is a nice song,' says one of the villagers. 'Yes,' says another, 'I heard it on the radio.' But it doesn't *mean* anything to them; and the secretary refuses to explain anything. In fact it would seem that he is determined to confuse them.

When the governor arrives the secretary deliberately mistranslates everything the governor has come to tell the villagers about how they must improve their village. He then pockets half of the money left by the governor for the villagers to dig wells and pit-latrines, make better homes and improve the road. The village headman, into whose custody the other half of the money is given, is told that it is for development, but he simply has no idea what to do with it. Maybe he would like to pocket some of it for himself, but he lacks experience in corruption. Instead, he distributes it, under pressure, to individual villagers for squandering in various ways which help them out of immediate personal difficulties.

The return of the district governor some weeks later brings retribution for the headman, which he does not really deserve, and, superficially at least, for the regional secretary – though there is plenty of evidence in the text that he is going to be able to wriggle out of it. The ending in the written text is ambiguous and suggests a sub-text in performance which runs counter to the actual words spoken.

The character of the district governor is shadowy in outline: he is, in fact, drawn from the point of view of the villagers – remote and unapproachable. He may be good or bad, intelligent or stupid, kindly or crass; but the villagers – and the audience – see nothing of this, merely his public demeanour. His only obvious fault is that he refuses to learn the language of the people who have been placed under his administration. This fault is one of the themes of the play. The task of the district governor is to translate the philosophy of Zambian humanism into the actual processes of rural development. If the district governor cannot communicate with the people then even though he may not be corrupt himself he creates a situation in which corruption can flourish and become a canker in the system. A philosophy which is concerned with the plight of those most economically disadvantaged is a good philosophy, but it can be easily contradicted and undermined if the top party man in the area cannot even communicate directly with the people.

The regional secretary, on the other hand, is a maniac in his compulsive venality. His arrogance towards the villagers is blatant, as is his exploitation of them. His character reflects another theme in the play: the power of the party is so great that opportunists in its sustaining bureaucracy can turn its operations at the local level against those people in whose name and for whose benefit the party was created.

The headman and his fellow peasants are ignorant and idle but well-meaning. Their horizons are amazingly limited and nothing much has changed for them since independence. Nobody thinks of getting them to articulate their needs and suggest the strategies by which they might be fulfilled. The various peasants are humorously but sympathetically conceived, and quite detailed characterization and complex relationships are established in a very economical way within the play. For example, the scene in which the farmers call on the headman, one after the other, for a bit of the 'development' money, shows vividly the conflict between 'development' for the village in the abstract, and their individual concrete crises. The second farmer to call, Tembo, arrives as the first farmer is just leaving:

Tembo: I have come to ask for some help. (**Chirwa** – *the headman – looks away, knowing what* **Tembo** *is going to say*)

Chirwa: Now, what help? What kind of help can you get from me?

Tembo: You must know my son Musonda.

Chirwa: Which one is Musonda, now?

Tembo: The eldest one. The one at secondary school.

Chirwa: Oh, that one! Yes, I know him very well. Now, what about him?

Tembo: What he has done, this son! He has eaten someone's *chisungu*. The daughter of Chembe.

Chirwa: Ah . . . ah . . . ah . . . That's bad. Has he been asked to pay?

Tembo: Oh yes. They want £10. To eat a girl's *chisungu* is quite an offence. That is why I asked you to help me. Just £10, or is it 20 K?

Chirwa: But I do not have the money.

Tembo: I was just thinking of the *Buyuntanshi money*.

Chirwa: But that money is for *Buyuntanshi*, not to pay for sons who eat girls' *chisungu*.

Tembo: But that is *Buyuntanshi*. These children will soon be allowed to marry. They will have a child and that is *Buyuntanshi*.

The headman feels that he has no option but to give Tembo the money, so he does, telling him '. . . don't tell anybody else in the village!' But the next caller is hard on Tembo's heels.

The play is very funny; but through the comedy gleams the hard light of an intellectual's despairing analysis. It is an expression of things as they really are, and of the penetration of the rhetoric to the contradictory reality that lies behind such slogans as 'unity!', 'freedom!', 'development!'. In the end they mean only individual gain.

Big Berrin is by Yulisa Amadu Maddy, Sierra Leone's leading theatre activist. He is a publishing playwright (and novelist), a theatre director, an actor, stage designer, musician – versatile and talented. His contribution to theatre has not only been in Sierra Leone but in other African countries as well, most notably Zambia and Nigeria, and also in Britain among the black and self-exiled African communities. His published plays – *Gbana Gbendu* and *Obasai* particularly – which were written and published in the late 1960s, are only now being given their due recognition – ironically by those theatre critics who see them in the context of the development of the African art theatre.

Maddy's career over the past fifteen years actually highlights the problem experienced by many African playwrights which we have repeatedly encountered. It shows him attempting to resolve the dichotomy of how to develop intellectually and artistically as a playwright while still remaining at one with the mass of the people. The national elites, after independence, increasingly distance themselves from the people, and they encourage an intellectual and artistic theatre in order to sustain their new position. Maddy sees himself, therefore, as serving two masters.

At first he attempted to get his plays published. Then he became the Director of the Zambian National Dance Troupe. After this, there followed years of (self-) exile in Europe, sustained by writing novels on the one hand and directing plays on the other. He returned to Sierra Leone. *Big Berrin*, Maddy's play of 1976, was performed in Freetown in May that year. It was written in Krio and it addressed the mass of the urban population about their hopelessness in the face of corruption, violence and brutality. Maddy himself was subsequently imprisoned. There is now also a text of the play in English, except for some of the songs which remain in either Krio or Pidgin, and the play is expected to be published in London in due course. (It is worth noting again, though, that plays which enjoy a wide popularity among mass urban audiences pose problems for international publishers, which, as we saw in Chapter 2, is partly to do with the difficulty of rendering performance into texts and partly due to the language of performance.)

In the opening stage direction Maddy specifically states that he is not just attacking Sierra Leone – he doesn't even mention that country by name – though Sierra Leone is the immediate point of reference for his audience and his play's thinly disguised particularity. He is attacking, he says, the whole of the third world. His scathing indictment of third world societies is unique in African drama in two ways: (1) he has an empathy with the poor and the destitute, and the rare talent to create characters and dialogue that make his fictional world totally real; the characters embody simultaneously people's misery and hope, and (2) whatever immediate and short-term solutions the characters within his plays devise for their social problems, they are always solutions which are inevitable in the real world of the people he writes for: his special ability is to objectify these solutions so that the audience can criticize them.

Maddy's plays, therefore, are in a real sense plays of and for the people. At least this is so in terms of their *content*, that is, the characters, and the social conditions that shape those characters' personalities and order their actions. What he brings to his audiences, which is new to them, is a detailed *theatricality*: a knowledge and use of theatrical style which we have previously noted in other West African theatre, especially the theatre experiments of Efua Sutherland in Ghana and the productions of Ola Rotimi's plays at his Ori Olokun Theatre in Ife, Nigeria.

This highly stylized theatre, which is technically dependent upon elaborate stage lighting and complex stage settings, and aesthetically dependent upon highly trained actors and musicians, has positive and negative attributes in the context of a genuinely popular theatre. It can be very effective in conveying a mood, a state of mind, and an atmosphere, through which a complexity of meaning within the play may be more easily comprehended. But it can also mystify the theatrical and dramatic processes, as far as the audiences are concerned, and remove them from the means of theatrical production when in fact the opposite is needed, namely, for the people themselves spontaneously to make the drama.

An analysis of *Big Berrin* should show this thematic and theatrical enrichment. It is the opposite of the process which we noted in Chifunyise's plays where the tendency is to simplify, in order to bring out more clearly the social contradictions.

'Big Berrin' is Krio for 'big death'; in this play it is taken to mean, symbolically, the living death of the urban poor whose representatives are the main characters in the drama. These are: a young school teacher called Teme, who has not been paid, like all the other state secondary school teachers, for the past two months, and who is the most politically conscious character in the play. Teme has a hustler friend called Awoko. There is a middle-aged woman called Moshorkpe, who has a teenage son. And there is a family of an old woman, called Granny Fanny, and her suspicious old man, called Pa or Papa Adeloju, and their teenage grand-daughter, Tabita (who is flirting with the school teacher). In addition, there is a large group of musicians and a chorus who participate not only in the many songs in the play but also in the action of the drama when the songs, the dances and the mime invade the fictional world of the characters.

The play is set in a back-yard in which there are three adjacent shacks, together known as 'Adjoiney'. On one side of the yard is a communal kitchen and on the other side is the wash-house. The facilities in the yard and Adjoiney are minimal; but the characters who live in them appear grateful to have a place they call their own. In one shack of the Adjoiney lives the school teacher Teme; Granny, Papa Adeloju and Tabita live in the middle shack; Moshorkpe and her son, Lans, live in the remaining shack. Awoko, the hustler, does not live in the Adjoiney, but is known by all the residents.

The story, such as it is, concerns Teme's decision, at the instigation of Awoko, to become a religious hustler, just as Awoko is a ju-ju hustler. They plan to go into business together. The time of the action within the story is late afternoon; then the middle of the night; and finally the following morning. However, the story is frequently penetrated by songs and mime which more generally confront the audience with the details of oppression. The play's title, 'big death', and the stylized music and mime, support the playwright's own initial description of the play in the first stage direction as 'ritual' (or, on another occasion, 'a ritual movement'). Maddy seems to be suggesting that the poor are attending their own funeral.

Nevertheless, the play starts as a straightforward dialogue drama. The characters of Teme and Awoko are quickly estab- lished – as is the rather naturalistic location of the action, the back-yard of the Adjoiney. The first mime only takes place when each of the residents of the Adjoiney has entered the yard in his or her particular characterization. Gradually, everyone on stage freezes into a 'statuesque pose'; the darkness closes in, leaving the figures silhouetted against a sky lit by a red glow and distant lightning; and their silence is heightened by the sound of distant thunder. A transition is made from naturalism to symbolism. The actors and the chorus begin a chant about the 'big death' which is equated with human suffering and poverty through the gestures and the mime. A child's coffin is carried on to the stage by the pall-bearers, which has a sign on it:

CHILD VICTIM OF THE ONE MAN ONE VOTE REVOLUTION

A little later, a pall-bearer trips, the coffin is dropped. It bursts open, and out of it spills – *papers, receipt books, newspaper clippings, banned books, secret conf. government publications, revolvers, rifles, grenades, empty acid sprayers, pocket-knives, matchets, whips, torturing electrocuting implements. . . .*The chorus chants 'We are dead. . . . We have been killed. . . . ', and they itemize the manner of their death:

- I was hanged by the neck
- I was shot in the back
- I was poisoned
- It was arranged so that I had an accident
- They clubbed me to death
- They took me out to sea and I never saw land again.

Teme picks up the litany:

But, there was no obituary announcement on the radio. . . . No 'In Memoriam' appeared in the popular national *Una Yone Press.* . . . Big Berrin, Grand death. . . .

Independence is then signified by the thunder and lightning ceasing, and the appearance of 'A rainbow of extraordinary proportion' – but it is still the same dispensation, and nothing in the end seems to have changed. Christian liturgies and rituals suffuse the whole scene, culminating in what the stage direction calls 'heightened spiritual ecstasy'.

The mime closes somewhat ambiguously, though by the end of the play the significance of the religious fervour has been made clear.

The long middle section of the play takes place in the middle of the night. Awoko becomes as Master of Ceremonies, as it were, a sort of commentator, who guides us round the supposedly secret activities of the play's characters who are in pursuit of the fantasies born out of their poverty and sense of hopelessness. Mis

Moshorkpe, the middle-aged woman, goes to the ju-ju man – actually Awoko himself in disguise – in order that she may give birth to a son by the big man in the government she is presently going around with. If she gives him a son, he will give her a big house, a Honda car, and so on.

Tabita's grandfather, Papa Adeloju, goes to his Ronsho devil – a mask or masquerade – who is supposed to give the old man money in exchange for vaguely described 'sacrifices'. Papa grabs the devil's hands and dances with him, having demanded of it:

> What do you want me to do ehn? I mean, for all these forty-two years that we have been together, haven't I given you your demands and fulfilled your wishes . . . you have no right to complain . . . no right at all . . . I have sacrificed my two sons, one daughter and how many other relatives to our long friendship and self-help project.

The Ronsho whispers to him with slow gestures, obviously demanding now his grand-daughter Tabita. Papa tells him:

> Don't worry, that child will soon leave school. As soon as she graduates, she is all yours, I promise you faithfully, cross my heart, take my own life.

Granny, too, is in pursuit of her own fantasies; but unlike her old man she does it through African Christian rituals:

> (*She kneels, takes the cup of water in her hand and goes through the usual 'African Mama' ritual of calling on God, communing with the Holy Spirit, and calling all her dead relatives to unite, listen and help her.*)

She wants her son, Tabita's father, to acknowledge her existence and send her some money.

Tabita herself has been in pursuit of much more readily satisfied desires in Teme's part of the Adjoiney. As she sneaks out of his place, all the residents, all with the secrets of their guilty fantasies, briefly come together, by accident, in the back-yard; but they are scattered by the masquerade, the Ronsho devil, who gives Papa a bag full of paper money – 'payment' for Tabita. Awoko sings about consumerism, greed – and 'Big Berrin'. This gives way to a song, *Time Marches On*; and day breaks in the Adjoiney.

People begin to emerge from their shacks. Petty squabbles and the abiding problems of the Adjoiney residents occupy their minds in the early moments of their awakening. Papa threatens Granny over Tabita's suspected affiliation with Teme; Morshorkpe's son,

Lans, announces that their chicken has died (actually, he killed it deliberately); residents fight over the hot water which Lans has boiled up for his mother. When Tabita and Papa Adeloju have gone off, Granny calls Morshorkpe to witness the warning which she is about to give Teme concerning Tabita. Teme and Tabita have actually taunted the older residents with their informality and relaxed friendship. The discussion between Granny, Teme and Morshorkpe is initially comfortable, and leads to a wider discussion of present social ills; at which point Teme becomes increasingly bitter and articulate. The three of them all give vent to their frustrations, in dialogue and song, and with the help of the chorus and the musicians.

However, although all complain about the social conditions, they are all shown to be part of the social system; and their values are shown to be those of the very elites which they so despise. Teme brutally reminds Morshorkpe about her current affair with one of these:

Morshorkpe: Who is to blame?

Teme: People like your boy-friend, kai!

Morshorkpe: He is incorruptible. . . . He does not have any Syrian, Lebanese or Indian friends. . . . I tell you he does an honest job for which he is handsomely paid and he is satisfied.

But Teme overrules her objections, and Morshorkpe is beaten down by his aggression against her boy-friend:

Morshorkpe: I'll tell him what you have said. . . .

Teme: Tell him just as I have told you,
Talk to him like a mother who has been hurt because an only child has betrayed her,
Tell him that, if they want to rule, they must learn to serve,
We are tired of too many incapable obdurate masters.

(It is important to remember that the quotations are from the playwright's English version of the play which, of course, was in Krio in performance.)

The protest shifts into another song, or recitative, between the characters and the chorus, until the chorus bitterly sing, about Granny:

Your sex is not old
They have raped the constitution
They can rape you

They have murdered democracy
They can penetrate and mutilate your aged sanctuary
They have no morals . . . no compunction . . . no scruples
No decency . . . no respect for human rights or human lives. . . .

Teme comments in exasperation: '. . . I wonder whether there is God. . . .' Granny tells him that he is young and his own time will soon come; but Morshorkpe comments bitterly: '. . . and when that time comes he will be found guilty of the same malpractices . . . !', to which Teme emphatically replies 'Never!'

But Teme lies. He is already planning his own corruption and deceit. When everyone has left the back-yard, Awoko re-emerges, and he and Teme finalize their plans for Teme to become a powerful bogus prophet. This is now Teme's own fantasy; he is no different from any of the others, except that his superior education will make him one of the exploiters in his fantasies, rather than one of the exploited:

Awoko: There are only two kinds of lucrative businessmen today in this country apart from being politician . . . they are profiteering false prophets and deceitful juju practitioners.

Teme: With my church, I know I won't fail. . . . I will continue from where the white colonialist missionaries left off, just as our politicians have continued in the same manner and spirit from where their colonial predecessors left off.

The two of them plan their joint operation of the Muslim–Apostolic prophet and the juju practitioner; and as the play nears its conclusion, Teme has already swung into action for the benefit of the by now returning residents of the Adjoiney. Finally, the police come in and beat up all the people as the chorus sing:

Sailing along
Sailing along in one boat . . .
To di new utopia
    to di new utopia. . . .

It is a very ironic ending.

The play's bitter amoral stance is far removed from the moralistic people's theatre of Hubert Ogunde; and it is much more passionately critical of society than the other successful West African play about a false prophet, *The Trials of Brother Jero* by Wole Soyinka. But *Big Berrin* has its own problems, not least of which is the way the playwright finally abandons the residents of the Adjoiney to their various fantasies. Although the play avoids the moralizing and easy solutions of less honest plays about and for the proletariat, nevertheless, it is not at all clear in the play if Teme could have done anything else – anything ultimately more subversive, in fact, of the system he so despises – other than to become a bogus prophet and manipulating for his own ends people's superstitions and their still 'colonized' minds.

Furthermore, the play is daunting in the demands it makes upon even a professional theatre company in terms of human and material resources. Indeed, even as a production of the play lavishly entertains its audiences it sets a barrier between them and the 'product' they are 'consuming'. What can they possibly contribute to the dramatic process, if it requires such highly-trained performers as these? It is possible that the play is 'complete' – complete in its depiction of nihilism as well as in its theatrical form – and too 'finished' to allow an alternative development of the ideas and concepts which have been set in train. And even if it occurs to the audience to challenge Teme's final capitulation to his own selfish fantasy, how could they do it?

This question carries us to the next stage in our discussion of popular theatre; for we must move on from simply taking theatre to the people – category (3) of our earlier list – to a theatre which actually involves people in the making of theatre.

Rural Development and Self-Help: The Botswana Popular Theatre Campaigns – *Laedza Batanani*[9]

The use of the performing arts of the rural people by developers anxious to achieve their development objectives almost always has the blessing of the national government, as well as of local government agencies. Inevitably, the popular culture so used becomes further undermined, as a means of expression for the masses, by being invaded by the values of the dominant culture. There is no point, really, in pursuing examples of this sort of coercive use of theatre. There is, however, a much more positive side to the use of live theatre and the traditional performing arts in development work amongst rural communities.

In the mid 1970s, a 'popular theatre campaign', as it was then called, was tried out in one of the most depressed regions in Botswana. This project, which was initiated by adult educators in the territory, was partly influenced by the Zambian *Chikwakwa* rural theatre workshops, but mainly by the writings of the Brazil-ian adult educator, Paulo Freire, who has continued to develop a philosophy of revolution in the third world that makes use of radical literacy programmes in a particularly critical way.[10] Freire has expressed through the notion of *conscientization* the *process* by which the oppressed of the third world are able to generate their own political consciousness along the path of revolution. Con-scientization enables the peasants, in the process of achieving literacy, to identify their problems as resulting from a particular social order. Their approach to learning must involve a rejection, through direct experience, of a fatalistic universe and of a mechan-istic concept of society. It is crucial, for Freire, that the peasants must help devise the very ways in which they are going to learn; and this starts with basic literacy.

Freire has also developed, in the context of his overall phil-osophy, a theory of culture which is summed up in his concept of a *culture of silence*. Through it he describes how the values of the metropolitan society, the technologized west, are not only main-tained in third world countries, but actually reinforced through the attitudes of the particular third world country's ruling elite towards the masses. He is actually using culture in a more generalized sense than we are when we refer to the traditional culture in Africa. Nevertheless, we can observe the ways in which the traditional performing arts of the African people are used against them; and how the very preservation of the traditional culture by the new elites and intellectuals allows it to be abstracted, rendered functionless, transposed into literature, performed at the Inter-national Airport or shifted into art galleries overseas. However, Freire suggests, as the masses move from '. . . a semi-intransitive state to a naive transitive state of consciousness . . .' progressive intellectuals also experience a critical consciousness on their own part:

As the contradictions typical of a society in transition emerge more clearly, these groups multiply and are able to distinguish more and more precisely what makes up their society. They tend more and more to join with the popular masses in a variety of ways: through literature, the plastic arts, the theatre, music, education, sports and folk art. What is important is the communion with the people which some of these groups are able to achieve.[11]

The theatre work of Yulisa Maddy, clearly, would fall into this analysis. The next stage after this, according to Freire, is the actual participation of the people themselves in all creative work for and about them.

In fact it is another Latin American, Augusto Boal,[12] who is specifically a theatre activist (though he has participated in Freirian-inspired literacy campaigns in Peru). He carries the discussion further in theatre terms. He is concerned with theatre as an instrument in the process of achieving radical social change. For him, popular theatre is only significant in so far as the people are not just the audiences, but also, collectively, the actors and creators of the drama. Boal sees theatre as a *language*, 'capable of being utilized by any person, with or without artistic talent. . . .' Boal refers to his participation in the Peruvian literacy campaign:

We tried to show in practice how the theatre can be placed at the service of the oppressed, so that, by using this new language, they can also discover new concepts. . . . I believe that all the truly revolutionary theatrical groups should transfer to the people the means of production in the theatre so that the people themselves may utilize them. The theatre is a weapon, and it is the people who should wield it.[13]

Laedza Batanani

'Laedza Batanani' means 'The sun is already up. It is time to come and work together'. It is derived from the theme song of the first development festival, or campaign, in Botswana. The song continues:

Build your villages together;
Leave staying on the lands and build homes;
Attend meetings and hear what's happening in your country.
Men should work and give money to their wives.
Leave fighting in the *Gumba-Gumba*,
Teach your children to respect adults –
Awake and come together to build Botswana.

The development campaign itself was soon known by the title of the song; and the whole campaign had a considerable impact in the depressed north of Botswana.

The *Laedza* popular theatre movement, which the campaign grew into, has now extended all over Botswana. This has happened through similar campaigns, like *Bosele Tswaraganang* in the Kgatleng region; and through the 1978 National Popular Theatre Workshop in Molepolole. At the same time a critique of the work was developed which assessed the success of the project in terms of actual improvement in the lives of individuals as well as in the life of the community in which the campaign took place. Once it was established that real gains could be made in rural development – specifically in self-help projects – through the use of theatre, then a Popular Theatre Committee was constituted in the University College of Botswana with a brief to devise ways of improving the techniques of both the theatre and development aspects of the movement, and thus extend the work.

Laedza campaign techniques have always been concerned with showing extension workers – in health, agriculture, education and co-operatives – how they can use popular theatre for community and village renewal programmes. The focus in the campaigns has been on participation and self-reliance, with the Freirian objective of motivating people to improve their lives through improving the life of the community.

The first stage of the process is to collect first-hand data from the people themselves concerning problems in the villages in which the performance of the plays is going to take place. These problems will form the basis of the drama. Certain skills and techniques are required in the data-gathering process and it is at this stage that the nature of the campaign and its objectives need to be communicated to the villagers. Ideally, the villagers and the activists (the extension workers) should achieve a shared commitment to the work from the start; though in practice it is not always easy to achieve this the first time a campaign is taken to a particular village. The most that can ever be expected as a final outcome is a successful self-help project which will provide some amenities for a village and perhaps a greater awareness of rural and communal responsibilities. Unfortunately, these projects must ultimately be considered in the context of the flight from the land to either Gaborone or the South African mines. Rural Botswana is probably a more deadening experience for young Batswana than rural Zambia is for young Zambians.

The problems of the village or villages are then constituted as a performance of dramatic sketches, role-play, songs and some dances. The techniques and skills needed involve scenario-making and acting; composing and singing songs; making various kinds of puppets and learning to operate them; and learning some local dances. In the early *Laedza* campaigns these skills were accepted as adequate at a very basic level, so that everybody would have sufficient confidence to get up and join in, especially in the singing and the dancing. Ross Kidd and Martin Byram, who were the original instigators of the *Laedza* campaigns acknowledge a conflict in the aims of the movement in this respect. On the one hand, there is a concern to show the people that they themselves can dramatize their own problems. On the other hand, in order to convey the complexity of the issues and show the contradictions in the social conditions, a certain degree of professional performance skill is needed. Initially the *Laedza* campaigners opted for the first and went to great lengths to persuade villagers that they could act and sing and operate puppets; but it is now generally agreed that the performances which resulted became message-orientated: 'Build pit latrines', 'Support your headman', 'Co-operate!' – which is all in the end a sort of development moralism. There was little in the way of a detailed social analysis in which the villagers could participate.

However, in 1977, Kidd and Byram carried the process of getting the audience to participate to its logical – and in this instance very successful – conclusion. They engaged in some community work among the Basarwa (formerly called the Bushmen) in the west of Botswana across the Kalahari desert. Even in the initial discussion with the villagers, the Basarwa were encouraged to drift into role, thus dramatizing the problems they were attempting to articulate. The whole village group, sitting round the fire, became increasingly involved in improvising their problems, by showing, through characterization, exactly what was supposed to have taken place when they met the government authorities. Byram and Kidd accepted roles of the outsiders who were responsible, in part, for the Basarwa's backward state. The men were able to halt the improvisation they were taking part in at any time, in order to discuss the implications of each little scene and how their role in it might be changed. Understanding grew as they re-enacted certain situations, this time changing their own behaviour. Every man around the fire in that remote scrubland was simultaneously actor and audience in the 'play' of his life.

In the more conventional campaigns, which culminated in performances for audiences, it was necessary to have basic skills in order to capture and hold the attention of the audience: the drummers had to have a sense of rhythm, the dancers needed to be lithe, actors needed powerful voices, projection and a sense of timing, and singers needed tuneful voices.

The Popular Theatre Movement in Botswana now recognizes

that in addition to these basic skills, a particular type of performance skill is needed. This is the ability to constitute the world, in
the action of the drama, as though we – actors and audience – are
seeing it for the very first time. Once the familiar seems strange
then people begin to see that things which hitherto had appeared
unchangeable could in fact be changed. There is a similarity here
with the dramatic theory of Bertolt Brecht; but it was arrived at in
Botswana as an outcome of practical experimentation, without
knowledge of Brecht's work, unlike the more conscious and
academic influence of his theories in East African theatre.

There is still a determination to use the existing skills of the
Extension Workers – and of the audience too – especially the
traditional arts of singing and story-telling. However, the Botswana theatre activists are aware that many of the traditional
performances are breaking down, especially because of the male
labour migration to the South African gold mines. Not only the
culture, but also the whole fabric of the society is being systemati-
cally corroded. This reality is actually reflected in the way the
Popular Theatre Movement uses music.

For instance, the Batswana compose many songs, harmonize
them beautifully and accompany them with hand-clapping. (There
is some drumming in the north, but on the whole there is not much
instrumental accompaniment.) However, all communities who
send their men-folk to the mines have to cope with the *Gumba-
Gumba* music which the returning miners bring back with them
and play on loud, speeded-up tape-recorders, usually in the
context of a liquor and drugs party which they organize. For
Botswana communities, the '*Gumba-Gumba* party' constitutes a
problem, not so much in itself, as in the chain of financial, family
and sexual woes that follow in its wake. The music itself is lively
and a response to the urban milieu of South Africa.

The *Gumba-Gumba* party, therefore, features often in the plays
of a Popular Theatre campaign – as do the traditional songs and
hand-clapping. In addition, many of the plays have been frank
about the sexual mores of these disrupted communities and open
about advice. In one play which was concerned with a nexus of
issues on sex – family-planning, promiscuous youth and the high
incidence of venereal disease – an extension worker who is
acting the role of a nurse, tries, at one point, to persuade the
embarrassed lover to use a condom. She shows him one. He looks
at it, then mutters in a loud stage whisper: 'Too small!' 'Too small

for you?' asks the nurse in a loud voice as the fellow looks away in embarrassment. 'Yes,' he mutters, 'it'll burst.' 'We shall see,' says the nurse, as she takes a kettle of hot water which she has been boiling on the stage and slowly pours the water into the condom, which distends. The hero – and also the audience – are convinced. With her authority established she is able to persuade the two lovers who have VD (in the play's story) to come to the 'clinic' for treatment. The frank presentation of these issues on the stage at least served to instigate a constructive discussion about sexual relationships in the community.

In the end, this type of popular theatre can only be successful if it generates community action. It is, therefore, often restricted to a discussion on those community problems which can be immediately solved by self-help schemes: community involvement in decision-taking, better hygiene in the village, admitting to VD and accepting treatment, as well as construction projects like building a school house, or a clinic, or digging pit latrines. The Popular Theatre Movement in its very structure is committed to follow-up – theatre activists do not simply go and perform plays, they actually get involved in the community action. Many of them would do so anyway, since they are extension workers.

But Botswana exists in juxtaposition with the wider social and political system of South Africa, which constantly seeks to extend its hegemony over the whole region. South Africa is certain to be hostile to a growing consciousness among peasant communities in independent African states along its borders; and all sorts of constraints – especially economic – exist within Botswana to prevent any radical change. Radical extension workers may well find it difficult to carry their fellow extension workers in a wider consciousness-raising process in rural and urban communities. For the time being, therefore, it seems likely that the Popular Theatre Movement in Botswana will be a coming together of the community to work only for those social improvements which can be achieved through their own efforts.

Theatre and the raising of political consciousness: *Wasan Maska, Wasan Samaru, Wasan Bomo* (the plays of the communities of Maska, Samaru and Bomo in Hausaland)

There has been some experimentation in theatrical form in relation to a growing political awareness in various parts of Africa.

I have chosen the example of the work in the north of Nigeria, partly because I have been associated with it, but mainly because it exemplifies some of the constraints upon this sort of work in Africa at the moment. The work has been initiated by a group of university drama teachers on an unofficial basis; and it involves university students, adult educators and literacy officers, and young peasant farmers, in making plays which situate the problems of oppressed groups in a wider social analysis. Everybody, no matter what his social 'level', is involved in presenting this critique. It is the actual *process* of making these plays which is crucial, because it carries the thinking of the whole group forward.

In the first project, or workshop, undertaken, the emphasis was on the performance given to the rural village audiences, even though facts about, and opinions within, the communities formed the basis of the improvisations for performance. Now the actual performances are considered less important than the 'rehearsals' themselves, though performance is still an integral part of the wider process of enabling the people to think things out for themselves.

Salihu Bappa, a Nigerian theatre critic and theatre activist working among the Hausa peasantry has written about this process of play-making, after his experience in the first Popular Theatre Workshop (as the projects are now called) which involved adult literacy officers.[14] The whole workshop – working sessions and informal discussions – had to be conducted bilingually, in Hausa and English, because many of the literacy officers could not speak English. (They were, in fact, teaching basic literacy in Hausa to adults in their various rural areas.) Most of the participants in the workshop had never before encountered dialogue drama, improvisation and role-play, so it was necessary to translate the most basic concepts and techniques relating to theatre and drama into Hausa, but only after defining these afresh in English.

Those participants who could speak English as well as Hausa played a vital role in the process: they made an effort to grasp the explanation of a particular term or concept in English, then helped Bappa, through questions and answers in Hausa, to arrive at an explanation in Hausa that was as precise as possible. This led to defining the processes of play-making in terms of their overall function in rural conscientization. Eventually Bappa was able to withdraw from translating which was taken over by the participants themselves. They were actively involved in making the terms and the concepts their own.

About this process Bappa then wrote:

Gradually the workshop group came to understand both the practical and theoretical problems of *scenario-making*. Scenario-making is at the root of all basic techniques of drama which are used in improvising a play. The crucial nature of the scenario in formulating the abstract social problem as a play was the single most important discovery of the workshop. It lies at the very heart of the work we are trying to do and is the most difficult aspect of the work. By scenario-making we mean not only such dramatic techniques as *conflict, irony, characterization* and *dialogue* but, more significantly, the way in which an abstract social problem is

    (*a*) identified;

then

    (*b*) made concrete and particular in the form of a story;

then

    (*c*) made into a series of dramatized situations;

which then

    (*d*) articulate the contradictions of the society.

Actually, turning social problems into a critique of society through the drama processes is as difficult for university students as it is for adult literacy officers, though for different reasons. Another workshop, this time with university drama students, performed plays in a once-rural area near the university, Samaru, which is now experiencing rapid and unplanned urban development. The plays were about the community which comprises many peasants who have been displaced from their lands in the north, as well as a thoroughly urbanized population of southerners. Oga Abah, one of the Nigerians in charge of the workshop, commented on its significance for the students as follows:

For the first time the Drama students performed for the people of Samaru. The Samaru project introduced the students to community or 'popular' theatre through active involvement with that particular community. More significantly, it brought the students face to face with their own élitism; and a realisation of the distance their own 'superiority' will inevitably place between them and the people. Many students thought that the workers and displaced peasants in Samaru, especially in Hayin Dogo, would be incapable of appreciating plays. They were proved wrong, and in Hayin Dogo especially, when the peasants, who made up the main body of the audience, got into serious discussions with some of the students right after the performance.

There was, however, some criticism of the analysis which the plays offered; but it seemed important in the context of the project that the group developing the plays achieved a level of analysis which was their own.

Subsequently, Brian Crow and I tackled the problem of dramatic *form* and its relation to ideology in popular drama in a paper which we presented at conference in Benin city and in Zaria, Nigeria. In it we argue that the form of 'plays' of the popular theatre (which we try to define carefully) is 'incompleteness'. By developing thought through the dramatic processes, activists and their audiences can discover the key contradictions. Laying bare one contradiction through modes of drama raises others, either in rehearsals or in an actual performance, which then have to be brought out through discussion among the activists and between the activists and the audience. This is followed by a restructuring of the play. The process continues. Thus, a 'play' is never complete. (This notion, in terms of aesthetics, is much more complex than this outline suggests.)

Peeling off the layers of contradiction becomes the shared activity of the theatre activists and their audiences; and therein lies the process of acquiring true consciousness, no matter what level of formal education one has reached. Thus, the *process* of making drama, outlined in this way, becomes a valid alternative to the imposition of an ideology through the 'ready-made', 'complete' play.

Wasan Bomo

We were able to experiment with these ideas, briefly, in the workshop in the village of Bomo. Four adult literacy officers, ten drama students and fifteen young peasant farmers from the village of Bomo came together to tackle, through the drama process, an analysis of some of the problems of these young farmers. The working sessions of the workshop were probably more valuable than the single final performance we gave in Bomo. We 'talked' about the problems through the medium of drama, peeling away layer after layer of inadequate analysis. Through the realization that easy solutions never worked, the people came to understand the need for much wider information and a deeper analysis.

The following long quotation from a paper presented by two of the theatre activists involved in organizing the workshop, Oga Abah and Saddiq Balewa, indicates through a concrete example taken from the workshop experience what this process is, and also its present limitations:

. . . Each scene was further discussed and acted out. But at this point more emphasis was given to acting than endless talks. It was discussion through performance. The method we adopted was akin to what Augusto Boal employed in his 'People's Theatre in Peru'. The actors in the scene would first act the scene and the other members of the group would then say what they thought was wrong with the scene. Our Bomo participants were very active in this criticism. After all it was their own experience. We would then go back and do the scene again following the corrections. And, in fact, other participants were free to intervene when they thought something was not right. In this way the scenario was constantly being re-written. . . .

The Hajiya [a Moslem woman who has made the pilgrimage to Mecca; the literacy officer had herself been to Mecca and she kept her title in the character she played] had gone to the police station to seek redress for her market stall which had been taken away from her through the permission of the *Iyan Gari* (councillor) and the *Sarkin Kasuwa* (the Chief of the Market). But the corporal standing guard at the charge office would not let the Hajiya see the Police Inspector until she had offered a little bribery. Hajiya did, finally.

The participants from Bomo stopped the play and said that they would not offer bribery; they would instead join forces against the authority by refusing to offer any bribes and to insist on their rights. One man from Bomo now took the role of the trader whose market stall had been seized. He went to the Inspector's office and explained to the corporal why he wanted to see the boss. Tukur Mu'asu, who was playing the part of the police corporal, changed his demeanour from the smiling and friendly look he wore when the Hajiya came to a hard and stony countenance. The trader explained his problem all over again, but showed no inclination towards giving the corporal any 'tip'. The corporal listened and grunted his answers in monosyllabic 'huh!' and 'hums'. He could not be bothered. He busied himself at nothing. Our trader continued to feign ignorance of bribery and insisted on his 'rights'. The corporal merely led him on:

'If you want to see the Inspector you must do what will make you see him.'

(Tukur Mu'asu, one of the participants, was improvising all this for the first time.)

Realising that he would never see the Inspector unless he bribed his way, the trader acquiesced and offered the corporal some money. It was only then the corporal became friendly and smiled for once. The trader was allowed in to see the Inspector.

The Inspector listened and said that the matter was a serious one which must be taken to the Local Government Office. The trader insisted that the problem be solved by the Inspector. Now it was the Inspector who was expecting a little something from the trader, but nothing was forthcoming.

Disappointed and infuriated by the trader's lack of understanding of the system, the Inspector called the corporal to escort the man out of his office. When the trader had gone the Inspector described his disappointment to the corporal:

'Worthless! These people are worthless! They think they can just run into my office here and unreel their problems! Well, I thought he was going to extend his hand to me like this. [*Demonstrates*] Alright. Nothing gets done. Nothing! Don't even write that letter I talked about! And if he comes back, tell him I have gone out.'

Now then, the Bomo participant as our trader has done exactly what he said he would not do, and still his problem has not been solved. His fellow farmers from Bomo, watching the improvisation, argued that if the man did not succeed by himself then the solution was to team up. So they now all assumed the role of traders who has lost market stalls or land, joined forces, and marched on the Inspector's office. When the corporal would not let them in they became unruly. The corporal began to lash out with his baton. The traders were soon bashed into submission and one of the traders calmed his colleagues. He went into dialogue with the corporal. (It must be remembered that this was the first time the Bomo farmers had entered into improvised dialogue drama.)

The trader soon came out to announce to his colleagues that they must bribe the corporal before they can go in to see the Inspector. Some vehemently opposed that method; but others agreed. Those that agreed bought their way in to see the Inspector. But even then their problem was not solved: the Inspector just sent them back to the Local Government Offices.

What is important to note here is that co-operation amongst the traders had failed.

The participants began to realise that high-blown rhetoric was quickly contradicted by reality.

So, recourse to the police for help in redressing their wrongs was out. The participants now argued that if they maintained ranks before the Local Authority officers, who were civilians and wouldn't beat them up, if they stuck together, they would force the Authority, which comprised the Chairman of the Local District Council, the Secretary and the *Sarkin Kasuwa*, to back down.

Spirits revived and the 'crowd' marched on the Local Government Offices. . . .

The Chairman agreed to meet their representatives. Hajiya, still playing the part of the original woman trader who had been dispossessed of her stall, manoeuvred herself into the front-line and got elected as the traders' representative. Once inside the office Hajiya did her own separate deal with the Chairman. . . .

For the rest, their case would go back to the *Sarki Kasuwa* – the man who had cheated them out of their holdings in the first place.

To refuse to offer bribes proved impossible. To team up did not work; and neither violence nor begging worked. We then asked what their next line of action would be. The answer was a frustrated 'Forget it!'.

But the scene had worked on a number of levels: empty rhetoric, Hajiya's self-seeking at a crucial moment; the failure of co-operation; the corruption of the police; everybody's minds had been concentrated to an intense degree on all these levels of analysis.

This work is obviously in its very early stages. There are more developed examples of this work in places where there is a greater degree of class consciousness. In particular, mention should be made of the work of Ngugi wa Thiong'o and Ngugi wa Mirii at the Kamiriithu Community Educational and Cultural Centre, Kamiriithu village, Kenya. There, the play *Ngaahika Ndeenda* (literally 'I will marry when I feel like it') was created and staged through the co-operation of the two Ngugis with the villagers of Kamiriithu (and other people from nearby villages). In the play they were attempting an analysis of their problems. The participation of Ngugi wa Thiong'o was critical both for the form of the drama and for the analysis; and his detention without trial, after the performances of *Ngaahika* to thousands of rural people, was obviously a blow. But the significant fact was that the Centre continued undeterred: the organization and the initiatives in the work in all its educational and cultural aspects were the initiatives of the people themselves.

There is also increasing interest in the work of theatre activists in the countries of Latin America. There is probably a much greater degree of class consciousness there as a result of the Cuban revolution and the subsequent revolutionary movements of the past two decades. These movements have been considerably transformed in recent years by a greater awareness of the economic and political forces operating in the area. The failure of the revolutionary movements of the 1960s, epitomized by the Bolivian campaign of Che Guevara, was partly the result of the wider interests of the USA being threatened by them and partly due to the inability of the intellectual leaders to transfer the objectives and initiatives of the revolution to the peasantry whom they were intending to liberate. An intellectualized and romanticized version of class warfare has almost always brought a worsening of conditions for the peasants, those on the land who are the despised base of the society.

The most adventurous work in popular theatre now addresses iteself to this base and from this comes a recognition that, paradoxically, an ethnic consciousness can lead to a class consciousness. It is only a bourgeois class consciousness that actually replaces ethnic consciousness, which occurs through the acquisition of a metropolitan bourgeois culture. Therefore, as some of the Latin American activists would advocate, that which still exists in the people's culture needs to be strengthened, particularly those cultural activities with a strong organizational mode, so as to allow rural populations not only to come to a more effective analysis of their societies, but also to have their own organizational means to sustain new developments based on that analysis. This involves the whole question of 'development' in the third world, for it is tantamount to saying that those at the base must teach themselves to take the initiative in any further social development. This entirely contradicts the existing world order.

These concepts have been given a detailed critique in, for instance, the radical theories and work of Augusto Boal and Raul Alberto Leis, or of Carlos and Augusto Nuñez.[15] Boal was involved in consciousness-raising campaigns in Peru, using theatre in literacy programmes. Leis and the Nuñez have been most recently involved in the use of theatre to achieve some of the objectives of the present revolution in Nicaragua. This work, as well as similar work in many Asian countries, needs a further critique which will relate it to conditions and needs here in Africa.

If I allowed myself a final speculative paragraph I would identify, on the basis of experiments so far undertaken, two major constraints which would seem to apply generally to this theatre for consciousness and which would need to be tackled as a priority:

Unlike Latin America, where unofficial radical political and cultural organizations already exist, in Africa there seems to be an absence of any effective organizational framework to provide continuity – apart from the ruling or dominant political parties. Theatre work needs to be keyed into organizations which are concerned with raising consciousness and strengthening people's culture, rather than with acquiring and holding on to political power. The drama may well become a key *methodology* for developing thought across a broad front as a basis for future collective action; but the drama group, the theatre company, the university drama department are all politically inadequate organizations.

The process of turning a problem of social analysis into a play is achievable but complex. Experiments so far have resulted in only limited achievements, both in Africa and elsewhere; and this is often a major constraint upon otherwise successful projects. This process requires skills, but at the same time a demystification of those skills, and a constant sharing of techniques and talents. There is a need to pursue the form of this new drama along the lines already suggested, namely towards the 'incomplete' play: the play which is continually undermined by the revelation of new contradictions in each performance. People's consciousness thus continues to articulate a new reality.

This brief summary of popular theatre in Africa leaves off where in future, perhaps, the study of African drama might begin.

Notes and references

1 Unfortunately, this play is not published. Its present title is *Danger*. The narrative form was suggested to me by Stephen Chifunyise during a discussion about the play.
2 Wilikilifi Ludaka (Mkandawire) was an honoured and most distinguished *Vimbuza* dancer. The name 'Mkandawire' was mistakenly given to him by Zambians who, in 1964, had been impressed by Ziyayo Mkandawire, the uncle of Ludaka, who had come from Malawi and popularized *Vimbuza* in Zambia.
3 The seminar, on the Use of Indigenous Social Structures and Traditional Media in Non-Formal Education and Development, took place in Berlin (West), 5–12 November 1980. It was jointly organized by the German Foundation for International Development and the International Council for Adult Education. The quotation comes from the report of the Latin American sub-group. A report of the whole seminar is to be published shortly, entitled *Cultivating Indigenous Structures and Traditional Media for Non-Formal Education and Development* and edited by Ross Kidd and Nat Colletta; some of it is relevant to the discussion in this chapter.
4 This refers to the discussion on Ogunde's theatre in Chapter 1.
5 There are a number of theatre experiments, in Africa and elsewhere, which consciously relate to the process of social revolutions, both during the period of armed struggle and subsequently during the period of social reconstruction. We have to wait for the publication of Ross Kidd's comprehensive

research into this third world movement, *Poplar Theatre in the Third world: its role in adult education and social changes*, to be published shortly by Longman, London.

Some articles on specific projects are: Marian Sedley, 'Theatre as a revolutionary activity: the Escambray', in John Griffiths and Peter Griffiths (eds.), *Cuba: the second decade* (London: Writers and Readers Publishing Co-operative 1979); Kateb Yacine (in interview), 1979, 'Le théâtre révolutionnaire Algérien: un entretien de Jaques Alessandra avec Kateb Yacine', *Travail Théâtral*, no. 32–3, pp. 91–102; Carlos Nuñez, 'Popular theatre, conscientization and community organization in Mexico and Nicaragua', case study presented at the Berlin Seminar (ibid).

In addition, the following two articles make interesting references to other aspects of popular theatre: Anthony Akerman, 'Refuge theatre in Tanzania', *Theatre Quarterly*, vol. 8 no. 30 (1978), pp. 36–41; Rick Salutin, 'Theatre language and song in Mozambique', *This Magazine*, vol. 13 no. 1 (1979) pp. 26–30.

6 None of these plays had appeared in print at the time of writing. The quotations come from the manuscripts. We repeatedly come upon the problem of getting significant dramatic experiments published.

7 *Katongo Chala* has not been published, to my knowledge, but it has been successfully performed in Zambia.

8 *I Resign* was first written for television; then, I understand, it was toured as a stage play.

9 Ross Kidd, who was one of the original animators of *Laedza Batanani*, has written extensively on the Botswana work in collaboration with other animators of the campaigns. In particular, see: Ross Kidd and Martin Byram, '*Laedza Batanani*: popular theatre for development', *Convergence*, vol. 10 no. 2, pp. 20–31; Kidd and Byram, 'Popular theatre as a tool for community education in Botswana', *Assignment Children* (UNICEF), no. 44 (1978), pp. 35–66.

An excellent handbook for all levels of workers in the field, presented with diagrams and cartoon illustrations is: Kidd, Byram and Rohr-Rouendaal, *Organizing Popular Theatre: the Laedza Batanani experience 1974–77* (Gaborone, Botswana: Popular Theatre Committee 1978).

Kidd's attitude towards the Laedza work has changed recently. See especially: Kidd and Byram, 'Demystifying pseudo-Freirian non-formal education: a case description and analysis of *Laedza Batanani*', paper presented to the International Symposium on Anthropology and Primary Health Care, Inter-congress of the International Union of Anthropological and Ethnological Sciences, Amsterdam, April 1981; a slightly edited version appeared in *Rural Development Participation Review*, vol. 3, no. 1 (September 1981); and Ross Kidd and Krishna Kumar, 'Co-opting Freire: a critical analysis of pseudo-Freirean adult education', *Economic and Political Weekly*, Bombay 3–10 January 1981, pp. 27–36.

10 See particularly: Paulo Freire, *Cultural Action for Freedom*, (Cambridge, Mass.: Harvard University Press 1970, also, Harmondsworth: Penguin 1972). Textual references in the chapter are to the later English edition. The other major work is Freire, *Pedagogy of the Oppressed* (New York: Herder and Herder 1970, also, Harmondsworth: Penguin) and *Pedagogy in Process: The letters to Guinea-Buissau* (New York: Seabury Press 1978). See also Freire, *Oppression, Dependence and Marginalization*, LADOC, no. 60 (1975).

11 Paulo Freire, *Cultural Action for Freedom*, p. 68.

12 Augusto Boal, *Theatre of the Oppressed* (New York: Urizen Books 1979, also, London: Pluto Press 1979). This is a collection of Boal's writings translated into English. Boal's original works are: Augusto Boal, *Categorias del Teatro Popular* (Buenos Aires: Edition CEPE 1972); Augusto Boal, *Technicas Latinoamericanas del Teatro Popular Lima: ALFIN*, 1973, also Buenos Aires: Corregidor 1975). Augusto Boal, *Teatro de Oprimido* (Buenos Aires: Ediciones de la Flor 1975).

13 Boal, *Theatre of the Oppressed*, p. 122.

14 *Wasan Maska* is discussed in: Salihu Bappa, 'The Maska Project: drama workshop for adult educators', *Work in Progress*, no. 3 (Zaria: Department of English, Ahmadu Bello University 1980). The Soba Workshop is in: Brian Crow and Michael Etherton, 1979, 'Wasan Manoma: Community Theatre in the Soba District, Kaduna State', *Savanna*, Zaria, vol. 8 no. 1 (June 1979). Crow and Etherton, 'Ideology, form and popular drama' is to be published in the Report on the Berlin Seminar (ibid.). Bomo is mentioned in Chapter 1 in this book. It is the *Kalankuwa* village.

Bibliography

Adedji, J. A., 'The Alarinjo theatre: the study of a Yoruba theatrical art from its earliest beginnings to the present times', PhD. thesis, University of Ibadan 1969

Adedeji, J. A., 'Trends in the content and form of the opening glee in Yoruba drama', *Research in African Literatures*, vol. 4, no. 1 (1973)

Aeschylus, *The Oresteian Trilogy*, trans. Philip Vellacott, Harmondsworth: Penguin 1956

Aidoo, Ama Ata, *The Dilemma of a Ghost*, London: Longman 1965

Aidoo, Ama Ata, *Anowa*, London: Longman 1970

Ajayi, J.F.A., and Smith, R., *Yoruba Warfare in the Nineteenth Century*, Cambridge: Cambridge University Press 1964

Anderson, Perry, *Lineages of the Absolutist State*, London: New Left Books 1974

Anderson, Perry, *Passages from Antiquity to Feudalism*, London: Verso Editions 1978

Aristotle, 'Poetics', in T. S. Dorsch (ed.), *Classical Literary Criticism*: *Aristotle, Horace, Longinus*, Harmondsworth: Penguin 1965

Badian, Seydou, *Sous l'orage suivi de la mort de Chaka*, Paris: Présence Africaine 1972

Bain, David, *Actors and Audience: A study of asides and related conventions in Greek drama*, London: Oxford University Press 1977

Banham, M., and Wake, Clive, *African Theatre Today*, London: Pitman 1976

Barnett, Donald L., and Njama, Kariari, *Mau Mau from Within*, New York and London: Modern Readers Paperback 1966

Beier, Ulli, 'Yoruba theatre', in Ulli Beier (ed.), *Introduction to African Literature*, London: Longman 1967

Benjamin, Walter, *Understanding Brecht*, introduction and trans. Stanley Mitchell, London: New Left Books 1977

Bentley, Eric (ed.), *Songs of Bertolt Brecht and Hanns Eisler*, New York: Oak Publications 1967

Bevington, David M., *From Mankind to Marlowe: growth and structure in the popular drama of Tudor England*, Cambridge, Mass.: Harvard University Press 1963

Bithell, Jethro, *Modern German Tragedy, 1880–1950*, London: Methuen 1959

Boal, Augusto, *Theatre of the Oppressed*, London: Pluto Press 1979

Bond, Edward, *Lear*, London: Eyre Methuen 1972

Brecht, Bertolt, *Coriolanus*, in R. Manheim and J. Willett (eds.), *Bertolt Brecht: Collected Plays Vol. 9*, New York: Vintage Books 1973

Brecht, Bertolt, *The Threepenny Opera*, trans. H. MacDiarmid, London: Eyre Methuen 1973

Brecht, Bertolt, *The Caucasian Chalk Circle*, in R. Manheim and J. Willett (eds.), *Bertolt Brecht: Collected Plays Vol. 7*, New York: Vintage Books 1975

Brecht, Bertolt, *The Good Person of Szechuan*, in R. Manheim and J. Willett (eds.), *Bertolt Brecht: Collected Plays Vol. 6*, New York: Vintage Books 1976

Brook, Peter, *The Empty Space*, Harmondsworth: Penguin 1968

Cawley, A. C., *Everyman*, Manchester: Manchester University Press 1961

Cissé, Ahmadou, *Les derniers jours du Lat Dior; La mort du Damel*, Paris: Présence Africaine 1965

Clark, Ebun, *Hubert Ogunde: the making of Nigerian theatre*, London: Oxford University Press 1979

Clark, J. P., *Ozidi*, London: Oxford University Press 1966

Clark, J. P., *The Ozidi Saga: collected and translated from the Ijo of Okabou Ojobolo*, Ibadan: Ibadan University Press 1977

Cornevin, R., *Le théâtre en Afrique noire et à Madagascar*, Paris: Le livre africain 1970

Dadié, Bernard B., *Monsieur Thôgô-gnini, comédie*, Paris: Présence Africaine 1970

de Graft, Joe, *Through a Film Darkly*, London: Oxford University Press 1970

Duerden, Dennis, *African Art and Literature: the invisible present*, London: Heinemann Educational Books 1977 (first published by Harper and Row 1975)

Eades, J. S., *The Yoruba Today*, Cambridge: Cambridge University Press 1980

Echeruo, Michael, 'Dramatic limits of Igbo ritual', in Bernth Lindfors (ed.), *Critical Perspectives on Nigerian Literatures*, London: Heinemann Educational 1979

Eliot, T. S., *The Family Reunion*, London: Faber 1970

Euripides, *Bacchae*, ed. E. R. Dobbs, London: Oxford University Press 1970

Euripides, *The Bacchae and Other Plays*, trans. Philip Vellacott, London: Penguin 1972

Freire, Paulo, *Cultural Action for Freedom*, Harmondsworth: Penguin 1972

Freire, Paulo, *Pedagogy of the Oppressed*, Harmondsworth: Penguin 1972

Freire, Paulo, *Pedagogy in Process: The Letters to Guinea-Buisau*, New York: Seabury Press 1978

Fugard, Athol, Kani, John, and Ntshona, Winston, *Statements: three plays*, London: Oxford University Press 1974

Furst, Lillian R., and Skrine, Peter N., *Naturalism*, London: Methuen 1971

Gay, John, *The Beggar's Opera*, ed. Edgar V. Roberts (music ed. Edward Smith), London: Edward Arnold 1969

Gibbs, James (ed.), *Critical Perspectives on Wole Soyinka*, Washington: Three Continents Press 1980

Grotowski, Jerzy, *Towards a Poor Theatre*, London: Methuen 1969

Hagher, I. O., 'The Kwagh hir: an analysis of a contemporary indigenous puppet theatre and its social and cultural significance in Tivland in the 1960s and 1970s', PhD thesis, Ahmadu Bello University, Zaria, 1981

Harlowe, V., and Chilver, E. M. (eds.), *History of East Africa Vol. II*, London: Oxford University Press 1965

Henderson, John A., *The First Avant-Garde 1887–1894: sources of the modern French theatre*, London: Harrap 1971

Hevi, Jacob, *Amavi*, in Michael Etherton (ed.), *African Plays for Playing I*, London: Heinemann Educational Books 1975

Hussein, Ebrahim N., *Kinjeketile*, Dar es Salaam: Oxford University Press 1970

Igbafe, Philip Aigbona, *Benin under British Administration*, London: Longman 1979

Ijimere, Obotunde, *The Imprisonment of Obatala and Other Plays*, trans. Ulli Beier, London: Heinemann Educational Books 1966

Iliffe, John, *Tanganyika under German Rule 1905–1912*, Cambridge: Cambridge University Press 1969

Jones, Eldred Durosimi, *The Writing of Wole Soyinka*, London: Heinemann Educational Books 1973

Jones, Eldred (ed.), *African Literature Today, No. 8: Drama in Africa*, London, Heinemann Educational Books 1976

Jones, Eldred (ed.), *African Literature Today, No. 10: Retrospect and Prospect*, London: Heinemann Educational Books 1979

Kasoma, Kabwe, *Black Mamba Two*, in Michael Etherton (ed.), *African Plays for Playing II*, London: Heinemann Educational Books 1975

Kavanagh, Robert, *South African People's Plays*, London: Heinemann Educational Books 1981

Kiel, Charles, *Tiv Song*, Chicago: Chicago University Press 1979

Ladan, Umaru, and Lyndersay, Dexter, *Shaihu Umar*, London: Longman 1975

Ladipo, Duro, *Moremi*, in Ulli Beier (ed.), *Three Nigerian Plays*, London: Longman 1967

Ladipo, Duro, *Oba Ko So/The King Did Not Hang*, Ibadan: Institute of African Studies, University of Ibadan 1972

Ladipo, Duro, *Èdá/Everyman*, Ibadan: Institute of African Studies, University of Ibadan 197?

Leys, Colin, *Underdevelopment in Kenya: the political economy of neo-colonialism 1964–1971*, London: Heinemann Educational Books 1975

Lindfors, Bernth (ed.), *Dem Say: interviews with eight Nigerian writers*, Austin: Occasional Publication, African and Afro-American Studies and Research Center, University of Texas 1974

Maddy, Pat Amadu, *Obasai and Other Plays*, London: Heinemann Educational Books 1971

Masiye, Andreya, *Singing for Freedom*, Lusaka: NECZAM 1977

Mitchell, J. C., *The Kalela Dance: aspects of social relationships among urban Africans in Northern Rhodesia*, Rhodes-Livingstone Papers no. 27, Manchester: Manchester University Press 1956

Moore, Gerald, *Wole Soyinka*, London: Evans 1971

Morell, Karen L. (ed.), *In Person: Achebe, Awoornor and Soyinka at the University of Washington*, Seattle: Institute of Comparative and Foreign Area Studies, University of Washington 1975

'Mshengu', 'After Soweto: people's theatre and the political struggle in South Africa', *Theatre Quarterly*, vol. 9, no. 33 (1979)

Mulford, David C., *Zambia, the Politics of Independence*, London: Oxford University Press 1967

Nadeau, Maurice, *The History of Surrealism*, trans. Richard Howard, London: Jonathan Cape 1968 (originally published in French as *Histoire du Surréalisme* 1964)

Nasiru, Isaac Oluwalalaaro Akanji, 'Communication and the Nigerian drama in English', PhD thesis, University of Ibadan 1978

Odinga, Oginga, *Not Yet Uhuru*, London: Heinemann Educational Books 1967

Ogunba, Oyin, *The Movement of Transition*, Ibadan: Ibadan University Press 1975

Ogunba, Oyin, and Irele, Abiola (eds.), *Theatre in Africa*, Ibadan: Ibadan University Press 1978

Ogunba, Oyinade, 'Ritual drama of Ijebu people: a study of indigenous festivals', PhD thesis, University of Ibadan 1967

Ogunmola, Kola, *The Palmwine Drinkard*, Ibadan; Institute of African Studies, University of Ibadan 1972

O'Neill, Eugene, *Mourning Becomes Electra*, London: Jonathan Cape 1966

Osofisan, Babafemi Adeyemi, 'The origins of drama in West Africa: a study of the development of drama from traditional forms to the modern theatre in English and French; Ph.D thesis, University of Ibadan 1973

Osofisan, Femi, *The Chattering and the Song*, Ibadan: Ibadan University Press 1977

Osofisan, Femi, *Who's Afraid of Solarin?*, Ibadan: Scholars Press 1978

Owusu, Martin, *The Sudden Return and Other Plays*, London: Heinemann Educational Books 1973

Pascal, Roy, *From Naturalism to Expressionism: German literature and society 1880–1918*, London: Weidenfeld and Nicolson 1973

Pliya, Jean, *Kondo le requin*, Cotonou: Les Editions du Benin 1966

Ranger, T. O., *Dance and Society in Eastern Africa 1890–1970: the Beni Ngoma*, London: Heinemann Educational Books 1975

Roberts, Andrew, *A History of Zambia*, London: Heinemann Educational Books 1976

Rotimi, Ola, *The Gods are not to Blame*, London: Oxford University Press 1971

Rotimi, Ola, *Kurunmi*, Ibadan: Oxford University Press 1971

Rotimi, Ola, *Ovonramwen Nogbaisi*, Ibadan: Oxford University Press 1974

Rugyendo, Mukotani, *The Barbed Wire and other plays*, London: Heinemann Educational Books 1977

Ryder, Alan, *Benin and the Europeans 1485–1897*, London: Longman 1969

Sartre, Jean-Paul, *Three Plays*, Harmondsworth: Penguin 1981

Saul, John S., *The State and Revolution in Eastern Africa*, London: Heinemann Educational Books 1979

Smith, Robert S., *Kingdoms of the Yoruba*, London: Methuen 1969

Sophocles, *The Theban Plays: King Oedipus, Oedipus at Colonus, Antigone*, trans. E. F. Watling, Harmondsworth: Penguin 1947

Soyinka, Wole, *A Dance of the Forests*, London and Ibadan: Oxford University Press 1963

Soyinka, Wole, *The Road*, London and Ibadan: Oxford University Press 1965

Soyinka, Wole, *Kongi's Harvest*, London and Ibadan: Oxford University Press 1967

Soyinka, Wole, *Madmen and Specialists*, London: Methuen 1971

Soyinka, Wole, *The Bacchae of Euripides*, London: Eyre Methuen 1973

Soyinka, Wole, *Camwood on the Leaves*, London: Eyre Methuen 1973

Soyinka, Wole, *Collected Plays I: The Swamp Dwellers; The Strong Breed; The Road; The Bacchae of Euripides*, London: Oxford University Press 1974

Soyinka, Wole, *Collected Plays II: The Lion and the Jewel; Kongi's Harvest; The Trials of Brother Jero; Jero's Metamorphosis; Madmen and Specialists*, London: Oxford University Press 1974

Soyinka, Wole, *Death and the King's Horseman*, London: Eyre Methuen 1975

Soyinka, Wole, *Myth, Literature and the African World*, Cambridge: Cambridge University Press 1976

Soyinka, Wole, *Opera Wonyosi*, London: Rex Collings 1981

Strobel, Margaret, *Moslem Women in Mombasa in 1890–1975*, New Haven, Conn.: Yale University Press 1980

Sutherland, Efua, *Edufa*, London: Longman 1967

Sutherland, Efua, *The Marriage of Anansewa*, London: Longman 1975

Swantz, Marja-Liisa, and Jerman, Helena (eds.), *Jipemoyo: development and cultural research 1/1977*, Tanzania: Department of Research and Planning, Ministry of National Culture and Youth 1977; Finland: Academy of Finland 1977; *Jipemoyo: development and cultural research 2/1980*, ed. A. O. Anacleti, Tanzania: Department of Research and Planning, Ministry of National Culture and Youth 1980; Finland: Academy of Finland 1980

Thiong'o, Ngugi wa and Mugo, Micere Githae, *The Trial of Dedan Kimathi*, London: Heinemann Educational Books 1977

Traore, Bakary, *The Black African Theatre and its Social Functions*, trans. Dapo Adelugba, Ibadan: Ibadan University Press 1972 (originally published in French as *Le théâtre Négro-Africain et ses fonctions sociales* 1958)

U Tam'si, Tchicaya, *Le Zulu, suivi de Vivène le Fondateur*, Paris: Nubia 1977

L'Université d'Abidjan, *Actes du colloque sur le théâtre négro-africain 1970*, Paris: Présence Africaine 1971

Vickers, Brian, *Towards Greek Tragedy: drama, myth and society*, London: Longman 1973

Wickham, Glynne, *The Medieval Theatre*, London: Weidenfeld and Nicolson 1974

Willett, John, *The Theatre of Bertolt Brecht*, London: Methuen 1959

Willett, John, (ed. and trans.), *Brecht on Theatre: the development of an aesthetic*, London: Eyre Methuen 1964

Williams, Raymond, *Keywords: a vocabulary of culture and society*, Glasgow: Fontana 1976

Williams, Raymond, *Marxism and Literature*, London: Oxford University Press 1977

Williams, Raymond, *Modern Tragedy*, London: Verso Editions 1979

Williams, Raymond, *Problems in Materialism and Culture: selected essays*, London: Verso Editions 1980

Index